MICROPROCESSORS AND LOGIC DESIGN

Dr. Ronald L. Krutz

Director, Computer Engineering Center
Carnegie-Mellon Institute of Research
Carnegie-Mellon University

MICROPROCESSORS AND LOGIC DESIGN

John Wiley & Sons

New York · Chichester · Brisbane · Toronto

I dedicate this book to my wife and daughters
for all the usual reasons and for many many more.

Library of Congress Cataloging in Publication Data:

Krutz, Ronald L   1938-
  Microprocessors and logic design.

  Includes index.
  1. Microprocessors. 1. Logic design. I. Title.
QA76.5.K77   001.6'4'04   79-17874
ISBN 0-471-02083-4
Printed in the United States of America
10 9 8 7 6 5 4 3 2 1

PREFACE

The microprocessor field is emerging from an initial period of relatively rudimentary designs and techniques to a time of sophisticated "systems-on-a-chip" and advanced support software. The area of logic design is, obviously, greatly impacted by the microprocessor and its methods of application.

A need exists to relate and merge the two areas, since the microprocessor is actually a digital building block that can be applied effectively to solve a wide variety of problems. Furthermore, the microprocessor and the microcomputer system, which is built around it, are themselves the results of logic design techniques that utilize fundamental digital building blocks. The goal of this book is to meet this need by presenting the basic logic design techniques—first by explicitly emphasizing the understanding of the internal design and operations of different types of microprocessors and then by examining the systems implementation of microprocessors. The coverage of combinational and sequential logic design is presented at a level that establishes the relationship of the fundamental digital building blocks to microprocessor architecture and accomplishes the transition from logic design to microprocessor systems design and application. In the latter area, particular emphasis is placed on software, input/output techniques, interface standards, and communications.

This approach supports the two fundamental aspects of this book. The first is that no background in digital systems is assumed, since the text provides the reader with the material necessary to progress through logic design to microprocessor system development. Thus, in addition to electrical engineering and computer science students, it is intended that individuals in other engineering disciplines, as well as in chemistry, physics, and mathematics, who have an interest in microprocessors can proceed through the material to develop an in-depth understanding of microprocessors and their implementation. The second aspect of the book is that students are provided with a background of fundamentals and then are involved in developing the architecture and detailed instruction set of an advanced 16-bit microprocessor. Furthermore, by developing an assembly language for this processor and by participating in software examples that utilize the microprocessor, the student should be able to understand and successfully apply newer, more complex microprocessors as they are introduced, as well as the existing devices. Therefore, in contrast to other books on this subject, this text is not a survey of existing microprocessors and their corresponding assembly languages, but instead discusses principles, structure, and techniques that can be applied to a variety of microprocessor types and applications, both present and future.

Chapter 1 is aimed at putting the microprocessor into perspective relative to custom devices and standard small-scale and medium-scale digital circuits. Basic definitions of terms relative to microprocessors are presented along with a description of the structure of a microcomputer. The concept of programmed logic is discussed, and a simple example of a microprocessor program to implement a logic device is presented. Chapter 2 is an in-depth development of number systems with specific emphasis on arithmetic operations performed with microprocessor accumulators and registers. Chapter 3 covers switching algebra, Karnaugh-map techniques, and combinational and sequential logic design. The fundamentals of switching algebra, the Karnaugh-map method, and combinational logic are dealt with in detail, and sequential circuit and finite state machine concepts are introduced and related to microprocessor building blocks, such as counters, shift registers, and control circuits. (A discussion of sequential circuit synthesis and analysis are left to texts devoted specifically to the subject.) Chapter 3 concludes with an examination of combinational and sequential circuits as they appear in a microprocessor context.

More than ever before, the designer and the user of microprocessors must be familiar with the process technology used in their fabrication. Today's computer engineer must be involved with computer hardware, software, and technology. Chapter 4 provides the reader with the basics of the important technologies used in the fabrication of microprocessors from the viewpoint of how these technologies affect microprocessor cost and performance. The emphasis is on developing the ability of the student to intelligently consider technology when he or she is evaluating and using a microprocessor. The treatment in this chapter is particularly useful, but is not required as a background for the discussion of memories in Chapter 5, since references to memory performance, cost, and power consumption are tied to chip process technology. The many definitions associated with semiconductor memories are presented in Chapter 5 along with a breakdown of the categories and types of semiconductor memory devices. Then, the means of implementing data storage for each major type of semiconductor memory are considered, followed by the organization of these storage means into memory systems. Throughout the chapter, memories are viewed from the perspective of a subsystem of a microcomputer system, thus accentuating interrelationships with the other major system elements.

The background developed to this point in the book culminates by involving the student with the specification and design of a 16-bit microprocessor and its instruction set in Chapter 6 and the related software topics in Chapter 7. Key concepts such as addressing modes and register transfers are emphasized in the instruction set development. Prior to the 16-bit architecture design in Chapter 6, fundamentals of data and instruction representations and basic architectural considerations are presented along with examples of specific 8- and 16-bit microprocessor architectures. For completeness, the concept of a bit-slice architecture concludes the chapter with an illustration of a general, bit-slice microcomputer.

Using the development of an assembly language for the 16-bit microprocessor of Chapter 6 and corresponding examples as a starting point for imparting basic software/firmware concepts, Chapter 7 progresses through high level languages, such as PL/M, BASIC, and PASCAL, to examine compilers, interpreters, and program structuring. These languages are discussed at a familiarization level that enable students to understand the principles and characteristics of high level languages and the trade-offs of using these languages relative to assembly language. PASCAL and its structured character are emphasized, and a complete example using PASCAL is developed. Other software related topics such as simulators and editors are also examined in Chapter 7. To consolidate the material developed to this point in the text, examples of microprocessor selection and trade-offs for specific applications are presented.

The very important subject of interfacing is addressed in Chapter 8. Since interfacing is involved with a variety of topics, such as communications hardware, protocols, and bus standards, the material in Chapter 8 is selected to cover the most widely used or important emerging techniques. With an introduction to interfacing that includes basic interfacing methodology, the material in Chapter 8 also covers fundamental I/O structures, IEEE 488 and CAMAC standards, USARTS and UARTS, SLDC network communication protocol, DMA, and a magnetic bubble memory interface. Chapter 8 concludes with a complete interfacing example utilizing the 16-bit microprocessor of Chapter 6 in a real-time, industrial, video-processing application.

This book can be used in three principal ways. The first is in a one-semester undergraduate logic design/microprocessor course based on the merging of these two areas and the need to provide the student with fundamentals that encompass and interrelate the two topics. In many instances, undergraduate students will be required to take only one digital course. However, they should be versed in the basics of logic design and microprocessors to prepare them for the industrial environment. A single course emphasizing only one of these two areas will severely limit students in their encounters with real world requirements. For students with no previous background in number systems or switching algebra, the recommended one-semester course sequence is Chapters 1 to 3, 5 to 7 (Sections 7.1 through 7.3), and 8 (Sections 8.1, 8.2.1, 8.2.2, 8.3, 8.4.1, and 8.5). For the one-semester course with students who have had basic number systems and switching algebra, the sequence should be Chapters 1, 2 (Section 2.4), 3 (Sections 3.4 through 3.6), 4, 5, 6, 7 (Sections 7.1 through 7.4), and 8 (Sections 8.1, 8.2.1, 8.2.2, 8.3, 8.4.1, and 8.5 through 8.8).

The second approach in using the text is in a two-semester course sequence covering the areas of fundamentals of logic design and microprocessors. Chapters 1 to 5 would constitute the first semester's work, and the three remaining chapters would be covered in the second semester.

A third application of the material in the text is in a course for industrial personnel of many disciplines who want to upgrade their knowledge of microprocessors. Naturally, the amount of material and the depth of coverage is a function of the time allotted for the course, but a recommended basic course structure is Chapters 1, 2 (Sections 2.1, 2.2.3, 2.3, 2.4.1, and 2.4.2), 3 (Sections 3.4, 3.5.3, and 3.6), Chapter 4 (highlights only) to 6 (Sections 6.1, 6.2, 6.3, 6.4.1 through 6.4.4), 7 (Sections 7.1 through 7.4, highlights of 7.5, and 7.6 through 7.8), and 8 (Sections 8.1 through 8.3, 8.4.1 and 8.5).

I extend my appreciation to my wife, Hilda, and to Diane Byrnes for their parts in typing the manuscript and its revisions, to Dr. Alberto Guzman for his review of Chapter 4 on technology, to Regis Leonard for his review of the microprocessor selection criteria of Chapter 7, to Mary Ann Kowalski for her review of the PASCAL coverage in Chapter 7 and the development of the PASCAL example in Chapter 7, and to Charles Morrow for the interfacing example of Chapter 8. I also wish to thank Dean Angel Jordan of Carnegie-Mellon University and Dr. Theodore Hermann of Carnegie-Mellon Institute of Research for their support during the preparation of the manuscript.

Ronald L. Krutz

ACKNOWLEDGMENT

I wish to acknowledge the special contribution of Mr. Dave Wecker, a graduate student at CMU, in taking the basic concept of the instruction set and developing it into a workable tool for conveying the software ideas in Chapters 6 and 7. The comprehensive examples in Section 7.3, the microcomputer monitor program, and the problems at the end of Chapter 7 were additional contributions of Dave's that provide clear and imaginative illustrations of the application of the instruction set. In addition to these specific areas, Dave provided constructive feedback information relative to the instruction set and programming with it.

R.L.K.

CONTENTS

MICROPROCESSORS AND LOGIC DESIGN

INTRODUCTION

Improvements in integrated circuit design methods and processing techniques have made possible a low-cost versatile component, the *microprocessor*. This *processor-on-a-chip* evolved with the ability of the semiconductor industry to fabricate reliably and in quantity thousands of transistors on a silicon chip less than two-tenths of an inch square. A chip of this scale of transistor density is referred to as a *Large Scale Integration (LSI)* chip or a *Very Large Scale Integration (VLSI)* chip. In terms of logic gates such as AND or OR circuits, an LSI chip is defined as having a complexity of greater than 100 gates and a VLSI chip, greater than 1000 gates. Think about it. If you were an integrated circuit designer and had this capability before you, what would you build? Your choices would probably narrow to two areas. You could design an extremely powerful and complex custom chip that would be aimed at performing a series of specialized tasks very efficiently and very well; or, you could generate a general-purpose chip that could be programmed to meet the requirements of different applications. In either case, there would have to be a large volume market for your device, since chip design costs are typically in the $50,000 range.

An example of a custom chip would be a microwave oven controller for a particular manufacturer. If 100,000 custom chips were needed for use as microwave oven controllers, the design cost could be spread out over the 100,000 units, resulting in a cost of 50 cents per chip. Most semiconductor manufacturers feel that approximately 20,000 chips annually is the minimum volume necessary to justify custom chip design.

The alternate design approach of producing a general-purpose chip that could be sold off the shelf and used in many diverse applications would be another means of providing a large volume market for the product. The way to make this chip truly general-purpose would be to give it the ability to perform many functions and to provide the means to select and execute these functions in a sequence specified by a program. Thus, if the time required for the sequential execution of the functions (or *instructions*) is not a factor, this general-purpose chip could be used in instruments, vending machines, and home heating and cooling systems and in a myriad of other applications limited only by one's imagination. Even though the general-purpose programmed device that is exemplified by the microprocessor might not perform the functions as efficiently as a custom-designed chip, its universality and resulting low cost would make it available to numerous users who heretofore could not have justified economically a small, programmed computing device in their products or applications. Custom chips and microprocessors both have their places in the marketplace because of their efficiency and programmability, respectively. Figure 1.1 summarizes the cost–volume relationship among the three main approaches to logic function implementation: Small Scale Integration *(SSI)*

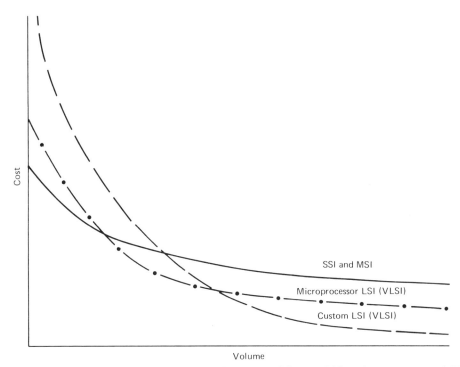

FIGURE 1.1 Cost-volume relationship among SSI and MSI, microprocessor LSI (VLSI), and custom LSI (VLSI) logic function implementation.

and Medium Scale Integration *(MSI)* such as AND gates and Counters, respectively (typically an SSI device has a complexity of less than 50 gates and an MSI device has a complexity of 50 to 100 gates); *Microprocessor LSI* or *VLSI*; and *Custom LSI* or *VLSI*.

It should be noted that, because of the programmable nature of the microprocessor, it is employed in many areas where the development of a custom LSI chip can be justified. The ability to change the program executed by the microprocessor is an attractive alternative to having to rewire or redesign in order to modify the operation of a system. Also, by expanding the program, one can add tasks and performance options incrementally to those already being run on the microprocessor without extensive hardware modifications.

In addition to the high-density or LSI semiconductor technology, the electronic calculator chips made possible by this technology were also a driving force for the development of the microprocessor. The microprocessor met the requirements of programmable and preprogrammed calculators on the market scale between high volume four-function calculators using custom chips and lower volume minicomputers that use SSI and MSI circuits. The microprocessor provided a means to implement a family of machines that were programmable at a chip level to provide a variety of features. The microprocessor, then, filled a gap where the combination of volume, performance, speed, and cost could not be effectively addressed by either custom chips or SSI and MSI technology.

1.1 DEFINITIONS

Before proceeding further, we offer the following necessary definitions.

A *bit* is an acronym for the term *binary digit*. A binary digit can have only two values, which are represented by the symbols 0 and 1, as compared to a decimal digit, which can have 10 values, represented by the symbols 0 through 9. The bit values are easily implemented in electronic and magnetic media by two-state devices whose states portray either of the binary digits, 0 or 1. Examples of such two-state devices are a transistor that is conducting or not conducting, a capacitor that is charged or discharged, or a magnetic material that is magnetized North-to-South or South-to-North.

The *bit size* of a microprocessor refers to the number of bits which can be processed simultaneously by the basic arithmetic circuits of the microprocessor. A number of bits taken as a group in this manner is called a *word*. For example, the first commercial microprocessor, the Intel 4004, which was introduced in 1971, is a 4-bit machine and is said to process a 4-bit word or have a 4-bit word length Central Processing Unit (CPU). Because two particular word lengths are commonly used, they are given specific names. An 8-bit word is referred to as a *byte* and a 4-bit word is known as a *nibble*. It should be noted that a processor can perform calculations involving more than its bit size, but must perform them sequentially, thus taking more time to complete the operation. In general, longer word lengths or bit sizes provide higher system throughput while shorter word lengths require less hardware and interconnections in the CPU.

An *Arithmetic Logic Unit (ALU)* is a digital circuit which performs arithmetic and logic operations on two n-bit digital words. The value of n is normally 4, 8, or 16. Typical operations performed by the ALU are addition, subtraction, ANDing, ORing, and comparison of the two words.

With these basic terms defined, the important distinction between a *microprocessor* and a *microcomputer* can be made. A *microprocessor* is the *Central Processing Unit (CPU)* of a *microcomputer* and normally must be augmented with peripheral support devices in order to function. In general, the CPU contains the Arithmetic and Logic Unit (ALU) and control circuitry for the ALU. The number of peripheral devices depends upon the particular application involved. As the microprocessor industry matures, more of these functions are being integrated onto LSI chips to reduce the system package count. In general, a *microcomputer* consists of a microprocessor (CPU), input means, output means, timing circuits, and memory, in which to store programs and data. Other devices such as communications adapters and modems (which actually fall under input and output means) are also being provided by manufacturers. Some microcomputers are implemented on a single chip containing a CPU, program and data memory, timing circuitry, and input/output means. The relationship between a microprocessor and a microcomputer is illustrated in Figure 1.2.

An *address* is a pattern of 0's and 1's that represent a specific location in memory or a particular input/output device. Many microprocessors have 16 address lines and, recalling that a bit can have a value of either 0 or 1, one sees that these 16 lines can produce 2^{16} unique 16-bit patterns from 0000000000000000 to 1111111111111111, representing 65,536 different addresses.

Read Only Memory or *ROM* is a storage medium for the groups of bits called words, and its contents cannot normally be altered. A typical ROM is fabricated on an LSI chip and can store, for example, 2048 eight-bit words that can be individually accessed by presenting one of 2048 addresses to it. This ROM would be referred to as a 2K-word by 8-bit ROM. An example of an 8-bit word that might be stored in one location in this memory is 10110111. A ROM is also a *nonvolatile* storage device, which means that its contents are retained in the event of a loss of power to the ROM chip. Because of this characteristic, ROM's are used to store instructions (programs) or data tables that must always be available to the microprocessor.

Random Access Memory or *RAM* is also a storage medium for groups of bits or words whose contents can be read and also dynamically altered at specific addresses. A RAM normally provides *volatile* storage in that its contents are lost in case of a power failure. RAM's are fabricated on LSI chips and have typical densities of 4096 to 65,536 bits per chip. These bits can be organized in many ways: for example, as 4096 by 1-bit words, or as 2048 by 8-bit words. RAM is normally used as *scratchpad* memory for storage of temporary data and intermediate results as well as programs which can be reloaded from a back-up non-volatile source.

A *register* can be considered as volatile storage for a number of bits. These bits may be entered into the register simultaneously (in *parallel*), or sequentially *(serially)* from right to left or left to right, one bit at a time. An 8-bit register storing the 8 bits, 11110000 is represented as follows.

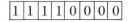

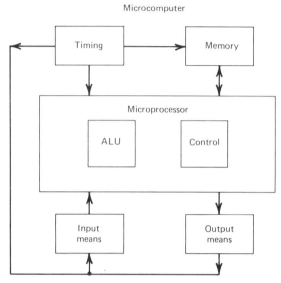

FIGURE 1.2 Microcomputer versus microprocessor.

The term *bus* refers to a number of conductors organized to provide a means of communication among different elements in a system of elements. The conductors in the bus can be grouped in terms of their functions. A microprocessor normally has an *address bus*, a *data bus*, and a *control bus*. The address bits to memory or to an external device are sent out on the address bus; instructions from memory and data to and from memory or external devices normally travel on the data bus; and control signals for the other buses and among system elements are transmitted on the control bus. Buses are sometimes bidirectional; that is, information can be transmitted in either direction on the bus but normally only in one direction at a time.

The *instruction set* of a microprocessor is the list of commands that the microprocessor is designed to execute. Typical instructions are **ADD, STORE,** and **ROTATE.** Individual instructions are coded as unique bit patterns that are recognized and executed by the microprocessor. If a microprocessor had three bits allocated to the representation of instructions, then the CPU could recognize a maximum of 2^3 or eight different instructions and would be said to have eight instructions in its instruction set. It is obvious that some instructions would be more suitable to a particular application than others. For example, if a microprocessor is to be used in a calculating mode, instructions such as **ADD, SUBTRACT, MULTIPLY,** and **DIVIDE** would be desirable. In a control application, a **COMPARE** instruction that would read digitized signals into the processor easily and quickly and write digital control variables to external circuits would be valuable. The number of instructions and their mix directly influence the amount of hardware in the chip set, the number and organization of the interconnecting bus lines, and the applications in which the microprocessors would perform well.

A microcomputer requires synchronization among its components and this is provided by the *clock* or timing circuits. The signals provided by the clock circuits are either *single-phase* or *multi-phase*. A *single-phase clock* is a periodic signal and is distributed throughout the microcomputer on a single line. A *multi-phase clock* consists of multiple periodic signals synchronized with each other but normally out of phase. Examples of a single-phase and a two-phase clock are given in Figure 1.3.

These definitions serve as a background for the remaining introductory discussions. All additional definitions are presented in the chapter relating to the particular subject matter.

1.2 PROGRAMMED LOGIC

In 1951 at the University of Manchester in England, M. V. Wilkes presented a paper entitled "The Best Way to Design an Automatic Calculating

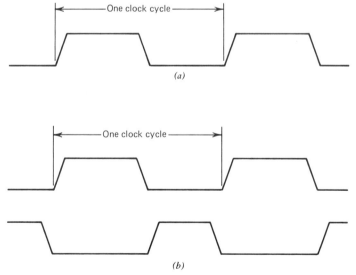

FIGURE 1.3 Microcomputer clock signals. (*a*) Single-phase clock signal. (*b*) Two-phase clock signal.

Machine."* In his paper, Wilkes questioned the conventional ad hoc or random logic methods applied to the design of a digital computer control section and proposed the use of *Read Only Storage (ROS)* or ROM to generate the control signals that determine the signal paths or routes among the functional elements comprising the control section of the CPU. Wilkes realized that each instruction in the computer instruction set could be broken down into a sequence of primitive operations that define the transfer of information between the functional elements in the CPU. Wilkes proposed that these information paths be specified and set up by output lines from Read Only Memories. These output lines would have either a 1 or 0 on them and would activate specific gates in the path structure thereby setting up a particular data path in the CPU. When another address in ROM is specified, a new pattern of 1's and 0's on the ROM output lines would configure another routing path among the CPU functional elements. Since this technique involved the use of *microprograms* in ROM to execute an instruction in the computer instruction repertoire, the technique was termed *microprogramming.* Microprogramming was to have a profound effect on computer design, but only after technological advances had made possible low-cost and fast Read Only Memory. In fact, it was not until the announcement of the microprogrammed IBM System/360 in 1964 that any major interest in microprogrammed computer control implementation occurred. In 1966, the microprogrammed RCA Spectra/70 was introduced. Following these machines, many other microprogrammed computers were announced, including the Interdata 2, 3, and 4; Burroughs 2500 and 3500; and the TRW-130 and TRW-530.

With the continued lowering in cost and increase in density of semiconductor memories in the late 1960s, it was inevitable that the microprocessor would emerge and provide a new dimension to logic design. In addition to using ROM to efficiently implement the logic of the computer control section, it was possible to use the same techniques to perform logic functions previously in the domain of SSI and MSI integrated circuits. Thus, the control, data acquisition, and logic functions being performed in instruments, controllers, point-of-scale terminals, and similar pieces of equipment were now amenable to logic implementation by means of the microprocessor. This transfer of logic circuit configuration from the physical realm of interconnections among SSI and MSI building blocks to program sequences in ROM is referred to as *programmed logic.* The concept is sometimes exaggeratingly referred to as logic implementation by memory instead of by soldering iron.

* Wilkes, M. V., The Best Way to Design an Automatic Calculating Machine, Manchester University Computer Inaugural Conference, July 1951. Published by Ferranti, Ltd., London.

1.3 EVOLUTION OF THE MICROPROCESSOR

Intel Corporation is generally acknowledged as the company that introduced the microprocessor successfully into the market place. Its first microprocessor, the 4004, was announced in 1971 and evolved from a development effort for a calculator chip set. The 4004 microprocessor was the central component in the chip set, which was called the MCS-4. The other components in the set were a 4001 ROM, a 4002 RAM, and a 4003 Shift Register.

Shortly after the 4004 appeared in the commercial marketplace, three other general-purpose microprocessors were announced. These devices were the Rockwell International 4-bit PPS-4, the Intel 8-bit 8008, and the National Semiconductor 16-bit IMP-16. Other companies such as General Electric, RCA, and Viatron had also made contributions to the development of the microprocessor prior to 1971.

The microprocessors introduced in 1971 to 1972 were the *first generation* systems. In 1973, the *second generation* systems, typified by the Motorola 6800 and the Intel 8080 8-bit units, were introduced. The distinction between the first and second generation devices was primarily the use of newer semiconductor technology to fabricate the chips. This new technology resulted in a fivefold increase in instruction execution speed and higher chip densities. Since then, microprocessors have been fabricated using a variety of technologies and designs. The *second and one-half generation* of microprocessors, typified by the Zilog Z-80, was introduced in 1976. The *third generation,* introduced in 1978, is represented by the Intel 8086 and the Zilog Z8000, which are 16-bit processors with minicomputerlike performance. A precursor to these microprocessors was the 16-bit Texas Instruments 9900 microprocessor introduced in the 1976 time frame. The various technologies and architectures of microprocessors will be discussed in detail in Chapters 4 and 6, respectively.

A question tha often arises is, "What is the difference between a microcomputer and a minicomputer?" The answer is not clear cut, since, with the increased capabilities of today's microcomputers, there is an overlap of performance, price, and architecture between microcomputers and minicomputers. The situation is identical to the overlap between some large computers and today's minicomputers. Some defining characteristics for the microcomputer have emerged, however, and they serve as guides to its classification. The microprocessor or CPU portion of the microcomputer is normally implemented on one LSI or VLSI chip but, in some instances, can require in excess of 20 chips. The word length is usually between 4 and 16 bits in a microcomputer whereas minicomputers generally employ word lengths of 16 bits or greater. The instruction execution times of most microcomputers are 2 to 10 times slower than those of a minicomputer, and ROM's are used more extensively with microcomputers than with minicomputers, both to store instructions and to hold the micro-programs which effect the execution of these instructions. Then RAM implemented with semiconductor or magnetic core memory is predominantly used in minicomputers for instruction storage. The consequences of these microcomputer characteristics relative to minicomputers are the two most prominent differences between the two products, **cost** and **size.** A minimum microcomputer can be implemented with one or two LSI chips on a 3-in. by 5-in. printed circuit board plus power supply in contrast to a minimum minicomputer configuration that would require a number of larger printed circuit boards, necessitating a higher capacity power supply and mounting in a case or rack-mountable enclosure. Although some microcomputer configurations can be made to equal or exceed the cost of a minicomputer, the cost of a minicomputer can be 2 to 10 times that of a microcomputer in an application where both systems are capable of performing the required task.

The distinction between minicomputers and microcomputers will become exceedingly less distinct since VLSI techniques have made possible 32-bit microcomputers with speeds approaching those of minicomputers.

1.4   GENERAL STRUCTURE

The organization of a microcomputer system is a function of the particular microprocessor being utilized and the requirements of its intended application. To show the relationships among the elements comprising a microcomputer, however, a general structure is given in Figure 1.4. This organization is typical of many microcomputers and serves as a basis for the following discussion of microcomputer operation.

As discussed earlier, the microprocessor executes one instruction at a time in a specified order. It does this by *fetching* an instruction from program memory, *decoding* the instruction to identify it, and then *executing* the instruction. This sequence of events is synchronized by the clock signal(s) distributed throughout the microcomputer. The fetch operation is accomplished by the microprocessor's sending out on the address bus the address of the next instruction to be executed, allowing enough time for the program memory to respond, and receiving the binary code for the instruction on the data bus.

The source of the binary pattern of 1's or 0's presented on the address bus and pointing to the location of the next instruction to be executed is the *Program Counter (PC)*. The PC is a counting register commonly located in the microprocessor. The PC is incremented after the instruction address

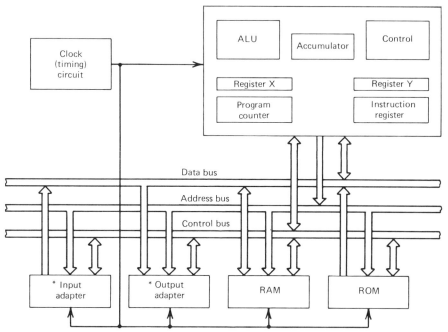

FIGURE 1.4 General microcomputer structure. *Note:* Input and output adapter functions may be physically contained in one chip.

is sent out and is, therefore, ready to address the next instruction in the sequence. If there are no branches in the program sequence, this new address will be presented to the address bus at the proper time to point to the next instruction to be executed. For example, if the present instruction being executed was fetched from location 197 and the next instruction was stored at location 198, the PC would be incremented from 197 to 198 after presenting the binary equivalent of 197 to the address bus. On the other hand, if the instruction fetched from address 197 specified that the location of the next instruction to be executed was address 243, the binary equivalent of 243 would be *jammed* into the PC. The binary equivalent of 198, which was resident in the PC, would be written over and the address 243 would be stored in the PC and sent out on the address bus at the start of the next instruction fetch cycle. One type of instruction which accomplishes the above modification of the instruction sequence is the **unconditional JUMP** instruction. This instruction can be represented by a symbol that aids in remembering the operation performed by the instruction. This type of symbol is called a *mnemonic* or memory aid. A mnemonic for the **JUMP** instruction would be **JMP.** The **JUMP** instruction is normally written with the mnemonic followed by the address to which control of the program is transferred or by a symbol representing that address. In the example above, the instruction would be **JMP 243** or **JMP TEMP**, where TEMP would be equivalent to location 243. The preceding discussion can be illustrated as follows.

	ADDRESS	INSTRUCTION	
	– – –	– – – – – –	
	– – –	– – – – – –	
	195	– – – – – –	
	196	– – – – – –	
Addressing sequence	197	JMP 243	Instruction execution sequence
	198	– – – – – –	
	199	– – – – – –	
	– – –	– – – – – –	
	– – –	– – – – – –	
		– – – – – –	
TEMP	243	– – – – – –	

When the address of the instruction to be executed is presented to program memory (which can be either ROM or RAM), the binary code for the instruction is gated onto the memory output lines that are connected to the microprocessor data bus. Since the data bus is normally bidirectional, it must have been previously placed in the input mode in order to permit transfer of information into the microprocessor. The binary code for the instruction is received in the microprocessor and stored in the *Instruction Register (IR)*. The binary representation of the instruction is then decoded to identify the particular instruction. The decoded information is then used to generate control signals in the microprocessor for such functional elements as the ALU and internal storage registers. These control signals can be generated either by random logic or by microprograms stored in an additional ROM (or, in some cases, RAM) as discussed in Section 1.2 of this chapter.

Of the internal registers in the microprocessor, the principal one is the *Accumulator*. The accumulator stores the results of operations involving the ALU, serves as intermediate memory for transfer of data, provides the capability to perform tests on data it holds, and permits shifting of a binary pattern one bit at a time to the left or right. The word size in bits of the microprocessor is usually synonymous with the word size of the accumulator. Thus, an 8-bit microprocessor contains an 8-bit accumulator.

1.5 FIELDS OF APPLICATION

In order to put the microprocessor into perspective, it is important to explore its areas of application. It was noted previously that the microprocessor lies between the calculator and the minicomputer on the scale of computing power, ease of programming, and speed. Since most calculators operate on data one bit at a time in a serial fashion, they are 10 to 100 times slower than a microprocessor, which itself is 2 to 10 times slower than a minicomputer. *Thus, regardless of all the advantages a microprocessor may be able to bring to a product, it must be fast enough to perform its required tasks.* Remember, the microprocessor, like any single processor, is a device that executes one instruction at a time in a sequential fashion and typical instruction execution times are 500 nanoseconds to 2 microseconds. If the time to execute the necessary instructions is greater than the minimum time allowed to handle the data, the microprocessor itself cannot meet the requirements of the application. Consider the example where binary data are being transmitted serially over a communications line to a microcomputer at a 2-MHz rate. This rate means that a new bit value is appearing at the input of the microcomputer every 500 nanoseconds. If the execution time for each instruction used to read in data from an input port is also 500 nanoseconds, but two such instructions are required to read in the data and store it in memory, the microcomputer will fall behind the incoming data. Thus, the microcomputer alone without some other means of reading the data into its memory at a higher rate would not be suitable for this application.

In the spectrum of applications, the microprocessor is well suited to dedicated controllers, point-of-sale terminals, intelligent terminals, low to moderate speed data communications systems, small dedicated processors (such as in instruments, automobiles, etc.), and programmed logic replacement of random logic systems.

An example of a programmed logic application of a microcomputer illustrates some of the concepts discussed in this chapter. The logic function chosen would not alone justify a microcomputer but provides a means to study the approach to such a problem and illustrate a simple microcomputer program. The logic function to be implemented in this example is a 2-line to 4-line decoder. This function is available as a single MSI chip and activates 1 of 4 output lines according to the binary pattern on the 2 input lines. The pin diagram and table in Figure 1.5 completely define the logic function and its random logic implementation.

There are 2^2 or 4 possible input combinations of 1's and 0's. Each of these combinations produces a 0 state or *active low*, as it is sometimes

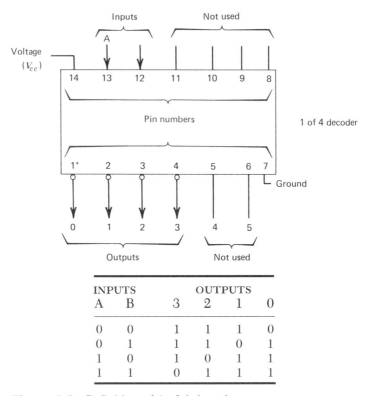

Figure 1.5 Definition of 1 of 4 decoder.

INPUTS		OUTPUTS			
A	B	3	2	1	0
0	0	1	1	1	0
0	1	1	1	0	1
1	0	1	0	1	1
1	1	0	1	1	1

called, on a unique output pin and a 1 state on all other output pins. The circles on output pins 1, 2, 3, and 4 are used to indicate an active low output. In conventional MSI circuits, a logic 1 output is approximately 2.4 volts and a logic 0 output is approximately 0.4 volts. The 1 of 4 decode function is implemented on the MSI chip by interconnections among logic gates and is therefore considered a random logic implementation of the decode function.

To develop the programmed equivalent of the 1 of 4 decode function the general microcomputer structure described in Figure 1.4 will be utilized.

The two input lines A and B of the decoder function are transferred onto the microcomputer data bus by an input interface adapter, and the four output bits are transferred from the data bus to an output adapter where they are presented as the four output lines of the decoder. Since the data bus is bidirectional, data are transferred into and out of the microprocessor on the data bus lines, but at different times. Since the data bus on our general processor is 8 bits wide, the excess bits transferred in or out are ignored. Data can be transferred to and from either of general-purpose registers X and Y in the microprocessor.

The following subset of instructions is defined for the microprocessor. The instructions are specified by mnemonic labels that relate to the operation performed by the instruction. Note that an 8-bit memory word is required to hold the code for each instruction mnemonic. If the instruction also includes 8 bits of data, two memory words are required, which, then, take up two memory locations. The two-byte instructions in the subset are noted with asterisks.

INSTRUCTION MNEMONICS

LDX IN	Load Register X with 8 bits from input adapter
LDY IN	Load Register Y with 8 bits from input adapter
STX OT	Send contents of Register X to output adapter
STY OT	Send contents of Register Y to output adapter
SXL	Move (shift) all bits in Register X left one position
SYL	Move (shift) all bits in Register Y left one position
LDX N＊	Load Register X with 8-bit pattern *nnnnnnnn*
LDY N＊	Load Register Y with 8-bit pattern *nnnnnnnn*
JXZ N＊	Transfer program control to instruction at address specified by *nnnnnnnn* if register X contains 00000000; otherwise execute next instruction in sequence
AZX N＊	Set Register X equal to 00000000 if pattern in Register Y matched pattern specified by *nnnnnnnn;* otherwise leave Register X unchanged
JMP N＊	Transfer program control unconditionally to instruction at address specified by *nnnnnnnn*

Given the mnemonics for the general microcomputer, let us develop a flowchart that traces the operations necessary to implement a programmed logic version of a 1 of 4 decoder. In the flowchart the following assumptions are made:

The microprocessor has an 8-bit address bus and an 8-bit data bus. The data bus sends 8 bits to the output adapter and receives 8 bits from the input adapter.

＊ NOTE: *N* represents the 8-bit pattern *nnnnnnnn.*

Eight output bits are available on the output adapter and are labeled 0 through 7. Output bits 0 through 3 correspond to the 1 of 4 decoder outputs 0 through 3, respectively. Output bits 4 through 7 are ignored.

Eight input bits are available on the input adapter and are labeled 0 through 7. Input bits 0 and 1 correspond to decoder inputs B and A, respectively. Input bits 2 through 7 are permanently connected to provide 0's as inputs.

In writing a string of 8 bits, one labels the individual bits 0 through 7 going from right to left. For example, if Register X contained the 8-bit word 00001011, each bit is labeled as shown.

| Bit | 7 | 6 | 5 | 4 | 3 | 2 | 1 | 0 |

| Register X | 0 | 0 | 0 | 0 | 1 | 0 | 1 | 1 |

Thus, bit 0 is a 1, bit 1 is a 1, bit 2 is a 0, and so on.

Using three assumptions, one possible flowchart for the 1 of 4 decode problem is given below.

The flowchart begins by initializing the X and Y registers. Initialization is the first step in any flowchart and puts the registers in known states from which we can proceed in developing the program. Register Y is set to 00000000 to clear it of previous data. Register X is set to a nonzero state, in this case 11111111, since one of the instructions JXZ N transfers program control if Register X contains all 0's. Since we desire Register X to contain all 0's only as a result of identifying the decoder inputs, at least one bit in Register X must be a 1 at the start of the program.

Following initialization, 8 bits are read from the input adapter and placed in Register Y. The two rightmost bits, bits 0 and 1, are only of concern since they correspond to the decoder inputs B and A, respectively. Once these two bits are resident in Register Y, a test procedure is entered which is represented by the four diamond-shaped figures. In these four decision situations, the input pattern is tested to see if bits 0 and 1 in Register Y match any of the four possible decoder input combinations, namely 00, 01, 10, and 11. When the particular input combination is found, the program jumps to an address that is unique to the particular input pattern and sends out the 4-bit decoder output corresponding to one of the four input patterns on bits 0 through 3 of the output adapter. Since eight output lines are available, 1's are transmitted to bits 4 through 7 of the output adapter.

In the event that no pattern match is found (which is not possible unless there is a malfunction in the system), an error condition is entered.

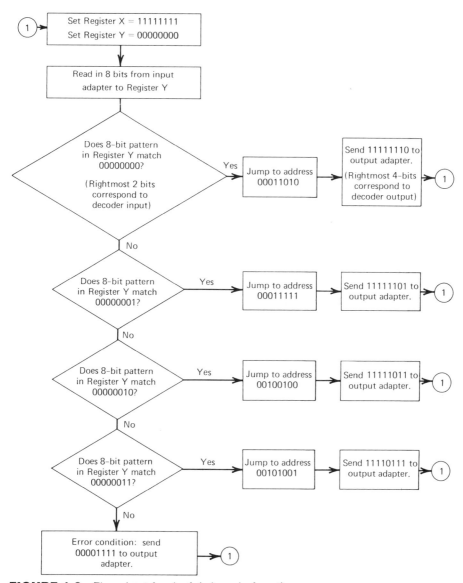

FIGURE 1.6 Flowchart for 1 of 4 decode function.

In order to indicate the error, 1's are transmitted to bits 0 through 3 of the output adapter and 0's to bits 4 through 7. Since bits 4 through 7 are 1's in all normal situations, the 0's in these positions can be used to detect an error condition.

In all cases, after data are sent to the output adapters, the program returns to the initialization block and begins the testing cycle again.

Refined programming techniques applied to the 1 of 4 decoder could reduce the number of steps required to produce its programmed logic equivalent. The straightforward method given in the flowchart was chosen, however, to relate the use of instructions to the microcomputer organization and demonstrate the concept of programmed logic.

Now, the flowchart must be translated into a sequence of instructions using the mnemonics of the microprocessor instruction set. There are many sequences of the given instructions that accomplish the 1 of 4 decode function as defined by the flowchart. The program given below is one solution.

ADDRESS	INSTRUCTION	COMMENTS
00000000 00000001	LDX 11111111	; Register X made nonzero
00000010 00000011	LDY 00000000	; Register Y = 00000000
00000100	LDY IN	; Read in decoder inputs to Register Y
00000101 00000110	AZX 00000000	; Test if pattern in Register Y is 00
00000111 00001000	JXZ 00011010	; If pattern is 00, jump to address 00011010
00001001 00001010	AZX 00000001	; Pattern ≠ 00, try 01
00001011 00001100	JXZ 00011111	; If pattern is 01, jump to address 00011111
00001101 00001110	AZX 00000010	; Pattern ≠ 01, try 10
00001111 00010000	JXZ 00100100	; If pattern is 10, jump to address 00100100
00010001 00010010	AZX 00000011	; Pattern ≠ 10, try 11
00010011 00010100	JXZ 00101001	; If pattern is 11, jump to address 00101001
00010101 00010110	LDY 00001111	; Load error pattern 00001111 in Register Y
00010111	STY OT	; Send error pattern to output adapter
00011000 00011001	JMP 00000000	; Return to beginning of program

00011010 00011011	LDY 11111110	; Load decoder output pattern 1110 into Register Y
00011100	STY OT	; Send pattern to output adapter
00011101 00011110	JMP 00000000	; Return to beginning of program
00011111 00100000	LDY 11111101	; Load decoder output pattern 1101 into Register Y
00100001	STY OT	; Send pattern to output adapter
00100010 00100011	JMP 00000000	; Return to beginning of program
00100100 00100101	LDY 11111011	; Load decoder output pattern 1011 into Register Y
00100110	STY OT	; Send pattern to output adapter
00100111 00101000	JMP 00000000	; Return to beginning of program
00101001 00101010	LDY 11110111	; Load decoder output pattern 0111 into Register Y
00101011	STY OT	; Send pattern to output adapter
00101100 00101101	JMP 00000000	; Return to beginning of program

This example illustrates the interaction between the instruction sequence or *program* or *software* of the microcomputer and the physical components or *hardware* that comprise the microcomputer. Skills in both of these areas are required and the remaining chapters of this text are aimed at providing the material necessary for acquisition of these skills.

REFERENCES

1. Ronald L. Krutz, *Microprocessors—Out of Control*, Proceedings of ACM 75, Minneapolis, Minn. 1975.

2. Gene Bylinsky, "How Intel Won Its Bet on Memory Chips," *Fortune*, November 1973.

3. Staff, "New Leaders in Semiconductors," *Business Week*, March 1, 1976.

4. A. O. Williman and H. J. Jelinek, "Introduction to LSI Microprocessor Developments," *Computer*, June 1976.

5. S. S. Husson, *Microprogramming Principles and Practices*, First Edition, Prentice-Hall, Englewood Cliffs, N.J., 1970.

6. *MCS—4 Users Manual*, Intel Corporation, Santa Clara, Cal., 1974.

NUMBER SYSTEMS

A microcomputer, like almost all digital machines, utilizes two states to represent information. These two states are given the symbols 1 and 0. Which particular state is assigned the symbol 1 or 0 is arbitrary, but the convention adopted must be specified beforehand and consistently adhered to throughout the microcomputer system.

It is important to remember that these 1's and 0's are symbols for the two states and have no inherent numerical meaning of their own. When these symbols are used to represent the two digits, 1 and 0, of the binary number system, however, they must be manipulated according to the number system rules. Also, since other number systems can be used to represent a string of binary digits more compactly, rules of these other number systems must be utilized.

Thus, in this chapter, the basics of number systems needed to effectively implement and use a microcomputer are presented.

2.1 METHODS OF NUMBER REPRESENTATION

In general, a number N can be represented in the form following.

$$N = d_{p-1} \times b^{p-1} + \cdots + d_{p-2} \times b^{p-2} + \\ \cdots + d_0 \times b^0 + d_{-1} \times b^{-1} + \cdots + \\ d_{-q} \times b^{-q} \tag{2.1}$$

where

> b is the *base* or *radix* of the number system;
> the *d's* are the *digits* of the number system in which there are b *allowable digits;*
> p is the *number of integral digits;*
> q is the *number of fractional digits;*
> and $(b-1) \geq d_i \geq 0$ where $(p-1) \geq i \geq (-q)$

N can also be written as a string of digits whose integral and fractional portions are separated by the symbol $\cdot$, which is called a *radix point* and takes on the name of the base or radix of the number system being utilized. In the binary or *base 2* system this point is called a *binary point*, and in the decimal or *base 10* system, it is called a *decimal point*. In this format, a number N is represented as

$$N = d_{p-1}d_{p-2} \cdots d_1 d_0 \cdot d_{-1} \cdots d_{-q} \tag{2.2}$$

where

d, p, and q are as previously defined and $\cdot$ is the radix point

If a number has no fractional portion [i.e., $q = 0$ in form (2.1)], then the number is called an *integer number* or an *integer*. Conversely, if the number has no integer portion [i.e., $p = 0$ in form (2.1)], the number is called a *fractional number* or a *fraction*. If both p and $q \neq 0$, then the number is called a *mixed* number.

Since some digits may be common to more than one number system, the base or radix usually is written as a subscript following the number except in cases where it is specified beforehand or it is obvious. For example, the decimal number 147.25 could be written as 147.25_{10}. Because the decimal number system is used in everyday practice, the subscript 10 is usually omitted.

2.1.1 Decimal Number System

In the decimal number system, which is most familiar to us, the number 147.25 can be represented in both forms (2.1) and (2.2). As it is written, it is already in form (2.2). Translating the number to form (2.1) yields:

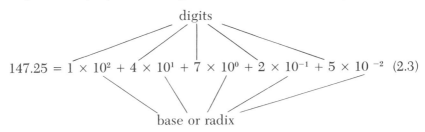

$$147.25 = 1 \times 10^2 + 4 \times 10^1 + 7 \times 10^0 + 2 \times 10^{-1} + 5 \times 10^{-2} \quad (2.3)$$

or

$$147.25 = 100 + 40 + 7 + 2/10 + 5/100 \quad (2.4)$$

From form (2.4), it can be seen that the decimal number 147.25 can also be looked upon in terms of *weights* corresponding to the position to the left or right of the decimal point occupied by a digit. For example, the 7 in the first position to the left of the decimal is the *units* digit; the next digit to the left, 4, is the *tens* digit; and so on. Table 2.1 is a table of weights showing the value of each digit in terms of its position.

TABLE 2.1 Weighted Representation of N = 147.25_{10}

10,000	1000	100	10	1	0.1	0.01	0.001
0	0	1	4	7	2	5	0

By virtue of their respective positions in the table, the digit 1 represents 1×100, the digit 4 represents 4×10, the digit 7 represents 7×1, the digit 2 represents 2×0.1, and the digit 5 represents 5×0.01. A zero in a column means that no contribution to the value of N is made by the corresponding weight of that column. Therefore, the value of the resulting number, N, is the sum of the value contributed by each digit in its respective position. The positions could be extended to the left or right as needed with the weight of each additional column increasing or decreasing by a factor of ten from the preceding column.

2.1.2   Binary Number System

In terms of form (2.1), the binary number system has a base or radix of 2 and has two allowable digits, 0 and 1. The binary number 101.01 can be written as 101.01_2 to indicate that each digit in the number corresponds to a power of 2 as opposed to a power of 10 in the decimal number system. Thus, from form (2.1), 101.01_2 is interpreted as:

$$1 \times 2^2 + 0 \times 2^1 + 1 \times 2^0 + 0 \times 2^{-1} + 1 \times 2^{-2}$$

The decimal or base 10 value of 101.01_2 is found from the above summation as:

$$4 + 0 + 1 + 0 + \frac{1}{4}$$

or

$$5.25_{10}$$

Looking at this binary number in a weighted representation with the weight of each position now being a power of 2 yields Table 2.2.

**TABLE 2.2   Weighted
Representation of N = 101.01$_2$**

16	8	4	2	1	0.5	0.25	0.125	0.0625
0	0	1	0	1	0	1	0	0

Note that the value contributed by each binary digit to N is determined by its position relative to the binary point. The procedure for determining N is identical to that described in Section 2.1.1, Decimal Number System, except that each position has a weight corresponding to a power of 2 instead of to a power of 10.

The binary numbers corresponding to the decimal numbers 0 through 15 are listed in Table 2.3. It is important to become familiar with the counting sequence of binary numbers and also to note the patterns of alternating 0's and 1's in each weight column of the binary number patterns. These repetitive patterns are useful in implementing logic functions, detecting particular counts, and determining enabling criteria for other circuits.

**TABLE 2.3 Binary-Decimal
Equivalent Numbers**

BINARY NUMBER				DECIMAL NUMBER
(POSITIONAL WEIGHT)				
8	4	2	1	
0	0	0	0	0
0	0	0	1	1
0	0	1	0	2
0	0	1	1	3
0	1	0	0	4
0	1	0	1	5
0	1	1	0	6
0	1	1	1	7
1	0	0	0	8
1	0	0	1	9
1	0	1	0	10
1	0	1	1	11
1	1	0	0	12
1	1	0	1	13
1	1	1	0	14
1	1	1	1	15

2.1.3 Binary Coded Decimal (8421 Code)

The 10 decimal digits, 0 through 9, can be represented by their corresponding 4-bit binary numbers. The digits *coded* in this fashion are called *Binary Coded Decimal* digits in 8421 code or BCD digits. Table 2.4 lists the BCD representation of the 10 decimal digits.

The six possible remaining 4-bit codes as shown in Table 2.4 are not used and represent illegal BCD codes if they occur.

Since binary numbers can be very long, the binary digits are usually

**TABLE 2.4   BCD Representation
of the 10 Decimal Digits**

DECIMAL DIGITS	BCD REPRESENTATION
0	0000
1	0001
2	0010
3	0011
4	0100
5	0101
6	0110
7	0111
8	1000
9	1001
not used	1010
	1011
	1100
	1101
	1110
	1111

grouped to form a more compact representation. This grouping results in the use of other number systems, particularly the *octal (base 8)* and *hexadecimal (base 16)* systems.

2.1.4   Octal Number System

The radix or base of the octal number system is 8 and there are 8 digits, 0 through 7, allowed in this number system. In a manner similar to that employed in the decimal and binary number system discussions, the number 543.11_8 is interpreted as:

$$5 \times 8^2 + 4 \times 8^1 + 3 \times 8^0 + 1 \times 8^{-1} + 1 \times 8^{-2}$$

The decimal value of this number is found by completing the above summation of

$$5 \times 64 + 4 \times 8 + 3 \times 1 + 1 \times \frac{1}{8} + 1 \times \frac{1}{64}$$

producing

$$320 + 32 + 3 + 0.12500 + 0.015625$$

or

$$355.140625_{10}$$

The weighted representation of the octal number is given in Table 2.5.

TABLE 2.5 Weighted Representation of N = 543.11$_8$

4096	512	64	8	1	0.12500	0.015625
0	0	5	4	3	1	1

Again, each octal digit contributes to the value of N an amount weighted by a power of 8. The particular power of 8 contributed is determined by the digit's position relative to the octal point.

The octal number system is useful as a means of compacting binary numbers. To accomplish this compacting, the binary number is converted to an octal number and utilized in this form until it is absolutely necessary to revert back to binary representation. In many cases, the octal representation will be used exclusively, with programs in the microcomputer performing the octal-to-binary conversion.

One converts a number from binary to octal representation easily and mechanically by taking the binary digits in groups of three beginning at the binary point and converting each group of three bits to an octal digit.

The octal digit is obtained by considering each group of three bits as a separate binary number capable of representing the octal digits 0 through 7. The radix point remains in its original position.

The following example illustrates the procedure.

It is desired to represent the number 11001101.11010$_2$ in the shorter octal form. First, take groups of three bits starting at the radix point.

$$0\ 1\ 1\quad 0\ 0\ 1\quad 1\ 0\ 1\ .\ 1\ 1\ 0\quad 1\ 0\ 0$$

Where there are not enough leading or trailing bits to complete the triplet, 0's are appended as shown. Now, each group of three bits is converted to its corresponding octal digit.

$$0\ 1\ 1\quad 0\ 0\ 1\quad 1\ 0\ 1\ .\ 1\ 1\ 0\quad 1\ 0\ 0$$
$$3\qquad 1\qquad 5\quad .\quad 6\qquad 4$$

Thus, we can convert the original string of 13 bits to a representation requiring only 5 digits in octal form. Keep in mind that the two numbers are equivalent; that is, 11001101.11010$_2$ = 315.64$_8$. Also, the conversion back to binary representation from octal is simply the reverse of the binary-to-octal process. For example, conversion from 713.02$_8$

to binary is accomplished by expanding each octal digit to its equivalent binary values as shown:

$$\underbrace{7}_{111} \quad \underbrace{1}_{001} \quad \underbrace{3}_{011} . \underbrace{0}_{000} \quad \underbrace{2}_{010}$$

or

$$713.02_8 = 111001011.000010_2$$

2.1.5 Hexadecimal Decimal System

The *hexadecimal* or *base 16* number system has 16 individual digits. Each of these digits, as in all number systems, must be represented by a single symbol unique from the other symbols in the number system. The digits in the hexadecimal or *hex* number system are 0 through 9 and the letters A through F. Letters were chosen to represent the hexadecimal digits greater than 9 since a *single* symbol is required for each digit. The numbers 10, 11, 12, and so on are composed of two symbols and are not permissible as individual hexadecimal digits.

Table 2.6 lists the 16 digits of the hexadecimal number system and their corresponding decimal values.

TABLE 2.6 Hexadecimal Digits and Corresponding Decimal Values

HEXADECIMAL DIGIT	DECIMAL VALUE
0	0
1	1
2	2
3	3
4	4
5	5
6	6
7	7
8	8
9	9
A	10
B	11
C	12
D	13
E	14
F	15

An example of a hexadecimal number is D56.A2. By subsituting into form (2.1), we can write D56.A2 as:

$$D \times 16^2 + 5 \times 16^1 + 6 \times 16^0 + A \times 16^{-1} + 2 \times 16^{-2}$$

Substituting the decimal values for hex digits D and A yields:

$$13 \times 16^2 + 5 \times 16^1 + 6 \times 16^0 + 10 \times 16^{-1} + 2 \times 16^{-2}$$

The next number D56.A2, then, corresponds to a decimal value of

$$13 \times 256 + 5 \times 16 + 6 + \frac{10}{16} + \frac{2}{256}$$

or

$$3328 + 80 + 6 + 0.6250 + 0.0078$$

which equals

$$3414.6328_{10}$$

The weighted representation of $D56.A2_{16}$ is shown in Table 2.7.

TABLE 2.7 Weighted Representation of $N = D56.A2_{16}$

4096	256	16	1	0.0625	0.0039
0	D	5	6	A	2

As with the octal form, a binary number can be represented by fewer digits when converted to hexadecimal form. The conversion from binary to hexadecimal representation is accomplished in a way identical to the binary-to-octal number conversion except that groupings of four bits instead of three bits are taken starting at the binary point. As illustrated in the binary-to-octal example, the grouping proceeds to the left for the integer portion of the number and proceeds to the right for the fractional part of the number. Each group of four bits is then replaced by its corresponding hexadecimal representation with the radix point remaining in its original position. If the number of bits in the binary number is such that the extreme right or left groupings do not contain the full four bits, zeros must be appended to complete the group. For example, conversion of the binary number 1011010101.1110100 to hexadecimal representation is accomplished as follows.

$$\underbrace{0\ 0\ 1\ 0}_{2}\ \underbrace{1\ 1\ 0\ 1}_{D}\ \underbrace{0\ 1\ 0\ 1}_{5}.\ \underbrace{1\ 1\ 1\ 0}_{E}\ \underbrace{1\ 0\ 0\ 0}_{8}$$

Note that two leading zeros and one trailing zero are appended to the binary number to complete the four bit groupings. This conversion shows that $1011010101.1110100_2 \equiv 2D5.E8_{16}$.

Also, the 17 bits comprising the binary number can be represented by five hexadecimal digits, thus reducing the possibility of error in transcribing or interpreting the number.

Conversion from hexadecimal form to a binary representation is the reverse of the previous procedure and is illustrated below.

$F3C.9A_{16_{=2}}$

$$\underbrace{F}_{1\ 1\ 1\ 1}\ \underbrace{3}_{0\ 0\ 1\ 1}\ \underbrace{C}_{1\ 1\ 0\ 0}\ .\ \underbrace{9}_{1\ 0\ 0\ 1}\ \underbrace{A}_{1\ 0\ 1\ 0}$$

Therefore, $F3C.9A_{16} \equiv 111100111100.10011010_2$.

The hexadecimal number representation is widely used in microcomputer systems. It provides an efficient means of specifying addresses, instructions, and data as well as displaying the contents of the various buses. A hexadecimal display utilizing *Light Emitting Diodes* or *LED's* is commonly used to display the address and data buses on most microcomputer systems. The hex number 1F on the address display would indicate that memory location $1F_{16}$ is being addressed. In binary number form, this location would be at address 00011111 or, in decimal form, at address 31.

In any number representation, the digit contributing the most weight is the *most significant digit* or *msd*. This digit corresponds to digit $(p-1)$ in form (2.1) and is usually the leftmost digit in the number as conventionally written. The digit contributing the smallest weight to the number is, then, the rightmost digit and is called the *least significant digit* or *lsd*. This digit corresponds to digit $(-q)$ in form (2.1). Since the digits of a binary number are called *bits*, the terms *most significant bit* or *msb* and *least significant bit* or *lsb* are used to refer to the bits contributing the largest and smallest weights, respectively, to the binary number. The number 101100_2, for example, has an msb of 1 and an lsb of 0.

Depending on the location of the radix point, the msd or lsd could be integers, fractions, or both. In most computers, the radix point is not physically existent in the hardware, but computations involving mixed numbers are accomplished by the software with cognizance of the hardware organization.

2.2 ADDITIONAL CONVERSION TECHNIQUES AMONG NUMBER SYSTEMS

In addition to the conversion techniques presented in the discussions of decimal, binary, octal, and hexadecimal numbers in this chapter, three more conversion methods are useful in the application of microcomputers. These methods are **decimal-to-binary**, **decimal-to-octal**, and **decimal-to-hexadecimal** conversion. Any other conversions between these four number representations can be accomplished by combinations of the methods presented.

In some instances a finite fractional number, N, in a number system of base b_1 may not have a finite fractional equivalent in a number system of base b_2. When this situation occurs, the base b_2 number is carried out to the number of fractional digits necessary to produce an acceptable error between the two number system representations of N.

2.2.1 Decimal-to-Binary Conversion

Conversion of integral and fractional decimal numbers to binary is accomplished by successive division and multiplication by 2, respectively.

To convert an *integral decimal number N to a binary number*, the decimal number is divided by 2. As a result of this division, a quotient, Q_0, and remainder, R_0, are obtained. The remainder is an integer that is always less than the divisor. In this case, since the divisor is 2, the remainder is either 1 or 0. This remainder, R_0, is the lsd, d_0, of the desired binary number. Division of quotient Q_0 by 2 yields a quotient Q_1 and another remainder, R_1. Then R_1 is the next least significant digit, or digit d_1 of the binary number. This successive division by 2 continues until the quotient Q_{p-1} becomes 0. The remainder, R_{p-1}, resulting from this last quotient is d_{p-1}, the most significant digit of the binary number.

The emergence of the binary digits during the successive division of N by 2 can be easily illustrated. The integer decimal number, N, can always be expressed as a binary number in the form

$$N = d_{p-1}2^{p-1} + \cdots + d_1 2^1 + d_0 2^0$$

where the d_i are either 0 or 1 and $(p-1) > i > 0$. Division of N by 2 the first time yields

$$N/2 = \underbrace{d_{p-1}2^{p-2} + \cdots + d_1 2^0}_{Q_0} + \underbrace{d_0 2^{-1}}_{R_0}$$

As shown, the digit d_0 is the remainder of the first division and is the lsb of the equivalent binary number. Successive division of the ensuing quotients produces the remaining binary digits.

$$\underbrace{Q_0/2 = d_{p-1}2^{p-3} + \cdots}_{Q_1} + \underbrace{d_1 2^{-1}}_{R_1}$$

$$\underbrace{Q_{p-2}/2 = \underbrace{0}_{Q_{p-1}} + \underbrace{d_{p-1}2^{-1}}_{R_{p-1}}}$$

In general, then, the sequence of operations for conversion of an integer decimal number, N, to an integer binary number is as follows.

$$\frac{N}{2} = Q_0 + R_0; \qquad d_0 = R_0$$

$$\frac{Q_0}{2} = Q_1 + R_1; \qquad d_1 = R_1$$

$$\frac{Q_1}{2} = Q_2 + R_2; \qquad d_2 = R_2$$

$$\frac{Q_{p-2}}{2} = Q_{p-1} + R_{p-1}; \qquad d_{p-1} = R_{p-1}$$

where

$$d_i = 0 \text{ or } 1, (p-1) \geq i \geq 0,$$

and

$$N = d_{p-1}d_{p-2}\cdots d_1 d_0$$

This method can be illustrated by converting the number 147_{10} to a binary number.

$$N = 147_{10} = \text{?}_2$$

Successive division by 2 produces

$$\frac{147}{2} = 73, \text{ remainder } 1$$

$$Q_0 = 73, R_0 = d_0 = 1$$

$$\frac{73}{2} = 36, \text{ remainder } 1$$

$$Q_1 = 36, R_1 = d_1 = 1$$

$$\frac{36}{2} = 18, \text{ remainder } 0$$

$$Q_2 = 18, R_2 = d_2 = 0$$

$$\frac{18}{2} = 9, \text{ remainder, } 0$$

$$Q_3 = 9, R_3 = d_3 = 0$$

$$\frac{9}{2} = 4, \text{ remainder, } 1$$

$$Q_4 = 4, R_4 = d_4 = 1$$

$$\frac{4}{2} = 2, \text{ remainder } 0$$

$$Q_5 = 2, R_5 = d_5 = 0$$

$$\frac{2}{2} = 1, \text{ remainder } 0$$

$$Q_6 = 1, R_6 = d_6 = 0$$

$$\frac{1}{2} = 0, \text{ remainder } 1$$

$$Q_7 = 0, R_7 = d_7 = 1$$

The binary equivalent of 147_{10} is then $d_7 d_6 d_5 d_4 d_3 d_2 d_1 d_0$ or 10010011.

A fractional decimal number is converted to its binary representation by successive multiplication by 2. The first multiplication of the fractional number by 2 will produce a product with a fractional portion X_{-1} and an integral portion I_{-1}. This integer portion will be a single digit whose value is either 0 or 1. This digit is d_{-1}, the *most significant digit* of the resulting fractional binary number. Multiplication of only the fractional portion X_{-1} by 2 again produces a fractional number X_{-2} and an integer digit I_{-2}. As before, I_{-2} can take on values of 0 or 1. This binary digit, I_{-2}, is digit d_{-2} of the desired binary number. The multiplication by 2 continues until the fractional product X_{-q} is 0. The integer I_{-q} resulting from the last multiplication is digit d_{-q}, the least significant digit of the desired binary fraction. The basis of this technique is illustrated by assuming that the fractional decimal number N can be represented by a fractional binary number as follows.

$$N = d_{-1}2^{-1} + d_{-2}2^{-2} + \cdots + d_{-q}2^{-q}$$

The initial multiplication by 2 leaves the msb of the equivalent binary number as the integer portion of the product.

$$2N = \underbrace{d_{-1}2^0}_{I_{-1}} + \underbrace{d_{-2}2^{-1} + \cdots + d_{-q}2^{-q+1}}_{X_{-1}}$$

The successive multiplications of the fractional portion of the products produce the remaining bits of the fractional binary number as shown in the following sequence.

$$2X_{-1} = \underbrace{d_{-2}2^0}_{I_{-2}} + \cdots \underbrace{d_{-q}2^{-q+2}}_{X_{-2}}$$

$$2X_{-q+1} = \underbrace{d_{-q}2^0}_{I_{-q}}$$

As an example, the conversion of 0.25_{10} 0 to a binary number is given as follows.

$$N = 0.25_{10} = ?_2$$

The conversion is accomplished by successive multiplication of 0.25_{10} by two.

$$2 \times 0.25 = 0.50 \qquad X_{-1} = 0.50, \qquad I_{-1} = d_{-1} = 0$$

$$2 \times 0.50 = 1.00 \qquad X_{-2} = 0.00, \qquad I_{-2} = d_{-2} = 1$$

The number 0.25_{10} can then be exactly represented by 0.01_2.

In many cases, a finite fractional number in one number system cannot be exactly represented by a finite fractional number in another number system. The following example illustrates this point.

$$0.257_{10} = ?_2$$

$$2 \times 0.257 = 0.514 \qquad X_{-1} = 0.514, \qquad I_{-1} = d_{-1} = 0$$

$$2 \times 0.514 = 1.028 \qquad X_{-2} = 0.028, \qquad I_{-2} = d_{-2} = 1$$

$$2 \times 0.028 = 0.056 \qquad X_{-3} = 0.056, \qquad I_{-3} = d_{-3} = 0$$

$$2 \times 0.056 = 0.112 \qquad X_{-4} = 0.112, \qquad I_{-4} = d_{-4} = 0$$

$$2 \times 0.112 = 0.224 \qquad X_{-5} = 0.224, \qquad I_{-5} = d_{-5} = 0$$

In this example, the successive multiplication of a previous fractional product by 2 will not yield a zero fractional result. Therefore, 0.257_{10} cannot be represented by a finite binary number. The error between the decimal and binary representations is reduced, however, as more binary digits are added to the binary number representation.

2.2.2 Decimal-to-Octal Conversion

Decimal-to-octal conversion of integral and fractional numbers is performed in a manner similar to decimal-to-binary conversion with the exception that successive division and multiplication are by 8 instead of by 2. An example of integral and fractional conversion illustrates the method.

$$N = 147.25_{10} = ?_8$$

The integral conversion is performed by successive division by 8.

$$\frac{147}{8} = 18, \text{ remainder } 3$$

$$Q_0 = 18, \qquad R_0 = d_0 = 3$$

$$\frac{18}{8} = 2, \text{ remainder } 2$$

$$Q_1 = 2, \qquad R_1 = d_1 = 2$$

$$\frac{2}{8} = 0, \text{ remainder } 2$$

$$Q_2 = 0, \qquad R_2 = d_2 = 2$$

The octal equivalent of 147_{10} is 223_8. Fractional conversion is accomplished by successive multiplication by 8.

$$8 \times 0.25 = 2.00 \qquad X_{-1} = 0.00, \qquad I_{-1} = d_1 = 2$$

Thus, $0.20_8 = 0.25_{10}$

Another convenient method of converting from decimal to octal form is to convert from decimal to binary and then from binary to octal.

2.2.3 Decimal-to-Hexadecimal Conversion

This conversion is accomplished by successive division and multiplication of N, the number to be converted, by 16 to obtain the integer and fractional results. An example again suffices to illustrate the technique.

$$N = 3414.6328_{10} = ?_{16}$$

Integral conversion by successive division by 16:

$$\frac{3414}{16} = 213, \text{ remainder } 6$$

$$Q_0 = 213, \qquad R_0 = d_0 = 6$$

$$\frac{213}{16} = 13, \text{ remainder } 5$$

$$Q_1 = 13, \qquad R_1 = d_1 = 5$$

$$\frac{13}{16} = 0, \text{ remainder } 13 = D$$

$$Q_2 = 0, \qquad R_2 = d_2 = D$$

The hex equivalent of 3414_{10} is $D56_{16}$.

As discussed before, the conversion of the fraction 0.6328_{10} to a decimal fraction is accomplished by successive multiplication by 16.

$$16 \times 0.6328 = 10.1248 \qquad X_{-1} = 0.1248, \qquad I_{-1} = d_{-1} = 10 = A$$

$$16 \times 0.1248 = 1.9968 \qquad X_{-2} = 0.9968, \qquad I_{-2} = d_{-2} = 1$$

$$16 \times 0.9968 = 15.9488 \qquad X_{-3} = 0.9488, \qquad I_{-3} = d_{-3} = F$$

$$16 \times 0.9488 = 15.1808 \qquad X_{-4} = 0.1808, \qquad I_{-4} = d_{-4} = F$$

Since there is not an exact representation of 0.6328 in the hexadecimal number system, the multiplication can continue until the desired number of digits is obtained. As far as we have computed, $0.6328_{10} = 0.A1FF_{16}$, where $0.A1FF$ carried out to six decimal places is equal to 0.632797. Note that, in the example put forth under the hexadecimal number system discussion in this chapter, $D56.A2_{16}$ was shown to be equivalent to 3414.6328_{10}. As can be seen, the accuracy obtained depends on the number of digits utilized. The fractional solution A2 obtained in the earlier discussion is the result that would be obtained by rounding off A1FF to the next highest hexadecimal number, which is A200.

2.2.4 General Conversion Method from a Number in Base b_1 Number System to a Number in Base b_2 Number System

If the examples of number conversion among the decimal, binary, octal, and hexadecimal number systems discussed throughout this chapter are extended to the general case, the following rules can be formulated.

To convert from an integral number N in base b_1 to its equivalent in base b_2, perform successive division by b_2. One can show this method to be valid by first writing the following general expression.

$$N_{b_1} = d_{p-1}b_2^{p-1} + \cdots + d_1 b_2^1 + d_0 b_2^0$$

The initial division of N_{b_1} by b_2 produces d_0 as the remainder. Division of the resulting quotient by b_2 leaves d_1 as the next remainder. This process is repeated until a quotient of zero is obtained. The last remainder is the msd of the desired equivalent number. This procedure can be written in general form as:

$$\underbrace{\frac{N_{b_1}}{b_2} = d_{p-1}b_2^{p-2} + \cdots}_{Q_0} + \underbrace{d_1 b_2^0 + d_0 b_2^{-1}}_{R_0}$$

$$\underbrace{\frac{Q_0}{b_2} = d_{p-1}b_2^{p-3} + \cdots}_{Q_1} + \underbrace{d_1 b_2^{-1}}_{R_1}$$

$$, \quad , \quad ,$$
$$, \quad , \quad ,$$
$$, \quad , \quad ,$$

$$\underbrace{\frac{Q_{p-2}}{2} = 0}_{Q_{p-1}} \quad \underbrace{+ d_{p-1}b_2^{-1}}_{R_{p-1}}$$

To convert from a fractional number, N, in base b_1 to its fractional equivalent in base b_2, perform successive multiplication by b_2. Keep in mind, again, that a finite fractional equivalent of a finite fractional number in the base b_1 number system may not exist in the base b_2 number system. When this situation arises, the base b_2 number is carried out to as many places as required to obtain an acceptable error between it and the base b_1 number. If the fractional number N in base b_1 is to be converted to a q-digit fractional representation in base b_2, then we can write:

$$N_{b_1} = d_{-1}b_2^{-1} + d_{-2}b_2^{-2} + \cdots + d_{-q}b_2^{-q}$$

Successive multiplication of N_{b_1} and resulting remainders X_{-i}, where

$$1 \geq i \geq q$$

results in

$$b_2 N_{b_1} = \underbrace{d_{-1}b_2^0 +}_{I_{-1}} \cdots + \underbrace{d_{-q}b_2^{-q+1}}_{X_{-1}}$$

(msd of base b_2 number)

$$b_2 X_{-1} = \underbrace{d_{-2}b_2^0 +}_{I_{-2}} \cdots + \underbrace{d_{-q}b_2^{-q+2}}_{X_{-2}}$$

$$b_2 X_{-q+1} = \underbrace{d_{-q}b_2^0}_{I_{-q}}$$

(lsd of base b_2 number)

2.2.5 Number Representation Efficiency

The various number systems can be considered as having different efficiencies of representing a given number. For example, the number 84_{10} can be represented by two decimal digits, seven binary digits (1010100), three octal digits (124), and two hexadecimal digits (54). If a maximum number, N, of discrete numbers can be represented in binary form by b digits, in octal form by t digits, in decimal form by d digits, in hexadecimal form by h digits, and in base r form by x digits, the following expression can be written.

$$N = 2^b = 8^t = 10^d = 16^h = r^x$$

Using this expression, we can calculate the ratio of the number of digits needed to represent N in one number system to the number of digits required to represent N in another system. If the hexadecimal and binary systems were to be compared, the ratio h/b is found as $h/b = 1/4$. This result states that the maximum number that one hexadecimal digit can depict requires four binary digits for representation. Other interesting ratios are:

$$d/b = \log_{10}2 = 0.301$$

$$h/d = 1/\log_{10}16 = 0.8304$$

$$h/t = 3/4 = 0.75$$

$$t/b = 1/3 = 0.333$$

$$x/b = 0.301/\log_{10}r$$

$$x/t = 0.903/\log_{10}r$$

$$x/d = 1/\log_{10}r$$

$$x/h = 1.204/\log_{10}r$$

2.2.6 Conversion Tables

For convenience, a binary-to-decimal conversion table, a table of powers of sixteen, and a hexadecimal-to-decimal integer conversion table are given in Appendices A, B, and C, respectively.

2.3 COMPLEMENTS

Up to this point, the different methods of representing numbers and converting among the different representations have been presented. Implicit in these discussions were that the numbers were positive or that magnitudes without respect to sign were being considered.

Since the binary symbols 1 and 0 are the only elements available in the microcomputer to represent information, various conventions utilizing these 1's and 0's exist to designate positive and negative numbers. When working with binary numbers, we find that an obvious method is to have one bit of the number represent the sign and the remaining bits represent the magnitude. The *sign bit*, as it is called, is normally the leftmost bit of the binary number. If the sign bit is a 1, a binary number is considered negative and, if the sign bit is a 0, the binary number is positive. This representation of a number is called the *signed-magnitude* representation.

For example, the binary number equivalents of +8 and −8 in the signed-magnitude form with four magnitude bits and one sign bit are as follows:

DECIMAL NUMBER	BINARY NUMBER	
	SIGN	MAGNITUDE
+8	0	1000
−8	1	1000

In writing the number in signed-magnitude form, one usually does not physically separate the sign and magnitude bits. The number −8, for example, is written as 11000. Table 2-8 shows the range of equivalent decimal numbers that can be represented by four magnitude bits and a sign bit.

TABLE 2.8 Binary Signed-Magnitude Representation of Decimal Numbers 0 through 15

POSITIVE NUMBERS		DECIMAL EQUIVALENT	NEGATIVE NUMBERS		DECIMAL EQUIVALENT
SIGN	MAGNITUDE		SIGN	MAGNITUDE	
0	0000	0	1	0000	− 0
0	0001	1	1	0001	− 1
0	0010	2	1	0010	− 2
0	0011	3	1	0011	− 3
0	0100	4	1	0100	− 4
0	0101	5	1	0101	− 5
0	0110	6	1	0110	− 6
0	0111	7	1	0111	− 7
0	1000	8	1	1000	− 8
0	1001	9	1	1001	− 9
0	1010	10	1	1010	−10
0	1011	11	1	1011	−11
0	1100	12	1	1100	−12
0	1101	13	1	1101	−13
0	1110	14	1	1110	−14
0	1111	15	1	1111	−15

Even though the signed-magnitude approach is straightforward, other means of representing numbers provide hardware and software advantages. These means are the radix complement and the diminished radix complement. In the decimal or radix 10-number system, the corresponding terms to describe these complements are the *ten's complement* and the *nine's complement*, respectively. For binary numbers, the two's and one's complement are utilized.

2.3.1 Radix Complement

The general definition for the *radix complement*, N' of a number N is

$$N' = b^p - n$$

where p is the number of integral digits of N and b is the base or radix of the number system as definited in form (2.1).

For a decimal number N_{10}, b is equal to 10, and the ten's complement, $N_{10'}$, is found from

$$N'_{10} = 10^p - N_{10}$$

For example, the *ten's complement* of 125_{10} is equal to $10^3 - 125_{10}$ or 875_{10}. The same holds true if N is a fractional number. To illustrate this procedure, the ten's complement of 14.73_{10} is found as follows.

$$N'_{10} = 10^2 - 14.73_{10}$$

$$= 100 - 14.73_{10}$$

$$= 85.27_{10}$$

Similarly, the *two's complement*, N'_2, of a binary number, N'_2, is given by the expression

$$N'_2 = 2^p - N_2$$

Using this expression, the two's complement of 1001_2 is found as follows:

$$N'_2 = 10000_2 - 1001_2$$

$$= 0111_2$$

or

$$N'_2 = 16_{10} - 9_{10}$$

$$= 7_{10}$$

There are two other popular methods for deriving the two's complement of a binary number N_2. One approach is to complement each bit individually and then to add a value equal to 2^{-q}, the lsb of N_2, to the result. This method is illustrated below for $N_2 = 1001$.

1001
↓↓↓↓ (complementing each bit individually)
0110

0110
+1 (adding 1)
‾‾‾‾
0111

Thus, the two's complement of 1001_2 is 0111_2. The second means of deriving the two's complement of a binary number is to perform the following steps.

1. Beginning with the least significant digit of N_2 and proceeding to the higher order bits, copy each bit until the first 1 is encountered.
2. Copy the first 1.
3. Proceed from the first 1 and copy the complement of each of the remaining bits.
4. The resultant binary number is the two's complement of N_2.

The following two examples illustrate the procedure for $N_2 = 1001_2$ and $N_2 = 101100_2$.

For $N_2 = 1001_2$, the lsb is the first 1. Keep this 1, and complement individually all the remaining bits of N_2 proceeding to the left. This method yields $N_2' = 0111_2$.

For $N_2 = 101100_2$, the two 0's in the 2^0 and 2^1 positions are retained. The first 1, in the 2^2 position, is retained. The remaining three bits, 101, are complemented. The resulting number is 010100_2, the two's complement the 101100_2.

2.3.2 Diminished Radix Complement

In general form, the *diminished radix complement*, N'', of a number N is

$$N'' = b^p - b^{-q} - N$$

where b is the base or radix of the number system, p is the number of integral digits in N, and q is the number of fractional digits in N as described in Form (2.1). In the decimal number system, the expression for the *nine's complement*, N_{10}'', of a decimal number, N_{10}, is defined as:

$$N_{10}'' = 10^p - 10^{-q} - N_{10}$$

The nine's complement of 136.21_{10} is, then,

$$10^3 - 10^{-2} - 136.21_{10}$$

or

$$1000 - 0.01 - 136.21_{10} = 863.78_{10}$$

Correspondingly, the *one's complement*, N_2'' of a binary number, N_2, is given as

$$N_2'' = 2^p - 2^{-q} - N_2$$

The one's complement of the binary number 1011.01_2 can be calculated as

$$N_2'' = 2^4 - 2^{-2} - 1011.01_2$$
$$= 10000_2 - 0.01_2 - 1011.01_2$$
$$= 0100.10_2$$

or, looking at the calculation in decimal form

$$N_2'' = 16_{10} - 0.25_{10} - 11.25_{10}$$
$$= 16_{10} - 11.50_{10}$$
$$= 4.50_{10}$$

An alternate method of obtaining the one's complement of a binary number, N_2, is to complement each bit of N_2 individually. For example, for N_2 = 1011.01, N_2'' = 0100.10.

2.3.3 Complements As Negative Numbers

Since binary numbers are the basis for all microcomputer operations, this section will concentrate on number representations in the base two number system. The two's and one's complements of positive binary numbers are used to represent negative numbers in the microcomputer. If the two's complement of positive binary numbers is chosen to represent negative numbers by the microcomputer designer, the two's complement, N_2', of each positive binary number, N_2, is the negative or additive inverse of N_2. If four bits maximum are available to represent numbers, for example, the following number line (Figure 2.1) shows the relationship between positive and negative binary numbers using the two's complement.

Note that, in the two's complement representation, *all negative numbers have a 1 in the msb position* and one more negative number can be represented than positive numbers. In the 4-bit case, a negative 8_{10} exists

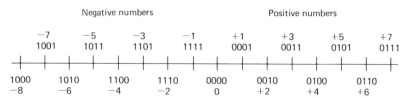

FIGURE 2.1 Two's complement representation of 4-bit numbers. (Negative numbers are two's complement of corresponding positive numbers)

whereas the largest positive number is 7_{10}. *In the two's complement form of a binary number N, if the sign bit position is assigned a weight of -2^{p-1} where p in the number of integral digits in N including the sign bit, the algebraic value of N can be found by summing the weights of all bit positions in normal fashion.* The algebraic value of the negative number 1011 in two's complement form in Figure 2.1 can then be found from summing the weights as follows.

$$1 \times (-2^3) + 0 \times 2^2 + 1 \times 2^1 + 1 \times 2^0 = -8_{10} + 0 + 2_{10} + 1_{10} = -5_{10}$$

For positive numbers, the sign bit is 0 and no weight is contributed by the term -2^{p-1}.

The one's complement of a positive binary number is also used in some microcomputers to represent the negative or additive inverse of that number. The number line in Figure 2.2 shows the corresponding positive and negative 4-bit numbers using the one's complement to represent negative numbers.

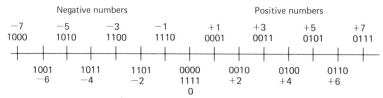

FIGURE 2.2 One's complement representation of 4-bit numbers. (Negative numbers are one's complement of corresponding positive numbers.)

Once again it is important to note that *all negative numbers in the one's complement representation have an msd of 1.* In addition, there are two representations for the number 0 using the one's complement.

The algebraic value of a one's complement number, N, can also be found by assigning a value of $(-2^{p-1} + 1)$ to the weight of the sign bit of N and summing weights conventionally. For example, the algebraic value of 1100 in Figure 2.2 is:

$$1 \times (-2^3 + 1) + 1 \times 2^2 + 0 \times 2^1 + 0 \times 2^0 = -7_{10} + 4_{10} + 0 + 0$$
$$= -3_{10}$$

Positive numbers in the one's complement notation have a sign bit of 0 and therefore the term $(-2^{p-1} + 1)$ contributes nothing to value of positive numbers.

Table 2.9 summarizes the signed-magnitude, two's complement, and one's complement representation for 4-bit binary numbers. It can be seen from Table 2.9 that *positive numbers in all three representations are identical* and only the negative number representations differ. Although the tabulation is for 4-bit numbers, it could be easily extended to other word lengths using the rules for obtaining the desired complements of the number.

TABLE 2.9   Signed-magnitude, one's complement, and two's complement representations of 4-bit binary numbers.

DECIMAL NUMBERS	SIGNED-MAGNITUDE BINARY REPRESENTATION	ONE'S COMPLEMENT BINARY REPRESENTATION	TWO'S COMPLEMENT BINARY REPRESENTATION
0	$\begin{cases} 0000 \\ 1000 \end{cases}$	$\begin{cases} 1111 \\ 0000 \end{cases}$	0000
+1	0001	0001	0001
+2	0010	0010	0010
+3	0011	0011	0011
+4	0100	0100	0100
+5	0101	0101	0101
+6	0110	0110	0110
+7	0111	0111	0111
−1	1001	1110	1111
−2	1010	1101	1110
−3	1011	1100	1101
−4	1100	1011	1100
−5	1101	1010	1011
−6	1110	1001	1010
−7	1111	1000	1001
−8	− − − −	− − − −	1000

It is clear from Table 2.9 that four bits, which can produce 2^4 or 16 possible combinations of 1's and 0's, can represent seven positive and seven negative numbers plus two zero's (positive and negative) in the signed-magnitude and one's complement form. In the two's complement column, these 16 combinations stand for seven positive numbers, eight negative numbers, and a zero. In general, using an $(n + 1)$ bit word including the sign bit, one can represent numbers in the range from $(2^n - 1)$ to $-(2^n - 1)$ inclusively with combinations for a positive and negative zero by the signed-magnitude and one's complement approach, totaling $2^{n + 1}$ combinations. Using the two's complement format, numbers from $(2^n - 1)$ to (-2^n) inclusive along with one combination for a zero are represented, again totaling $2^{n + 1}$ combinations.

With this background in the representation of positive and negative numbers, arithmetic operations using these numbers can now be discussed.

2.4 ARITHMETIC OPERATIONS

To perform arithmetic operations in any computer, a method of representing numbers in the computer must be chosen. Normally in a microcomputer, the Arithmetic Logic Unit (ALU), which is the heart of the microprocessor chip and performs the arithmetic and logical functions, operates in either an integer binary or Binary Coded Decimal (BCD–8421 Code) mode. In both cases, the numbers are usually treated internally as integers and any fractional arithmetic must be implemented by the programmer in the software. The ALU's perform functions such as addition, subtraction, magnitude comparison, ANDing, and ORing of two binary or Binary Coded Decimal numbers. The means of executing these functions will be covered in detail in Chapter 3, but the procedures involved will be discussed now to provide an understanding of the basic arithmetic operations performed in the microcomputer.

2.4.1 Binary Addition

If two numbers, M and N, are to be added together to obtain the sum, S, as follows

$$\begin{array}{r} M \\ +N \\ \hline S \end{array}$$

then M is termed the *augend* and N the *addend*. Binary addition is accomplished in the same manner as decimal addition, except that the carries involve powers of 2 instead of powers of 10. In general terms, carries from a summation in the 2^i column of binary digits denote the accrual of a multiple of $2^{i + 1}$ to be added to the existing digits in the $2^{i + 1}$ column.

The four possible combinations of augends, addends, and sums for two 1-bit binary numbers are:

(Weight)

	2^0	2^0	2^0	2^1 2^0
Addend	0	0	1	1
Augend	+0	+1	+0	+1
Sum	0	1	0	(1) 0

$$\curvearrowleft \text{carry}$$

Note that only in the case of $1 + 1$ is a carry of 1 produced. This occurrence indicates that summing $1 + 1$ yields a carry to the 2^1 position from the 2^0 position, resulting in a sum of 10_2 or 2_{10}. If more than two digits are to be added, the summing continues down the particular 2^i column with each carry being added to the digits in the 2^{i+1} column. An example of this addition is the summation of 1, 1, 0, and 1. Summing $1 + 1$ yields a subtotal of 0 in the 2^0 column and a 1 to carry to the 2^1 column. This 0 subtotal in the 2^0 column added to the next two bits, 0 and 1, produces a sum of 1 in the 2^0 column. Since only one carry was produced in the 2^1 column, the sum of the addition is 11_2. This sequence is illustrated below.

$$
\begin{array}{rcc}
 & 2^1 & 2^0 \\
1 & & \\
1 & 1 & 0 \\
0 & & 0 \\
+\,1 & +\,1 \\
\hline
 & 1 & 1
\end{array}
$$

For addition of larger binary numbers such as $1011011 + 1101111$, the carries propagate as shown.

$$
\begin{array}{ccccccccc}
1 & 0 & 1 & 1 & 0 & 1 & 1 & \text{or} & 91_{10} \\
1 & 1 & 0 & 1 & 1 & 1 & 1 & & +111_{10} \\
\hline
1\;1 & 1 & 0 & 0 & 1 & 0 & 1 & 0 & 202_{10}
\end{array}
$$

Since the number to be added may be in signed-magnitude, two's complement, or one's complement form, addition rules for each situation must be established.

Let M be represented in binary form by

$$d_p 2^p + d_{p-1} 2^{p-1} + \cdots + d_0 2^0 + d_{-1} 2^{-1} + \cdots + d_{-q} 2^{-q}$$

N by

$$b_p 2^p + b_{p-1} 2^{p-1} + \cdots + b_0 2^0 + b_{-1} 2^{-1} + \cdots + b_{-q} 2^{-q}$$

and S, the sum of M and N, by

$$s_p 2^p + s_{p-1} 2^{p-1} + \cdots + s_0 2^0 + s_{-1} 2^{-1} + \cdots + s_{-q} 2^{-q}$$

where d_p, b_p, and s_p are sign bits and the d's, b's, and s's are either 1 or 0. Also, let $/M/$, $/N/$, and $/S/$ denote the absolute value or magnitude of M, N, and S, respectively. Also, since a finite number of values of positive and negative numbers can be represented by n bits, an _overflow_ condition, which indicates that the range of possible positive and negative numbers has been exceeded, must be detected. The following binary addition examples illustrate the different cases that can occur. Then general rules will be established to handle these cases. The examples assume an 8-bit accumulator and ALU in the microprocessor. The methods are extendable to n-bit devices.

Example 1

No sign bits used. All bits comprise magnitude of number. All numbers assumed positive.

(a)	Range of 8 bits (255_{10}) not exceeded		(b)	Range of 8 bits (255_{10}) exceeded	
	11001101	205_{10}		11001101	205_{10}
	+00011101	+ 29_{10}		+01000001	65_{10}
	11101010	234_{10}		(1)00001110	270_{10}

carry or overflow
2^8 digit position

In part (a) of the example, the sum did not exceed the maximum number (255_{10}) that can be represented by eight bits if no sign bits are used. In part (b), the sum, (270_{10}), exceeds 255_{10} and a *carry* or *overflow* is generated indicating that the sum is larger than can be represented by eight bits and that a ninth bit is necessary to fully represent the number. Since no sign bits are involved in either summation, the terms *carry* and *overflow* can be used interchangeably. In other instances involving one of the three sign representations (signed-magnitude, two's complement, or one's complement), the terms *carry* and *overflow* as used in the microprocessor do not, in all cases, refer to the same bit.

2.4.1.1 Signed-Magnitude Addition

In most microprocessors, the carry bit is captured in a 1-bit register that acts as an extension of the accumulator. This bit is called the *carry* or *link bit*. In (b) of the example above, the carry bit would be set to a 1 to indicate that the range of eight bits was exceeded. The carry bit could then be examined to determine its status. The carry and accumulator register would appear schematically as follows in the microprocessor.

Accumulator

Carry   7   6   5   4   3   2   1   0   (Bit designation)

The next examples illustrate cases utilizing bit 7 as a sign bit. Thus, only seven bits (bits 0 to 6) are available to represent magnitude. These bits, 0 to 6, correspond to the weights 2^0 to 2^6, respectively, comprising a binary number, with bit 7 representing the sign of the binary number. Thus, the bit with a weight of 2^7 must be held in the carry bit and will not be bit 7 in the accumulator.

Example 2

Signed-magnitude representation. [Recall that numbers from $(2^n - 1)$ to $-(2^n - 1)$ inclusive can be represented in signed-magnitude form by a binary number with $(n + 1)$ bits including the sign bit. In this case, $n + 1 = 8$, so that the numbers ranging from $+127_{10}$ to -127_{10} can be represented by the seven bits and a sign bit.] This representation is not widely used, but is presented for completeness.

(a) Range of seven bits and sign ($+127_{10}$ to -127_{10}) not exceeded—both numbers are positive.

$$
\begin{array}{rr}
01110000 & +\ 112_{10} \\
\underline{00000111} & \underline{+\quad 7_{10}} \\
01110111 & +\ 119_{10}
\end{array}
$$

(b) Range of seven bits and sign ($+127_{10}$ to -127_{10}) exceeded—both numbers are positive.

$$
\begin{array}{rr}
01110000 & +\ 112_{10} \\
\underline{00110000} & \underline{+\ 48_{10}} \\
10100000 & -\ 32_{10}
\end{array}
$$

(should be 160_{10})

Note that in Example 2b the positive range of $+127_{10}$ is exceeded by the sum. The carry from bit 6 was propagated over to bit 7, the sign bit, and bit 7 became a 1, indicating incorrectly that the sum is a negative number. The result, therefore, appears as -32_{10} in signed-magnitude form. Also, no carry was generated from bit 7 into the carry register. The carry register would contain zero and would give no indication that the range was exceeded. What is required, then, is a separate, one-bit *overflow register* or *overflow bit* that would be set to a 1 if the range were exceeded by the sum as in Example 2b. For signed-magnitude addition not utilizing one's or two's complement representation of negative numbers, the condition for setting the overflow bit to a 1 is that a carry occurs from bit 6 to bit 7 (msb to sign bit) of the number in the accumulator. Assuming both a carry and an overflow bit are existent in the microprocessor, the sum of Example 2b would appear as:

Carry   Accumulator

| 0 | | 1 | 0 | 1 | 0 | 0 | 0 | 0 | 0 | Sum

Overflow

| 1 |

The overflow bit equal to a 1 would then indicate that the range was exceeded and corrective action should be taken in the program or hardware to modify the existing sum to be the correct answer. In the case of Example 2b, this action would be to interpret the carry bit as the sign bit (+) and the bit 7 position in the accumulator as the msb of the result. In other words, under this condition, the sign bit migrates to the carry bit. The corrected register picture in the microprocessor would then be:

Carry   Accumulator

| | | 7 | 6 | 5 | 4 | 3 | 2 | 1 | 0 | |
| 0 | | 1 | 0 | 1 | 0 | 0 | 0 | 0 | 0 | Sum |

Overflow
| 1 |

(c) Range of seven bits and sign ($+127_{10}$ to -127_{10}) not exceeded—both numbers are negative.

$$\begin{array}{ll} 11101011 & -107_{10} \\ \underline{10001010} & \underline{-\ 10_{10}} \\ (1)01110101 & +117_{10} \end{array}$$

The result of the addition of the two signed-magnitude negative numbers of Example 2c shows that an incorrect sign result was obtained and a correction must be applied. As discussed in Example 2b, this correction is easily accomplished in hardware or software since the addition of two numbers of identical sign must yield a sum of the same sign. In this case no overflow is generated and the carry bit can be interpreted as the sign bit and the bit 7 position in the accumulator as the msb of the result. Alternatively, bit 7 could be set to a 1 as a sign correction and the carry reset to a 0. The corrected microprocessor registers in this case would appear as:

Carry   Accumulator

7	6	5	4	3	2	1	0

| 0 |

| 1 | 1 | 1 | 1 | 0 | 1 | 0 | 1 | Sum

Overflow

| 0 |

(d) Range of seven bits and sign ($+127_{10}$ to -127_{10}) exceeded—both numbers are negative.

$$\begin{array}{ll} 11101111 & -\ 111_{10} \\ \underline{10100111} & \underline{-\ \ 39_{10}} \\ (1)10010110 & -\ 150_{10} \end{array}$$

In Example 2d the overflow bit would be set to a 1 as a result of the addition. As in the previous examples, the carry bit is interpreted as the sign bit and the bit 7 position in the accumulator as the msb of the result. In this particular case where both signed-magnitude numbers are negative, the carry bit will always be set to a 1 from the addition since the sign bit (bit 7) of the addend and augend will always be 1 and will generate a carry of 1 out of accumulator bit 7 when summed.

(e) Range of seven bits and sign (127_{19} to -127_{10}) not capable of being exceeded—numbers are of opposite sign.

If one's or two's complement representation of the negative number is not utilized and both the addend and augend are in signed-magnitude form, one magnitude must be subtracted directly from the other and not added in order to obtain the correct result. This subtraction must be implemented by a subtraction routine or directly with logic circuits. The alternative is to use one's or two's complement arithmetic as described in the following discussions.

2.4.1.2 Two's Complement Addition

Most of the deficiencies that have now become apparent when one utilizes signed-magnitude numbers in arithmetic operations are eliminated or reduced in two's complement arithmetic. That is the reason that two's complement arithmetic is widely used in microprocessors. The following examples will highlight the characteristics of two's complement addition operations.

Example 3

Two's complement representation. [Recall that numbers from $(2^n - 1)$ to (-2^n) inclusive can be represented in two's complement form by a binary number with $(n + 1)$ bits including the sign bit. In this case, $n + 1 = 8$, so numbers ranging from $+127_{10}$ to -128_{10} can be represented by the seven bits and sign bit.]

(a) Range of seven bits and sign ($+127_{10}$ to -128_{10}) not exceeded—both numbers are positive.

$$
\begin{array}{ll}
01110000 & +\ 112_{10} \\
\underline{00000111} & +\ \underline{\ \ \ 7_{10}} \\
01110111 & +\ 119_{10}
\end{array}
$$

This example is identical to 2a since the signed-magnitude, two's complement, and one's complement representations of positive numbers are identical.

(b) Range of seven bits and sign ($+127_{10}$ to -128_{10}) exceeded—both numbers are positive.

$$
\begin{array}{ll}
01110000 & +\ 112_{10} \\
\underline{00110000} & +\ \underline{\ \ 48_{10}} \\
10100000 & -\ \ 96_{10}
\end{array}
$$

$$\text{(should be } 160_{10})$$

The range of positive numbers ($+127$ maximum) has been exceeded and the result appears as a -96_{10} instead of $+160_{10}$. What is again required is an overflow indication. In two's complement arithmetic, however, the overflow bit set to a 1 always *indicates that a sign correction is required in addition to indicating that the range has been exceeded.* For two's complement addition, the overflow bit is set to a 1 if there is a carry from bit 6 to bit 7 in the accumulator and none out of bit 7 to the carry bit or if there is a carry out of bit 7 into the carry bit but not from bit 6 to bit 7. This relationship is called an *EXCLUSIVE OR function* and is written as overflow bit = C_6 EXCLUSIVE OR C_7 or overflow bit = $C_6 \oplus C_7$

where C_6 is the carry out of bit 6 to bit 7 in the accumulator,

C_7 is the carry out of bit 7 in the accumulator, and $\oplus$ is the symbol for the EXCLUSIVE OR operation.

In tabular form (Table 2.10), the overflow bit determination is given as:

TABLE 2.10 Overflow Bit Determination for Two's Complement Addition

C_6	C_7	OVERFLOW BIT = $C_6 \oplus C_7$
0	0	0
0	1	1
1	0	1
1	1	0

When this overflow bit is set equal to a 1, which would be the case in this example, the carry bit can be interpreted as the sign bit (+) and the bit 7 position in the accumulator as the msb of the result. The registers in the microprocessor would now appear as follows, representing a sum of positive 160_{10}:

Carry   Accumulator

        7   6   5   4   3   2   1   0

| 0 | | 1 | 0 | 1 | 0 | 0 | 0 | 0 | 0 | Sum

Overflow

| 1 |

(c) Range of seven bits and sign ($+127_{10}$ to -128_{10}) not exceeded—both numbers are negative.

$$
\begin{array}{ll}
10010101 & -107_{10} \\
\underline{11110110} & \underline{-\ 10_{10}} \\
(1)10001011 & -117_{10}
\end{array}
$$

Thus, two's complement numbers used in arithmetic operations have the desirable characteristic that, if the maximum range of the number of bits including sign that are available to represent numbers is not exceeded, the sign bit of the algebraic sum of the number is always correct. In general terms, if M and N are two $(n + 1) -$ bit numbers including sign, in two's complement number representation, and if $M + N = S$ where $(2^n - 1) \geq S \geq (-2^n)$, then the sign bit, bit $(n + 1)$ of S, is the true sign of S, no overflow indication is generated, and the carry bit is set to 0. If the sign of S is negative (1), then S is a binary number in two's complement representation and the magnitude of S in binary form can be found by taking the two's complement of S.

Applying these results to Example 3c, where $(2^7 - 1) \geq S \geq (-2^7)$, and $S = 10001011_2$, $|S|$ = two's complement of S = $01110101_2 = 117_{10}$.

(d) Range of seven bits and sign (127_{10} to -128_{10}) exceeded—both numbers are negative.

$$
\begin{array}{r}
10010001 \\
11011001 \\
\hline
(1)01101010
\end{array}
\qquad
\begin{array}{r}
-111_{10} \\
-\ 39_{10} \\
\hline
+106_{10}
\end{array}
$$
$$(\text{should be } -150_{10})$$

Since the sum exceeded the limit of the range of negative numbers (-128_{10}), it appears to be a positive number $+106_{10}$ with a carry into the 2^7 bit position. Remember that the numerical 2^7 bit position is in the carry bit since the physical bit 7 position of the accumulator is taken by the sign bit. Since the overflow bit is set in this addition, the carry bit can be interpreted as the sign bit and the bit 7 position in the accumulator as the msb of the result. This sum is negative and is in the two's complement form for a negative number. To find the magnitude of S, the two's complement of 101101010_2 is taken, yielding 010010110_2 or -150_{10}. The contents of the accumulator register and the carry and overflow bits in the microprocessor appear as follows after the sign correction is made with the value of the sum in two's complement form.

Carry		Accumulator								
		7	6	5	4	3	2	1	0	
1		0	1	1	0	1	0	1	0	Sum

Overflow

1

(e) Range of seven bits and sign ($+127_{10}$ to -128_{10}) not capable of being exceeded—numbers of opposite sign.

$$
\begin{array}{rr}
10010000 & -112_{10} \\
01111000 & +120_{10} \\
\hline
(1)00001000 & +8_{10} \\
\end{array}
$$

$$
\begin{array}{rr}
10010000 & -112_{10} \\
01100000 & +96_{10} \\
\hline
11110000 & -16_{10} \\
\end{array}
$$

As discussed in Example 3c, arithmetic using two's complement number representation has the property of always resulting in the correct sign if the range of the number of bits of the accumulator is not exceeded. Because the numbers in this case are of opposite sign, the range of seven bits and sign cannot be exceeded and, therefore, no overflow indication will occur. the first example in 3e yields a sum of $+8_{10}$. The second example in 3e results in a negative answer in two's complement form. This negative result 11110000_2 has a magnitude of 00010000_2 (16_{10}), which is found by taking its two's complement.

Closely related to two's complement addition is one's complement addition. In fact, it embodies essentially the same concepts as two's complement arithmetic as illustrated in the following example corresponding to the five cases in Examples 1, 2, and 3.

Example 4

One's complement representation. [Recall that numbers from $+(2^n-1)$ to $-(2^n-1)$ inclusive can be represented in one's complement form by a binary number with $(n + 1)$ bits including the sign bit. In this case, $n + 1 = 8$ so numbers ranging from $+127_{10}$ to -127_{10} can be represented by the seven bits and the sign bit.]

(a) Range of seven bits and sign ($+127_{10}$ to -127_{10}) not exceeded—both numbers are positive.

$$
\begin{array}{rr}
01110000 & +112_{10} \\
00000111 & +7_{10} \\
\hline
01110111 & +119_{10} \\
\end{array}
$$

This result is identical to Examples 2a and 3a since the signed-magnitude, two's complement, and one's complement representation of positive numbers are identical.

(b) Range of seven bits and sign ($+127_{10}$ to -127_{10}) exceeded—both numbers are positive.

$$
\begin{array}{ll}
01110000 & +112_{10} \\
00110000 & +\ 48_{10} \\
\hline
10100000 & -\ 95_{10} \\
\end{array}
$$

(should be $+160_{10}$)

The range of positive numbers ($+127_{10}$) has been exceeded and the result appears as a -95_{10} in one's complement form instead of $+160_{10}$. The same overflow criterion applies in one's complement addition as in two's complement addition, namely that the overflow bit equals $C_6 \oplus C_7$ where C_6 and C_7 are carries out of accumulator bits 6 and 7, respectively. In Example 4b, the overflow bit will be set to a 1 and the accumulator, carry, and overflow registers will appear as follows immediately after the addition.

Carry   Accumulator

		7	6	5	4	3	2	1	0	
0		1	0	1	0	0	0	0	0	Sum

Overflow

1

Interpreting the carry bit as the sign bit and the bit 7 position in the accumulator as the msb of the result yields the correct sum.

(c) Range of seven bits and sign ($+127_{10}$ to -127_{10}) not exceeded—both numbers negative.

$$
\begin{array}{ll}
10010100 & -107_{10} \\
11110101 & -\ 10_{10} \\
\hline
(1)10001001 & -117_{10} \\
\end{array}
$$

Even though the sign of the result is correct (negative) indicating that the available range has not been exceeded, and the overflow bit is 0, the magnitude of the answer is not correct as it stands. This condition can be verified by taking the one's complement of the eight bit result and obtaining 01110110_2 or 118_{10}.

The magnitude of the desired result is 117_{10} or 01110101_2. The negative representation (one's complement) of 117_{10} is 10001010_2, which is obtained by adding 1 to the original result. This modification can be achieved by always adding the carry bit in one's complement addition to the original sum or as it is sometimes called, executing an *end around carry* operation. If this method is used, proper correction to the magnitude of the sum will automatically be made since, in cases where the addition of 1 to the sum is not required, the carry will be a 0 and, then, not affect the sum. The corrected accumulator and carry registers would appear as follows in the microprocessor.

Carry   Accumulator

	7	6	5	4	3	2	1	0	
0	1	0	0	0	1	0	1	0	Sum

Overflow

0

(d) Range of seven bits and sign (127_{10} to -127_{10}) exceeded—both numbers are negative.

$$\begin{array}{rr} 10010000 & -\ 111_{10} \\ \underline{11011000} & \underline{-\ \ \ 39_{10}} \\ (1)\ \overline{01101000} & +\ 104_{10} \\ & (\text{should be } -150_{10}) \end{array}$$

The range of negative numbers (-127_{10}) has been exceeded and, therefore, the sum appears positive. The overflow bit is set indicating a sign correction is necessary. The magnitude correction is again accomplished by adding the carry (end-around carry) to the sum and obtaining the correct magnitude in one's complement form. Interpreting the carry bit as the sign bit, the corrected sum in the accumulator would appear in the microprocessor as:

Carry   Accumulator

	7	6	5	4	3	2	1	0	
1	0	1	1	0	1	0	0	1	Sum

Overflow

1

(e) Range of seven bits and sign ($+127_{10}$ to -127_{10}) not capable of being exceeded—numbers are of opposite sign.

$$\begin{array}{ll} 10001111 & -112_{10} \\ 01111000 & +120_{10} \\ \hline (1)\ 00000111 & +\ \ 8_{10} \end{array}$$

The correct sign will always result in this instance. If the end-around carry is added to the sum 00000111_2, the corrected sum of 00001000_2 or 8_{10} is obtained. When the carry is a 0, the result is still correct as shown in the addition below.

$$\begin{array}{ll} 10001111 & -112_{10} \\ 01100000 & +\ 96_{10} \\ \hline 11101111 & -\ 16_{10} \end{array}$$

2.4.2 Binary Subtraction

In the expression $M - N = D$ where M and N are two numbers, M is termed the *minuend,* N the *subtrahend,* and D the *difference* of M and N. For binary numbers, the four possible combinations of minuends, subtrahends, and differences for two 1-bit binary numbers are:

	2^0	(Weight) $2^1 2^0$	2^0	2^0
Minuend	0	0	1	1
Subtrahend	-0	-1	-0	-1
Difference	0	$(1)1$	1	0
		Borrow		

Only in the case of $0 - 1$ is a borrow generated. This borrow means that the subtrahend is larger than the minuend and a power of two has to be borrowed from the next higher bit position, 2^1 in this instance.

Subtraction in most computers and microcomputers is accomplished by addition of the two's or one's complement of the subtrahend (negative or additive inverse of the subtrahend) to the minuend. Thus, subtraction is performed according to the addition procedures described in Section 2.4.1 of this chapter.

If the microprocessor instruction set includes a SUBTRACT instruction, as most do, the subtraction is usually accomplished by complement addition. The complementing of the subtrahend is performed in the ALU as part of the instruction execution and need not be obtained by a separate instruction. A typical SUBTRACT instruction involves a borrow bit (physically the carry bit of the microprocessor) that is either set or reset as a result of a previous subtraction or by an initialization instruction. In the execution of the SUBTRACT instruction, a borrow generated by a previous subtraction or by the initialization instruction is normally represented by the carry bit reset to 0. The absence of a borrow is then indicated by the carry bit set to a 1. This procedure is opposite from that of addition as discussed in Section 2.4.1 of this chapter. The reason for this convention is illustrated in the following examples.

Example 5:

(a) Let $M = +6$, $N = +4$, and no initial borrow (carry = 1). Find $M - N$ using the SUBTRACT instruction. Assume an 8-bit accumulator and the use of two's complement notation. The operation $M - N$ is executed as follows by the SUBTRACT instruction.

$N = 00000100$
N' (one's complement of N) = 1111011
$M = 00000110$

$M - N$ is obtained by adding the one's complement of N to M with the carry set to a 1 in the addition.

$$
\begin{array}{lr}
\text{Carry} & \left. 1 \right\} \text{ two's complement of } N \\
N' & 11111011 \\
+\ M & \underline{00000110} \\
\hline
\text{Difference} & (1)00000010
\end{array}
$$

The difference is a positive 2_{10} as indicated by a 0 sign bit and the carry bit set to a 1, which indicates *no borrow* according to our convention.

(b) If $M = +6$ and $N = +8$ and the initial borrow = 0 (carry = 1), an example of a negative result is obtained.

$N = 00001000$
N' (one's complement of N) = 11110111 taken in ALU)
$M = 00000110$

$$
\begin{array}{lr}
\text{Carry} & \left. 1 \right\} \text{ two's complement of } N \\
N' & 11110111 \\
+M & \underline{00000110} \\
\hline
\text{Difference} & 11111110
\end{array}
$$

The difference is negative as indicated by the sign bit (1) and the generation of a borrow (carry of 0 according to the defined convention). The magnitude of the difference is found by taking the two's complement of the differences and obtaining 00000010_2 or 2_{10}. So, the difference is -2_{10}.

2.4.3 Multiword Binary Addition and Subtraction

In many cases the word length of a particular microprocessor may not be large enough to represent the desired magnitude of a number. Suppose, for example, that numbers in the range from 0_{10} to $65,535_{10}$ are to be used in an 8-bit microprocessor in binary addition and subtraction operations using two's complement number representation. This can be accomplished by storing the 16-bit addends and augends each in two 8-bit memory locations. Addition or subtraction of the two 16-bit numbers is implemented by adding or subtracting the lower 8 bits of each number, storing the result in an 8-bit memory location or register, and then adding the two higher order parts of the addend and augend with any carry generated from the first addition. The latter partial sum will be the high order portion of the sum. Therefore, the two 8-bit sums together comprise the 16-bit result. This use of two computer words in arithmetic operations to increase the number of bits available to represent numbers for computation is called *double precision* arithmetic. The 16-bit words can be in signed-magnitude, one's complement, or two's complement form with the most significant bit of the 16 bits being the sign bit. Overflow and carry conditions would be identical to those in 8-bit arithmetic with the modification that overflow detection and sign correction are performed on the high order 8-bit summation. The low order 8-bit summation involves no sign bits and no overflow detection. A carry bit of 1 resulting from the low order 8-bit summation is simply added to the two high order 8-bit numbers when they are summed. Example 6 illustrates two's complement addition and subtraction of two double word numbers.

Example 6

  (a) Add $18,599_{10}$ to $25,224_{10}$ using two's complement double precision binary arithmetic. Assume that only eight bit registers are available to store the data and that the msb of both numbers is the sign bit.

$$18,599_{10} = 0100100010100111_2$$
$$25,224_{10} = 0110001010001000_2$$

Since only eight bit registers are available, the addition must take place between the lower eight bits of the two numbers and then between the upper eight bits including any carry propagated from the addition of the low order eight bits of the numbers. The addition is accomplished as follows.

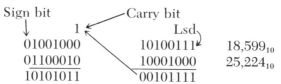

Overflow bit set to a 1, carry bit = 0, sign correction required, carry bit interpreted as sign bit.
Overflow bit = 1, represents a carry into bit position having a weight of 2^{15} or 32,768.

01010101100101111   Signed-corrected sum
= $43,823_{10}$.

Because the addition had to be performed as two separate half-additions, the increase in resolution of the numbers is gained at the expense of execution time.

(b) Add $18,599_{10}$ to $-25,224_{10}$ using two's complement addition (implementing subtraction by addition of the two's complement of the subtrahend). The binary representation of $25,224_{10}$ is stored in two separate 8-bit registers in this example. If the two's complement of this number is to be taken, the 8-bit register holding the lower order eight bits of the number must be individually complemented and the resulting 8-bit number incremented by one. Then, to complete the operation, any carry generated out of bit 7 of the complemented lower order eight bits by the increment operation must be added to the higher order 8 bits of the number *after* they have been complemented individually. The two resulting 8-bit numbers in their respective registers are, then, the high and low order portions of the 16-bit number that is the two's complement of $25,224_{10}$.

Two's complement of $25,224_{10}$ = 1001110101111000_2

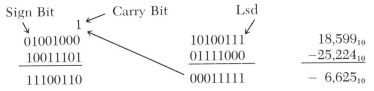

No overflow is generated according to the criterion given in Example 3b. The sign of the result is negative (1), which means that the sum is in two's complement form.

The magnitude of the result is the two's complement of 1110011000011111_2 or 0001100111100001_2, which is equivalent to $6,625_{10}$.

All the techniques discussed in Section 2.4.1 of this chapter relating to single word binary addition apply to multiword binary addition except that in the latter the sign bit appears as the msb of the highest order word of the numbers and the final carry and overflow conditions are tested on the msb and next msb of the highest order word.

2.4.4 BCD Addition

In order to perform addition in the Binary Coded decimal (BCD-8421 mode), the sum output of the conventional binary adder must be modified. Recalling that the BCD digits, 0 through 9, are represented by 4-bit binary numbers in 8421 code and that the binary numbers 1010, 1011, 1100, 1101, 1110, and 1111 are invalid combinations in BCD representation, one can determine the correction to be applied to the binary adder. There are three cases to be considered. These cases are situations in which the sum of two BCD digits is between 0 and 9 inclusive, the sum is between 10 and 15 inclusive, and the sum is between 16 and 18 inclusive. The desired corrections will be developed in the three parts of Example 7.

Example 7

(a) Sum is between 0 and 9 inclusive.
Add 6 and 2 in BCD.

$$
\begin{array}{rr}
0110 & 6 \\
+\ 0010 & +\ 2 \\
\hline
1000 & 8
\end{array}
$$

No correction necessary.

(b) Sum is between 10 and 15 inclusive.
Add 8 and 4 in BCD.

$$
\begin{array}{rr}
1000 & 8 \\
+\ 0100 & 4 \\
\hline
1100 & 12
\end{array}
$$

(invalid BCD number)

Since 4 bits represent one digit and this sum requires two digits, 1 and 2, the result of the summation should be a BCD digit of 0010_2 or 2_{10} in the units position with a carry of 1_{10} into the tens BCD position. The result will be the sum 12_{10} or 0001   0010 in BCD form. Thus, the correction required is the conversion of the initial or *apparent sum* of 1100, as it is sometimes termed, to a 0001 (carry into the tens position) and 0010 (representation of BCD 2). *The correction is accomplished by adding a 6 in binary form (0110) to the apparent sum.* This operation is illustrated in the continuation of Example 7b.

$$
\begin{array}{lr}
\text{Apparent sum} & 1100 \\
\text{Correction} & +\ 0110 \\
\text{Sum} \quad (1) & \overline{0010} \\
\text{Tens digit} & \\
\end{array}
$$

2 ←Units digit

Therefore, the sum is 1   0010 or

$$
\begin{array}{ccc}
 & 0001 & 0010 \\
\text{or} & 1 & 2
\end{array}
$$

(c) Sum is between 16 and 18 inclusive.
Add 9 and 8 in BCD.

$$
\begin{array}{cc}
1001 & 9 \\
+\ 1000 & +\ 8 \\
\hline
(1)0001 & 17
\end{array}
$$

A carry is produced in the apparent sum. This carry is retained and represents a 1 in the tens position of the apparent sum as a BCD 10. The desired sum is 17 or 0001   0111 in BCD. This sum is again obtained by adding a 6 or 0110 to the apparent sum. The result of this addition will produce no carry.

$$
\begin{array}{lr}
 & \text{Carry from apparent sum} \\
\text{Apparent sum} & (1)\quad 001 \\
\text{Correction} & +\ 0110 \\
\text{Sum} & 1\leftarrow 0111 \\
 & \text{Tens digit}\qquad 7\leftarrow\text{Units digit}
\end{array}
$$

The correct sum is, then, 0001 0111 or 17.

Summarizing the results of Example 7, the addition of 0110 to the apparent sum is required when the apparent sum and carry are one of the following values.

CARRY	APPARENT SUM				DECIMAL VALUE
	b_8	b_4	b_2	b_1	
0	1	0	1	0	10
0	1	0	1	1	11
0	1	1	0	0	12
0	1	1	0	1	13
0	1	1	1	0	14
0	1	1	1	1	15
1	0	0	0	0	16
1	0	0	0	1	17
1	0	0	1	0	18

From these patterns, it can be seen that the correction of + 0110 must be applied when carry bit $c = 1$, or when b_8 and $b_4 = 1$, or when b_8 and $b_2 = 1$. These bits can, then, be used to control software or hardware correction of the apparent sum.

In multi-digit BCD addition, the correction of 0110, if required, must be applied individually to each BCD digit and the carry propagated to the next higher order BCD digit. Example 8 illustrates the procedure.

Example 8

Add 179_{10} to 463_{10} using BCD addition.

179_{10} in BCD form is	0001	0111	1001
463_{10} in BCD form is	0100	0110	0011

Adding:		0001	0111	1001
	+ 0100	0110	0011
Apparent sum	0101	1101	1100

The tens and units digits, 1101 and 1100, in the apparent sum are invalid BCD digits. They are greater than 9 and the correction of 0110 is added individually to both of these digits with propagation of the carry. Since the most significant digit, 0101, is a valid BCD digit, no correction is required.

	1 ← Carry	1 ← Carry	
Apparent Sum	0101	1101	1100
Correction		0110	0110
Sum	0110	0100	0010
	6	4	2

The sum, then, in BCD form is

0110   0100   0010

or

642_{10}.

If a microcomputer has an 8-bit organization, then two BCD digits can fit into the 8-bit accumulator registers or 8-bit memory locations. A 16-bit microcomputer can pack four BCD digits into its internal registers or memory locations. The BCD digits handled in this manner are called *packed BCD digits*. In these cases, the numbers are unsigned and positive. An additional register or memory location is required to store the sign bit of the BCD number. Also, in an arithmetic operation involving packed BCD digits, carries and borrows among these digits may be generated among the internal bits of the accumulator. For example, an 8-bit accumulator holding one BCD digit in bits 0 through 3 and another in bits 4 through 7 may have an interdigit carry generated from bit 3 to bit 4 as a result of an addition. Some means of detecting this *half carry* must be employed. This detection can either be done with software or be performed by circuits in the microprocessor chip that automatically indicate when a half carry is generated. The overflow detection logic in BCD arithmetic using the ten's complement representation for negative numbers as discussed in Section 2.4.5 is identical to that in binary two's complement arithmetic; that is,

OVERFLOW $= C_s \oplus C_{msb}$ where C_s is the carry out of the BCD sign bit and C_{msb} is the carry out of the most significant BCD digit (bit position immediately preceeding the sign bit).

2.4.5 BCD Subtraction

Subtraction of BCD numbers can be accomplished in a number of different ways. One method is to utilize hardware subtraction circuitry to perform the decimal subtraction with borrow. Another method is to add the ten's complement of the subtrahend to the minuend using BCD addition as described in Section 2.4.4.

One means of finding the ten's complement of a d-digit BCD number, N, is to take the two's complement of each digit individually, producing a number, N'. Then, ignoring any carries, add the d-digit factor, M, to N' where

the msd of M is 1001 and
all remaining digits of M are 1010.

The resulting sum is the ten's complement of N in BCD form.

For example, the ten's complement of 0100   0001 or 41_{10} is found as follows:

	1100	1111	Two's complement of 41_{10}
	+ 1001	1010	BCD addition of correction factor, M
	(1) 0101	(1) 1001	
(Ignore)	5	(Ignore) 9	Ten's complement of 41_{10} (59_{10})

If the result of the BCD addition utilizing the ten's complement produces a carry out of the most significant BCD digit (borrow = 0), the sum is equal to the magnitude of the number in BCD form. If the addition produces no carry out of the msd, the sum is in ten's complement form. The magnitude of the sum can be found by taking its ten's complement.

Example 9 illustrates these two different BCD subtractions.

Example 9

(a) Find $84_{10} - 26_{10}$ using BCD subtraction.

0010	0110	26_{10}
1110	1010	Two's complement of digits 26_{10} (BCD)
+ 1001	1010	Addition of factor to find ten's complement
(1) 0111	(1) 0100	Ten's complement of 26_{10} (74_{10})
(Ignore) 7	(Ignore) 4	

0111	0100	Ten's complement of 26_{10} (74_{10})
+ 1000	0100	+ 84_{10}
1111	1000	
0110		+ BCD addition correction factor (0110)
(1) 0101	1000	Difference, 58_{10}
5	8	

Carry = 1

(No borrow indicates + answer)

(b) Find $26_{10} - 84_{10}$ using BCD subtraction.

1000	0100	84_{10}
1000	1100	Two's complement of digits 84_{10} (BCD)
+ 1001	1010	Addition of factor to find ten's complement
(1) 0001	(1) 0110	Ten's complement of 84_{10} (16_{10})
↑ (Ignore) 1	↑ (Ignore) 6	

0001	0110	Ten's complement of 84_{10} (16_{10})
+ 0010	0110	+ 26_{10}
0011	1100	
	0110	+BCD correction factor (0110)
(0) 0100	0010	Difference in ten's complement form

Carry = 0 (Borrow = 1)

Indicates negative answer in ten's complement form

1100	1110	Two's complement of difference (BCD)
+ 1001	1010	Addition of factor to find ten's complement
(1)0101	(1)1000	Magnitude of difference in BCD form, 58_{10}
↑ (Ignore) 5	↑ (Ignore) 8	

2.4.6 Floating Point Representation

Up to this point the numbers used in the arithmetic operations had their radix point fixed in a particular location. It was assumed that the numbers used were integers or that the radix points were aligned in addition and subtraction operations. Number representation assuming a fixed location of the radix point is called *fixed point representation.* The range of numbers that can be represented in fixed point notation is severely limited. As we have seen, $(n + 1)$ bits including a sign bit can represent integer numbers from $(2^n - 1)$ to (-2^n) in two's complement form. If q of these bits are used to represent a fraction, then the range of representable mixed numbers is reduced to the numbers from $[(2^n - 1)/2^q]$ to $(-2^n/2^q)$ inclusive. The following numbers are examples of fixed point numbers.

$$1011.1101_2$$

$$96.27_{10}$$

$$AF.1C_{16}$$

An alternate approach to number representation is to adopt the equivalent of scientific notation in the microprocessor. A number would then be represented as $N \times r^p$ where N is the *mantissa,* r is the *base* or *radix* of the number system, and p is the *exponent* or power to which r is raised. Some examples of numbers in floating point notation and their fixed point decimal equivalents are:

FIXED-POINT DECIMAL NUMBER	FLOATING-POINT REPRESENTATION
1760_{10}	0.1760×10^4
0.0538_{10}	0.538×10^{-1}
-235.8316_{10}	-0.2358316×10^3
101.11_2	0.10111×2^3
-0.001101_2	-0.1101×2^{-2}
$FA.1C_{16}$	$0.FA1C \times 16^2$

In converting from fixed to floating point number representation, we *normalize* the resulting mantissas; that is, the digits of the fixed point numbers are shifted so that the highest order nonzero digit appears to the right of the decimal point and, consequently, a 0 always appears to the left of the decimal point. This convention is normally adopted in floating point number representation. Assuming this convention, then, we have to make a decision regarding the storage of the floating point number in the microcomputer. Initially, the following observations can be made.

1. Numbers resulting from floating point operations should be put in the normalized form.

2. Since all numbers will be assumed to be in normalized form, the binary point is not required to be represented in the microcomputer registers.

3. The base r is known and assumed constant; therefore, it need not be stored in the number representation.

4. The numbers N and p can be either positive or negative and, thus, sign bits must be utilized. Conventional two's complement number representation can be used for negative numbers.

5. In order to eliminate the need for a sign bit of the exponent, an offset ($+64_{10}$, for example) can be added to the exponent so that both negative and positive exponents are represented in the microcomputer by positive numbers.

6. Floating point numbers to be added or subtracted must have identical exponents. To accomplish this, the bits representing the mantissa of one of the numbers must be shifted a number of places equal to the difference in the initial values of the exponents. The decision on which mantissa is to be shifted and the direction of the shift should be aimed at minimizing the loss of the high order significant digits. The consequences of these considerations are that the algebraically smaller of the exponents should be increased in the positive direction to equal the larger exponent and the digits of the mantissa of the smaller exponent be shifted right the corresponding number of places.

7. Following an operation, a carry out from the digit position to the right of the radix point of a floating point number requires that the radix point be moved one position to the left (all digits shifted to the right one position) and that the exponent of the number be increased by one.

8. Multiplication of two numbers using floating point arithmetic is accomplished by multiplying the mantissas of the two numbers together (as discussed in Section 2.4.7) and algebraically adding the exponents of the numbers. In floating point multiplication, the exponents need not be made identical as in floating point addition.

A comprehensive example serves to clarify and illustrate these observations. In the example, an 8-bit microcomputer is assumed and each floating point number is represented by the 8-bit words in the following convention.

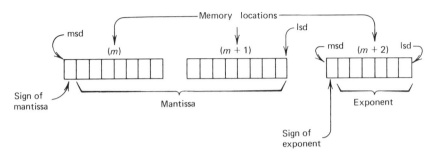

The floating point number is to be interpreted in the following manner.

●
$$\underbrace{\phantom{\hspace{6cm}}}_{\text{Binary point}} \quad \underbrace{\text{16-bit mantissa including sign in two's complement form}} \qquad 2 \begin{cases} \text{8-bit exponent including} \\ \text{sign in two's complement} \\ \text{form} \end{cases}$$

Binary point   16-bit mantissa including
                sign in two's complement
                form

Thus, the largest positive number that could be represented by this convention is $(1 - 2^{-15}) \times 2^{127}$ or $0.9999694824 \times 2^{127}$ or $0.1701359912 \times 10^{39}$. The most negative number representable is -1×2^{127} or $-0.170141183 \times 10^{39}$. The smallest nonzero magnitude that can be represented is $2^{-15} \times 2^{-128}$ or 2^{-143} or $0.8968310172 \times 10^{-43}$.

Example 10

Given two floating point numbers, M and N, stored consecutively in six memory locations according to the predefined coventions above, predict the result of a floating point addition between the two numbers.

	1A00									1A01									1A02							
M	1	1	1	1	0	0	0	1		1	0	0	1	0	0	0	0		0	0	0	1	1	0	0	1

	1A03									1A04									1A05							
N	0	1	1	1	1	1	0	0		0	1	1	0	0	0	0	1		0	1	0	0	0	0	0	0

According to the information given, the first number, M, is stored in memory locations 1A00, 1A01, and 1A02, and the second number, N, is stored in memory locations 1A03, 1A04, and 1A05. Interpreting the binary numbers in these locations as defined in the conventions yields:

$$M = 1.111000110010000 \times 2^{00011001} \quad = -0.1127929688 \times 2^{25}$$

$$= -3784704.002$$

?'s complement of .

Sign

$$N = 0.111110001100001 \times 2^{0100000} \quad = 0.9717102051 \times 2^{32}$$

$$= 4173463552$$

Since the exponent of M (+25) is less than the exponent of N (+32), the exponent of M must be increased by 7 to be equal to 32 and the bits of the mantissa of M must then be shifted right seven positions. The seven rightmost bits, the least significant bits of the mantissa of M, will be lost. Because M is negative and in two's complement form, 1's must be used to fill in the seven vacant positions to the right of the imaginary binary point. If M were positive, 0's would be used. These adjustments to M are made by transferring each of the memory locations 1A00, 1A01, and 1A02 into the accumulator and executing microprocessor instructions such as SHIFT RIGHT, ADD, and others to accomplish the required modifications. It is obvious that careful attention must be paid to carries resulting from execution of these instructions since each number is split among three 8-bit memory locations. After the proper adjustments are made, M will now be $1.111111111100011 \times 2^{01000000}$.

Now that the exponents of both the addend and augend are identical, the mantissas can be added using two's complement arithmetic. The addition is:

Sign bit

$$M \qquad 1.111111111100011 \times 2^{0100000} = -0.008850098 \times 2^{32}$$

$$= -3801088$$

$$+ N \qquad 0.111110001100001 \times 2^{0100000} = 0.9717102051 \times 2^{32}$$

$$= 4173463552$$

$$\text{Sum} \quad (1)\ 0.111110001000100 \times 2^{0100000} = 0.9708251953 \times 2^{32}$$

$$= 4169662464$$

Using the test described in Example 3b of Section 2.4.1, Binary Addition, we find the overflow bit is not set.

The actual sum of the addition before shifting the mantissa of M right seven bit positions and, therefore, losing the seven least signif-

$e = y - x$

$\frac{e}{x} \times 100 =$

icant bits of M is 4169678848. Thus, a difference in the two sums of 16384 or 0.00039293% of the actual sum resulted from the equalization of the exponents of M and N.

2.4.7 Multiplication

Multiplication of two positive binary numbers is essentially an adding and shifting operation using the basic binary multiplication rules.

1	1	0	0	*(Multiplicand)*
× 1	× 0	× 1	× 0	*(Multiplier)*
1	0	0	0	*(Product)*

Given two positive binary numbers, M and N, with p and q bits, respectively, the multiplication can be accomplished by a step-by-step procedure for calculation or *algorithm*. Assume that M and N are stored in two registers (or memory locations) in the microprocessor. If M is the multiplicand and N is the multiplier, then N would be stored in a q-bit register and M should be effectively (whether or not actually) stored in a $p + q - 1$ bit register with the $q - 1$ vacant bits to the left of the msb of M as shown.

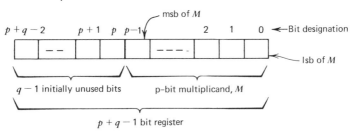

In the multiplication algorithm, the $p + q - 1$ bit register that contains the multiplicand M will be added to the contents of a $p + q$ bit partial product register that will accumulate the sums, that are the intermediate and final results. Pictorially, the registers appear as:

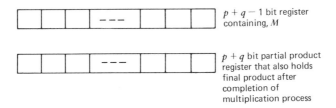

The multiplication algorithm for two positive binary numbers is:

[Set partial product register (intermediate result) = 0.]

1. Test if the lsb of the multiplier is a 1 or 0.
2. If the tested bit of the multiplier is a 1, add the multiplicand to the intermediate result and go to step 4, otherwise go to step 3.
3. If the tested bit of the multiplier is a 0, go to step 4.
4. Shift the multiplicand one bit to the left and fill the vacated lsb position with a 0.
5. If all bits of the multiplier have been tested, the product is present in the partial product register and the multiplication is complete— END.
6. If all multiplier bits have not been tested, determine if the next msb of the multiplier is a 1 or 0 and go to step 2.

An example multiplication will illustrate the procedure.

(Set partial product register = 0.)

1010	(Multiplicand)	=	10_{10}
× 101	(Multiplier)	=	5_{10}

    1010   Intermediate result or partial product (lsb of
    ⋮   multiplier = 1; add multiplicand to intermediate
    ⋮   result—shift multiplicand one bit to the left)

    ⋮   Next lsb of multiplier = 0; shift multiplicand one
    ⋮   bit to the left

    1010   Msb of multiplier = 1; add multiplicand to
            intermediate result or partial product
110010   (Product) = 50_{10}

2.4.8 Division

There are many algorithms for performing the division, $M \div N$, of two positive binary numbers. One commonly used algorithm is to repetitively subtract the *divisor N* from the *dividend M* until a borrow is observed. The borrow indicates that the divisor was subtracted from the dividend "one-too-many-times," thereby permitting determination of the *quotient* or result of $M \div N$. Again, assuming that the divisor and dividend are stored in appropriate registers in the microprocessor and that the quotient will be developed in a partial quotient register, we find that the division algorithm is as follows.

[Set partial quotient register (intermediate result) = 0.]

1. Subtract the divisor from the dividend (addition of two's complement).

2. The difference of the subtraction is to be the new minuend of the next subtraction.

3. Determine if a borrow (no carry) has occurred.

4. If a carry has occurred, add 1 to the intermediate result or partial quotient; go to step 6, otherwise, go to step 5.

5. If a carry has not occurred, the quotient is the number in the partial quotient register, and the magnitude of the remainder, if any, is the result of the next to last subtraction—END.

6. Subtract the divisor from the new minuend and go to step 2.

The following division will demonstrate the algorithm.

Sign bit

$$011011_2 \div 000101_2 = Q + R$$

(Dividend)   (Divisor)   (Quotient)   (Remainder)

or

$$27_{10} \div 5_{10} = Q + R$$

Implementing the algorithm:

(Set partial quotient register = 0.)

011011	(Dividend) = 27_{10}
111011	(Two's complement of Divisor = -5_{10})
(1)010110	Subtraction of 5_{10} from 27_{10} by two's complement addition produced no borrow (carry = 1)—add 1 to partial quotient and
111011	subtract divisor from new minuend
(1) 010001	No borrow (carry = 1)—add 1 to partial quotient (partial quotient now is = 2)
111011	subtract divisor from new minuend
(1) 001100	No borrow (carry = 1)—add 1 to partial quotient (partial quotient now is = 3) and
111011	subtract divisor from new minuend
(1) 000111	No borrow (carry = 1)—add 1 to partial quotient (partial quotient now is = 4) and
111011	subtract divisor from new minuend

(1) 000010 ⤶ No borrow (carry = 1)—add 1 to partial quotient
    111011   (partial quotient now is = 5) and
    ——————   subtract divisor from new minuend
    111101   Borrow (carry = 0) is generated—division is
              ended. Quotient (5_{10}) is held in partial product
              register and remainder (R) is the result of the
              next-to-last subtraction.

Remainder $= 2_{10}$.

2.5 ALGORITHM EXAMPLE

In utilizing microprocessors, one finds that there are a number of algorithms that are extremely useful in a wide variety of applications. One such algorithm is delay generation. The algorithm for delay generation is presented in general form to permit application to any microprocessor.

2.5.1 Delay Generation

Delay generation by software is accomplished by having the program execute a certain set of instructions repeatedly. Since the length of time required to execute each of the instructions is known, the amount of delay time generated can be calculated as the sum of the products of each instruction and its execution time. Having the microprocessor execute a particular sequence of instructions over and over again is called a *loop*. The following algorithm implements a simple delay loop.

1. Load the accumulator register with a number, N (this instruction will take n microseconds to execute).
2. Decrement the accumulator (d microseconds required for execution).
3. If accumulator = 0, delay timing is completed. If not, go to step 2 (m microseconds required for completion.

The total delay time required to execute this algorithm is, then, $n + N (d + m)$ microseconds. In many microprocessors, the step 3 instruction execution time will vary, depending on whether or not the "go to step 2" path is taken. For critical timing loops, this difference in execution time should be taken into consideration.

REFERENCES

1. R.K. Richards, *Digital Design*, John Wiley & Sons, New York, 1971.

2. Yaohan, Chu, *Digital Computer Design Fundamentals*, McGraw–Hill Book Company, New York, 1962.

3. R.K. Richards, *Arithmetic Operations in Digital Computers*, D. Van Nostrand Company, Princeton, N.J., 1955.

COMPUTER LOGIC

The microprocessor, like any computing device, is composed of basic decision-making cells or logic elements. The intelligence in the microprocessor chip is derived from the interconnection of these logic elements enabling the performance of relatively more complex functions such as instruction interpretation and control. In this chapter, the classical means of designing these logic elements and using them to implement microprocessor functions is highlighted. The techniques involved form the nucleus of sophisticated *computer-aided design* (*CAD*) and analysis programs used by the semiconductor manufacturers in the development, production, and testing of microprocessors and related chips. In addition, the logic design principles involved are relevant to the understanding of the microprocessor and to the design of interface functions that are necessary to bring data into and to send data out of the microprocessor.

3.1 SYMBOLIC STATE REPRESENTATIONS

Since the physical properties of the electrical, mechanical, magnetic, optical, and fluidic components available to implement stable and reliable logic elements are conducive to ON–OFF operation, most computer logic elements operate in the *binary* or *two-state* mode; that is, the state of a logic element can be represented by a transistor conducting or not conducting, by a mechanical switch closed or open, by a ferrite core magnetized North-to-South or South-to-North, or by the binary states of other physical devices. These states can be further classified into *active* or *inactive* categories. For example, a transistor conducting, a mechanical switch closed, and a ferrite core magnetized North-to-South can be said to be in the active state whereas a transistor not conducting, an mechanical switch open, or a ferrite core magnetized South-to-North can be defined as in the inactive state. Keep in mind that these categorizations are purely arbitrary and the designations *active* and *inactive* can be applied to physical states at the discretion of the definer. The important point to remember in making and using the active and inactive state assignments is that they be applied and interpreted *consistently* in the analysis and design of logic elements and the functions implemented with these elements.

In order to represent the binary states, the *symbols 1* and *0* are used. The symbol 1 is normally assigned to the active state and 0 assigned to the inactive state. Again, this assignment is arbitrary and can be reversed when advantageous to do so. When used in the design and analysis methods discussed in this chapter, the symbols 1 and 0 will be treated as binary digits, but it is important to remember that they are *symbols* representing binary states inherent in the microprocessor logic circuits.

3.2 BOOLEAN ALGEBRA

At one time, design using logic elements, or logic design, was a skill that was acquired through years of experience. Among the devices used to represent the binary states were switches, magnetic cores, vacuum tubes, and relays (electromagnetically operated switches.) Since switches and relays were commonly used in logic applications, the logic circuits are called *switching circuits*. Then, in 1938, Claude E. Shannon published a paper in which he developed a calculus applicable to switching circuits.* His calculus was based on the algebra of logic or *Boolean algebra* proposed by George Boole in 1847 and 1854.† Shannon's work provided for a systematic approach to logic design using a two-element Boolean algebra in which the variables are restricted to only two values, 1 and 0. This two-element subset of Boolean algebra or *switching algebra,* as it is called, became a powerful tool in the analysis and design of digital circuits. In the following developments, the terms *two-element Boolean algebra* and *switching algebra* are used interchangeably.

Formally, two-element Boolean algebra or switching algebra can be termed as the set S with the operations $+$ (OR, the Boolean sum), $\cdot$ (AND, the Boolean product), and $'$ (NOT, the Boolean inversion or complement) defined on the two elements, 1 and 0, of S such that the property of closure holds for the given operations over the elements of S. This definition states that for any variables x and y ϵS, $x \cdot y$, $x + y$, and x' ϵS; x and $y = 0$ or 1, and $x \cdot y$, $x + y$, and $x' = 0$ or 1.

3.2.1 Switching Algebra Posulates

As in any algebra a set of *postulates* or *assumptions without proof* must be established initially. From these postulates, the *theorems* or *propositions* of switching algebra can be proved.

Recall that the operations $+$ and $\cdot$ are **not** the operations of conventional algebra but that, in many instances, the results of these operations among the *symbols* 1 and 0 of S are identical to those of conventional algebra. Examples of these identical results are given in postulates 2, 3, 3a, 4, and 4a.

The switching algebra postulates are:

* C. E. Shannon, *A Symbolic Analysis of Relay and Switching Circuits,* Transactions of the AIEE, Vol. 57, 1938, pp. 713–723.

† George Boole, *The Mathematical Analysis of Logic,* Cambridge, England, 1847 (reprinted 1948, Oxford); George Boole, *An Investigation of the Laws of Thought,* London, 1854 (reprinted 1954, Dover Publications, New York).

1. $x = 0$ if $x \neq 1$ This defines two-valued Boolean algebra
1a. $x = 1$ if $x \neq 0$

2. $0 \cdot 0 = 0$ These next six postulates define reults of
2a. $1 + 1 = 1$ operations among elements 1 and $0 \in S$

3. $1 \cdot 1 = 1$
3a. $0 + 0 = 0$

4. $1 \cdot 0 = 0 = 0 \cdot 1$
4a. $0 + 1 = 1 = 1 + 0$

5. $0' = 1$ These postulates define the complement of
5a. $1' = 0$ the elements 1 and $0 \in S$

3.2.2 Switching Algebra Theorems

Now that the postulates have been established, the theorems of switching algebra can be stated. These theorems can be proved by using the postulates and any preceding proven theorems. In the following theorems, the variables x, y, and $z \in S$ with $+$, $\cdot$, and $'$ the defined operations of the algebra.

1. $x + 0 = x$ The existence of a unique zero
                                  element of S
1a. $x \cdot 1 = x$ The existence of a unique
                                  identity element of S

2. $1 + x = 1$
2a. $0 \cdot x = 0$

3. $x + x = x$ Idempotence
3a. $x \cdot x = x$

4. $[x]' = x'$ The complement of the variable x
                                    $\in S$ is identical to NOT x
4a. $[x']' = x$ The complement of the
                                    complement of the variable $x \in S$
                                    is identical to x

5. $x + x' = 1$ Existence of a unique
5a. $x \cdot x' = 0$ complement, x', of $x \in S$

6. $x + y = y + x$ Commutativity of elements x and
6a. $x \cdot y = y \cdot x$ $y \in S$ over $\cdot$ and $+$

7. $x + x \cdot y = x$

7a. $x \cdot (x + y) = x$

8. $(x + y') \cdot y = xy$

8a. $x \cdot y' + y = x + y$

9. $x + y + z = (x + y) + z$ Associative property
       $= x + (y + z)$

9a. $x \cdot y \cdot z = (x \cdot y) \cdot z = x$
       $\cdot (y \cdot z)$

10. $x \cdot y + x \cdot z = x \cdot (y +$ Distributive property
       $z)$

10a. $(x + y) \cdot (x + z) = x + y$
       $\cdot z$

11. $(x + y) \cdot (y + z) \cdot (z +$
       $x') = (x + y) \cdot (z + x')$

11a. $x \cdot y + y \cdot z + z \cdot x' = x$
       $\cdot y + z \cdot x'$

12. $(x + y)(x' + z) = xz +$
       $x'y$

13. $(x + y + z \cdots)' = x' \cdot y'$ DeMorgan's theorem
       $\cdot z' \cdot \ldots \cdot$

13a. $(x \cdot y \cdot z \cdots)' = x' +$
       $y' + z' + \cdots +$

14. $[f(x_1, x_2, \ldots, x_n, +, \cdot)]'$ Shannon's theorem—a
       $= f(x_1', x_2', \ldots, x_n', \cdot, +)$ generalization of DeMorgan's
                                          theorem

15. $f(x_1, x_2, \ldots, x_n) = x_1 \cdot f(1,$
       $x_2, \ldots, x_n) + x_1' \cdot f(0, x_2, \ldots, x_n)$

15a. $f(x_1, x_2, \ldots, x_n) = [x_1 + f$
       $(0, x_2, \ldots, x_n)] \cdot [x_1' + f(1, x_2, \ldots,$
       $x_n)]$ Expansion theorem

      Theorems 13 and 13a, DeMorgan's theorems, and their generalization in Theorem 14 are particularly useful in logic design and analysis. Theorem 13 states that the complement of a logic or switching function (as opposed to the complement of a single variable) that is the logical sum of any number of switching variables can be found by taking the complement of each of the switching variables and changing the + operator to the · operator. Conversely, the complement of a function that is the logical product of any number of switching variables can be found by taking the complement of each of the switching variables and changing the · operator to the + operator. For example, the complement of the expression $w' + x + y + z'$ is $w · x' · y' · z$ and the complement of $w · x' · y · z'$ is $w' + x + y' + z$. The generalization of DeMorgan's theorems in Theorem 14 states that the complement of a switching function where the variables and groups of variables are joined by the + and · operators is found by taking the complements of the variables and groups of variables and interchanging the + and · operators connecting them. Care must be taken in applying Theorem 14, and parentheses and brackets should be used liberally to insure no errors are made. The technique is illustrated in the following example.

$$f(w,x,y,z) = (w' + x · z) · (y + z · w) + x · z$$

$$f'(w,x,y,z) = ?$$

Rewriting $f(w,x,y,z)$ with brackets and parentheses prior to using Theorem 14 yields:

$$f(w,x,y,z) = [(w' + x · z) · (y + z · w)] + (x · z)$$

Applying Theorem 14,

$$f'(w,x,y,z) = [(w' + x · z)' + (y + z · w)'] · (x · z)'$$
$$= [(w ·(x' + z')) + (y' · (z' + w'))] · (x' + z')$$
$$= [w · x' + wz' + y' · z' + y' · w'] · (x' + z')$$
$$= w · x' + w · x' · z' + x' · y' · z' + w' · x' · y'$$
$$+ w · x' · z' + wz' + y'z' + w'y'z'$$

Using theorems to reduce the function:

$$= w · x' (1 + z') + wz' (x' + 1) + y' z' (x' + 1 + w') + w'x'y'$$
$$= w · x' (1 + z') + y'z' (x' + 1 + w') + wz'(x' + 1) + w'x'y'$$
$$= w · x' + y' · z' + w · z' + w'x'y'$$
$$= x' · (w + w' · y') + y' · z' + w ·z'$$
$$= x' · (w + y') + y' ·z' + w ·z'$$
$$= x' ·w + x' ·y' + y' ·z' + w ·z'$$

or

$$x' · (w + y') + z' · (w + y')$$
$$= (x' + z') · (w + y')$$

Theorems 15 and 15a are expansion theorems and are used to expand an n-variable switching function about any of the variables. These theorems can be proven by first substituting 1 for x_1 or 0 for x_1' and then 0 for x_1 and 1 for x_1' as follows.

For Theorem 15, letting $x_1 = 1$ and $x_1' = 0$:

$$f(1, x_2, \ldots, x_n) = 1 \cdot f(1, x_2, \ldots, x_n) + 0 \cdot f(0, x_2, \ldots, x_n)$$
$$= f(1, x_2, \ldots, x_n)$$

For Theorem 15, letting $x_1 = 0$ and $x_1' = 1$:

$$f(0, x_2, \ldots, x_n) = 0 \cdot f(1, x_2, \ldots, x_n)$$
$$+ 1 \cdot f(0, x_2, \ldots, x_n)$$
$$= f(0, x_2, \ldots, x_n)$$

Similarly, for Theorem 15a, letting $x_1 = 1$ and $x_1' = 0$:

$$f(1, x_2, \ldots, x_n) = [1 + f(0, x_2, \ldots, x_n)]$$
$$\cdot [0 + f(1, x_2, \ldots, x_n)]$$
$$= [1 \cdot 0 + 1 \cdot f(1, x_2, \ldots, x_n)$$
$$+ 0 \cdot f(0, x_2, \ldots, x_n)$$
$$+ f(0, x_2, \ldots, x_n) \cdot f(1, x_2, \ldots, x_n)]$$
$$= f(1, x_2, \ldots, x_n)[1 + f(0, x_2, \ldots, x_n)]$$
$$= f(1, x_2, \ldots, x_n)$$

Now, for $x_1 = 0$ and $x_1' = 1$:

$$f(0, x_2, \ldots, x_n) = [0 + f(0, x_2, \ldots, x_n)]$$
$$\cdot [1 + f(1, x_2, \ldots, x_n)]$$
$$= [0 \cdot 1 + 0 \cdot f(1, x_2, \ldots, x_n)$$
$$+ 1 \cdot f(0, x_2, \ldots, x_n) + f(0, x_2, \ldots, x_n)$$
$$\cdot f(1, x_2, \ldots, x_n)]$$
$$= f(0, x_2, \ldots, x_n)[1 + f(1, x_2, \ldots, x_n)]$$
$$= f(0, x_2, \ldots, x_n)$$

From the expansion theorem, four additional theorems can be proved.

16. $x_1 \cdot f(x_1, x_2,...,x_n) = x_1 \cdot f(1, x_2,...,x_n)$

16a. $x_1 + f(x_1, x_2,...,x_n) = x_1 + f(0, x_2,...,x_n)$

17. $x_1' \cdot f(x_1, x_2,...,x_n) = x_1' \cdot f(0, x_2,...,x_n)$

17a. $x_1' + f(x_1, x_2,...,x_n) = x_1' + f(1, x_2,...,x_n)$

The proofs of all of the theorems are not derived, but a few example proofs are given to illustrate typical methods.

3.2.3   Example Proofs

Since the variables in the two-element Boolean algebra can take on only the values 0 or 1, all possible combinations of these values can be substituted into a theorem to verify that the theorem holds for all the combinations. This method of proof is called *perfect induction*. For example, proof of Theorem 3, $x + x = x$, by perfect induction is accomplished by first substituting 0 for x and then 1 for x and verifying that the results are valid in terms of a previously proven theorem or a postulate. Applying this method yields:

$$0 + 0 = 0 \text{ (true by postulate 3a)}$$

$$1 + 1 = 1 \text{ (true by postulate 2a)}$$

Therefore, Theorem 3 is valid. Perfect induction applied to Theorem 10 establishes the distributive law of the switching algebra.

(Theorem 10)

x	y	z	$xy + x \cdot z = x \cdot (y + z)$	
0	0	0	$0 \cdot 0 + 0 \cdot 0 = 0 \cdot (0 + 0)$	(postulates 2,3a)
0	0	1	$0 \cdot 0 + 0 \cdot 1 = 0 \cdot (0 + 1)$	(postulates 2,4,4a,3a)
0	1	0	$0 \cdot 1 + 0 \cdot 0 = 0 \cdot (1 + 0)$	(postulates 4,2,4a,3a)
0	1	1	$0 \cdot 1 + 0 \cdot 1 = 0 \cdot (1 + 1)$	(postulates 4,2a,3a)
1	0	0	$1 \cdot 0 + 1 \cdot 0 = 1 \cdot (0 + 0)$	(postulates 4,3a)
1	0	1	$1 \cdot 0 + 1 \cdot 1 = 1 \cdot (0 + 1)$	(postulates 4,3,4a)
1	1	0	$1 \cdot 1 + 1 \cdot 0 = 1 \cdot (1 + 0)$	(postulates 3,4,4a)
1	1	1	$1 \cdot 1 + 1 \cdot 1 = 1 \cdot (1+1)$	(postulates 3,2a)

Again, note that, for the case where the variables are restricted to the values 0 and 1, the number of possible combinations of those variables $= 2^n$ where $n =$ the number of variables.

As in conventional algebra, the $\cdot$ sign or Boolean AND operation can be omitted between variables in switching algebra; that is, $x \cdot y$ can be written as xy. Parentheses and brackets can and should be used in the same manner as in conventional algebra.

Another method of proving the switching algebra theorems is to use previously proven postulates and theorems alone without applying perfect induction. Examples of proofs of Theorems 7a and 8a in this manner are given as follows.

Theorem 7a

$$x(x + y) = x$$
$$xx + xy = x \qquad \text{(Theorem 10, distributive property)}$$
$$x + xy = x \qquad \text{(Theorem 3a)}$$
$$x + xy = x \qquad \text{(proven, since this is Theorem 7)}$$

Theorem 8a

$$xy' + y = x + y$$
$$xy' + y \cdot 1 = x + y \qquad \text{(Theorem 1a)}$$
$$xy' + y\,(x + x') = x + y \qquad \text{(Theorem 5)}$$
$$xy' + yx + yx' = x + y \qquad \text{(Theorem 10, distributive property)}$$
$$xy' + yx + yx + yx' = x + y \qquad \text{(Theorem 3)}$$
$$xy' + xy + yx + yx' = x + y \qquad \text{(Theorem 6a)}$$
$$x(y' + y) + y(x + x') = x + y \qquad \text{(Theorem 10, distributive property)}$$
$$x \cdot 1 + y \cdot 1 = x + y \qquad \text{(Theorem 5)}$$
$$x + y = x + y \qquad \text{(Theorem 1a)}$$

The visualization of some of the switching algebra theorems and postulates is aided by associating a 0 with an open switch, a 1 with a closed switch, the $\cdot$ or AND operation with switches in series, and the + or OR operation with switches in parallel. Using these conventions, some postulates and theorems can be visualized as shown.

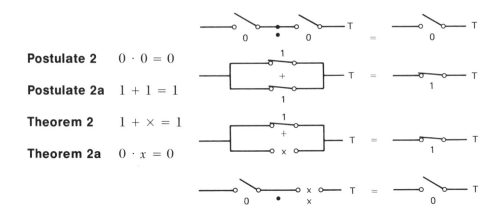

Postulate 2	$0 \cdot 0 = 0$
Postulate 2a	$1 + 1 = 1$
Theorem 2	$1 + \times = 1$
Theorem 2a	$0 \cdot x = 0$

3.2.4 Transmission and Standard or Canonical Forms

Using the previous examples, we introduce the concept of *transmission* (T). The *transmission of a circuit is 1 if there is a connection or short circuit from the input to the output and it is 0 if there is no connection or an open circuit from the input to the output.* In the examples of Postulate 2a and Theorem 2, the transmission or T = 1, and, for Postulate 2 and Theorem 2a, $T = 0$. When the transmission is a function of switching variables, it is termed a *transmission function*. For instance,

$$f(x,y) = x'y + xy'$$

and

$$T = A'BC + AB'C'$$

are transmisson functions. Two *standard* or *canonical* forms of a transmission function are commonly used. One is the *standard* or *canonical* sum, which is the *sum of products* of *all* the n variables of an n-variable problem, and the other is the *standard* or *canonical* product, which is the *product of sums* of the n variables. The following are examples of standard sums and standard products of a three-variable switching problem.

$f(x, y, z) = x'y'z' + xyz + x'yz$	(standard sum)
$T = A'BC' + ABC + AB'C$	(standard sum)
$f(x,y,z) = (x' + y' + z')(x + y + z)(x' + y + z)$	(standard product)
$T = (A' + B + C')(A + B + C)(A + B' + C)$	(standard product)

The product terms of the standard sum are called *minterms* and the sum terms of the standard product are called *maxterms*. Remember, minterms and maxterms contain all n variables of an n-variable switching function.

Terms of an n-variable switching function that contain n or less variables are called P *terms* if they are product terms and S *terms* if they are sum terms. Thus, a minterm is always a P term but a P term may not necessarily be a minterm. The *order* of a P term or S term is defined as the number of missing variables of the P term or S term. For an n-variable switching function, a P term of $n - m$ variables where $m < n$ is said to have an order of m. The following P terms and S terms further illustrate the definition of order.

$f(x,y,z)$	$= xy$	P term of 1st order
$f(a,b,c,d,e)$	$= ab'c$	P term of 2nd order
$f(u,v,w,x,y,z)$	$= uv'$	P term of 4th order
$f(x,y,z)$	$= (x + z)$	S term of 1st order
$f(a,b,c,d,e,f)$	$= (a + d + f')$	S term of 3rd order
$f(a,b,c)$	$=(a' + b' + c')$	S term of 0 order

3.3 KARNAUGH MAP METHOD

The use of switching algebra in analyzing and minimizing switching functions was greatly enhanced by a method developed by M. Karnaugh which permits the visual perception of minterns (or maxterms) that can be combined to form the simpler P terms (or S terms).* In order to use the Karnaugh method effectively, a numerical technique for representing the standard sum, minterms, or P-terms is introduced. The same techniques can also be applied to the standard product, maxterms, and S terms, but since switching functions are expressible using minterms and P terms and these forms are commonly used in design, the remaining material in this chapter is presented using the sum of products functional form.

3.3.1 Numerical Representation of Minterms and P-Terms

Since switching functions may involve a large number of minterms or P terms, it is convenient to represent minterms or P terms numerically. If the symbol for a variable is defined as a *literal*, then the rules for numerical representation of minterms and P terms can be given as:

---

* M. Karnaugh, *The Map Method for Synthesis of Combinational Logic Circuits*, A.I.E.E. Transactions, Part I: Communications and Electronics, Vol. 72, November 1953, pp. 593–599.

(a) Uncomplemented or unprimed literals in a minterm or P term are replaced by a 1.

(b) Complemented or primed literals in a minterm or P term are replaced by a 0.

(c) A missing literal in a minterm or P term is replaced by a $-$ or a 2; then, assuming that each $-$ or 2 is replaced by a 1, write the full number followed by parentheses that enclose the decimal equivalents of the binary positions of the missing literals in the minterm or P term.

These rules assume that the minterms or P terms are always written in the *consistent order* ABCD or wxyz as opposed to DCBA or zyxw. Some four-variable examples of this numerical representation are:

MINTERM OR P TERM	BINARY EQUIVALENT REPRESENTATION	DECIMAL EQUIVALENT REPRESENTATION
ABCD	msb → 1111	15
A'BC'D'	0100	4
AC'	1-0- or 1202 $\Big\}$ ≡1101 (1,4)	13(1,4)
$wx'z$	10-1 or 1021 $\Big\}$ ≡1011 (2)	11(2)

The number of digits in the parentheses is also the order of the P term. This technique can be applied to provide a shorthand method of writing transmission functions in the standard or canonical sum form.

$$f(w,x,y,z) = w'x'y'z' + w'x'yz + w'xy'z + wxy'z'$$

$$+ wxyz + wx'y'z$$

$$= 0000 + 0011 + 0101 + 1100 + 1111 + 1001$$

$$= 0 + 3 + 5 + 12 + 15 + 9$$

$$= \sum_1 (0, 3, 5, 12, 15, 9)$$

The symbol $\sum_1$ indicates that the numbers inside the parentheses are minterms whose logical or Boolean sum (OR) produces a transmission of 1. Similarly, a transmission function of the type $T' = \sum_0 (0, 3, 12, 14 , \ldots)$

would represent the logical or Boolean sum of minterms that would yield a transmission of 0.

A third situation that arises is one in which certain combinations of input variables cannot occur or, if they do occur, the output can be arbitrarily assigned to be either a 0 or 1. These input conditions are called *don't care* or *phi* (pronounced phe) *conditions* and are denoted by the symbol ϕ and by $\sum_\phi$ in the transmission function numerical representation. An example of a "don't care" input situation is a liquid level indicating circuit. Suppose that, in the following illustration, it is desired to know when the level of the liquid is above sensor A and below sensor B. The sensors are designed such that their output will be 1 volt (which will be defined as a logic 1) when they are in contact with the liquid and 0 volts (a logic 0) when they do not sense any liquid.

Liquid level sensors

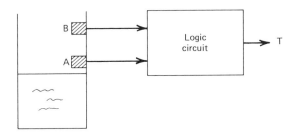

(T = 1 if liquid level is at or above sensor A and below sensor B and T = 0 if liquid level is otherwise)

INPUT		OUTPUT	
A	B	T	
0	0	0	
0	1	ϕ	Cannot occur
1	0	1	Liquid level at or above sensor A and below sensor B
1	1	0	

The output corresponding to the "don't care" input condition can arbitrarily be assigned a value of 0 or 1. The proper assignment of the "don't care" output can, in many instances, lead to a more efficient logic circuit solution than if it were not used or properly assigned. The means of using the "don't care" conditions will be covered in the following portions of this chapter. The different numerical representations of the transmission function of this example are:

$$T = \sum\nolimits_1 (2)$$

or

$$T' = \sum\nolimits_0 (0,3) + \sum\nolimits_\phi (1)$$

If a "don't care" output is assigned a 0 value, it should not then be used as a 1 value in the expression for T or vice versa.

3.3.2 Venn Diagram

A pictorial method of representing the logical operations among switching variables is the *Venn diagram.* The Venn diagram for one variable is:

One variable

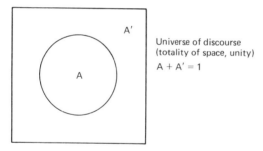

Universe of discourse
(totality of space, unity)

$A + A' = 1$

Venn diagrams for two and three variables are:

Two variables

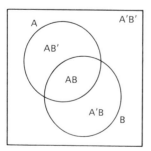

Three variables

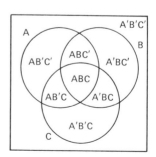

$$AB' + AB + A'B + A'B' = 1$$

$$AB'C' + ABC' + A'BC' + AB'C + ABC + A'BC + A'B'C + A'B'C' = 1$$

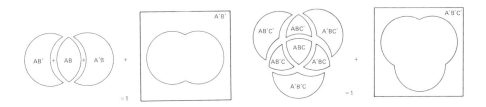

The Venn diagram pictorially illustrates which minterms can combine to form a *P* term with a reduced number of literals. Minterms that can combine in this manner are physically *adjacent* in the Venn diagram and differ algebraically by the complement of one variable. For example, in the three-variable Venn diagram, the following minterms are some of those that are adjacent.

ABC′ and AB′C′	(110 and 100)
A′BC′ and ABC′	(010 and 110)
A′B′C′ and A′B′C	(000 and 001)
ABC and A′BC	(111 and 011)

Numerically, these *adjacent* minterms differ by a power of 2. Looking at the same three variable minterms in numerical form:

6 and 4	(differ by 2)
2 and 6	(differ by 4)
0 and 1	(differ by 1)
7 and 3	(differ by 4)

3.3.3 Karnaugh Map

If the Venn diagrams for one through three variables are redrawn in a rectangular fashion, one-, two-, and three-variable *Karnaugh maps* result.

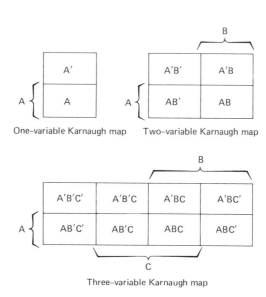

One-variable Karnaugh map   Two-variable Karnaugh map

Three-variable Karnaugh map

Now, if numerical representations for the minterms in each square or cell of the map are used, the following forms of the Karnaugh map are obtained for one, two, and three variables.

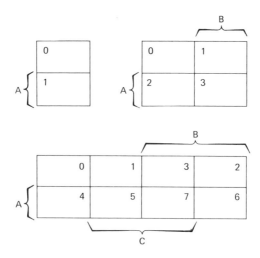

The adjacencies described in the Venn diagram are preserved in the Karnaugh map and thus provide a simple, visual means of reducing or minimizing switching functions.

To illustrate the application of the Karnaugh map, consider the three-variable transmission function.

$$T = AB'C + ABC + A'B'C' + A'BC'$$

Converting to numerical form produces

$$T = 101 + 111 + 000 + 010$$
$$= 5 + 7 + 0 + 2$$
$$= \Sigma_1 (0,2,5,7)$$

Since these minterms each will produce a transmission of 1, a 1 is placed in the map cell corresponding to that minterm. All the remaining minterms produce a transmission of 0 and would have a 0 placed in their positions in the map. Conventionally, the 0's are usually omitted from the map. The Karnaugh map for the given transmission function is:

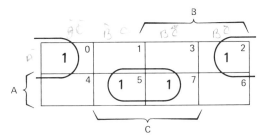

Karnaugh map of $T = \Sigma_1 (0,2,5,7)$

Note that the map "wraps around" so that minterms 0 and 2 and 4 and 6 are adjacent. By grouping minterms 0 and 2 and 5 and 7, one can produce a transmission function with a reduced number of literals. This minimized transmission function can be obtained by determining the intersections of areas (P terms) that define each group and by joining them as a sum of products. From the map of $T = \Sigma_1 (0,2,5,7)$, the intersection of areas A and C produces P term AC and defines the group composed of minterms 5 and 7. Similarly, P term A'C' defines the group composed of minterms 0 and 2. Thus, the reduced transmission function is

$$T = AC + A'C'$$

The reduced or minimized transmission function obtained by the Karnaugh map method is not necessarily unique. In many cases, groupings can be made differently for the same canonical sum, resulting in a different minimized sum of products. This method also guarantees that the resulting circuit will be a *two-level* realization. A *two-level realization* is one in which any logic signal will pass through only two levels of gating from the input to the output of the circuit. This definition assumes that the variables and their complements are available at the input of the circuit.

By extending the Venn diagram–Karnaugh map development, one obtains four- and five-variable Karnaugh maps.

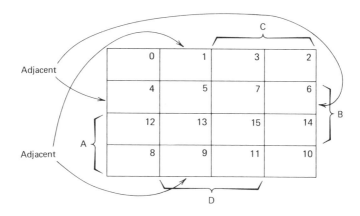

Four-variable Karnaugh map

Besides the physically adjacent cells in the four-variable map, cells 0 and 2, 4 and 6, 12 and 14, 8 and 10, 0 and 8, 1 and 9, 3 and 11, and 2 and 10 are adjacent. These adjacencies can be visualized by "wrapping the map around" vertically and horizontally.

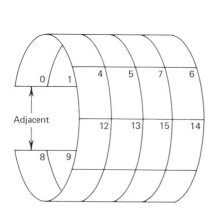

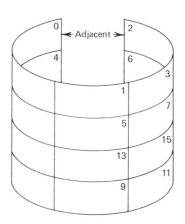

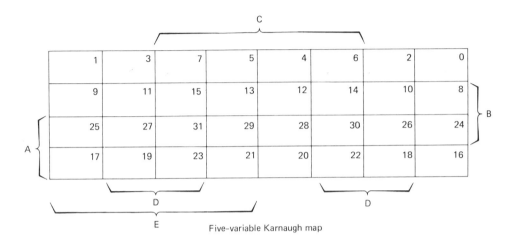

Five-variable Karnaugh map

Care must be exercised in applying the five-variable map since, in addition to the obvious and "wrap-around" adjacencies, the five-variable map has additional internal adjacencies that are not immediately obvious. Examples of these adjacencies are minterms 3 and 2, 11 and 10, 27 and 26, 19 and 18, 7 and 6, 15 and 14, 31 and 30, and 23 and 22.

From observation, it can be seen that *the number of cells to which any cell of an n variable map is adjacent is equal to n.*

There are necessary and sufficient conditions for grouping on the Karnaugh map. These are:

Necessary condition—the number of minterms in a group must be equal to a power of 2. This requirement results from the fact that a P term of order m resulting from a combination of adjacent minterms must be derived from the combination of 2^m minterms.

Sufficient condition—the extreme minterms of any row or column in the group must be adjacent.

The objectives of the grouping should be to make the smallest number of groups with each group containing the largest number of minterms possible.

Some examples are now presented to illustrate the preceding concepts.

Minimize by Karnaugh map:

(a) $f(w,x,y,z) = \sum_1 (0,2,4,6,8,10,11,12,14,15)$

Solution:

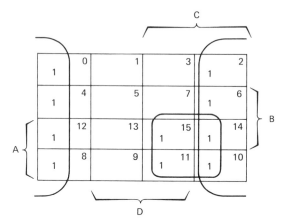

$$T = D' + AC$$

(b) $T = B'D' + AC'D' + AC'D$

Solution:
This transmission function is given as a sum of P terms. To enter it on the Karnaugh map, the reverse procedure of writing P terms from the map is applied. For example, B'D' specifies the four corners of the map—minterms 0,2,8, and 10; AC'D' specifies minterms 12 and 8; and AC'D specifies minterms 9 and 13.

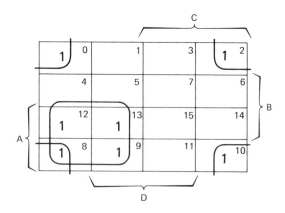

Writing P terms from the two groupings,

$$T = B'D' + AC'$$

(c) $T = \sum_1 (0,1,9,10) + \sum_\phi (2,3,4,15)$

Solution:

The "don't care" conditions in this example can be used as 1's as required to reduce the number of literals in the resulting P terms.

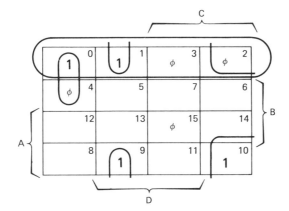

The four groupings in this map are minterms 0,1,3,2; 0,4; 1,9; and 2,10.

The minimized function is, then,

$$T = A'B' + A'C'D' + B'C'D + B'CD'$$

(d) $f(w,x,y,z) = \sum_1 (4,5,6,12,13,14)$

Find $f'(w,x,y,z)$.

Solution:

$f'(w,x,y,z)$ is found by grouping all 0's on the map. The 0's are all the minterms except those given in the $\sum_1$ parentheses.

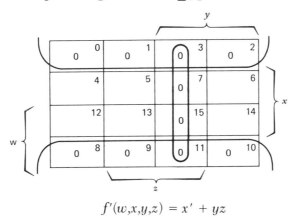

$$f'(w,x,y,z) = x' + yz$$

(e) $f(A,B,C,D,E) = \sum_1 (6,7,8,15,22,24,31) + \sum_\phi (1,14,17,23,30)$

Solution:

The "don't care" conditions minterms 14, 23, and 30 can be utilized to make an eight-minterm grouping. The remaining "don't care" conditions do not serve to make a larger grouping of 1's and are, therefore, not used.

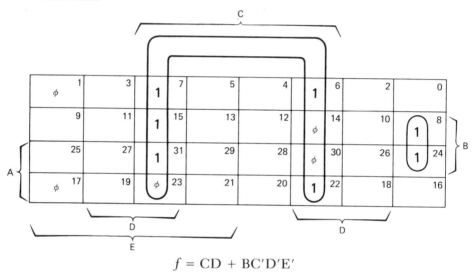

$$f = CD + BC'D'E'$$

3.4 COMBINATIONAL LOGIC CIRCUITS

Using the concept of transmission as defined in Section 3.2.4 of this chapter, we can now study an important class of digital circuits. In this class of digital circuits, the output is completely defined by the combinations of input variables and not by the sequence in which they are applied. This type of digital circuit is called a *combinational circuit*. Other terms used to describe a combinational circuit are *combinational logic or combinatorial logic*.

3.4.1 Table of Combinations

In order to completely define the output of a combinational circuit for each of the 2^n combinations of the n input variables, a *table of combinations or truth table* is used. Table 3.1 illustrates the table of combinations for seven of the basic digital logic building blocks—AND, OR, NAND, NOR, NOT, EXCLUSIVE OR, and EXCLUSIVE NOR (COINCIDENCE). These and other digital circuits are often referred to as *gates*. The symbols used are according to military standard 806B.

TABLE 3.1   Table of Combinations of the Seven Basic Logic Functions

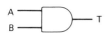

$$T = A \cdot B$$

INPUT		OUTPUT
A	B	T
0	0	0
0	1	0
1	0	0
1	1	1

AND

$$T = A + B$$

INPUT		OUTPUT
A	B	T
0	0	0
0	1	1
1	0	1
1	1	1

OR

$$T = A'$$

INPUT	OUTPUT
A	T
0	1
1	0

NOT (Logic Inverter)

$$T = (A \cdot B)'$$

INPUT		OUTPUT
A	B	T
0	0	1
0	1	1
1	0	1
1	1	0

NAND

$$T = (A + B)'$$

INPUT		OUTPUT
A	B	T
0	0	1
0	1	0
1	0	0
1	1	0

NOR

Table 3-1   Continued

INPUT		OUTPUT
A	B	T
0	0	0
0	1	1
1	0	1
1	1	0

INPUT		OUTPUT
A	B	T
0	0	1
0	1	0
1	0	0
1	1	1

EXCLUSIVE OR (XOR)

(Sometimes the symbol ⊕ is also used to designate the EXCLUSIVE OR function.)

EXCLUSIVE NOR (COINCIDENCE)

(Sometimes the symbol ⊙ is also used to designate the EXCLUSIVE NOR or COINCIDENCE function.)

Since the values of T,A, and B are limited to either 0 or 1, the table of combinations completely defines any combinational logic function in the **ideal** situation, namely, that all inputs and corresponding outputs change **instantaneously.** In reality, a *propagation delay,* or the time delay from the application of a level change at the input (A or B in the table of combinations examples—Table 3.1) to the change of state at the output of a digital circuit (T in the table of combinations examples), is on the order of tens of nanoseconds (one nanosecond = 10^{-9} seconds). This number is an average value and some logic families have delays that are lower or higher.

The number of inputs to a logic gate can be increased and the output defined by applying Theorems 9 and 9a, the associative laws of switching algebra. For example, the transmission function of a three-input OR gate can be defined as:

$$T = A + B + C$$

$$= (A + B) + C$$

The equivalent symbols for a three-input OR circuit are, then:

The table of combinations is also useful as a means to obtain the transmission function of any arbitrary logic device. First, all combinations of the input variables and the output (or outputs, if there is more than one output) corresponding to each combination of input variables must be put in the table. The transmission function is then written as a standard or canonical sum by applying the following rules.

Rule 1: For each 1 and only each 1 in the output column of the table of combinations, the corresponding input variables are used to form a minterm of the standard sum.

Rule 2: If the value of the variable in the **input** column is a 1, the variable is written as an unprimed or uncomplemented variable in the minterm; if the value of the variable in the **input** column is a 0, the variable is written as a primed or complemented variable in the minterm.

This procedure can be illustrated by the next example, given a specified table of combinations:

INPUT		OUTPUT	
A	B	T_1	T_2
0	0	1	1
0	1	1	0
1	0	0	1
1	1	0	0

Applying Rules 1 and 2, one can derive the transmission functions for the two-output logic circuit as the standard sums

$$T_1 = A'B' + A'B$$

and

$$T_2 = A'B' + AB'$$

Note that the transmission functions obtained in this manner are not necessarily minimized and they can be simplified ($T_1 = A'$, $T_2 = B'$).

By a similar procedure, the table of combinations can be used to obtain the transmission function in the standard or canonical product form by using the following rules.

Rule 3: For each 0 and only each 0 in the output column of the table of combinations, the corresponding input variables are used to form a maxterm of the standard product.

Rule 4: If the value of the variable in the input column is a 0, the variable is written as an unprimed or uncomplemented value in the maxterm; as if the value of the variable in the input column is a 1, the variable is written as a primed or complemented variable in the maxterm.

Referring to the previous example, T_1 and T_2 can be written as:

$$T_1 = (A' + B)(A' + B')$$
$$T_2 = (A + B')(A' + B')$$

By taking the logical products of the maxterms of T_1 and T_2 and manipulating the results using the theorems and postulates, one can show that T_1 and T_2 in the standard product form are equivalent to T_1 and T_2 in the standard sum form:

$$
\begin{aligned}
T_1 &= (A' + B)(A' + B') \\
&= A' + A'B' + A'B \\
&= A'(1 + B' + B) \\
&= A' \\
T_2 &= (A + B')(A' + B') \\
&= AB' + A'B' + B' \\
&= B'(A + A' + 1) \\
&= B'
\end{aligned}
$$

The Karnaugh map can be used to obtain the transmission function in terms of all NAND or all NOR expressions. These realizations of switching functions are desirable since most integrated circuits are based on NAND or NOR gates.

To obtain an all NAND transmission function, group all 1's in the map and apply Shannon's theorem (generalization of De Morgan's theorem) to obtain all NAND functions. Using the result of Example b in Section 3.3.3

$$T = B'D' + AC'$$
$$T' = (B'D')' \cdot (AC')'$$
$$T = [(B'D')' \cdot (AC')']' \quad \text{(all NAND functions)}$$

To implement an all NOR transmission function, group all 0's, write a sum of products expression $= T'$, and then apply Shannon's theorem to obtain an all NOR realization. Taking the solution obtained in Example d in Section 3.3.3 by grouping 0's and applying this technique,

$$f'(w,x,y,z) = x' + yz$$
$$= x' + (y' + z')'$$

Thus,

$$f = [x' + (y' + z')']' \quad \text{(all NOR functions)}$$

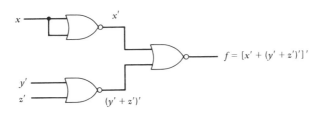

Again, it is important to note that these methods result in a two-level realization of the transmission function.

3.4.2 Important Combinational Logic Circuits

There are a number of combinational logic circuits in addition to the seven basic ones previously defined that are commonly used as components of a microprocessor and in other microcomputer elements. These circuits are also produced as packaged integrated circuits for use as constituents of more complex functions. The table of combinations, a brief description of the function(s) performed, and a diagram of the circuit implemented in the popular SN 54/74 family of SSI and MSI integrated circuits are given. Remember that the operations performed by these circuits are fundamental to the operation of a microcomputer and, in fact, form the basis of any logic or arithmetic systems.

Full Adder
In Chapter 2, binary addition was discussed. Recalling that the four possibilities of one-bit binary addition are

$$
\begin{array}{cccc}
1 & 1 & 0 & 0 \\
+\ 1 & +\ 0 & +\ 1 & +\ 0 \\
\hline
\text{Carry (1) } 0 & 1 & 1 & 0
\end{array}
$$

We can see that the sum is an EXCLUSIVE OR function and that the carry is an AND function. A circui⁺ that performs this addition is a *half adder*. In order to provide a general binary addition element that can be used as a building block in implementing an *n* bit adder, a carry must also be included in the addition. A half adder with a third or carry input is called a *full adder*. The table of combinations along with the block diagram of a full adder is:

INPUT			OUTPUT	
A	B	C_0 (Carry in)	Σ (Sum)	C_4 (Carry out)
0	0	0	0	0
0	0	1	1	0
0	1	0	1	0
0	1	1	0	1
1	0	0	1	0
1	0	1	0	1
1	1	0	0	1
1	1	1	1	1

Using four full adders, one can construct a binary adder to add two 4-bit numbers, $A_4 A_3 A_2 A_1$ and $B_4 B_3 B_2 B_1$, along with a carry input (if necessary) from a preceding adder stage. The logic diagram for this device and its implementation as the SN74/83 4-bit binary adder is:

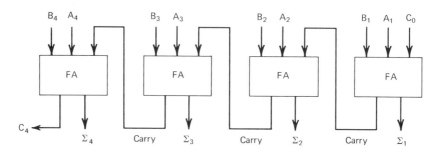

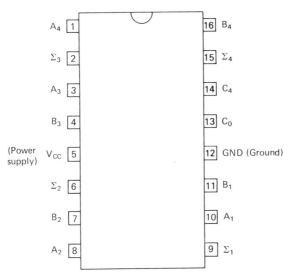

The summation or EXCLUSIVE OR function for obtaining each bit, Σi, of the sum is implemented by the logic cell,

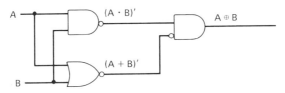

Decoder
A *decoder* is a combinational logic circuit that detects the occurrence of discrete states or patterns at its input and produces a unique output corresponding to each of the detected input states (Figure 3.1).

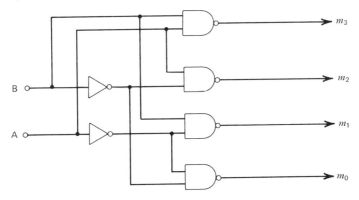

INPUT		OUTPUT				
A	B	m_0	m_1	m_2	m_3	
0	0	0	1	1	1	minterm 0 yields active low output on m_0
0	1	1	0	1	1	minterm 1_{10} yields active low output on m_1
1	0	1	1	0	1	minterm 2_{10} yields active low output on m_2
1	1	1	1	1	0	minterm 3_{10} yields active low output on m_3

FIGURE 3.1 Two to four line decoder.

In most cases, the decoder output corresponding to a specific input minterm is *active low*, i.e., it produces a low output while all other outputs remain high. Integrated circuit decoders of many types are available including three to eight line and BCD to decimal devices (Figure 3.2).

Encoder

An *encoder* is a combinational logic circuit that detects an active input on one of many input lines and produces a unique output code or address

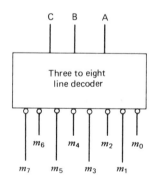

A	B	C	m_0	m_1	m_2	m_3	m_4	m_5	m_6	m_7
0	0	0	0	1	1	1	1	1	1	1
0	0	1	1	0	1	1	1	1	1	1
0	1	0	1	1	0	1	1	1	1	1
0	1	1	1	1	1	0	1	1	1	1
1	0	0	1	1	1	1	0	1	1	1
1	0	1	1	1	1	1	1	0	1	1
1	1	0	1	1	1	1	1	1	0	1
1	1	1	1	1	1	1	1	1	1	0

FIGURE 3.2 (a) Three to eight line and (b) BCD to decimal decoders.

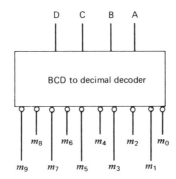

A	B	C	D	m_0	m_1	m_2	m_3	m_4	m_5	m_6	m_7	m_8	m_9
0	0	0	0	0	1	1	1	1	1	1	1	1	1
0	0	0	1	1	0	1	1	1	1	1	1	1	1
0	0	1	0	1	1	0	1	1	1	1	1	1	1
0	0	1	1	1	1	1	0	1	1	1	1	1	1
0	1	0	0	1	1	1	1	0	1	1	1	1	1
0	1	0	1	1	1	1	1	1	0	1	1	1	1
0	1	1	0	1	1	1	1	1	1	0	1	1	1
0	1	1	1	1	1	1	1	1	1	1	0	1	1
1	0	0	0	1	1	1	1	1	1	1	1	0	1
1	0	0	1	1	1	1	1	1	1	1	1	1	0

FIGURE 3.2 (continued).

corresponding to that input. The encoder can be designed such that only one or several inputs can be active at a time. If several inputs can be active, the output code generated corresponds to the input with the highest priority (*priority encoder*). The priority is determined by the position of the inputs. Encoders can have active low or active high inputs and outputs (Figure 3.3, Figure 3.4).

Arithmetic Logic Unit

The heart of a microcomputer is the Arithmetic Logic Unit (ALU) and associated control as defined in Chapter 1. The ALU combines arithmetic and logical operations in one device and is the center for execution of those operations in the microcomputer.

A typical ALU, the 74181, is a 4-bit ALU that performs 16 binary

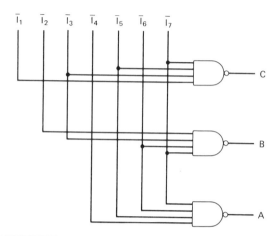

INPUTS (ACTIVE LOW)							OUTPUT (ACTIVE HIGH)		
I_1	I_2	I_3	I_4	I_5	I_6	I_7	A	B	C
0	1	1	1	1	1	1	0	0	1
1	0	1	1	1	1	1	0	1	0
1	1	0	1	1	1	1	0	1	1
1	1	1	0	1	1	1	1	0	0
1	1	1	1	0	1	1	1	0	1
1	1	1	1	1	0	1	1	1	0
1	1	1	1	1	1	0	1	1	1
1	1	1	1	1	1	1	0	0	0

FIGURE 3.3 Seven to three line encoder.

arithmetic operations on two 4-bit words. The operations are selected by four input lines, S0, S1, S2, and S3 and a mode line M providing a total of 2^5 or 32 functions. The 74181 functions include comparison and 16 functions of two Boolean variables. The 74181 is available in a 24-pin, Dual-In-Line (DIP) package. The two 4-bit input numbers are designated $A_3A_2A_1A_0$ and $B_3B_2B_1B_0$. The ALU can operate in both active low and active high modes. The block diagram and modes of operation are given in Figure 3.5. The outputs G and P are Carry Generate and Carry Propagate, respectively, and are used with external carry lookahead circuits to reduce carry propagation delay time. The bar (—) over a variable indicates the complement of the variable (i. e., $\overline{A} \equiv A'$).

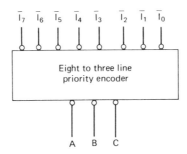

INPUTS (ACTIVE LOW)								OUTPUTS (ACTIVE LOW)		
$\overline{I}_0$	$\overline{I}_1$	$\overline{I}_2$	$\overline{I}_3$	$\overline{I}_4$	$\overline{I}_5$	$\overline{I}_6$	$\overline{I}_7$	A	B	C
X	X	X	X	X	X	X	0	0	0	0
X	X	X	X	X	X	0	1	0	0	1
X	X	X	X	X	0	1	1	0	1	0
X	X	X	X	0	1	1	1	0	1	1
X	X	X	0	1	1	1	1	1	0	0
X	X	0	1	1	1	1	1	1	0	1
X	0	1	1	1	1	1	1	1	1	0
0	1	1	1	1	1	1	1	1	1	1

FIGURE 3.4 Eight to three line priority encoder operation (X denotes "don't care").

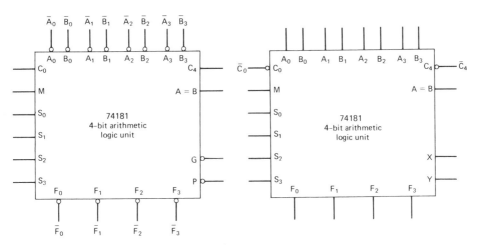

FIGURE 3.5 (a) ALU block diagram and (b) control/output table.

S_0	S_1	S_2	S_3	LOGIC (M = H)	ARITHMETIC (M = L, C_0 = INACTIVE)	ARITHMETIC (M = L, C_0 = ACTIVE)
L	L	L	L	$\overline{A}$	A minus 1	A
H	L	L	L	$\overline{A \cdot \overline{B}}$	$A \cdot B$ minus 1	$A \cdot B$
L	H	L	L	$\overline{A + B}$	$A \cdot \overline{B}$ minus 1	$A \cdot \overline{B}$
H	H	L	L	Logic '1'	minus 1 (2s comp.)	Zero
L	L	H	L	$\overline{A + \overline{B}}$	A plus $(A + \overline{B})$	A plus $(A + \overline{B})$ plus 1
H	L	H	L	$\overline{B}$	$A \cdot B$ plus $(A + \overline{B})$	$A \cdot B$ plus $(A + \overline{B})$ plus 1
L	H	H	L	$\overline{A \oplus B}$	A minus B minus 1	A minus B
H	H	H	L	$A + \overline{B}$	$A + \overline{B}$	$A + \overline{B}$ plus 1
L	L	L	H	$\overline{A \cdot B}$	A plus $(A + B)$	A plus $(A + B)$ plus 1
H	L	L	H	$A \oplus B$	A plus B	A plus B plus 1
L	H	L	H	B	$A \cdot \overline{B}$ plus $(A + B)$	$A \cdot \overline{B}$ plus $(A + B)$ plus 1
H	H	L	H	$A + B$	$A + B$	$A + B$ plus 1
L	L	H	H	Logic '0'	A plus A $(2 \times A)$	A plus A $(2 \times A)$ plus 1
H	L	H	H	$A \cdot \overline{B}$	A plus $A \cdot B$	A plus $A \cdot B$ plus 1
L	H	H	H	$A \cdot B$	A plus $A \cdot \overline{B}$	A plus $A \cdot \overline{B}$ plus 1
H	H	H	H	A	A	A plus 1

Active low inputs and outputs

L	L	L	L	$\overline{A}$	A	A plus 1
H	L	L	L	$\overline{A + B}$	$A + \overline{B}$	$A + \overline{B}$ plus 1
L	H	L	L	$\overline{A \cdot B}$	$A + \overline{B}$	$A + \overline{B}$ plus 1
H	H	L	L	Logic '0'	minus 1 (2s comp.)	Zero
L	L	H	L	$\overline{A \cdot B}$	A plus $A \cdot \overline{B}$	A plus $A \cdot \overline{B}$ plus 1
H	L	H	L	$\overline{B}$	$A \cdot \overline{B}$ plus $(A + B)$	$A \cdot \overline{B}$ plus $(A + B)$ plus 1
L	H	H	L	$A \oplus B$	A minus B minus 1	A minus B
H	H	H	L	$A \cdot B$	$A \cdot \overline{B}$ minus 1	$A \cdot B$
L	L	L	H	$\overline{A + B}$	A plus $A \cdot B$	A plus $A \cdot B$ plus 1
H	L	L	H	$\overline{A \oplus B}$	A plus B	A plus B plus 1
L	H	L	H	B	$A \cdot B$ plus $(A + \overline{B})$	$A \cdot B$ plus $(A + \overline{B})$ plus 1
H	H	L	H	$A \cdot B$	$A \cdot B$ minus 1	$A \cdot B$
L	L	H	H	Logic '1'	A plus A $(2 \times A)$	A plus A $(2 \times A)$ plus 1
H	L	H	H	$A + B$	A plus $(A + B)$	A plus $(A + B)$ plus 1
L	H	H	H	$A + B$	A plus $(A + \overline{B})$	A plus $(A + \overline{B})$ plus 1
H	H	H	H	A	A minus 1	A

Active high inputs and outputs

FIGURE 3.5 (continued).

3.5 SEQUENTIAL LOGIC CIRCUITS

Another important class of logic circuits that is fundamental to the understanding of microcomputer systems is *sequential logic*. In contrast to the
combinational logic circuits discussed in Sections 3.3 and 3.4 of this chapter, the **output of a sequential logic circuit is a function not only of the
combination of the input variables but of the sequence in which they are
applied.** Behaviorally, the sequential circuit output depends upon the past
history of the inputs and, thus, a memory capability must exist in the sequential circuit that is not required in a combinational circuit. If i, j, k, and
r are integers and the n input variables of a sequential logic circuit are
represented by x_i where $i = 1,2,...,n$, the m output variables are represented
by z_j where $j = 1,2,..., m$, the q *excitation* variables are represented by Y_r
where $r = 1,2,...,q$, and the p *state* (sometimes also referred to as memory,
feedback, secondary, or auxiliary) variables are represented by y_k where
$k = 1,2,...,p$, a sequential circuit can be represented diagrammatically as
in Figure 3.6.

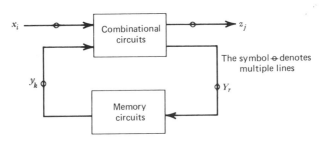

FIGURE 3.6 Sequential circuit model.

Thus, a sequential circuit consists of a memory or feedback portion
$Y_r = g(x_i,y_k)$ and a combinational portion whose output $z_j = f(x_i, y_k)$ with
the x's, y's, Y's, and z's functions of time. Note that a sequential circuit can
be in any one of a number of conditions or *states* that are "remembered"
by the memory circuits and characterized by the y_k's. The y_k's then provide
an input to the combinational portion of the sequential circuit. These y_k
inputs along with the x_i inputs to the combinational portion produce an
output or outputs, z_j, corresponding to the particular state of the circuit and
the input variables.

Since a sequential circuit generates state information necessary to
determine the corresponding output of its combinational portion, a sequential circuit, therefore, requires the two time dependent functional
expressions:

$$Y_r = g(x_i,y_k) \qquad (r = 1, 2, \ldots, q) \text{ next state equations}$$

and

$$z_j = f(x_i, y_k) \qquad (j = 1, 2, \ldots, m) \text{ output equations}$$

In contrast, a combinational circuit can be described by one functional expression of the type $z_j = f(x_i)$ where the x_i's are input variables and the z_j's are output variables.

Sequential circuits are normally subdivided into categories that attempt to distinguish between those circuits having equal or externally clocked times in each state and those circuits whose state times are a function of internal logic delays. Conventionally, these circuits have been referred to as *synchronous* or *clocked* sequential circuits and *asynchronous* sequential circuits, respectively. Another categorization is determined by whether or not the inputs and outputs to the sequential circuit are pulses or levels, thereby resulting in the terms *pulse mode* and *level mode* sequential circuits. Along these lines, sequential circuits can also be modeled as *Mealy* and *Moore* circuits. A *Mealy circuit is a sequential circuit whose outputs depend on the inputs to and the present state of the circuit.* A *Moore circuit is a sequential circuit whose outputs depend solely on the present state of the circuit.* A sequential circuit that is implemented as one of these models can also be implemented as the other. In general, the Mealy circuit will require less states than the Moore circuit to represent the same sequential function.

In this text, which is aimed at providing an understanding of microcomputers, programmed logic, and their application, the terms *synchronous* and *asynchronous sequential circuits* are utilized. This terminology is somewhat restrictive but serves as a vehicle for imparting the necessary concepts without developing a level of detail more appropriate to a text on sequential circuit or finite state machine design.

Specifically, a *synchronous sequential circuit* is defined *as a sequential circuit having equal times in each state or a time in each state determined by external timing means (clock).* An *asynchronous sequential circuit* is a sequential circuit whose state times are determined by *internal circuit delays. The inputs and outputs of an asynchronous sequential circuit are usually levels whereas the inputs to a synchronous sequential circuit are normally entered by a clocked source and the outputs are pulses or are meaningful only at the time of the clock pulses.* As used in these definitions, a *level* is a voltage or current that remains essentially constant for a period of time that is relatively long compared to circuit delay times or circuit pulse times. A *pulse* is a voltage or current that changes from one value to another and returns to the initial value in a relatively short period of time as referenced to circuit timing characteristics.

There are many methods of analyzing and synthesizing synchronous and asynchronous sequential circuits. Since detailed developments of the

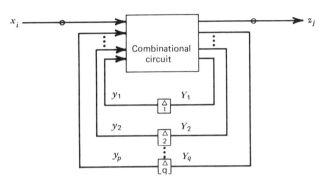

FIGURE 3.7 Asynchronous sequential circuit model.

analysis and synthesis approaches are beyond the scope of this text and are very well covered in works including sequential design (1,2,3), they are not treated in this text. Instead, definitions, descriptions, and modes of operation of asynchronous and synchronous sequential circuits used in microcomputer and programmed logic systems are presented with an emphasis on synchronous devices since they are predominant in those systems. State diagrams, which are used to analyze and design synchronous sequential circuits, are introduced in order to provide for a better understanding of the operation of these circuits.

3.5.1 Asynchronous Sequential Circuits

An asynchronous sequential circuit can be represented as shown in Figure 3.7, where the memory indicated in Figure 3.6 is implemented via delay elements, $\boxed{\Delta}$, in the feedback loop. These delay elements are not necessarily discrete components but may be the inherent delay of the combinational logic circuits themselves.

In order to illustrate the operation of an asynchronous sequential circuit, the Reset-Set (R-S) and J-K flip-flops along with a type D latch will be analyzed.

R-S Flip-Flop

The R-S flip-flop is itself a memory element that can store transient digital information. The NAND R-S flip-flop circuit is as follows (S' and R' indicate active low inputs) (Figure 3.8).

Redrawing this circuit to correspond to Figure 3.7, one can assume the NAND gates to be "ideal" elements with no inherent delay, with the $\boxed{\Delta}$'s in the feedback loops representing equal lumped delays of each NAND gate and associated wiring (Figure 3.9).

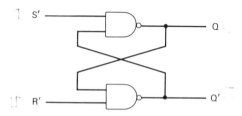

FIGURE 3.8 NAND RS flip-flop.

The operation of the circuit can be defined in Table 3.2. The 1 1 input situation is the "rest" state of the flip-flop and the output may be changed by setting one and only one of the inputs at a time to a 0. Arbitrarily assuming that the flip-flop is initially in the state where Q = 0 and Q' = 1, the R-S flip-flop operation is:

TABLE 3.2   NAND R-S Flip-Flop Function Table

INPUT		OUTPUT	
S'	R'	Q	Q'
1	1	0	1
0	1	1	0
1	1	1	0
1	0	0	1
1	1	0	1
0	0	1	1*

*An input of 00 produces an illegal output since Q and Q' are to be complementary but are both forced to a 1 state.

From Table 3.2 it can be seen that a change of either the S' or R' input from a 1 to a 0 can produce a change in the outputs. A change of S' from 1 to 0 will "set" the Q output of the flip-flop to a 1 if it was previously a 0 or will cause Q to remain at 1 if it was previously a 1. Similarly, a change of R' from 1 to 0 will "reset" the Q output of the flip-flop to a 0 if it was previously a 1 or will cause Q to remain at a 0 if it was previously a 0. Applying 0's to the R' and S' inputs simultaneously is an illegal procedure since it forces both Q and Q' to 1's. The memory feature of the flip-flop can be visualized from the first three entries of Table 3.1 by observing that

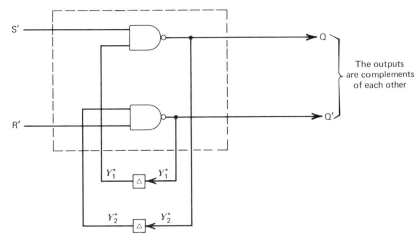

FIGURE 3.9 Asynchronous sequential circuit model of NAND R-S flip-flop. *Since, in an asynchronous sequential circuit, the y_k's are identical with the Y_r's except delayed in time, both the excitation variables (Y_r's) and the feedback or memory variables (y_k's) are represented by Y_r's.

a change of input S' from 1 to 0 to 1 ($\boxed{1}$$\boxed{0}$) will again cause the Q output to "set" or latch at a 1 value. Thus, a transient or pulse input to the S' input of the flip-flop will be sensed and retained after the pulse is gone. Similarly, a 1 to 0 to 1 transition on the R' input will "reset" the flip-flop by latching the Q output to a 0. In both the set and reset cases, the Q and Q' outputs are always complements of each other.

The two states of this asynchronous sequential circuit are Q = 1, Q' = 0 and Q = 0, Q' = 1. The values of Q and Q', which, in this case, are also the state variables, are returned to the inputs of the combinational circuit where they, along with the other inputs S' and R', will determine the output and next state of the sequential circuit. In some asynchronous sequential circuits, if the delay in the feedback loop was not present or was not large enough, the newly generated state variables would appear at the input to the combinational circuit and, along with the "old" values of S' and R', generate the next state output and state variables. This mode of operation is generally undesirable and may, in some cases, result in an oscillatory or runaway situation.

The sequential nature of the R-S NAND flip-flop can also be represented in a sequential table of combinations or *transition table* with inputs S, R, and Q^n and output Q^{n+1} where Q^n is the output of the flip-flip (which is fed back as an input) at the present time n and Q^{n+1} is the output of the flip-flop at a time $n + 1$. The time $n + 1$ means the time one clock period later or the time when a change has occurred in the input(s) of the circuit. Using this nomenclature, the R-S NAND flip-flop sequential table of combinations is:

INPUTS						OUTPUT
S	R	Q^n	S'	R'	Q^n	Q^{n+1}
0	0	0	1	1	0	0
0	0	1	1	1	1	1
0	1	0	1	0	0	0
0	1	1	1	0	1	0
1	0	0	0	1	0	1
1	0	1	0	1	1	1
1	1	0	0	0	0	ϕ
1	1	1	0	0	1	ϕ

Inputs S' and R' are not permitted to be 0 at the same time.

A Karnaugh map can now be used to minimize the next state function of the flip-flop. The map corresponding to the transition table is:

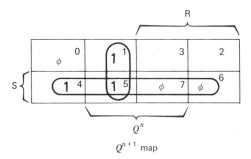

Q^{n+1} map

Grouping as shown, the next state or *characteristic* function of the R-S flip-flop implemented with NAND gates is

$$Q^{n+1} = S + R'Q^n$$

In a similar fashion, the transition table of a NOR R-S flip-flop and its characteristic function from a Karnaugh map are:

INPUTS			OUTPUT
S	R	Q^n	Q^{n+1}
0	0	0	0
0	0	1	1
0	1	0	0
0	1	1	0
1	0	0	1
1	0	1	1
1	1	0	ϕ
1	1	1	ϕ

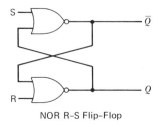

NOR R-S Flip-Flop

In a NOR R-S flip-flop, the S and R inputs cannot be 1 at the same time.

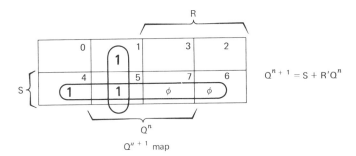

$$Q^{n+1} = S + R'Q^n$$

Q^{n+1} map

Note that, since the NAND and NOR R-S flip-flops are functionally identical, their characteristic equations are the same. The transition table, Karnaugh map, and characteristic function of other commonly used flip-flops and their derivatives are given along with a brief description of their operation. Positive logic will be assumed, i.e., that the inputs are normally a 0, and a 1 input is used to change the circuit state unless otherwise noted.

J-K Flip-Flop

The operation of the J-K flip-flop is identical to that of the NOR R-S flip-flop except that the two inputs can both have a value of 1 at the same time. When this input condition occurs, the flip-flop "toggles" or changes to the output opposite from the present output.

J-K Flip-Flop

INPUTS			OUTPUT
J	K	Q^n	Q^{n+1}
0	0	0	0
0	0	1	1
0	1	0	0
0	1	1	0
1	0	0	1
1	0	1	1
1	1	0	1
1	1	1	0

"Toggle" output

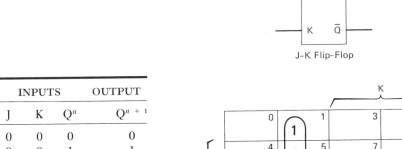

Q^{n+1} map

$$Q^{n+1} = JQ^{n\prime} + K'Q^n$$

D Latch

The D latch can be implemented by modifying the R-S NAND flip-flop circuit as follows.

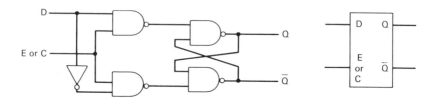

This type of circuit is called a *latch* since the circuit latches or holds the data present on the input (D in this case) **when it is either a 1 or a 0.** In other words, the output, Q, directly follows the D input and stores the status of the D input. The type D latch is enabled by a gating signal E (sometimes labeled as clock, C) that, when equal to a 1, allows the data on line D to enter the flip-flop circuit. This circuit can be used in both a synchronous and asynchronous manner.

INPUTS			OUTPUT
D	E	Q^n	Q^{n+1}
0	0	0	0
0	0	1	1
0	1	0	0
0	1	1	0
1	0	0	0
1	0	1	1
1	1	0	1
1	1	1	1

$$Q^{n+1} = ED + E' Q^n$$

The R-S and J-K flip-flops and the type D latch are commonly used as building blocks in more complex asynchronous circuits.

3.5.2 Synchronous Sequential Circuits

A widely used implementation of synchronous sequential circuits employs flip-flops to define the present state of the circuit. The general configuration of this implementation is given in Figure 3.10.

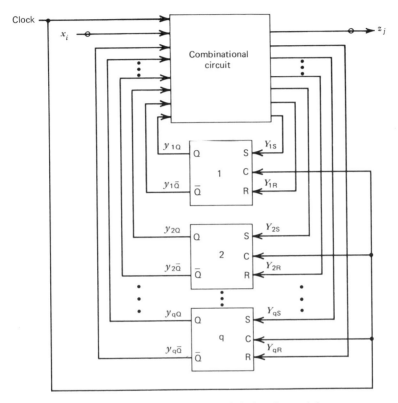

FIGURE 3.10 Synchronous sequential circuit model.

The circuit configuration of Figure 3.10 depicts the general case of both the Q and $\overline{Q}$ outputs of the flip-flops being used as state variables; however, many circuits will require only one of these outputs as an input to the combinational circuit to provide present state information. The flip-flops shown are clocked R-S flip-flops that themselves, are synchronous sequential circuits. Their operation is identical to that of the R-S flip-flop described in Section 3.51 with the exception that the inputs are entered into the flip-flop circuit only upon application of a clock pulse, thus providing synchronous operation. There are many other types of flip-flops that can be used as memory elements in place of the R-S flip-flops and these will be discussed later in this chapter.

The operation of the sequential circuit model is as follows.

1. The binary pattern on the outputs of flip-flops 1 through q represents the present state of the sequential circuit. This state is one of a num-

ber of possible states of the circuit and is given by the y_k, k = 1,2, . . . ,q, inputs to the combinational circuit.

2. The state variables, y_k, k = 1,2, . . . , q, and the input variables, x_i, i = 1,2, . . . , n, will, upon application of the next clock pulse, produce an output or outputs, z_j, j = 1,2, . . . , m. In addition, the Y_r, r = 1, 2, . . . ,q, set and reset inputs to the flip-flops will then be generated to cause the pattern for the next state to appear on the y_k lines and to stabilize before the occurrence of the next clock pulse.

One means of describing this operation is the *state diagram*. Each *state* or *time between clock pulses* is represented by a circle with a state label. The time between states is represented by a straight line connecting the state representations with specifications of the x_i inputs causing the transition between states and the output(s), z_i, corresponding to those inputs. This type of state diagram would be a Mealy model since each new state and output are determined by the present state and the input(s) to the circuit. In general, the state diagram would appear as:

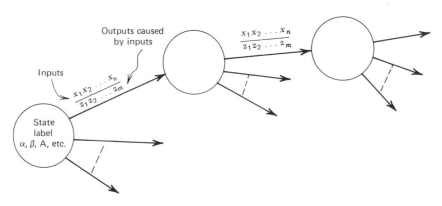

Note that, in this diagram, each state must have 2^n exit lines to account for all 2^n combinations of the n inputs to the sequential circuit. Also the occurrence of the clock pulses is not specifically shown but is implicit in the diagram. The inputs to and outputs of the synchronous sequential circuit occur between states (between the labeled circles) on the state diagram. Each state represents the time between clock pulses and is essentially the circuit "dead time" or "rest time" when inputs and outputs of the circuit do not occur, or, if they do occur, are ignored.

To illustrate the use of the state diagram, the operation of the synchronous or clocked R-S, J-K, and T type flip-flops is defined using this method. Since synchronism of these circuits by "clocking" the inputs is implied in the state diagram, the clock is not explicitly shown as an input.

Synchronous or Clocked R-S Flip-Flop

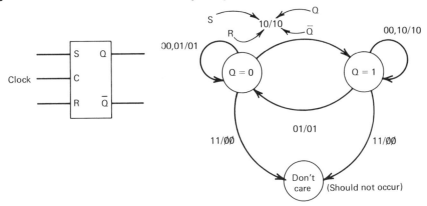

* NOTE: Outputs Q and $\overline{Q}$ are always complementary.

Since there are four possible combinations of the two inputs S and R (00,01,10,11), each state must have four exit combinations accounting for the possible occurrence of any of the four inputs. The exit line 10/10 from state $Q = 0$ to state $Q = 1$ denotes that, when an input of $S = 1$ and $R = 0$ is applied to the R-S flip-flop when it is in the state $Q = 0$, an output of $Q = 1$ and $\overline{Q} = 0$ will occur when the clock signal is applied and the flip-flop will be in the new state $Q = 1$. The two lines to the "don't care" state indicate that inputs to the R-S flip-flop of $S = 1$ and $R = 1$ simultaneously are not permitted and therefore would never occur if proper operation of the R-S flip-flop is desired. Therefore, the outputs are labeled $\phi\phi$ to indicate that these are "don't care" conditions. The characteristic function of the clocked R-S flip-flop is still

$$Q^{n + 1} = S + R' Q^n$$

with the clocked operation implicit in this function.

Synchronous J-K Flip-Flop

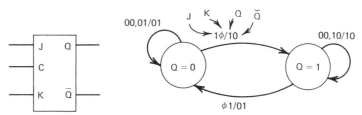

The operation of the clocked J-K flip-flop is identical to that of the clocked R-S flip-flop except that a 11 input is permitted. When a 1 is applied simultaneously to J and K inputs and a clock pulse appears on clock input C, the Q output changes, or "flips," or "toggles" to the state opposite from the present state.

The characteristic function of the clocked J-K flip-flop is

$$Q^{n+1} = JQ^{n\prime} + K'Q^n$$

with the clocked operation implicit in the equation.

T Flip-Flop

A T (toggle) flip-flop is a 1-input flip-flop whose output toggles each time a pulse is applied to the input.

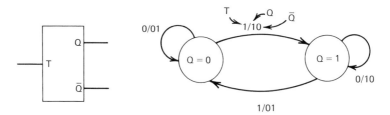

The T flip-flop can be implemented by tying the J and K inputs of a clocked J-K flip-flop to a logic 1 and using the clock input as the T input.

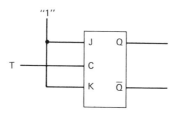

The derivation of the characteristic function of the T flip-flop is as follows.

INPUTS		OUTPUT
T	Q^n	Q^{n+1}
0	0	0
0	1	1
1	0	1
1	1	0

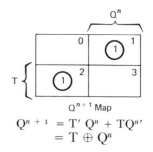

Q^{n+1} Map

$$Q^{n+1} = T' Q^n + TQ^{n\prime}$$
$$= T \oplus Q^n$$

3.5.3   Important Sequential Logic Circuits

Using the basic sequential logic circuits explained in Sections 3.5.1 and 3.5.2 of this chapter, we describe the other sequential logic circuits utilized in microcomputers.

Clocked D Flip-Flop with Direct Preset and Clear

The operation of the D flip-flop is similar to that of the D latch described earlier, except that the input data are transferred to the output, Q, when the enable or clock *changes* from a 0 to 1 in positive logic. In other words, a change in the output of the flip-flop will occur as a result of the *transition* of the clock or enable signal from a 0 to a 1. In the D latch, the output will follow the D input any time the enable or clock input is a 1. The dynamic or *edge-triggering* characteristic of the clock signal is indicated by a triangle on the clock input of the D flip-flop.

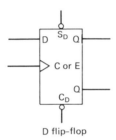

D flip-flop

If the D flip-flop is activated by the *falling edge* of the clock (the transition of the clock input from 1 to 0), this would be indicated by a small circle on the clock input. A circle on any input or output line indicates that the activating input or the active output of the digital circuit is a *low*. This type of input or output is termed *active low*. The absence of a circle indicates an *active high* input or output where the active state is high. The combination of a triangle and circle on an input indicates that the active state is the falling edge of the input signal.

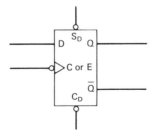

D flip-flop falling edge-triggered.

The *preset* or *direct set* (S_D) and *clear* or *direct clear* (C_D) inputs of the D flip-flop and of most flip-flops are active low. Thus, a *positive logic one* or *high* on the S_D and C_D inputs has no effect on the circuit and is the "rest" condition on these inputs. A 0 or low on the S_D input causes the output Q to be set to a 1 ($\overline{Q} = 0$) independent of the D and C inputs and, in fact, will override the D and C inputs until a 1 is restored to S_D. The C_D input operates in a similar manner except that Q is cleared to a 0 and $\overline{Q} = 1$. As in the case of the R-S flip-flop inputs, S_D and C_D should not be simultaneously connected to a low. The transition table of the leading edge-triggered D flip-flop is as follows with a symbol ↑ indicating the triggering of the flip-flop by a 0 to 1 transition of the clock input signal.

INPUTS					OUTPUT	
S_D	C_D	C	D	Q^n	Q^{n+1}	
0	0	ϕ	ϕ	ϕ	ϕ	This condition should not occur ($S_D = C_D = 0$)
0	1	ϕ	ϕ	ϕ	1	
1	0	ϕ	ϕ	ϕ	0	
1	1	0	ϕ	0	0	
1	1	0	ϕ	1	1	
1	1	↑	0	ϕ	0	
1	1	↑	1	ϕ	1	

Shift Register

A shift register is a series of flip-flops that are interconnected such that data are transferred or "shifted" from one flip-flop to another upon application of a "shift" or clock pulse. The shift register can be either a shift right or shift left register or both. The application of a clock pulse to a shift right register will cause the bits to move one position to the right. If the present output of flip-flop i in an n bit right shift register (with lsb in leftmost flip-flop) where $1 < i < n$ is Q_i^n, then the output, Q_i^{n+1}, of flip-flop Q_i after the application of the next clock pulse is Q_{i-1}^n. For a left shift register, the corresponding expression is $Q_i^{n+1} = Q_{i+1}^n$. Two implementations of a right shift register using D flip-flops and J-K flip-flops, respectively, are (Figures 3.11 and 3.12).

The shift register in Figure 3.11 has parallel data inputs through which binary information can be "jammed" into the shift register, thereby loading it with an initial pattern of 1's and 0's. In Figure 3.12, the direct clear inputs are tied in common and brought out as a reset line to initialize the shift register to all 0's. Both shift registers have parallel output lines that allow the contents of each flip-flop in the register to be monitored, and

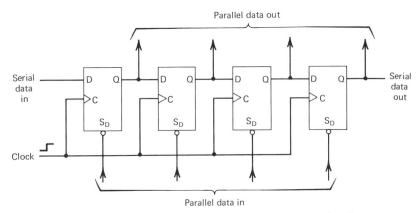

FIGURE 3.11 Right shift register implemented with D flip-flops.

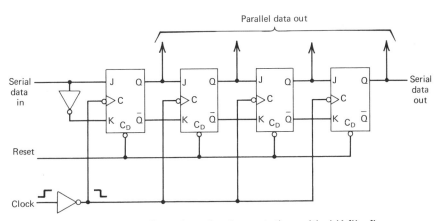

FIGURE 3.12 Right shift register implementation with J-K flip-flops.

they also have a serial output line that is the Q output of the last flip-flop in the chain. Bits transferred out of this flip-flop are lost unless provision is made to capture these data in other flip-flops or to recirculate them to the serial data input of the shift register. Data are entered into the shift register through this serial data input line. If, for example, the serial data input is tied permanently to a logical 1, the shift register will "fill up" with 1's from the left as each clock pulse is applied until every flip-flop in the shift register contains a 1.

In microcomputer systems, registers are utilized in many ways, among which are serial-to-parallel and parallel- to serial conversion, storage of data, delaying of digital data, and counting.

Counters

A *counter* is a sequential circuit that cyclically proceeds through its states and, thus, produces a repetitive sequence of patterns when activated by input pulses. Counters can be visualized as the circuit realization of the next state equation

$$Y_r = g(x_i, y_k)$$

as discussed in Section 3.5 of this chapter.

Counters are usually implemented with a number of clocked J-K flip-flops whose Q outputs collectively form the patterns corresponding to the counter states. For example, if a counter is implemented with two J-K flip-flops whose Q outputs cycle through the ascending binary patterns as shown, the counter is a *binary counter* (Figure 3.13).

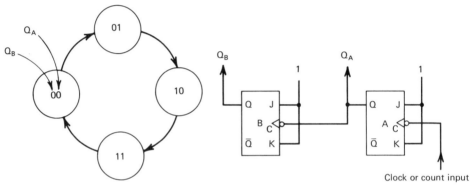

FIGURE 3.13 Binary counter.

The flip-flops shown are trailing (negative) edge-triggered and their outputs would appear as follows (Figure 3.14).

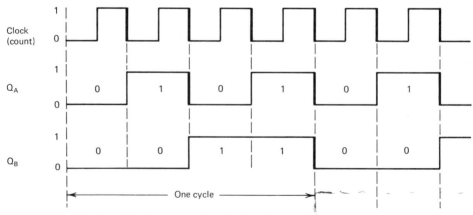

FIGURE 3.14 Two-bit binary counter timing diagram.

Note that, since the J-K inputs of the flip flops are permanently tied to a logical 1, the flip flops behave as T or toggle devices, changing outputs on the trailing edge of their respective C inputs. Because the output of flip-flop A is connected to the C input of flip-flop B, flip-flob B toggles at ½ the frequency of A. Similarly, flip-flop A toggles at ½ the frequency of the clock (count) input. Thus, the binary counter performs a *frequency division* by 2 at each flip-flop stage. This feature is useful in generating lower frequency clock pulses synchronized with a higher frequency source and for other timing purposes. Since this binary counter has a capacity of two bits, 2^2 or four different patterns can be generated. This counter is referred to as a *modulo* four or *mod* four counter since it has a *capacity* or *modulus* of four states (0 through 3_{10}). If two more identical flip-flops were added to the two original flip-flops, a modulo 16 (2^4) counter would result (Figure 3.15).

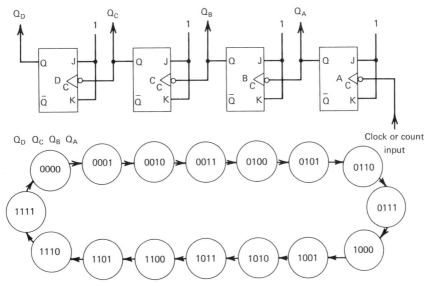

FIGURE 3.15 Mod 16 binary counter.

Thus, if a mod M binary counter were required, 2^M flip-flops would have to be used. Note that this rule applies only to binary counters. It is not true of counters with moduli that are not integer powers of two.

The type of binary counter illustrated in Figures 3.13 and 3.15 is referred to as an *asynchronous* or *ripple* counter since each flip-flop stage following the low order or lsb flip-flop of the counter is activated by the output of the previous stage. Thus, the C input signal ripples through the counter stages from the lsb to the msb. Since there is a propagation time delay, tp, from a level change at the C input of a flip flop to a change in the Q or $\overline{Q}$ output, the Q outputs of the counter will not change to a new pattern or count simultaneously but will ripple from the lsb to the msb flip-flop. The actual timing waveforms including propagation delay, tp, for the counter of Figure 3.13 are as follows (Figure 3.16).

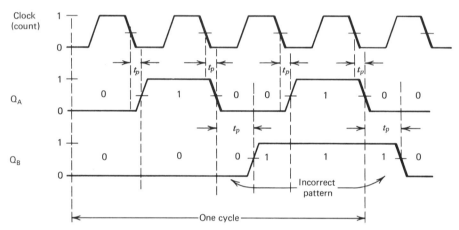

FIGURE 3.16 Two-bit binary counter timing diagram including propagation delay.

Note that unlike instances reflecting the ideal timing diagram of Figure 3.14 there are instances where the propagation delay introduces some incorrect patterns in the counting sequence. For example, as noted in Figure 3.16 the erroneous pattern 00 appears between pattern $Q_A = 1$, $Q_B = 0$ and $Q_A = 0$, $Q_B = 1$ because of the propagation delay of the flip-flops. Another incorrect pattern, 01 occurs between $Q_A = Q_B = 1$ and $Q_A = Q_B = 0$. If the counts 00 and 01 were used to indicate the occurrence of external events, false indications would be given following the 10 count and 11 count. One means of avoiding this situation in ripple counters is to delay sampling the count until a specified settling time following the negative transition of the input clock pulse. Typical values for tp are 10 to 20 nanoseconds (10^{-9} seconds) with the counter able to handle counting input pulses with frequencies of up to about 18 MHz (18 million or 18×10^6 pulses per second).

Another method of eliminating the false counts is to use a *synchronous* or *"lookahead-carry"* counter. With this type of counter, external logic is used to cause all outputs of the flip-flop stages to change simultaneously. With this technique, the counting frequency is limited by the delay of only one flip-flop and, therefore, can operate at higher frequencies (32 MHz). The logic of implementing a synchronous counter of this type is based on the fact that any bit, 2^m, of the binary counter must change or toggle only if bits 2^{m-1}, 2^{m-2}, . . . , 2^0 are all equal to a 1 and the next pulse to be counted arrives. For the 4-bit binary counter in Figure 3.17, then, the logic equations can be written as $J_B = K_B = Q_A$, $J_C = K_C = Q_A \cdot Q_B$, and $J_D = K_D = Q_A \cdot Q_B \cdot Q_C$.

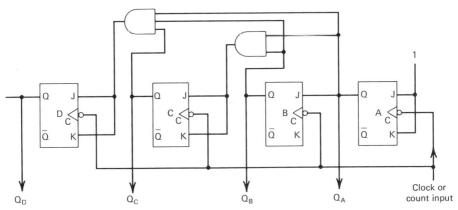

FIGURE 3.17 Synchronous lookahead carry counter.

Counters of other modulo can be implemented in a similar manner by utilizing flip-flops and external gating. The count sequence is obtained by resetting all the flip-flops with Q outputs of 1 on the count input following the modulus −1 count. This technique is illustrated in the ripple and synchronous *decade* (mode 10) counters (Figures 3.18 (a) and 3.18 (b)).

BINARY COUNT				DECIMAL EQUIVALENT	
Q_D	Q_C	Q_B	Q_A		
0	0	0	0	0	Reset of flip-flops
0	0	0	1	1	takes place when last
0	0	1	0	2	pattern is 1001 (9)
0	0	1	1	3	and on the occurrence
0	1	0	0	4	of the next count
0	1	0	1	5	input.
0	1	1	0	6	
0	1	1	1	7	
1	0	0	0	8	
1	0	0	1	9	
0	0	0	0	0	

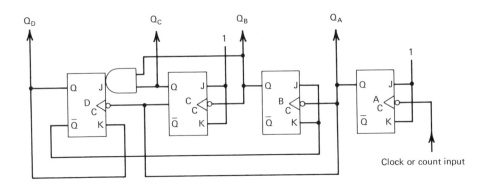

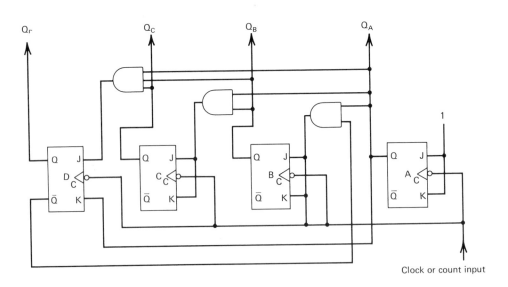

Up to and including the count of 8 (1000), each flip-flop representing bit 2^m of the binary count is set to a 1 (Q = 1) on the trailing edge of the next incoming count pulse following the condition where bits 2^{m-1}, 2^{m-2}, ... ,2^0 are equal to 1. The bits 2^{m-1}, 2^{m-2}, ... ,2^0 are then toggled to 0. Following a 9 (1001) count, flip-flop A will toggle to 0 and flip-flop D will be reset to 0 upon application of the next input pulse. Flip-flop D will reset to 0 in this instance since, on count 9, the K input of D will be 1 and the J input of K will be 0.

FIGURE 3.18 Ripple and synchronous decade counting. (a) Ripple decade counter. (b) Synchronous decade counter.

The types of counters described are sometimes referred to as *up counters* since the count is incremented upward on each count input. Following the same techniques, counters of a variety of modulo can be implemented along with counters that can count down one count at a time (*decrement*). Figure 3.19 is an example of a 4-bit binary synchronous down counter implemented with J-K master slave flip-flops. The counter is initialized to a 1111 state by placing a logic 0 on the preset inputs of the flip-flops.

The types of counters discussed up to this point are available in integrated circuit form in MSI (Medium Scale Integration) packages that can be used as building blocks for larger systems. If a count capacity larger than that available in one integrated circuit is required, the counters can

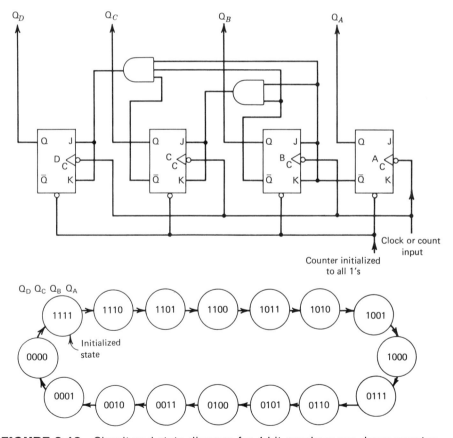

FIGURE 3.19 Circuit and state diagram for 4-bit synchronous down counter.

be cascaded by using the msb output or, if available, by using the carry output of one counter circuit as the input to the next counter circuit.

Most integrated circuit counters insert an inverter in the count (clock) input line so that, externally, the counter changes state on the 0 to 1 (low to high) clock transition instead of on the trailing edge. In addition, a clock gating input, COUNT ENABLE or EN, as it is sometimes labeled, is provided for cascading purposes. The carry output is fed into the EN input and thus enables the clock input to the next counter circuit only when the carry out is a 1, indicating a carry out from the previous circuit.

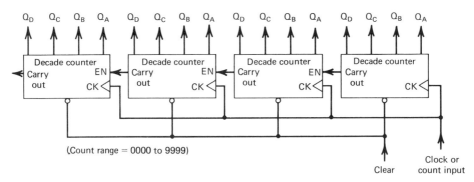

FIGURE 3.20 Four digit BCD counters.

The number of states possible when using cascaded counter circuits can be determined by multiplying the moduli of all the stages together. For a counter composed of four decade counter circuits, the total number of states is $10 \times 10 \times 10 \times 10 = 10,000$ with the largest number in the range equal to one less than 10,000 or 9,999. In general, for counter circuits with moduli of $M_1, M_2, \ldots, M_n$, the number of possible states available by cascading these circuits is equal to $M_1 \times M_2 \times \ldots \times M_n$ with the largest possible number in this range equal to $M_1 \times M_2 \times \ldots \times M_n - 1$.

3.6 TYPICAL UTILIZATION OF COMBINATIONAL AND SEQUENTIAL CIRCUITS IN MICROPROCESSOR STRUCTURE

There are a number of functions that a microprocessor must perform that are common to most microprocessor architectures. These functions are illustrated in the following general block diagram (Figure 3.21).

All of the functions depicted in the block diagram are implemented with the combinational and sequential circuits discussed in this chapter. Referring to the circled numbers in the diagram, we describe the functions and their related circuits.

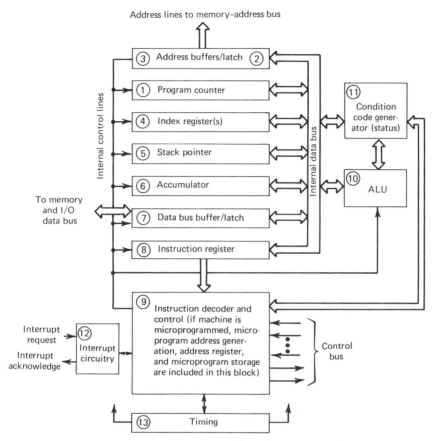

FIGURE 3.21 General block diagram of a microprocessor.

1 Program Counter (PC). A binary counter (ripple or synchronous) or flip-flop storage register that contains the address of the next memory location or I/O device to be accessed. This counter is incremented upon each current instruction fetch.

2 Address Latch or Memory Address Register. A storage register of latches which holds the address of the memory location or I/O device to be accessed. Its input may be from the Program Counter, Index Registers, results of calculations among the Index Registers and Program Counter, or the Stack Pointer. The capacity of this latch is usually m bits where m equals the number of address lines.

3 Address Buffers. Transistors or logic gates that are designed to supply the current necessary to drive the address bus and maintain proper

timing characteristics of this bus. In some microprocessors, these buffers have tri-state capability.

4 Index Registers. Storage registers implemented with latches, J-K, R-S, or D flip-flops. These registers may also be configured as shift registers to allow shifting of their contents right and/or left in addition to providing data storage. They are useful as temporary storage locations and for providing or modifying memory addresses to be sent out on the address buffers.

5 Stack Pointer (SP). A binary counter (ripple or synchronous) or flip-flop storage register that points to one of a series of memory locations called a *stack*. The stack can consist of a number of flip-flop storage registers in the microprocessor itself or a portion of external Random Access Memory (RAM).

6 Accumulator. Flip-flop storage register used to store results of arithmetic, logical, memory read and write, and I/O operations. The accumulator may also supply data for arithmetic and Boolean operations and may also have shift right and shift left capability. It usually holds one of ALU input operands.

7 Data Bus Buffer/Latch. Since the data bus is bidirectional (data can be sent out or received by the microprocessor bus), there are two modes of operation associated with it—input and output. In the output mode, data to be transferred are stored in the Data Bus Latch, which is a register composed of n latches where n is the number of data bus lines. The contents of the Latch then feed the Data Bus Buffers, which in turn provide the current needed to drive the data bus and maintain proper timing characteristics. These buffers are usually of the tri-state type. In the input mode, the data on the Data Bus lines are transferred either into the data latch or directly to the internal data bus.

8 Instruction Register (IR). This register is a register comprised of flip-flops that store the instruction that was fetched from memory. If the instruction occupies more than one memory word, one portion of the instruction is held in the Instruction Register. Subsequent fetches will retrieve the remainder of the instruction and these are usually stored in temporary registers in the microprocessor. The instruction register contents are fed into the Instruction Decoder.

9 Instruction Decoder and Control. The decoder circuit receives the coded portion of the instruction describing the operation to be performed (OPERATION CODE or OP CODE) by the microprocessor. The decoder outputs, in conjunction with the microprocessor clock or timing signals, enable the control circuits inside the microprocessor

in the proper sequence to execute the desired operation. For example, if the OP code were 8 bits long, 2^n or 256 possible combinations could be decoded and, thus, 256 different combinations of control lines could be activated.

The control portion of this block can be implemented in a hard-wired fashion with sequential circuits utilizing next state flip-flops, counters, and combinational circuits as described in Section 3.5 of this chapter or by *microprogramming*. If the microprocessor is micro-programmed, the control necessary to execute the instruction (*macroinstruction*) contained in the Instruction Register is generated by a series of *microinstructions* or *microcode* stored in another memory in the microprocessor. Note that this memory is separate from that containing the macroinstructions that were fetched on the data bus. Thus, each macroinstruction to be executed by the microprocessor "points to" a series of microinstructions that, in turn, produce the control signals needed to execute the desired macroinstruction.

10 ALU. Arithmetic Logic Unit, which performs the arithmetic and logic functions of the microprocessor. The ALU usually contains an n-bit full adder (where n is the data bus width), n-bit subtractor, Boolean, shift, and Decimal Adjust logic. Decimal adjust provides BCD arithmetic capability.

11 Condition Code Generator. Flip-flops and associated logic gating that store the results of operations in the microprocessor. Some typical indicators or *flags* stored in these flip-flops are:

- Result of previous operation = 0.
- Result of previous operation is negative.
- Carrying resulting from previous operation.
- Overflow of accumulator capacity resulting from previous operation.
- Parity error detected from previous operation.
- Half carry (for BCD calculation) resulting from previous operation.

12 Interrupt Circuitry. This circuitry includes a flip-flop that is set by an Interrupt Request signal from an external source. This signal can cause the microprocessor to leave its present program sequence and begin execution of a different series of instructions that *service* the interrupt. Usually, the setting of this flip-flop is synchronized with one of the microprocessor clock phases and requires that the interrupt

line be enabled. In many cases, an interrupt acknowledge signal is generated that acknowledges the external request.

13 Timing. This block utilizes counters to divide the frequency of external oscillator inputs in order to generate the clock phases required by the microcomputer. Logic gating (AND, OR NOR, NAND, etc.) and decoders are used to generate these phases and additional synchronized timing signals.

REFERENCES

1. G.E. Williams, *Digital Technology*, SRA, Chicago, Illinois, 1977.

2. S.C. Lee, *Digital Circuits and Logic Design*, Prentice–Hall, Englewood Cliffs, N.J., 1976.

3. R.K. Richards, *Digital Design*, John Wiley & Sons, New York, 1971.

TECHNOLOGY

When the term *technology* is used in relation to microcomputers or to any integrated circuit device, it refers to the chip fabrication processes that are the means of producing the device. An understanding of these processes is extremely important to a designer or user of microcomputers. The type of technology used will determine the following.

- The speed of operation of the device.
- The degree of integration (the number of transistors which can be integrated onto the chip).
- The power consumption.
- The cost of the chip.
- The interface requirements for the chip.
- The reliability of the device.

4.1 TYPES OF PROCESSES AND STRUCTURES UTILIZED

There are essentially only two main types of fabrication technologies for digital integrated circuits and microprocessors in particular. These technologies are bipolar and MOS (Metal-Oxide-Semiconductor.) Under these main headings are derivative processes that are used in manufacturing most of the present microcomputers and that will be used to produce a majority of the microcomputers in the near future. The most popular process technologies are given in Table 4.1.

TABLE 4.1   Types of Microcomputer Fabrication Processes

BIPOLAR	MOS
Bipolar (conventional)	P-channel MOS—PMOS
Schottky bipolar	N-channel MOS—NMOS
Integrated Injection Logic—I²L	Complementary symmetry MOS—CMOS
	Silicon on sapphire—SOS
	VMOS
	HMOS

All of these processes use the basic structure of a p–n junction to build the transistors and, from these, the digital logic circuits which comprise a microcomputer. The following sections explain the structure and operation of a p–n junction and these transistor elements.

4.1.1 P–N Junctions

The p–n juncton is the basic component of all semiconductor devices. Since most integrated circuits are fabricated utilizing the semiconductor silicon, this discussion will be limited to silicon in explaining the basic structures of integrated circuits. The concepts, however, can apply to other commonly used semiconductor materials such as germanium or gallium arsenide.

A semiconductor is defined as *n-type* or *p-type* depending on whether it has an excess or dearth, respectively, of electrons in its crystalline structure. Since silicon has a valence of four, addition of impurities to or "doping" of intrinsic (relatively "pure") silicon with an element such as phosphorus (in the form of PH_3), which has five valence electrons, will result in an excess of electrons in the doped silicon. Similarly, doping with an element such as boron that have three valence electrons (in the form of B_2H_6) will yield p-type silicon with "holes" or a net shortage of valence electrons. A hole or absence of an electron acts as a positive charge, producing a crystalline structure with an excess of positive charges. Doping levels range from approximately 10^{15} to 10^{21} impurity atoms per cubic centimeter of silicon. Elements such as phosphorus or arsenic that are used to produce n-type silicon are referred to as *donors* since they donate electrons to the silicon crystalline structure. Boron, on the other hand, is referred to as an *acceptor* since it "accepts" electrons from the silicon crystalline structure and produces excess positive charges or holes in the silicon.

A junction of p- and n-type silicon has the characteristic of conducting when a positive potential is applied to the p-type silicon with respect to the n-type silicon. A voltage applied in this direction is referred to as a *forward bias voltage.* For silicon, conduction takes place after a *threshold voltage* of approximately 0.7 volts is reached. If a voltage of opposite polarity or a *reverse bias* is applied to the p–n junction, the current flow Thus, a p–n junction acts as a *rectifying* junction or a *diode*, conducting when a voltage is applied across it in one direction and acting essentially as an open circuit when the voltage is applied in the opposite direction.

An important factor to note in relation to current flowing in an n- or p-type material is that the effective movement of positive charges (holes) in silicon is approximately three times slower than that of negative charges (electrons) in silicon. Thus, the *mobility*, μ_n, of electrons is said to be about three times greater than μ_p, the mobility of holes. This characteristic is due to the larger effective mass of holes relative to electrons in silicon and, therefore, results in a higher resistance conducting channel in p-type material than in n-type material (Figure 4.1).

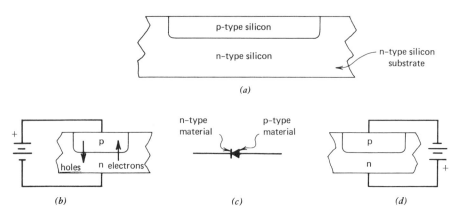

FIGURE 4.1 p–n junction and biasing modes.

4.2 BIPOLAR (CONVENTIONAL)

If two p–n junctions are fabricated such that there are n–p–n or p–n–p regions in a silicon crystalline structure, then a *bipolar* transistor is formed. This transistor is called a bipolar device since both hole and electron current (carriers of both polarities) flow take place in the transistor. This bipolar transistor has the characteristic that current supplied to the p- or n-type material in the center will control a much larger current flowing from one end region to the other. One of the end regions acts as a source or *emitter* of charges and the other end region acts as a *collector* of these charges. The center or *base* region controls the current flowing from the emitter to the collector (Figure 4.2).

Levels representing logical 1's or 0's are obtained by injecting enough current into the base to cause the transistor to turn *ON* and conduct heavily or by supplying no current or less than the minimum amount (*threshold*) necessary for emitter-to-collector conduction and turning the transistor *OFF*.

If a bipolar transistor is biased for amplifier applications, the base-emitter junction is forward biased and the base-collector junction is reverse biased. For conventional switching or digital logic applications, the bipolar transistor emitter-base junction is forward biased and its base-collector junction becomes forward biased when the transistor is turned ON. Under those circumstances, the transistor is said to be in *saturation.* In the forward biased base-collector junction, hole current flows from the p-type to n-type material and electron current flows from the n-type to p-type material. This bipolar current flow produces a *stored charge* or an excess of minority carriers (electrons in p-type silicon and holes in n-type silicon) in

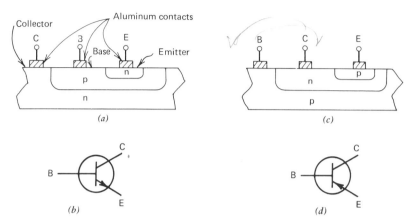

FIGURE 4.2 Bipolar transistor cross sections. (a) npn bipolar transistor. (b) npn bipolar transistor symbols. (c) pnp bipolar transistor. (d) pnp bipolar transistor symbol.

the vicinity of the forward-biased junction. If, after forward-biasing the base-collector, the bias voltage is reversed (as is the case when the transistor is to be turned OFF), the minority carriers flow back across the junction and, thus, a current continues to flow for a short period. The time for these minority carriers to recombine and, thus, for the minority carrier current flow to cease is called *storage time*. Typical storage time for a bipolar transistor is about 30 nanoseconds (30×10^{-9} sec). This storage time limits the frequency at which the transistor can switch from ON to OFF since it continues to conduct for a period of time equal to the storage time following the removal of base current. Two commonly used methods to overcome the storage time delay are gold doping and the Schottky bipolar process. The Schottky bipolar process will be discussed in Section 4.3.

Gold doping or diffusion of gold into the transistor reduces storage time to approximately 6 nanoseconds, which is a factor of five less that of a non-gold-doped bipolar transistor. It accomplishes this reduction by enhancing the minority carrier recombination process and, thus, shortening the time required for the transistor to return to its equilibrium carrier concentration. One of the disadvantages of gold doping is the reduction of the transistor gain, thereby requiring a narrow base region to improve gain. This requirement, then, generally excludes transistors with wide base regions such as lateral pnp devices (transistors formed by creating a pnp "sandwich" laterally across the silicon substrate rather than vertically) from gold doping. In addition, the ability of gold doping to reduce storage time decreases at high temperatures. For example, the storage time for a gold-doped bipolar transistor increases from about 6 nsec at 25°C to 15 ns at 125°C.

Since the storage time is a component of the *propagation delay time* (time for a logic level change at the input of a device to appear as a corresponding change at the output), a reduction in storage time can significantly reduce the propagation delay and, therefore, increase the frequency of pulses which the device can handle. A comparison of typical propagation delay and storage times for non-gold-doped and gold-doped bipolar transistors is given in Table 4.2. The numbers in Table 4.2 are average values and may vary with process methods.

4.3 SCHOTTKY BIPOLAR

In order to avoid the disadvantages of gold-doping and yet reduce or effectively eliminate charge storage in the base-collector junction of a bipolar transistor, a Schottky diode can be employed. The *Schottky diode* is a rectifying junction formed by placing a metal in contact with a semiconductor. This diode was named after a German scientist who developed the first valid theory of metal-to-semiconductor rectification. In most integrated circuits, the Schottky diode is fabricated by placing aluminum in contact with n-type silicon with forward current consisting of electrons flowing from the n-type silicon into the aluminum. These electrons then rapidly come to equilibrium with the other electrons in the metal, which effectively results in no stored charge. The symbol for the Schottky diode is

TABLE 4.2   Propagation Delay Time Components for Typical Non-Gold-doped and Gold-doped Bipolar Transistors

	PROPAGATION DELAY	DEVICE DELAY (EXCLUDING STORAGE TIME)	STORAGE TIME
Non-gold doped transistors	41 nsec	11 nsec	30 nsec
Gold-doped transistor	14 nsec	8 nsec	6 nsec

Propagation delay = device delay + storage time (device delay is nonzero time required for a transistor to change from ON to OFF excluding storage time).

as opposed to that of conventional p–n junction diode which is
. The Schottky diode also has a lower forward voltage drop (approximately 0.4 v) than that of a silicon p–n junction, which is about 0.7 v.

In the Schottky bipolar process, a Schottky diode is placed in parallel
with the base-collector junction of an npn transistor. A metal electrode is
placed across the base-collector junction with the rectifying junction
formed at the metal–collector interface.

Because the Schottky diode has a lower "turn-on" threshold or forward voltage drop than the base-collector p–n junction, the excess base
current that would normally drive the transistor into saturation is diverted
through the Schottky diode and does not flow into the base [See Figure
4.3*a*.] Thus, the base-collector p–n junction never becomes forward biased
and an excess of minority carriers does not build up at the junction. This
lack of minority carrier buildup at the base-collector junction and at the
Schottky metal-to-semiconductor junction results in no stored charge and,
therefore, effectively zero storage time for the Schottky transistor.

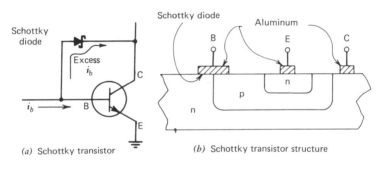

(a) Schottky transistor   (b) Schottky transistor structure

(c) Schottky transistor symbol

FIGURE 4.3 Schottky transistor structure and symbols.

The Schottky bipolar transistor also has the following advantages over
the gold-doped bipolar transistor.

- Storage time not increasing with temperature.
- Less sensitive to changes in power supply voltage.
- Ability to handle higher frequency pulse trains because of its lower
  propagation delay.
- Less inverse leakage current.

Table 4.3 contrasts typical values of propagation delay components among non-gold-doped, gold-doped, and Schottky bipolar transistors. These numbers are, again, average values subject to process method differences.

TABLE 4.3 Propagation Delay Time Components for Typical Non-Gold-doped, Gold-doped, and Schottky Bipolar Transistors

	PROPAGATION DELAY	DEVICE DELAY (EXCLUDING STORAGE TIME)	STORAGE TIME
Non-gold-doped transistor	41 nsec	11 nsec	30 nsec
Gold-doped transistor	14 nsec	8 nsec	6 nsec
Schottky transistor	7 nsec	7 nsec	0 nsec

4.4 MOS

The other major process used to fabricate transistors is the Metal-Oxide-Semiconductor (MOS) process. In this process, two heavily doped diffused "wells" of either n- or p-type (n+ or p+) are embedded in a silicon substrate of the opposite type. (See Figure 4.4.) The surface area between these wells is covered by a thin insulating layer of silicon dioxide on which, in turn, is deposited a layer of metal. This layer of metal is called the *gate*, the wells are referred to as the *source* and *drain*, and the substrate material between the wells is the *channel*. If the wells are p-type silicon in an n-type substrate, the device is a *PMOS* or *P-channel MOS transistor* or P-channel *insulated-gate field effect transistor (IGFET.)* If the opposite types of material are used for the source/drain diffusions and the substrate, the device is called an *NMOS* or *N-channel MOS transistor* or *N-channel IGFET.*

4.4.1 PMOS

If a potential is applied across the source and drain of a P-channel MOS transistor, the flow of current between the source and drain can be controlled by the gate potential with respect to the substrate. If a negative potential larger than the gate threshold voltage, V_T, is applied to the gate, positive charges (holes) are attracted to the surface of the silicon between the p-type source and drain and form a conductive channel between the

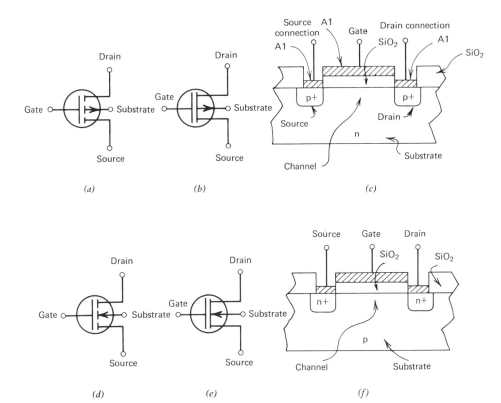

FIGURE 4.4 PMOS and NMOS transistor symbols and structures. (*a*) P-channel MOS transistor symbol (enhancement mode). (*b*) P-channel MOS transistor symbol (depletion mode). (*c*) P-channel MOS transistor structure. (*d*) N-channel MOS transistor symbol (enhancement mode). (*e*) N-channel MOS transistor symbol (depletion mode). (*f*) N-channel MOS transistor structure.

p regions. For an aluminum gate P-channel transistor, V_T is approximately equal to -2 v. When an MOS transistor operates in this manner, i.e., conducts when a gate voltage is applied and does not conduct when the gate voltage is zero, it is called an *enhancement mode* transistor. If the MOS transistor conducts current from source to drain when the gate voltage is zero or below V_T and does not conduct current when a voltage above V_T is applied to the gate, it is a *depletion mode* transistor. Because the enhancement mode MOS transistor offers higher immunity to noise and lower power dissipation characteristics than a depletion mode device, it is widely used in microprocessor and memory fabrication. Since the gate of the MOS transistor is insulated from the substrate, source, and drain by an insulating layer of silicon dioxide, the gate draws virtually no direct current and presents an essentially capacitive load to any driving device.

This PMOS technology was developed in the mid-1960s and was, therefore, used to fabricate the first microprocessors and calculator chips in the early 1970s. The PMOS process is the oldest of the MOS LSI processes. Early PMOS transistors were fabricated with aluminum gates and, since this required the accurate deposition of metal across the channel between the p-type source and drain, gate alignment was a critical factor in the performance of the transistors. If the aluminum was not deposited so as to completely span the channel region between the source and drain, channel conduction would be poor or would not take place. On the other hand, if the aluminum gate overlapped the source and drain diffusions more than necessary, gate-to-drain and gate-to-source capacitance would be increased and the switching speed of the transistor would be reduced. This reduction would, in turn, result in a decrease in the instruction execution time of the microprocessor.

The high work function of the aluminum gate also contributed to higher threshold voltages ($\simeq2$ volts), which then resulted in higher power supply voltages' being needed to operate the transistors (non-TTL compatible).

A method devised to eliminate or reduce some of the problems associated with aluminum gate MOS transistors is the silicon gate process. In this process, doped polycrystalline silicon is used as the gate of the MOS transistor and is deposited *before* the source and drain diffusion. Then, during these diffusions, the silicon gate serves as a diffusion mask for the source and drain resulting in a self-aligned silicon gate. The reduction in gate capacitance produced by this technique provides a switching speed increase of twice that of the aluminum gate process. The silicon gate also yields a lower gate threshold voltage (1 volt), which can permit circuit operation from a single +5-volt power supply and also results in smaller gate dimensions, which allows a higher packing density of transistors. The silicon layer used for the gate also provides another interconnecting level and immediate protection of the gate oxide from impurities. In conventional aluminum gate processing, the gate oxide remains exposed throughout one masking step.

As a relative figure of merit, a P-channel silicon gate processor operates on a clock frequency of approximately 500 KHz to 1 MHz with instruction execution times of about 10 microseconds.

4.4.2 NMOS

The NMOS transistor as shown in Figure 4.4d, 4.4e, and 4.4f operates in the same manner as the PMOS device except that electrons and not holes are the carriers in the channel between the source and drain when the transistor is conducting.

Because of the threefold increase in the mobility of the channel carriers in N-channel MOS, a speed increase of three over P-channel MOS is obtained. The N-channel silicon gate technology makes possible a minimum of a five times increase in speed over P-channel aluminum gate MOS technology. A typical NMOS microprocessor executes instructions on the average of 0.5 to 2 microseconds and operates on a clock frequency of 1 to 4 MHz.

The N channel process is the dominant MOS technology for microcomputer fabrication, even though NMOS has a high sensitivity to surface contamination that requires ultra clean processing. The N-channel silicon gate devices provide low threshold properties and, with other processing techniques, a single +5 volt power supply requirement (TTL compatible.)

4.4.3 HMOS

High Performance MOS or, HMOS, is achieved by scaling down of device dimensions in the NMOS process to achieve increased performance. By reducing the channel length of the NMOS transistor, one can achieve increased density and speed in LSI and VLSI circuits along with corresponding decreases in the speed–power product. Theoretically, the scaling down process is achieved by merely reducing the mask dimensions, but second-order effects (such as shifting in the value of V_T and electron trapping in the gate oxide) limit the degree of scaling. Some typical parameters that presently characterize the HMOS process are channel lengths of 3.5 μm, memory access times of approximately 50 nsec, and speed–power products of 1 picojoule at 5 volts power supply voltage. HMOS portends to be a dominant MOS technology for high density LSI systems on a chip such as memories and 16-bit microcomputers.

4.4.4 VMOS

Another approach to achieving short channel length and, thus, increased performance and density is V-groove MOS or VMOS. In the VMOS process, the NMOS transistor is formed vertically through a series of semiconductor layers as shown in Figure 4.5.

The n+ source region is the deepest layer and serves as a common ground for all VMOS transistors. The channel is the next layer, p, above the source diffusion and actually wraps around the periphery of the V-groove, providing a large area channel with a short channel length. The lightly doped π epitaxial layer (p-type) separates the p layer in which the channel is formed from the n+ drain region. The effect of this π layer is

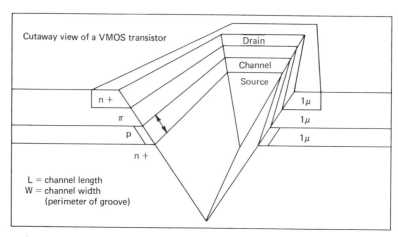

FIGURE 4.5 VMOS transistor structure.

to increase the breakdown voltage between the drain and substrate and to increase switching speed by reducing the capacitance of that junction. Thus, VMOS achieves high density by using a three-dimensional transistor that has a small surface area and obtains increased speed by virtue of the fact the channel is vertical ($\cong$ 1 μm) and the π layer reduces capacitance.

4.4.5 CMOS

CMOS or Complementary MOS is a technology which combines both P-channel and N-channel transistors on the same substrate in a complementary structure.

In the CMOS gate, the N-channel and P-channel transistors are connected so that, except for switching intervals when the output is changing state, only one transistor of the pair is ON at a time (Figure 4.6). If a logic 0 or a ground potential is applied to the gate inputs, the P-channel transistor will be turned ON, connecting the V_{DD} supply to the output and producing a logic 1. If V_{DD} = +5 volts, the output voltage will be approximately +4.99 volts. The N-channel transistor will be OFF since the gate voltage is not sufficiently positive with respect to the substrate. Conversely, if a logic 1 or +4.99 volts is applied to the gate inputs, the N-channel transistor is turned ON and the P-channel transistor is turned OFF. Thus, a logic 0 of approximately 0.01 volts is provided on the output lead.

This complementary arrangement means that during static operation there is always a high impedance between V_{DD} and ground and a very small

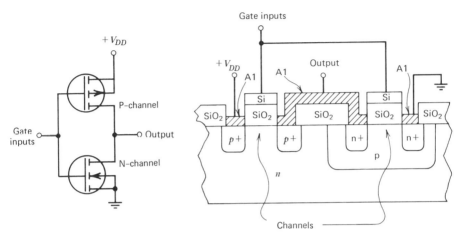

FIGURE 4.6 CMOS gate symbol and structure. (a) CMOS gate symbol. (b) CMOS gate structure.

amount of current flow (microamperes.) Since the output is normally connected to the high impedance (10^{12} ohms at 5 pf) gate inputs of another CMOS gate, there is virtually no static loading of the CMOS gate output. Thus, in the static or quiescent state, a CMOS gate draws a very small amount of power—on the order of 25 nanowatts (25×10^{-9} watts.) As the frequency of switching of the CMOS gate increases, however, the power requirements of the gate also increase. The dynamic power dissipation, P_{DD}, of a CMOS logic gate is given by the expression.

$$P_{DD} = CV^2 f \text{ watts}$$

where f is the switching frequency, V is the supply voltage, and C is the load capacitance. If the output of a CMOS gate with a V_{DD} supply = 5 volts is driving the input of an identical CMOS gate with a typical input capacitance of 5 picofarads (5×10^{-12} farads), the dynamic power dissipation is

$$P_{DD} = (5 \times 10^{-12})(25) \times f \text{ watts}$$

or

$$125 \times 10^{-12} \times f \text{ watts}$$

If the transistors were switching at a rate of 10 MHz, the dynamic power dissipation would be

$$P_{DD} = 125 \times 10^{-12} \times 10 \times 10^6 = 1250 \times 10^{-6} = 1.25 \text{ milliwatts}$$

This level of power dissipation is near the value of that for bipolar logic circuits.

Propagation delay time of a CMOS gate is a function of the power supply voltage. For a 10-volt supply, the delay is approximately 25 nsec and for a 5-volt supply it is typically 60 nsec.

The characteristics of the CMOS process are high immunity to noise (approximately 40% of supply voltage), insensitivity to temperature variations, low power dissipation in static or low frequency mode, operation over wide range of power supply voltages (+5 to +18 volts, typically), higher cost, and lower packing density than PMOS or NMOS. These features of the CMOS process make it a good candidate for use in automotive applications and low-power, battery-operated systems.

4.4.6 SOS

Silicon On Sapphire is a technology which is particularly amenable to CMOS designs since, in LSI applications, it can enhance the advantages of CMOS with higher speed and density. In this technology, islands of silicon are formed by an epitaxial process on an insulating substrate of sapphire (Al_2O_3) and complementary P- and N-channel transistors are formed from these islands (Figure 4.7). A particular SOS process that produces high-performance CMOS-on-sapphire circuits is the Hewlett-Packard Losos process (local oxidation of Silicon-on-Sapphire). As shown in Figure 4.7a, aluminum gates are employed in the Losos N- and P-channel transistors.

The main advantage of the SOS process is the effective elimination of the large drain-to-substrate capacitance that is present in other MOS processes. This elimination is achieved by diffusing the drain regions of the transistor islands down to the sapphire substrate and, thus, producing a very low capacitance silicon-to-insulator junction. Since there is less capacitance to charge and discharge in an SOS gate, the dynamic power requirements are less than that of a conventional CMOS gate and the speed of operation is higher. The low-capacitance characteristics of SOS can best be utilized in LSI circuits where there are a large number of interconnections whose capacitances can severely limit the maximum speed of operation. The SOS LSI devices can operate at speeds approaching 90 MHz with propagation delays of 1 to 2 nanoseconds.

4.5 INTEGRATED INJECTION LOGIC (I²L)

A bipolar technology which combines the density of MOS with the speed of bipolar is *Integrated Injection Logic* (I²L) or, as it is sometimes called, *Merged Transistor Logic* (MTL). This process was developed simultane-

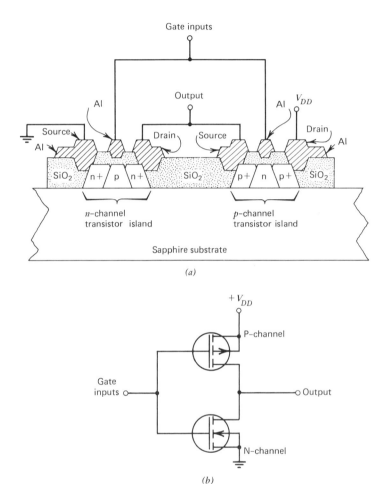

(a) SOS gate structure (Losos).
(b) SOS gate symbol.

FIGURE 4.7 SOS gate symbol and structure. (a) SOS gate structure (Losos). (b) SOS gate symbol.

ously and independently by teams working at IBM in West Germany and Philips Research in the Netherlands and was announced in 1972. The IBM researchers had the objectives of "merging" portions of components so that one semiconductor region would be common to two or more of them, thus producing a simple basic building block. The Philips approach was to eliminate load resistors required by some logic families and to replace them with current injector transistors. The result of these efforts was the I²L gate (Figure 4.8).

The I²L gate consists of an npn transistor with multiple open collectors that is integrated vertically into the silicon substrate. The difference between this type of transistor and the conventional type as shown in Figure 4.2 is that the I²L npn transistor is upside down, i.e., its emitter region is the deepest in the substrate and the collector diffusion is at the surface. This geometry is the reverse of conventional bipolar processing. Because of this structure, the inverse current gain or inverse beta of the vertical npn transistor has to be controlled during processing whereas the forward beta is optimized in standard bipolar processing. This vertical npn transistor is turned ON or OFF by controlling the current into its base, B_2. This current is supplied by the lateral pnp current injector transistor.

The pnp transistor is described as a lateral device since it is formed

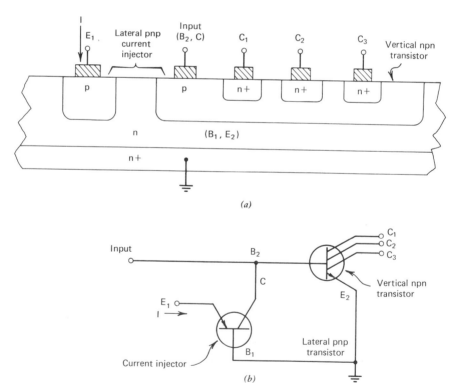

FIGURE 4.8 I²L gate symbol and structure. (a) I²L gate structure. (b) I²L gate schematic.

laterally across the silicon structure as shown in Figure 4.8*a*. Note that the base, B_1, of the lateral pnp transistor is common to and merged with the emitter, E_2, of the vertical npn transistor in the silicon substrate. The n+ region shown in Figure 4.8*a* provides a common ground plane for all the npn transistor gates and eliminates the need for metal runs on the surface to perform this function. Additional merging is achieved in the I²L gate with the collector area, C, of the lateral pnp transistor's being common with the base, B_2, of the vertical npn transistor. Because of this arrangement of elements and the polarity of the voltages applied to the various doped regions, no "isolation islands" between transistors are required as in conventional bipolar technology. This feature permits I²L to approach or exceed MOS packing densities.

The I²L gate operates as an inverter with a logic 1 or high being approximately 750 millivolts (0.750 volts) and a logic 0 or low a voltage of about 50 millivolts. Thus, if a voltage of 750 millivolts or greater is applied to the input of the I²L gate, the current from the injector will flow into the low impedance base-emitter junction of the npn transistor causing it to conduct or turn ON. This conduction will produce a voltage drop ($V_{ce,sat}$) from the collectors C_1, C_2, and C_3 to the emitter, E_2, of approximately 50 millivolts. Conversely, if a voltage of typically 50 millivolts is applied to the input of the gate, the current from the injectors will be diverted from the base, B_2, of the npn transistor to the input lead. In other words, current will flow from the injector out of the input lead. This type of operation is termed *current sourcing* since the input lead serves as a source of current. If the 50-millivolts logic 0 on the input lead were being supplied by one of the collectors of a second I²L gate, the npn transistor of the second gate would serve as a current *sink* since it would have to conduct the current sourced by the first gate (Figure 4.9).

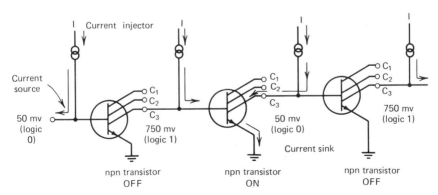

FIGURE 4.9 I²L gates' logical operation.

The current source to the emitter, E_1, of the lateral pnp transistor could be a programmable current power supply or a voltage source with a series dropping resistor. Since the switching speed of the I²L gate is a function of the injector current, the speed of operation of the gate can be programmed by controlling this current. Thus, ranges of low power to high speed operation can be selected. The density of I²L is comparable and, in some cases, better than N-channel silicon gate MOS. A typical gate in silicon gate NMOS requires approximately 5 square mils whereas a comparable I²L gate takes up 4.5 square mils of area. I²L also can operate over the full military temperature range of −55°C to +125°C.

As noted in Figure 4.9, I²L logic levels are not directly compatible with TTL bipolar logic levels and require conversion to obtain compatibility. This conversion consists mainly of a voltage divider on the input to the I²L gate and connecting a proper pullup resistor from the collector to the power supply of the I²L open collector output, which is essentially the

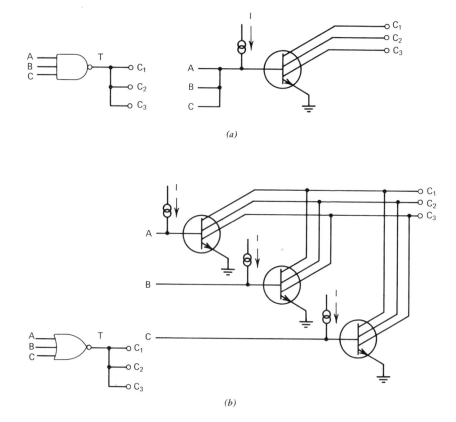

(a)

(b)

same as a TTL open collector device. These techniques can be easily implemented on the chip to provide TTL compatible I²L circuits. To date, I²L has not lived up to its expected potential.

Some implementations of conventional digital circuits with I²L gates are given in Figure 4.10.

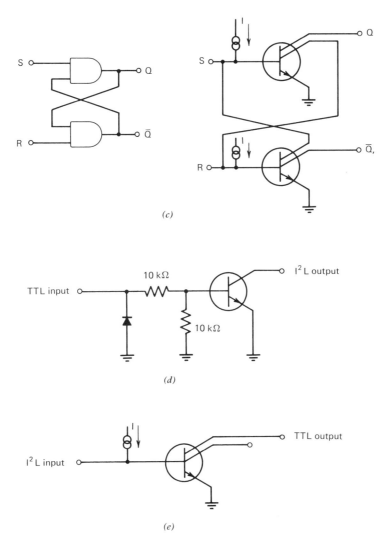

(c)

(d)

(e)

FIGURE 4.10 I²L digital circuit implementations. (a) NAND gate. (b) NOR gate. (c) NAND R-S latch. (d) TTL-to-I²L interface. (e) I²L to TTL interface.

TABLE 4.4 Characteristics of Major Fabrication Technologies

CHARACTERISTIC	TECHNOLOGY							
	SCHOTTKY BIPOLAR	PMOS	NMOS SILICON GATE	HMOS	VMOS	CMOS	SOS	i^2L
Logic voltage range (high-low)	5 volts	10 volts	5 volts	2-5 volts	5 volts	Supply voltage	Supply voltage	0.6-0.7 volts
Speed power product (pj)	10-100	50 to 100	5 to 50	0.5-1	0.5-1	2 to 40	0.5 to 30	0.2 to 2
Gate propagation delay (ns)	7	75	4 to 25	2	2	10 to 35	4 to 20	7 to 50
Gate power dissipation	1-5 mw	1.7 mw	1 mw	0.4-1 mw	1 mw	1 watt to 1 mw	0.05 mw	1 nw to 100 μw
Gate current	0.2 to 2 ma	50 μa to 1 ma	50 μa to 1 ma	0.2-1 ma	0.5-1 ma	nanoamperes	nanoamperes	1 na to 1 ma
Power supply voltage	5 volts typically	-5 to -15 volts	5 to 15 volts	2-5 volts	5 volts	3 to 18 volts	3 to 18 volts	1 to 15 volts
Gate area (mils^2)	20	10	5	2-3	2-3	10 to 30	15	5
Gates/mm^2	20-40	70-120	100-180	250	250	40 to 90	100 to 200	75 to 150
Comments	High speed, less dense, bit slice processor technology	High yield, proven technology low speed, good packing density	High yield, higher density and higher speed than PMOS, dominant microprocessor technology	Scaled-down NMOS resulting in higher performance, greater density and lower cost. One of dominant technologies of the 1980's.	More complex processing than NMOS. High-speed and high density NMOS process. Can sink higher currents than HMOS	Low power static operation, complementary N & P channel structure, wide operating range over temperature and power supply variations, less dense	Features of CMOS, higher speed and density	Programmable speed and power characteristics, eliminates discrete load resistors; has high speed capability of bipolar, high density of MOS

4.6 TABULAR COMPARISON OF IMPORTANT PARAMETERS

The technology used in the manufacture of a microprocessor determines directly, or indirectly, its price, performance, capabilities, size, and application.

A summary of the salient characteristics of the major fabrication technologies discussed in this chapter is provided for reference in Table 4.4. The values in Table 4.4 are average values and will change as device dimensions change due to improvements in process technology.

Note that in the table the characteristic called the *speed–power product* is given for each of the technologies. The *speed–power product* is the product of the typical gate propagation delay time in that technology and the average power dissipation of the gate. The units of the speed–power product are picojoules (pj) when the propagation delay is in nanoseconds and the power dissipation is in milliwatts. The speed–power product is a figure of merit that can be used to evaluate the performance of a typical microprocessor technology. The lower the value of the speed power product, the higher the speed and the lower the power of operation of the device.

REFERENCES

1. Lawrence Altman, "Digital Design: Scaling New Heights," *Electronics*, Vol. 51, No. 4, February 16, 1978.

2. E.A. Torrero, "Solid State Devices," *Spectrum*, Vol. 15, No. 1, January, 1978.

3. S.S. Eaton, "Silicon on Sapphire Stretches CMOS Performance," *Electronics*, Vol. 48, No. 12, June 12, 1975.

4. G.E. Williams, *Digital Technology*, ARA, Inc., Chicago, Illinois, 1977.

5. P.W. Verhofstadt, "Evaluation of Technology Options for LSI Processing Elements," *Proceedings of the IEEE*, Vol. 64, No. 6, June, 1976.

6. R.A. Pederson, "I²L—A MOS Competitive Bipolar Logic Technique," paper presented at 1975 IEEE Intercon, New York, April 18-20, 1975.

MEMORIES

Discussion of memories relative to microcomputers is essentially a discussion of semiconductor memories as opposed to core memories. Up to the 1970s, ferrite core memories were the dominant means of rapid, random access storage and retrieval of digital data. In the ferrite core or ring, the two possible directions of magnetic polarization are used to represent the logical 1 and logical 0 states. The binary state of the core is determined by the induction of current in a core sense winding when the core switches from one magnetic polarity to the opposite polarity and the conversion of this current pulse by a sense amplifier into a 1 or 0 indication.

Because of the cost, density, power, and speed limitations of core memory and because of the temperature instability of low-current core materials, semiconductor memories have become and will continue to be the principal means of random access, high speed data storage in digital systems.

5.1 TYPES OF SEMICONDUCTOR MEMORIES

The terminology used to identify the different types of memories is based on the means of accessing the stored data. The major categories of memories and their descriptions are given in Table 5.1.

5.2 DEFINITIONS

A pseudostandard terminology has developed for memories used in microcomputer systems. In this section, definitions of the major terms used in describing microcomputer memories are presented as a group for ease of reference. Some of these terms have been presented in Table 5.1 but are also given here in more detail.

MICROCOMPUTER MEMORY TERMS

Access Time — Delay interval from the time a stable memory address is presented to memory to the time valid information is available at the memory outputs. This time includes delays caused by chip select, address decoding, and chip enable circuits, along with buffering, wiring, and circuit capacitance delays. For a completely static memory, access time is equal to cycle time. In RAM with the automatic power down features (power dissipation of memory reduced when it is not being accessed) access time can

TABLE 5.1 Major Semiconductor Memory Categories

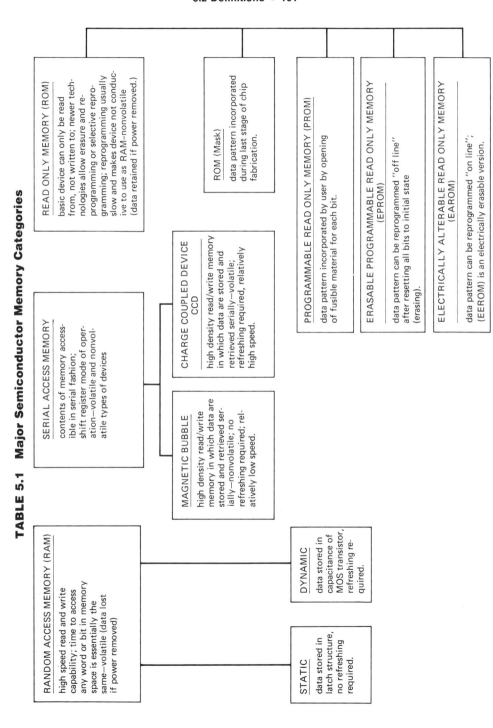

RANDOM ACCESS MEMORY (RAM)

high speed read and write capability; time to access any word or bit in memory space is essentially the same—volatile (data lost if power removed)

STATIC

data stored in latch structure, no refreshing required.

DYNAMIC

data stored in capacitance of MOS transistor, refreshing required.

SERIAL ACCESS MEMORY

contents of memory accessible in serial fashion; shift register mode of operation—volatile and nonvolatile types of devices

MAGNETIC BUBBLE

high density read/write memory in which data are stored and retrieved serially—nonvolatile; no refreshing required; relatively low speed.

CHARGE COUPLED DEVICE CCD

high density read/write memory in which data are stored and retrieved serially—volatile; refreshing required, relatively high speed.

READ ONLY MEMORY (ROM)

basic device can only be read from, not written to; newer technologies allow erasure and reprogramming or selective reprogramming; reprogramming usually slow and makes device not conducive to use as RAM-nonvolatile (data retained if power removed.)

ROM (Mask)

data pattern incorporated during last stage of chip fabrication.

PROGRAMMABLE READ ONLY MEMORY (PROM)

data pattern incorporated by user by opening of fusible material for each bit.

ERASABLE PROGRAMMABLE READ ONLY MEMORY (EPROM)

data pattern can be reprogrammed "off line" after resetting all bits to initial state (erasing).

ELECTRICALLY ALTERABLE READ ONLY MEMORY (EAROM)

data pattern can be reprogrammed "on line"; (EEROM) is an electrically erasable version.

be looked at as t_{AA} (address access time) and t_{ACS} (chip-select access time.) In some cases, t_{ACS} can be greater than T_{AA}, thus, limiting the memory access speed if chip select is part of address information.

Address Hold Time	Time between end of write signal and removal of address from address lines.
Address Setup Time	Time between presentation of stable address on memory address lines and initiation of memory write signal.
Byte	A grouping of eight bits taken as a unit.
CCD	Charge Coupled Device; a serially organized memory in which information is stored as charge in a potential well of an MOS device. Information is transferred serially from one well to another by the application of multiphase clock pulses to the structure. Since the data are shifted through the CCD memory, access to any bit is not random, but all other bits that are stored before the desired bit must be accessed. Typical access times of CCD memories are 15 to 100 μsec with shifting data rates of 2 to 20 MHZ. CCD storage is volatile and must be refreshed as is necessary for other MOS capacitive storage devices.
Chip Enable	One or more binary inputs to a chip that when active, enable the chip operation including control of clock and power applied to the chip circuits. Chip enable (CE) can either be active low ($\overline{\text{CE}}$) or active high (CE). It is sometimes used interchangeably with the term *chip select* but, in a strict sense, is not the same.
Chip Select	One or more binary inputs to a chip that, when active, connect the inputs/outputs of the chip to the proper bus (normally the data bus.) When the chip select (CS) line is not active, the outputs are usually in a tri-state high impedance mode and are essentially disconnected from the bus. The CS can either be active low ($\overline{\text{CS}}$) or active high (CS). It is

	sometimes used interchangeably with the term *chip enable* although CS does not affect operation or enable the internal circuit operation as does the CE. In RAM circuits with automatic power down (power dissipation of memory reduced when it is not being accessed) t_{ACS} (chip select access time) can be greater than t_{AA} (address access time) and reduce access speed if chip select is part of address information to the chip.
Cycle Time	Time to complete one cycle of operation. For a memory read operation, this is the time composed of the combination of memory addressing time, read enable, chip select and/or chip enable activation time, time for output data to be valid, read enable, and chip select and/or chip enable deactivation time. These delays are not usually sequentially totalled since some of the times overlap during the read sequence. Essentially, this time is the period of a read cycle. Similarly, the write cycle time consists of the same delays except that data are being sent to the memory instead of being read from the memory. This time is the period of a memory write cycle. For a static memory, cycle time equals access time. Otherwise, cycle time is greater than access time.
Data In Hold Time	Time between initiation of memory write signal and removal of data input.
Data In Setup Time	Time between presentation of stable data on data input lines and initiation of memory write signal.
Dynamic	Refers to Random Access Memories in which information stored can deteriorate with time and be lost. The memory, therefore, must be refreshed (recharged) at specific intervals to retain the information content. Commonly, the information is stored on parasitic capacitances of MOS structures.
EAROM	Electrically Alterable Read Only Memory; Read Only Memory whose contents can be

altered without removing the memory from its socket. Since these devices usually have much slower write times than read times, they are best used in applications where reading will be performed more frequently than writing. Because of this characteristic, these memories are sometimes referred to as *Read Mostly Memories* or RMM's. As with other ROM's, they are nonvolatile. The primary technologies used to fabricate EAROMS are Metal Nitride Oxide Semiconductor (MNOS) and technologies utilizing amorphous semiconductors such as tellurium.

EEROM

Electrically Erasable Read Only Memory; a ROM which can be erased electrically in place; requires special programming circuitry; similar to EAROM.

Edge-activated or Edge-enabled

Refers to ROM's whose internal peripheral circuits such as decoders, sense amplifiers, and output buffers are dynamic. This technique is used to save power since these circuits are activated only when chip is in operation.

EPROM

Erasable Programmable Read Only Memory; a ROM whose total contents can be erased and then reprogrammed. The erasure of the ROM and its reprogramming usually require removal of the memory chip from the microcomputer system. Erasure is accomplished by exposure of the EPROM to ultraviolet (UV) light with a wavelength of 2537 Å at a dosage of 10 watt-seconds/cm². A typical erase time ranges from 10 to 30 minutes. This exposure takes place through a quartz lid or window on the EPROM package. Programming of the EPROM is performed on a piece of equipment referred to as a *programmer*, which contains a socket into which the EPROM is inserted. Appropriate addresses and programming voltage pulses (−25 to −40 volts) are then applied to the EPROM. Each address in the EPROM is programmed in sequence and typical programming times range from approximately

	1½ to 2 minutes. The FAMOS or Floating gate Avalanche-injection MOS storage cell is used to implement the EPROM.
Field Programmable Logic Array	PLA that can be programmed in field by user. (See Programmable Logic Array)
Latency Time	Time to access the first bit of a memory word.
Mask	As referred to in semiconductor processing, a pattern that is placed over the chip during fabrication to define diffusion areas and interconnecting patterns. The programming of a 0 or 1 into a Read Only Memory (ROM) is accomplished during the late stages of chip manufacturing by selectively etching a mask-defined pattern in an interconnecting layer of aluminum.
Magnetic Bubbles	Serial access memory in which 1's or 0's are stored by the presence or absence of magnetic domains or "bubbles" in a thin garnet epitaxial layer on a semiconductor substrate. The bubbles are formed by applying a dc magnetic field to the epitaxial layer and they are circulated in shift register fashion on the bubble memory integrated circuit chip. Bubble memory devices have the features of nonvolatility and high density, but they are slower in shifting speed than other shift register devices such as CCD's. Typical shifting rate for a bubble memory device is in the 100 to 500 KHz range with access times of approximately 2 to 4 msec.
Nonvolatile	The ability of a memory device to retain its information content when power is removed.
Output Disable Time	Time between deactivation of Output Enable line and removal of valid data from data output(s).
Output Enable Time	Time between activation of Output Enable line and presentation of stable data on data output(s).
Programmable Logic Array (PLA)	Logical combination of AND/OR circuits capable of generating transmission functions in

	sum of product form. The P terms and their summation are selected by fusible links.
PROM	Programmable Read Only Memory; a ROM which can be programmed by the user with his particular information pattern but cannot be erased and used again. Programming is usually accomplished by opening metallic or polycrystalline silicon fusible links. A PROM is nonvolatile and information can be randomly accessed.
RAM	Random Access Memory; Read/Write scratchpad memory in which stored information can be accessed randomly. These memories are usually volatile in that they will lose their stored information if power is removed.
RMM	Read Mostly Memory; a nonvolatile memory that is used mainly as a ROM but whose information content can be changed. This type of memory usually requires a longer time for writing than for reading. See EAROM and EEROM in this section.
ROM	Read Only Memory; a nonvolatile memory whose information content is programmed during the final stages of semiconductor manufacturing by a mask pattern. Fabrication of this type of memory by the manufacturer entails an initial mask charge of approximately $500 to $1000, but then the cost of the individual units are lower than other types of read only devices. The data stored in the ROM at the factory cannot be changed once the device is fabricated.
Serial Access Memory	A memory whose information cannot be accessed randomly but must be acquired through a serial search of data preceding the desired information. Shift registers and magnetic tapes are examples of serial access memories.
Static	Random Access Memory in which the stored information is not lost with time, eliminating refreshing (recharging) requirements.

UV Source	Ultraviolet light source usually at wavelength of 2537 Å, used to erase EPROM's.
Volatile	The inability of a memory device to retain its information content when power is removed.
Word	A group of bits in memory organized as a unit. An 8-bit word is referred to as a *byte*.

5.3 METHODS OF DATA STORAGE

The "unit" of data storage in any memory system is referred to as a *storage cell*. The characteristics of a storage cell determine the characteristics of the memory devices comprised of these cells. Thus, a smaller, less power consuming cell with relatively small delay times will result in a higher density memory with less power consumption and higher access speed. Typical storage cells utilized in the different types of memory chips are described in this section.

5.3.1 RAMS

Even though the term RAM is commonly used to describe a volatile memory which has read or write capability, a better term for this type of memory would be *READ/WRITE* memory. A random access memory is either a *static* or *dynamic* device. A static memory stores the information in flip-flop or latch type structures and maintains the information without requiring any refreshing or restoring of data. A dynamic memory incorporates a storage medium, such as a capacitor, which loses its information content over a period of time and, therefore, must be refreshed at intervals to insure data retention. In most dynamic RAM's, the refresh is performed when a memory cell is read. A semiconductor RAM is normally a volatile storage medium whose data are lost when power is removed from the chip.

A typical storage cell for an MOS dynamic RAM is shown in Figure 5.1. This cell is used in Texas Instruments' TMS 4164 64 kbit (65,536 word by 1 bit) dynamic RAM. The chip is organized as two, 128 by 256 cell arrays with 256 sense amplifiers between the two arrays. A memory cell is selected by the coincidence of one of 256 outputs of the row decoder and one of 256 outputs of the column decoder. The individual RAM storage cell is basically a single transistor and single capacitor. A 1 is stored in the cell by a voltage level V_{CC} ($\cong$ 5 volts) on the capacitor while a 0 is represented by 0 volts stored on the capacitor. When the cell is selected, the voltage on the storage capacitor is applied through the transfer gate to the sense amplifier, which is a balanced flip-flop circuit. The sense amplifier then compares the stored charge level in the capacitor with charge level in a dummy cell connected to the flip-flop on the side opposite from the storage capacitor and detects whether a 1 or 0 was stored in the cell. A 1 is rewritten into the cell after a sense operation by the active pull-up network.

Refreshing of the 4164 is performed by executing a memory read cycle once every 4 ms for each of the 256 row addresses.

NMOS RAMS have achieved densities of up to 64 K bits with 256 K bit devices soon to follow. Access times of these RAMS range from 30 nsec to 450 nsec. The I²L bipolar RAMs are fabricated in densities of up to 4K bits with access times of down to 50 nsec.

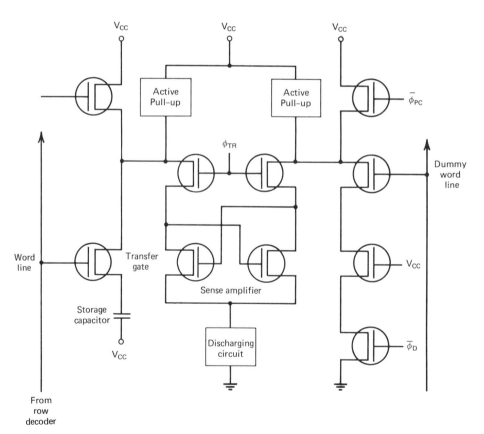

FIGURE 5.1 TMS 4164 single transistor dynamic storage cell.

5.3.2 ROMS and PROMS

In contrast to a dynamic RAM whose read/write data store is accomplished by the presence or absence of charge on a capacitance, a Read Only Memory or ROM stores a bit by the presence or absence of a connecting link between a row line and a column line in the memory array. This storage mechanism gives the ROM the characteristic of being nonvolatile. In Figure 5.2, a 4-word × 4-bit ROM is schematically depicted. The circuit represents only the functional operation of a ROM and is not intended to be a true electrical representation.

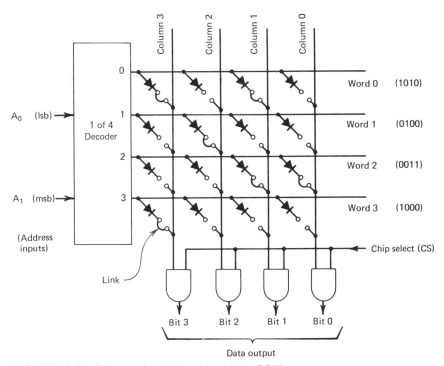

FIGURE 5.2 Schematic of 4-word × 4-bit ROM.

The two address bits, A_0 and A_1, can select one of the four rows or words to be read out by means of a 1 of 4 decoder. This decoder produces a logical 1 (+ voltage) on the output line corresponding to the address input pattern and a logical 0 on the other three output lines. If, for example, A_0 = 0 and A_1 = 1, a logical 1 would appear on decoder output 2 and word 2 line. The links from word 2 line to column lines 0 and 1 cause a logical 1 to appear on these column lines. Since there are no links from word 2 line to column lines 2 and 3, a logical 0 will appear on these lines. On the column lines, word 2 will be 0011 and will then appear at the inputs of the four AND gates which are enabled by the Chip Select (CS) signal. These output gates are normally tri-state devices that permit tying the output lines of multiple ROM's in parallel and activating the desired ROM by the Chip Select signal. The outputs of the nonselected ROM's would be in the high impedance state and would appear essentially as open circuits to the selected ROM outputs.

The diodes in the ROM array are used to provide isolation of each word line. If they were not present in this example, a logical 1 on the word 0 line from the decoder would be pulled to a logical 0 by the word 3 line since there would be a closed path through the links from word 0 line to word 3 line in column 3. This situation is shown in Figure 5.3.

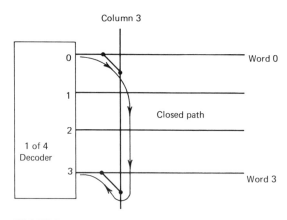

FIGURE 5.3 Need for diode isolation of ROM memory bits.

In some ROM's transistors are used to provide the required isolation in place of diodes.

Another type of ROM memory is the $n \times 1$ bit organization in which each individual bit of the memory can be accessed independently. Both column and row address decoders are required for this type of ROM. A typical 16×1 bit ROM organization is given in Figure 5.4.

In this ROM, the column and row decoders gate the bit located at address $A_3A_2A_1A_0$ (where A_0 is the least significant address bit) to the output buffer. The data will appear at the output of the buffer if the CS line for this particular ROM has been activated. The output buffer is normally a tri-state device, thus allowing the common connection of multiple ROM output lines.

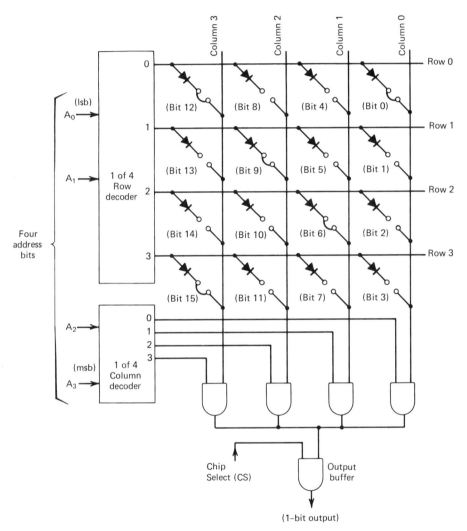

FIGURE 5.4 Typical 16 × 1 bit ROM organization.

Strictly speaking, a *ROM* is a *mask programmable* Read Only Memory in which the open or closed link pattern for the ROM cells is determined during chip manufacture by a mask overlay. This mask pattern will result in the selective etching of metal interconnections on the chip to produce the desired 1 or 0 in each ROM cell. Since a mask must be generated for each custom ROM pattern, a $500 to $1000 mask charge is usually required by the semiconductor manufacturer to produce a ROM. This charge, then, must be amortized over the total number of ROM's ordered to determine if the mask-programmed route is economically justifiable. Also, since the data pattern cannot be changed on a ROM after it has been manufactured, a ROM should be used primarily when the programs or data to be stored have been tested for a period of time and have been proven to be free of errors.

An alternative to a ROM that allows programming of the stored pattern by the customer is a *PROM* or *Programmable Read Only Memory.* In a PROM, the link corresponding to the storage of a bit in memory is fusible, i.e., it is a fuse which can be "blown" to open the link in a particular PROM cell (Figure 5.5). The fuse is typically either nichrome (a nickel/chrome alloy) or polycrystalline silicon (polysilicon) that is doped to provide good conduction properties. By addressing a specific storage cell of a PROM and applying the proper pulses of current through the fuse, the fuse will "blow," opening the cell link. The currents and current pulse widths required to blow the fuses vary with manufacturer and type of PROM, but representative values range from 20 to 200 ma programming current and from 1 μsec to 2 msec pulse widths, with some devices requiring linearly increasing current pulse widths at a specified rate of change.

5.3.3 PLA

A *Programmable Logic Array* is a circuit that can be programmed to implement transmission functions in the sum of products form. (See Chapter 3.) It consists of a series of AND gates that can be programmed by fusible links to generate P terms that, in turn, can be OR'ed together to form a sum

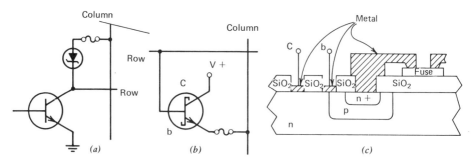

FIGURE 5.5 Typical bipolar PROM cells, (a) nichrome fusible link. (b) polycrystalline silicon fusible link. (c) fusible link structure of (b).

of products output. For example, consider the transmission function T = A'BC + ABC'. Figure 5.6 illustrates its implementation with AND, OR, and inverter gates.

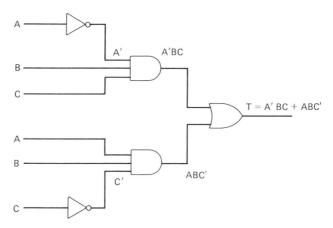

FIGURE 5.6 Minterm implementation using AND, OR, and inverter gates.

The same function could be obtained using AND and OR gates implemented with diodes as shown in Figure 5.7.

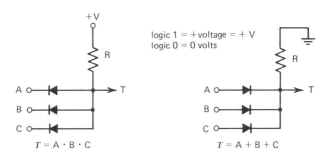

FIGURE 5.7 Diode implementation of AND and OR gates.

Using these diode AND–OR gates to implement the transmission function of Figure 5.6 would yield (Figure 5.8):

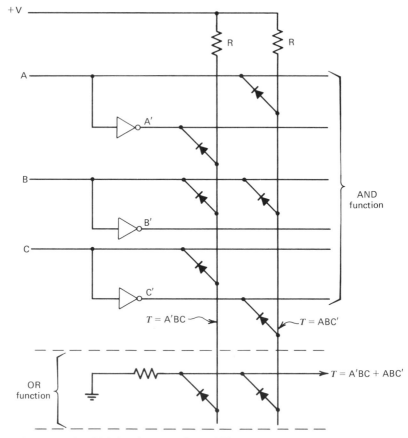

FIGURE 5.8 PLA implementation of T.

The circuit of Figure 5.8 is a simple PLA structure. In a general PLA, diode connections are present on both the variable and the variable complement lines and are disconnected by blowing the desired nichrome fusible links similar to PROM programming. "Don't care" conditions are programmed by fusing both links of a particular variable in the AND matrix. A PLA that can be programmed by the user in the field is called a *Field Programmable Logic Array* or an *FPLA*. A typical FPLA structure with 16-variable inputs capable of implementing forty-eight, 16-variable *P* terms, summing any 8 of these P terms to produce an output sum of products, and providing for 8 different outputs, is given in Figure 5.9.

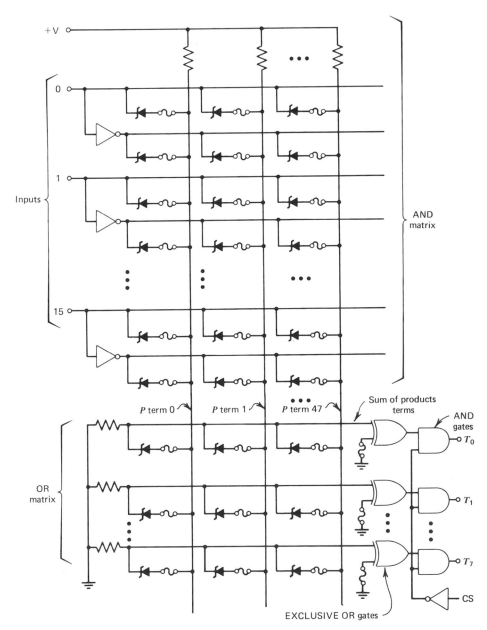

FIGURE 5.9 Typical PLA structure.

The EXCLUSIVE OR gates at the output of each of the sum-of-products terms in the OR matrix allow for selective inversion of any output by breaking the fusible link on one of the EXCLUSIVE OR gates' inputs. The Chip Select ($\overline{CS}$) input functions as in any memory circuit by placing the T outputs in a high impedance state when the FPLA chip is not selected.

A PLA can be used in programmed logic applications to implement specific combinational logic functions and, when used in association with flip-flops and storage registers, can implement sequential circuits. (See Chapter 3.) The PLA's are used as ROM's in cases where every address will not occur and, therefore, save cost and space. For example, if only 32 combinations of 16 input variables could occur, the FPLA described in Figure 5.9 could be used to detect those combinations and provide an 8-bit output on lines T_0 to T_7.

5.3.4 EPROMS and EAROMS

The ROM's and PROM's described in Section 5.3.3 of this chapter all have the characteristic that, once programmed, the contents of the memory cannot be reprogrammed. Two other types of Read Only Memories, the *Erasable Programmable Read Only Memory (EPROM)* and the *Electrically Alterable Read Only Memory (EAROM)* do provide the ability to alter the stored information and still retain the property of *nonvolatility*. The term *Electrically Erasable ROM* or *EEROM* refers to a device which is essentially the same as an EAROM although, strictly speaking, an EAROM should denote selective modification of a storage location without requiring total erasure of the chip. **The main differences between an EPROM and an EAROM are that the EPROM chip must be removed from its socket for both erasure and reprogramming, while the EAROM can selectively be erased and rewritten in place.** Erase and write times for both devices are relatively long, ranging from milliseconds to 30 minutes. Since the EAROM contents can be changed electrically under software control at the expense of a long write cycle, EAROM's are sometimes referred to as *Read Mostly Memories (RMM's)*.

The EPROM was introduced in 1971 by Intel Corporation and is implemented using the *Floating Avalanche Injection MOS (FAMOS)* storage principle (Figure 5.10).

In Section 4.4 of Chapter 4, the operation of a P-channel MOS transistor was discussed. Recalling that a negative potential applied to the gate produced a conducting channel of positive charges (holes) between the source and drain, we can describe the operation of the FAMOS device. The construction of the P-channel FAMOS device is similar to that of a PMOS transistor except that the gate is enclosed in an insulating volume of S_iO_2

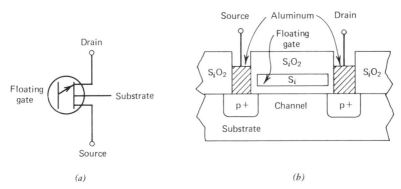

FIGURE 5.10   P-channel FAMOS EPROM symbol and structure. (a) Symbol. (b) Structure.

and cannot be accessed. Therefore, in order to cause the transistor to conduct from source to drain (which particular state will be referred to as a 0), another means of placing a negative charge on the gate must be devised. By applying a reverse bias voltage pulse of approximately 25 to 30 volts to either the source or drain p–n junction of the FAMOS transistor, we inject electrons into the floating gate. When the voltage is removed from the p–n junction, the electrons remain in the silicon gate since it is completely insulated by S_iO_2 and there is no discharge path. In reality, there is a small rate of discharge, but it is on the order of a 20% to 30% charge loss after 10 years at a temperature of 125°C. The programming pulse is applied through a program pin on the EPROM package while the address to be programmed is presented on the address pins and the data to be programmed are presented to the EPROM **output lines** as inputs. Typical programming pulse widths are 1 msec with approximately 100 such pulses required at each address to insure correct programming of the EPROM. Some EPROMs have the attractive feature that they can be programmed with single pulse TTL-compatible signals. The EPROM programming times range from 6.1 msec/bit or 49 msec/(8-bit word) to 59 msec/bit or 470 msec/(8-bit word). Using the 6 msec/bit time, a 2K word × 8-bit EPROM (16K bit) would require 49 × 2048 msec or 100 seconds to program.

In order to erase the EPROM, the electrons stored in the floating gate must be discharged. Since there is no connection to the gate, it must be discharged or erased by illumination with ultraviolet light at a dosage large enough to cause the electrons to flow back to the substrate, thus returning the gate to its original, uncharged condition. The wavelength of the UV light used for this purpose is 2537 Å with an integrated dosage of 6 to 10 watt-seconds/cm² applied to the chip. Erasure of a packaged chip is accomplished by illuminating it through a quartz window provided in the EPROM package. Erasure times range from 10 to 30 minutes.

Access times of the FAMOS EPROMS are typically 450 nsec to 1 μsec.

Another type of writable, nonvolatile storage is the *EAROM*, which can be electrically erased and rewritten without having to remove the device from its socket. The primary means of implementing an EAROM at the present time are with Metal Nitride Oxide Semiconductor (MNOS) technology and amorphous semiconductors.

MNOS is a modified MOS technology that uses capacitor charge storage and achieves a storage time half-life in the 20- to 30-year range. Access time of MNOS devices is approximately 2 μs with a write time of 15 msec and an erase time of 100 msec.

An amorphous semiconductor such as tellerium is one that can exist in either an amorphous (disordered) state or a structured polycrystalline state. The two states exhibit different electrical and optical properties that can then be used to "read out" the stored information. For example, in its disordered state, the amorphous material exhibits a resistivity of 5×10^4 ohm-cm compared to 0.5 ohm-cm in the polycrystalline state. The switching between the states is accomplished by applying some form of energy (electrical, optical, etc.) to the device.

Amorphous memories can be developed with access times of 15 to 20 nsec and write times of 2 to 10 msec.

5.3.5 CCD Memories

A CCD or Charge Coupled device memory is a volatile MOS shift register memory (serial access) in which the digital information is represented by packets of charge that are transferred along a string of storage cells or wells under control of a series of voltage pulses. Figure 5.11 illustrates a CCD structure whose shifting is controlled by three overlapped voltage pulses or phases. Two, three, and four phase CCD's are the most common. The three phase device, however, can serve to convey the general principles of CCD operation.

It is comprised of a metal or polysilicon gate—silicon dioxide—p-type substrate layering as with a typical MOS transistor except that there are no source or drain diffusions. Charge is stored in potential wells that are formed when, for the p-type substrate, a positive voltage is applied to a gate. This positive voltage repels the majority carriers (holes) in the substrate under the gate and forms a region that is depleted of charge or a *depletion region*. This depletion region or, as it is sometimes called, a

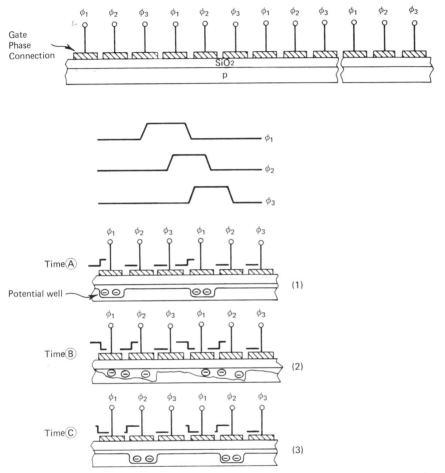

FIGURE 5.11 Three phase CCD. (a) CCD structure. (b) Three phase clock pulses. (c) Charge transfer in CCD.

potential well, is capable of storing electrons if they can be injected into the well.

The sequence in Figure 5.11c—(1), (2), (3)—illustrates the charge transfer operation. In step (1), a positive voltage is applied to $\emptyset_1$ (time Ⓐ in Figure 5.11c). A potential well is then formed under the $\emptyset_1$ electrodes.

Assuming an initial charge packet of electrons stored in this well, the charges can be transferred to the right as shown in step (2). At this time Ⓑ, a positive voltage has been applied to the $\emptyset_2$ electrode followed by a voltage reduction at $\emptyset_1$. This effectively decreases the depth of the potential well under the $\emptyset_1$ electrode while increasing the well depth under $\emptyset_2$, causing a "spilling" of charges to the right in step (2). At time Ⓒ in step (3), the $\emptyset_1$ potential well has been reduced to zero with the charge packet now stored in the $\emptyset_2$ potential well. Transfer of the electrons from the potential well under $\emptyset_2$ to the well under $\emptyset_3$ and then from $\emptyset_3$ well to $\emptyset_1$ well is accomplished in an identical manner and the cycle then repeats. **These three stages of transfer are equivalent to a one-bit position shift.**

Charge is injected into the first potential well of a CCD through a source diffusion/control gate combination at the beginning of the shift register string and is detected by a floating drain diffusion at the end of the string.

Since there is a certain amount of charge lost during transfer from one potential well to another, the *charge transfer efficiency* of a CCD is an important parameter, particularly if large capacity shift registers are to be implemented. The *charge transfer efficiency*, η, is defined as the ratio of the charge transferred from one well to the next to the total charge to be transferred. In order to estimate a typical value of η, assume that a 256-bit, 3 phase CCD shift register is to be fabricated with an overall acceptable charge loss from beginning to end of the shift register of 5%. If the initial charge value stored in the first potential well is Q_0 and the remaining charge after 256 bit position (3 phase position) shifts is Q_1, then

$$Q_1 = Q_0 \times \eta^{256 \times 3} = Q_0 \times \eta^{768}$$

or

$$\eta^{768} = Q_1/Q_0$$

or

$$\eta = \sqrt[768]{Q_1/Q_0}$$

Now since

$$Q_1 = 0.95\,Q_0$$
$$\eta = \sqrt[768]{0.95\,Q_0/Q_0} = \sqrt[768]{0.95} = 0.999933$$

Thus, charge transfer efficiencies of 0.9999 or inefficiencies of 10^{-4} to 10^{-5} are required and have been achieved to fabricate reasonable length CCD shift registers.

If the shifting chain is long enough, deterioration of a charge packet will require that it be *refreshed* or restored to the original level. Typical CCD memories incorporate shift registers up to 256 bits in length before refreshing the data with a maximum refreshing period of 2 to 10 msec. Because of this refreshing cycle, a CCD memory is a dynamic memory.

In addition to charge loss by transfer inefficiency, thermally generated background charge or *dark current* in each well is another potential source of data loss in CCD's. When a potential well under a CCD gate electrode is formed, thermal charges will begin building up in the well. If the shifting rate is fast enough, this charge will be transferred to the next well along with any data charge packet that is present and will not accumulate to any significant degree. Again, refreshing of the datum stored in each well at proper intervals eliminates any errors due to charge buildup. Typical dark current densities are $< 10 \text{na/cm}^2$. Shift rates for CCD devices range from 2 to 20 MHz with access times to the first bit (*latency* times) of 15 to 100 μsec.

The internal organization of a CCD memory chip is a function of the desired cost, power dissipation, shifting rate, and access time. Some possible organizations are given in Figure 5.12.

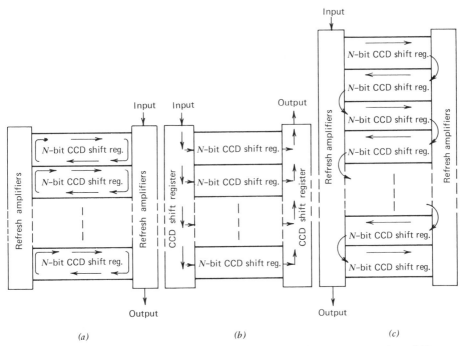

FIGURE 5.12 Possible CCD memory organizations. (*a*) Recirculating shift registers. (*b*) Straight through organization. (*c*) Serpentine configuration.

As with MOS dynamic RAM memories, CCD read and write operations are controlled by address decode, Chip Enable (CE), Chip Select (CS), Write Enable (WE), and I/O buffer logic signals.

Because of the rapid advances being made in speed and density of HMOS RAM's, CCD memories may not be as highly utilized as once anticipated.

5.3.6 Magnetic Bubble Memories

Another serial access type memory is the magnetic bubble memory, which stores 1's and 0's by means of magnetic domains or "bubbles" in a layer of magnetic garnet. This memory differs from a CCD memory in that it is nonvolatile and does not have to be continuously shifted to maintain data integrity. In fact, the magnetic bubble shift register can be stopped and started without loss of data. Since the stored data are not lost with time, a magnetic bubble memory is not a dynamic device.

A magnetic bubble device is fabricated by growing an epitaxial layer of magnetic garnet (such as calcium–germanium–garnet) on a nonmagnetic garnet substrate (gadolinium–gallium–garnet or G^3) as shown in Figure 5.13.

The magnetic bubbles or, more realistically, cylinders, ($\cong 3 \ \mu m$ in diameter) are formed in and shifted through this magnetic layer. The movement of the magnetic bubbles is produced by a rotating magnetic field which alternately attracts and repels the bubbles, thus shifting them in one direction through the layer. If the presence of a bubble were denoted by a 1 and its absence by a 0, then the 1's and 0's would be shifted in the magnetic material as in any shift register.

The bubble propagation is accomplished by magnetizing permalloy patterns that are deposited above the bubble layer with the rotating magnetic field. This field continuously changes the polarities of the permalloy patterns, which, in turn, attract and repel the magnetic bubbles to produce bubble movement in a particular direction. The direction of bubble movement is determined by the direction of rotation of the magnetic field.

Some typical permalloy patterns used for bubble propagation are given in Figure 5.14.

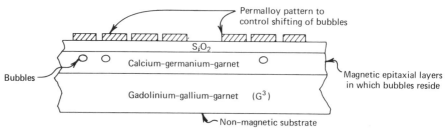

FIGURE 5.13 Magnetic bubble memory structure.

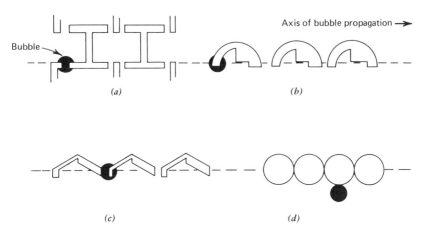

FIGURE 5.14 Permalloy patterns for magnetic bubble propagation. (a) T-bar. (b) Asymmetrical half disk. (c) Chevron. (d) Contiguous disk.

Note that the rotating magnetic field in the plane of the permalloy must be supplied either on or off a magnetic bubble memory chip for its operation.

Bubbles are generated or injected into the shift register by a number of means, including "stretching" an existing bubble until it "breaks" in two, thereby generating a new bubble and retaining the old. Bubbles are sensed by such means as a Hall effect probe, magnetic resistance sensing, and optical intensity detection. Since a magnetic bubble is nonvolatile, it must be destroyed or annihilated to erase the bit of data it represents. This erasure is performed by increasing the strength of a biasing magnetic field until the bubble collapses.

Magnetic bubble memories, being serial devices, have organizations similar to some CCD memories. A few examples are illustrated in Figure 5.15.

Depending upon the organization and fabrication characteristics of magnetic bubble memory, a range of performance parameters are obtained. Representative values are 100 KHz to 300 KHz shifting rates and 1 msec to 20 ms average access time. Typical bubble memory chip densities are 256 kilobits to 1 megabit/chip with higher densities feasible.

Typical support chips required with a bubble memory chip are a bubble memory controller, bubble sense amplifier, a current pulse generator, and a coil driver. The memory controller provides for system timing and control, accommodates external requests for data transfers (including address correlation), and interfaces to the processor bus. The sense amplifier incorporates circuits to sense the bubble information. The pulse generator and coil driver provide high current signals to the bubble memory

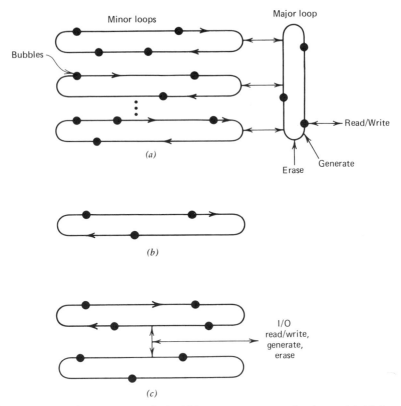

FIGURE 5.15 Some magnetic bubble memory organizations. (a) Major-minor loop (data are circulated as bubbles in minor loops and transferred to a major loop for read/write generation and erase functions). (b) Single loop. (c) Double loop.

chip. The coil driver provides two currents, 90° out of phase, to the bubble memory for use in bubble propagation. Discrete transistors are required between the coil driver and bubble memory to produce the necessary current levels.

New developments to eliminate the necessity of drive coils for bubble memories utilize thin conducting layers that are etched with patterns of holes. When current is applied to these layers, magnetic fields form around the holes with the polarity of these fields controlling the movement of the bubbles. This technique promises continued advances toward higher speed and higher density bubble memories.

5.4 ORGANIZATION

The various types of memory implementations discussed in the previous section of this chapter can be organized to build memory systems with particular size, performance, and cost characteristics. Some typical organizations for the serial access devices (CCD's and magnetic bubble memories) were given in Sections 5.3.5 and 5.3.6 and will not be discussed further. Specific organizations for those two classes of memories are in a state of evolution and, since they are mainly applicable to high-density, low-cost/bit storage similar to disks and magnetic tape, particular applications will have requirements that will result in different memory system designs. General organizations of RAM and ROM systems are more applicable to a wider variety of systems and are now discussed.

5.4.1 Addressing

As explained in Chapter 1, memory space in a microcomputer is accessed by sending the address of a particular location to the memory on the address lines. If a microprocessor has 16 address lines and the address is represented by patterns of 1's and 0's on these lines, there are 2^{16} or 65,536 possible locations that can be accessed. For n address lines, there would be 2^n possible addresses. In order to illustrate the addressing methods, a value of $n = 16$ will be used, but keep in mind that the same methods apply to any value of n (Figure 5.16).

Address representations are sometimes partitioned into hexadecimal (see Chapter 2) notation for ease of description. The hexadecimal form is further broken down into a *page* number and the particular *word* on a page. In Figure 5.17, page notations for some 16 bit addresses are illustrated.

5.4.2 Decoding and Chip Selection

The different patterns on the address lines are usually decoded **internal** to the memory chip by row and column decoders to select a particular word or bit in the chip. These address lines are normally connected in parallel

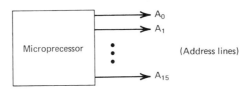

FIGURE 5.16 Microprocessor with 16-bit addressing.

PAGE	WORD	ACTUAL ADDRESS DECIMAL EQUIVALENT OF BINARY ADDRESS	HEX EQUIVALENT OF BINARY ADDRESS	PAGE (MSB) A_{15}	A_{14}	A_{13}	A_{12}	A_{11}	A_{10}	A_9	A_8	WORD A_7	A_6	A_5	A_4	A_3	A_2	A_1	A_0 (LSB)
0	0	0	0000	0	0	0	0	0	0	0	0	0	0	0	0	0	0	0	0
0	1	1	0001	0	0	0	0	0	0	0	0	0	0	0	0	0	0	0	1
0	2	2	0002	0	0	0	0	0	0	0	0	0	0	0	0	0	0	1	0
0	FF	255	00FF	0	0	0	0	0	0	0	0	1	1	1	1	1	1	1	1
1	0	256	0100	0	0	0	0	0	0	0	1	0	0	0	0	0	0	0	0
1	FF	511	01FF	0	0	0	0	0	0	0	1	1	1	1	1	1	1	1	1
FF	00	65,280	FF00	1	1	1	1	1	1	1	1	0	0	0	0	0	0	0	0
FF	FF	65,535	FFFF	1	1	1	1	1	1	1	1	1	1	1	1	1	1	1	1

FIGURE 5.17 Address page notation. Note that, using the page–word notation, we represent address locations 0 to 65,535 as 256 pages (0_{16} to FF_{16}) of 256 words each.

to multiple memory chips and an **external** decoding of the address lines provides the Chip Select (CS) and/or Chip Enable (CE) signal, which selects the desired memory chip. Figure 5.18 illustrates a method of addressing 4K bytes of RAM and 2K bytes of ROM in a microprocessor system. Memory chips used are 4K × 1 RAM (4096 × 1) and 1K × 8 ROM (1024 × 8). The ROM addresses are from locations 0_{10} to 2047_{10} (0000_{16} to $07FF_{16}$) and RAM addresses are from 2048_{10} to 6143_{10} (0800_{16} to $17FF_{16}$). Addresses > $32,768_{10}$ (address bit $A_{15} = 1$) are used to select input/output interface chips and external devices.

A discussion of the system in Figure 5.18 will serve to tie together the memory concepts covered in this chapter.

The microprocessor, ①, is an 8-bit device with a 16-bit address bus ② and an 8-bit data bus, ③. As the microcomputer program executes, addresses of instructions or data in memory are presented on the unidirectional address bus. Instructions and data are returned from memory to the microprocessor on the data bus. The data bus can also send data out of the microprocessor to RAM or output devices; hence, it is referred to as a *bidirectional data bus*. The direction of the data bus is determined by the particular instruction being executed at the time. The ROM locations, 0_{10} to 2047_{10}, are addressed by 11 address lines (A_0 to A_{10}), 10 (A_0-A_9) of which are connected in parallel to both ROM's. Since these 10 address lines are connected simultaneously to both ROM's, the same one out of 1024 (2^{10}) addresses in both ROM's will be selected by their byte select and row decoders. For proper operation, only one of the ROM's at a time should be returning information to the microprocessor on the data bus. The Chip Select (CS) lines on the ROM's perform this ROM selection. The 1K × 8 ROM's used in this example have two Chip Select lines, CS and $\overline{CS}$. CS is an active high input and $\overline{CS}$ is an active low input. A ROM is selected only when there is a logic 1 (high) on the CS input *and* a logic 0 (low) on the $\overline{CS}$ input. Address line A_{10} is utilized as one Chip Select input, ⑥. Since ROM 0 is designated as addresses 0_{10} to 1023_{10}, it should be selected when the address lines have the following binary patterns.

32,768		2048	1024	512	256	128	64	32	16	8	4	2	1 ⎰Binary
													⎱weights
A_{15}	←	A_{11}	A_{10}	A_9	A_8	A_7	A_6	A_5	A_4	A_3	A_2	A_1	A_0
0	...	0	0	X	X	X	X	X	X	X	X	X	X

all 0's

X denotes either a 0 or 1; address lines A_{10} through A_{15} must be at a logic 0 level. From these patterns it can be seen that address line A_{10} should be

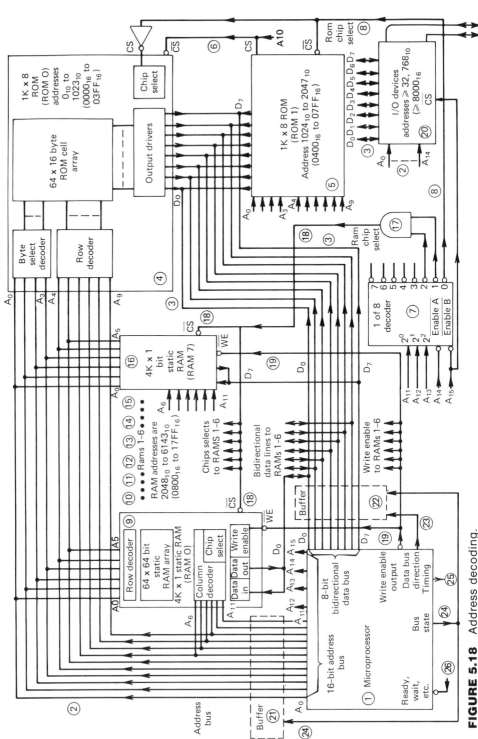

FIGURE 5.18 Address decoding.

connected to $\overline{CS}$ of ROM 0 and to CS of ROM 1. With this arrangement, a logic 0 will be applied to $\overline{CS}$ of ROM 0 when addresses $\leq 1023_{10}$ are requested and a logic 1 will be applied to CS of ROM 1 when addresses $\geq 1023_{10}$ but $\leq 2047_{10}$ are present on A_0 to A_{10}. Recalling that ROM memory had a maximum address of 2047_{10}, the patterns for addresses ≥ 1023 but $\leq 2047_{10}$ are:

32,768		2048	1024	512	256	128	64	32	16	8	4	2	1	$\left\{\begin{array}{l}\text{Binary} \\ \text{weights}\end{array}\right.$
A_{15}	$\leftarrow$	A_{11}	A_{10}	A_9	A_8	A_7	A_6	A_5	A_4	A_3	A_2	A_1	A_0	
0	...	0	1	X	X	X	X	X	X	X	X	X	X	

all 0's

The address line A_{10}, then, provides a mutually exclusive selection of ROM 0 or ROM 1 when A_{10} is a logic 0 or 1, respectively. In order to implement the upper limit boundary (2047_{10}) on ROM memory addressing, address lines A_{11} through A_{15} must be logic 0's. This function is accomplished by the 1 of 8 decoder, ⑦, which produces an active low output for each of the eight combinations of three binary inputs. The decoder also requires two active low enable inputs to enable the active low output. If both enable inputs, Enable A and Enable B, are not at an active low level, all decoder outputs will be at a high or logic 1 level. Address lines A_{11}, A_{12}, and A_{13} are applied to the three binary inputs of the decoder and lines A_{14} and A_{15} are applied to the ENABLE inputs. If A_{11} through A_{15} are at logic 0 level, output 0 of the decoder will be at a low level. This output, ⑧, is connected directly to $\overline{CS}$ of ROM 1 and, through an inverter, connected to CS of ROM 0. Thus, if address lines A_{11} through A_{15} are not all at a logic 0 level, ROM 0 and ROM 1 will not be selected. When either ROM is not selected, either by the levels on lines A_{11} through A_{15} or the level on A_{10}, the ROM outputs revert to a high impedance level since they incorporate tri-state drivers on the chip. Note that the internal ROM cell organization is that of 64 rows of 16 bytes/row. Therefore, out of the 10 address lines A_0 through A_9, lines A_0 to A_3 select one of 16 bytes in a row and lines A_4 to A_9 select one of 64 rows.

The RAM's, ⑨ through ⑯, used in this example are 4K word $\times$ 1 bit static RAM's. In order to achieve a 4K $\times$ 8 bit memory, 8 of these devices, RAM's 0 to RAM 7 are required. With this organization, each RAM chip contains one bit of the 4096 possible 8-bit words. In order to read out a particular 8-bit word, then, a bit at the same address in each of the RAM's must be accessed and presented on the data out line of each RAM. The one bit out of 4096 possible bits stored in each RAM is addressed by the 12 address lines A_0 through A_{11} ($2^{12} = 4096$) plus a $\overline{\text{Chip Select}}$ ($\overline{\text{CS}}$) RAM input to distinguish these addresses from ROM or I/O addresses. The $\overline{\text{CS}}$ logic signal is also derived from 1 of 8 decoder, (7). Since RAM addresses range from 2048_{10} to 6143_{10}, the following address line patterns are required for RAM accessing.

32,768		8192	4096	2048	1024	512	256	128	64	32	16	8	4	2	1
A_{15}	$\leftarrow$	A_{13}	A_{12}	A_{11}	A_{10}	A_9	A_8	A_7	A_6	A_5	A_4	A_3	A_2	A_1	A_0
0	...	0	0	1	X	X	X	X	X	X	X	X	X	X	X
0		0	1	0	X	X	X	X	X	X	X	X	X	X	X

all 0's

From these patterns it can be seen that $A_{11} \odot A_{12}$ and A_{13} through A_{15} = logic 0 are required for RAM addressing in this example. These requirements can be met using decoder (7) and AND gate (17). The table of combinations for the active low RAM chip select line (18), which is the output of AND gate (17), is given in Table 5.2.

TABLE 5.3 CD (18) Table of Combinations

					ACTIVE LOW OUTPUTS 1 AND 2 OF DECODER (7)		CHIP SELECT (18)
DECODER (7) INPUTS					(AND GATE (17) INPUTS)		(AND GATE (17) OUTPUT)
ENABLE B	ENABLE A	2^2	2^1	2^0			
A_{15}	A_{14}	A_{13}	A_{12}	A_{11}	1	2	
0	0	0	0	1	0	1	0
0	0	0	1	0	1	0	0
X	X	X	1	1	1	1	1
X	X	1	X	X	1	1	1
X	1	X	X	X	1	1	1
1	X	X	X	X	1	1	1

X denotes either a 1 or 0.

Table 5.2 shows that the desired RAM $\overline{\text{CS}}$ = 0 is generated only when locations 2048_{10} to 6143_{10} are addressed.

The 4K × 1 RAM used in this example, as all RAM's, must have an input or inputs to indicate whether a read from RAM or a write to RAM is being executed. The $\overline{\text{Write Enable}}$, $\overline{\text{WE}}$, input to each RAM chip performs this function. The $\overline{\text{WE}}$, (19), is an active low signal; therefore, the microprocessor must provide a logical 0 on this line when it is writing to RAM and a logical 1 when it is reading from RAM. In addition to enabling the write circuitry in the RAM chip, $\overline{\text{WE}}$ controls data in, data out circuitry to provide for data being transmitted to the chip. The particular RAM chip in this example has separate DATA IN and DATA OUT lines. The DATA OUT line has tri-state capability and enters the high impedance state when $\overline{\text{WE}}$ is a 0, indicating that a write is to be performed. Many RAM chips have a bidirectional data line which performs both the data in and data out functions under control of WE-type signals. The RAM's selected for this example are of the static type, i.e., they require no refreshing and no additional timing circuitry. Using static RAM's, therefore, simplifies the memory design problem. Dynamic RAM's made particularly for use as part of a microcomputer set of chips, usually have the refreshing circuitry and timing built in to the chip set.

Dynamic RAM's used in larger systems require refreshing at approximately 2-millisecond intervals and associated circuitry must be included to perform this function. A refresh cycle is essentially a memory read cycle (see Section 5.3.1) and, thus, a read of the entire memory must be accomplished every 2 milliseconds without interfering with the microcomputer operation. Memory refresh chips are available that are used to control refresh operations.

Input/output device addresses are specified as being $\geq 32,768_{10}$, which means that A_{15} must be a 1. The I/O devices, (20), are enabled by A_{15}, which is used as an active high chip select. When $A_{15} = 1$, lines A_0 to A_{14} can be used to address 32,768 different I/O devices. Data are transferred to and from the I/O devices through data bus (3).

When the data and address bus loading exceeds their drive capability (typically one TTL load), buffers, (21) and (22), are required on the address and data lines, respectively, to prevent performance degradation and/or improper operation. These buffers provide proper MOS logic levels and current capability for driving the accumulated capacitance on the buses. If the bus being buffered is a bidirectional bus such as the data bus, (3), the buffers must be bidirectional and controlled by a DATA BUS DIRECTION logic signal, (23), from the microprocessor. This signal selects the direction of data flow through the buffer as determined by the instruction being executed by the microprocessor. In some microprocessors, one direction logic output is used to perform the functions of Write Enable and buffer direction control. The buffers normally have the capability to be placed in the high impedance state by a BUS STATE-type logic signal,

㉔ , from the microprocessor. This operation essentially disconnects the microprocessor from the address and data buses throughout the system and permits external sources to insert memory addresses and read or write from memory independent of the microprocessor. This type of memory accessing is referred to as *Direct Memory Access (DMA)*.

Timing signal(s), ㉕ , are distributed throughout the microcomputer system for synchronization among the devices that comprise the system.

5.4.3 Access Time Considerations

When a microprocessor addresses a memory location, the instruction or data stored in that location has to be returned to the microprocessor within a specified time in the microprocessor timing cycle. For MOS processors, the time is on the order of hundreds of nanoseconds. Relative to the memory, this time to return the information following presentation of an address is the *access time*. The access time of most memories falls within the time allotted in most microprocessor fetch cycles. Some memories, however, cannot return the addressed information to the microprocessor in the time allowed; therefore, the waiting time must be extended by external influence on the CPU chip. This situation applies in particular to some EPROM's with access times ranging from 0.6 to 1.5 μsec. This extension of the fetch cycle is usually accomplished by a circuit additional to the "slow" memory that provides an active low to a microprocessor READY, WAIT, or similar input line, ㉖ , which, in effect, freezes the microprocessor in the memory access state until released by applying a logic 1 to that input. The active low to the READY or WAIT inputs of the microprocessor can be implemented by a counter or a one-shot multivibrator whose output is triggered to a low state whenever the particular memory is selected and that times out for an interval greater than the maximum memory access time before returning to the high state.

An interesting access time consideration is that many RAM's now exist with access times one-fifth of that allowed by the microprocessor for information fetching from memory. With RAM's of this speed, read/write memory could be accessed by properly synchronized multiple microprocessors in one fetch cycle without any loss of instruction execution speed on any one processor.

5.4.4 Power Requirements

Options regarding power supplied to memory subsystems must also be considered in developing a microcomputer system. For example, a standby mode of operation for some ROM or PROM memory chips can reduce the system power consumption when they are not being accessed. One means of implementing this feature is to place a transistor in series with the memory supply voltages and control the transistor's ON–OFF states with a chip select for the memory as shown in Figure 5.19.

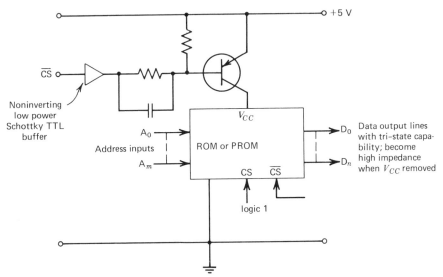

FIGURE 5.19 Chip Select control of PROM or ROM power supply.

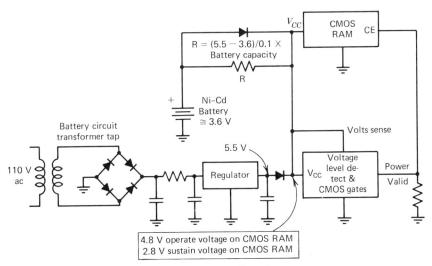

FIGURE 5.20 General Battery Backup Circuit.

This control usually adds 10 to 30 nsec to the memory access time. Other memory chips incorporate this standby feature internally and are placed in a low power mode when the chip is not selected ($\overline{CS} = 1$). When $\overline{CS} = 0$, the chip is activated with no increase in access time.

Another option is to provide nonvolatile RAM capability utilizing CMOS memory with a battery backup. The most popular types of batteries for this type of application are the sealed lead–acid batteries and the nickel cadmium (Ni-Cd) batteries. A typical battery backup arrangement for a CMOS memory is illustrated in Figure 5.20.

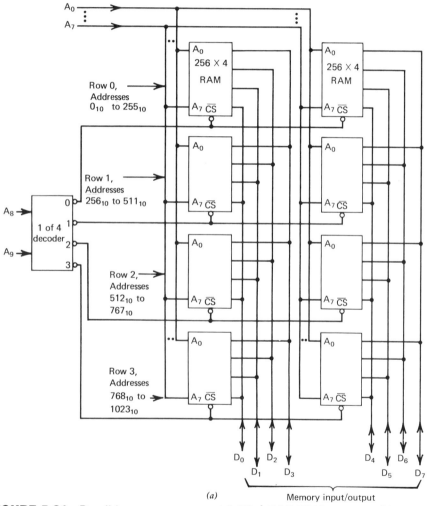

(a)

FIGURE 5.21 Possible memory arrays. (a) 1K × 8-bit RAM memory. (b) 4K × 8 PROM memory.

As the +5.5V supply begins to drop, the battery will start supplying power to the CMOS memory. Using available microcomputer-related support chips or a level detecting circuit (comparator) with hysteresis, an active high Power Valid signal can be generated. One function of this circuit would be to place and hold a low on the CMOS memory CE input during power failure and recovery to insure that no spurious data are written into the memory.

5.4.5 Memory Arrays

Generalizing on the memory system described in Figure 5.18, we can organize memory chips in a variety of ways to achieve the desired word and bit lengths. Figure 5.21 gives examples of possible memory array layouts.

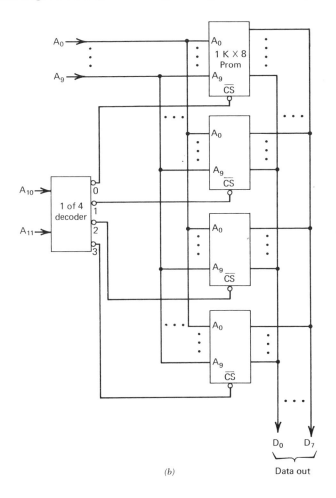

(b)

Memory systems are a large and critical portion of any microcomputer system. Selection of the proper technology of memory coupled with an organization well suited to the desired application can lead to high performance and cost-effective microcomputer design.

REFERENCES

1. Lawrence Altman, "New Arrivals in the Bulk Storage Inventory," *Electronics,* Vol. 51, No. 8, April 13, 1978.

2. E.A. Torrero, "Solid State Devices," *Spectrum,* Vol. 15, No. 1, January, 1978.

3. *Intel Memory Design Handbook,* Intel Corp., 1975.

4. *The MOS Memory Data Book,* Texas Instruments, Inc., 1978.

5. R. Papenberg, "Design and Application of Intel's 2416 16K CCD," Intel Corporation, 1975.

ARCHITECTURE

The word *architecture* or, more specifically, *computer architecture,* has different meanings to different people. To the computer scientist, it means *the characteristics of a computer as seen by the programmer.* To the computer systems engineer, *it means the result of the integration of computer hardware and software by a user to perform a particular task or set of tasks.* To the computer hardware designer, it means *the organization of the digital building blocks* (ALU, Index Registers, Accumulator(s), etc.) *and the controls, communication, and data flow among these blocks.* It is in the context of this last definition that microcomputer architecture is discussed in this chapter.

6.1 DATA AND INSTRUCTION REPRESENTATIONS

An important concept in the evolution of the computer is that data and instructions, many times, are stored in the same areas of memory and are, in fact, interleaved among these locations. Their correct interpretation by the microprocessor assumes a known starting address for the instruction and data sequences. The first instruction in the program is usually contained in this address and its interpretation provides the reference to properly distinguish among instructions and data in the following sequences of accesses throughout memory. (See Example in Section 1.5 of this text.)

6.1.1 Data Representations

Data are stored in the microcomputer in single or multiple words, depending on their values and their mode of representation (i.e., fixed point, floating point, binary, BCD, etc.—see Chapter 2). For an 8-bit microprocessor, one byte of data or a data word is stored in memory as:

Address Y $\boxed{b_7\,|\,b_6\,|\,b_5\,|\,b_4\,|\,b_3\,|\,b_2\,|\,b_1\,|\,b_0}$

If more than 8 bits are required to store the value of the number, multiple bytes or *multiple precision* storage can be used. In an 8-bit microcomputer, a *double precision* word could be stored in memory as:

Address Y $\boxed{b_7\,|\,b_6\,|\,b_5\,|\,b_4\,|\,b_3\,|\,b_2\,|\,b_1\,|\,b_0}$

Address Y + 1 $\boxed{b_{15}\,|\,b_{14}\,|\,b_{13}\,|\,b_{12}\,|\,b_{11}\,|\,b_{10}\,|\,b_9\,|\,b_8}$

Data can be part of an instruction, also, and examples of these types of data are given in Section 6.1.2.

6.1.2 Instruction Representations

Again, using an 8-bit microprocessor as an example, we find that an instruction can consist of one or two parts. The first portion, and one which always is present, is the *operation code* (*op code*). The op code is a pattern of 1's and 0's that denotes the particular operation to be executed. The number of bits available for the op code determines the number of possible distinct instructions that can be in the microprocessor's instruction set. If 4 bits were available, for example, 2^4 or 16 possible instructions could be provided. If 1 byte is allotted for the op code, 2^8 or 256 different instructions could be accommodated. A powerful utilization of the op code is to have some of the bits specify different addressing modes for the same operation, thus providing flexibility and tailoring of addressing used by a particular instruction. The second portion of an instruction is the *operand*. This part may or may not be present, depending upon the particular instruction. The operand consists of either an address or data, or both. Hypothetical codes for some typical instructions (three used in Chapter 1) demonstrate some of the different lengths of instructions.

INSTRUC-TION MNEMONIC	DESCRIPTION	REPRESENTATION IN MEMORY	
SXL (one byte instruction)	Shift all bits in Register X left one position	`1 1 0 0 0 0 0 0`	Op code
LDX N* (two byte instruction)	Load Register X with 8-bit pattern nnnnnnnn	`1 0 1 0 0 0 0 0`	Op code
		`1 1 1 1 0 0 0 0` 8-bit pattern nnnnnnnn$\equiv$FO$_{16}$	Operand (data)
JMP N* (two byte instruction)	Transfer program control unconditionally to instruction at address specified by nnnnnnnn	`0 0 0 1 0 0 0 1`	Op code
		`0 0 0 1 0 0 1 1` 8-bit pattern nnnnnnnn$\equiv$13$_{16}$	Operand (address)
JMP M*	Transfer program control unconditionally to instruction at	`0 0 0 1 0 0 1 1`	Op code
		`1 1 0 0 1 0 0 1` 1sb↗	Operand (low

address specified
by
$(msb) \rightarrow \underline{mmmmmmmm}$

$\underline{mmmmmmmm}_{\wedge}$
(16 bits)   lsb)

| 0 | 1 | 0 | 0 | 1 | 0 | 1 | 1 |
$^{\wedge}$msb

16-bit pattern of
m's$\equiv$4BC9$_{16}$

order
address)
Operand
(high
order
address)

* NOTE: N represents 8-bit pattern nnnnnnnn and M represents 16-bit pattern of m's.

There are many different variations on the interpretation of the operands in an instruction and these will be covered in Section 6.4 of this chapter.

6.2 ADDRESS, INSTRUCTION, AND DATA PATHS

The architecture of a microcomputer can be easily understood by observing the paths among its principal components and the controls for these paths for the execution of a particular instruction. Noting that architectures differ from microprocessor to microprocessor, we can begin tracing of an instruction among the architectural elements embodied in most microprocessors with an instruction fetch. At the beginning of a program, the address of the first instruction to be fetched is placed in the Program Counter (PC) and then, in some cases, to a Memory Address Buffer Register by applying the proper logic input to the Reset line as illustrated in the 8-bit microprocessor of Figure 6.1. This starting location is fixed for a particular device and can be address zero, for example. The address is then placed on the address bus, usually through an address buffer, where it initiates an access to the desired memory location. The Memory Read/Write line will be in the Read state.

After the memory access time delay, the instruction at the specified location in memory will be present on the data bus. It will then be transmitted through the data bus buffer and stored in the instruction register for decoding. The decoder may be hardwired or may be microprogrammed. If it is microprogrammed, the op code pattern will address a sequence of microinstructions in a microprogram control memory that will execute the required macroinstruction. This instruction execution will be accomplished by the decoder and the microprocessor control unit. Thus, the two main operations performed by the microprocessor are an instruction *fetch* and *execution*.

Continuing in the block diagram of Figure 6.1, assume that the instruction fetched was decoded and found to be an ADD memory location to the accumulator with Carry instruction. The decoded op code would indicate that this instruction is a three byte instruction (first byte being the

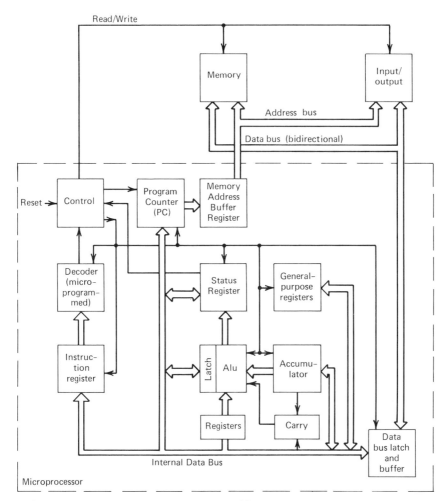

FIGURE 6.1 Basic microcomputer architecture.

op code) with the next two consecutive bytes in memory containing the low order and high order addresses of the data in memory to be added to the accumulator with carry. Two more fetches to memory are then executed and the required 16-bit data location is obtained and stored temporarily in registers in the microprocessor. This 16-bit address is then sent out to memory to fetch the 8-bit data word that is to be added to the accumulator. The data word is then sent through the data bus buffer into a register providing one input to the ALU. The other input to the ALU is gated from the accumulator and the carry input to the ALU is provided by the microprocessor carry bit. The result of the addition is temporarily stored in a latch and then gated back into the accumulator. The instruction execution is now complete. Table 6.1 summarizes the execution of the ADD with Carry instruction.

TABLE 6.1 Summary of ADD with Carry Instruction

Send out address of instruction: instruction stored in instruction register; Increment program counter; Begin instruction decode:	FETCH instruction
Send out address of low address of data: low address of data stored in register; Increment program counter;	FETCH Low order address
Send out address of high address of data: high address of data stored in register; Increment program counter;	FETCH High order address
Send out address of data: data stored in register; Increment program counter;	FETCH Data
Data and accumulator contents added together in ALU with carry bit and sum stored in accumulator.	Perform addition

This example shows that an instruction fetch and execution usually requires additional fetches to obtain addresses and data and also requires intermediate storage of data and results. It is obvious, therefore, that many different organizations and interconnections among the microprocessor's internal building blocks are possible and particular organizations can enhance the execution of one group of instructions and degrade the execution of others. The question is, then, "Which is the best microprocessor architecture?" This question prompts a counter question, "What is your application?" If your requirement is for a microprocessor that will handle incoming data, store the information, and output data, an architecture that is optimized for memory access and I/O operations is desirable. If arithmetic operations are the principle tasks of the microprocessor, an architecture oriented toward mathematical calculations is needed. Figures 6.2 to 6.7 illustrate some typical architectures.

6.2.1 ALU Data Paths

The heart of the microprocessor is the ALU, and typical data paths associated with it are given in Figure 6.8.

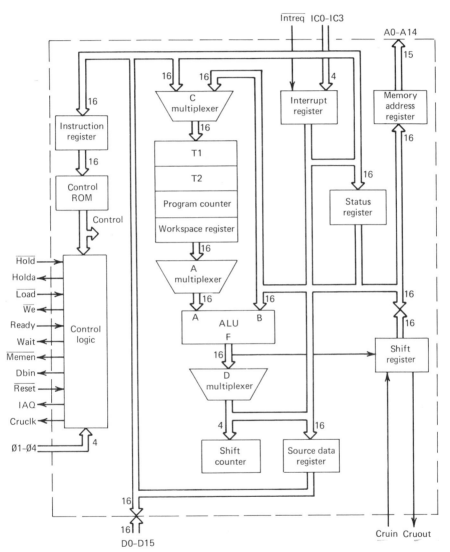

FIGURE 6.2 Texas Instruments' TMS 9900 16-bit microprocessor. (Copyright 1976, Texas Instruments, Inc.)

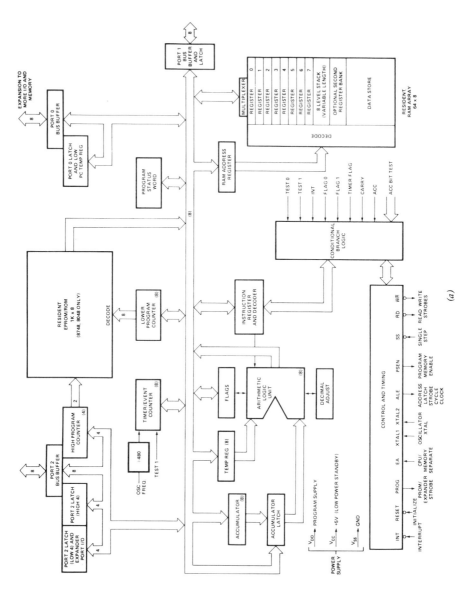

FIGURE 6.3 (a) Architecture of Intel 8748/8048 single chip microcomputer.

(a)

FIGURE 6.3 (*b*) Photograph of 8748 chip (Copyright Intel Corporation 1977, all rights reserved)

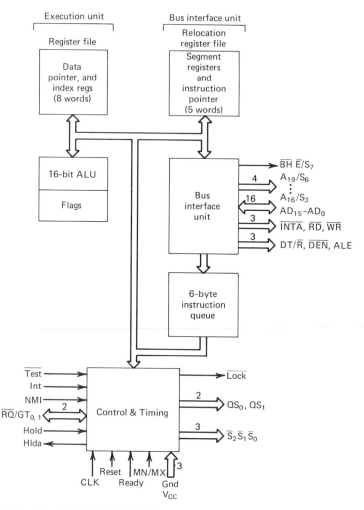

FIGURE 6.4 Intel 8086 16-bit HMOS microprocessor. (Reprinted by permission of Intel Corp., Copyright 1978)

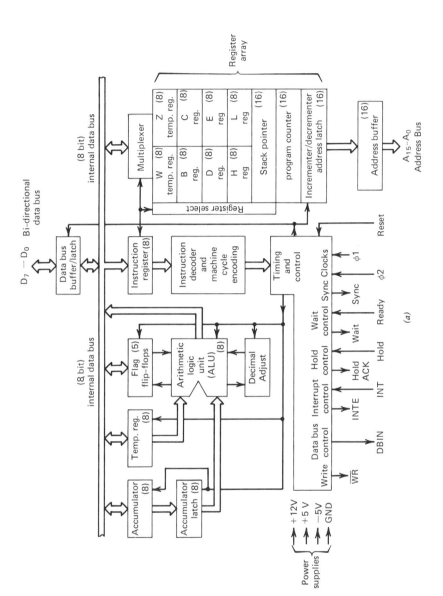

FIGURE 6.5 (a) Intel 8080A microprocessor.

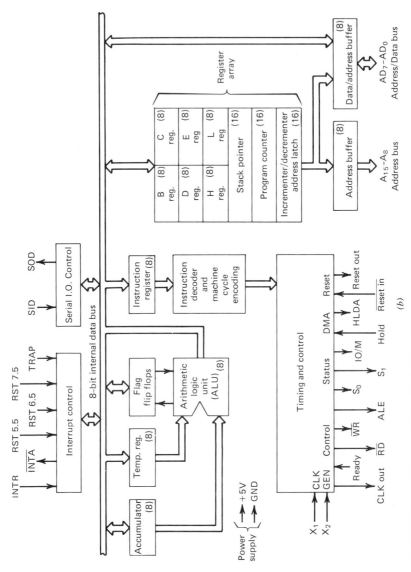

FIGURE 6.5 (b) Intel 8085 microprocessor.

FIGURE 6.5 (c) Photograph of 8085 wafer. (Copyright Intel Corporation, 1977, all rights reserved.)

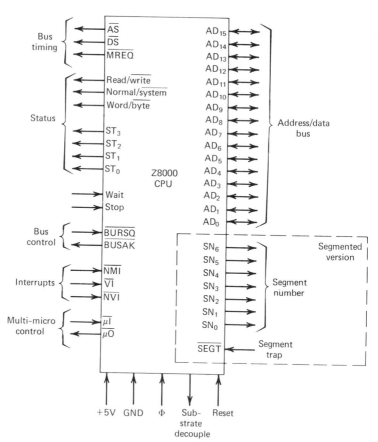

FIGURE 6.6 Zilog Z8000 16-bit microprocessor. NOTE: This CPU comes in two versions, a 40-pin nonsegmented version that directly accesses 64 K bytes per address space and a 48-pin version that directly accesses 8 megabytes per address space. (Reprinted by permission of Zilog Corporation.)

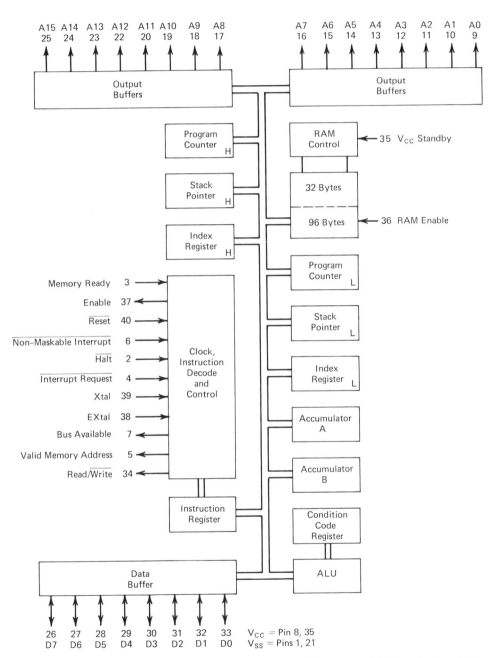

FIGURE 6.7 Motorola 6802 microprocessor. (Courtesy of Motorola Inc., Integrated Circuits Division.)

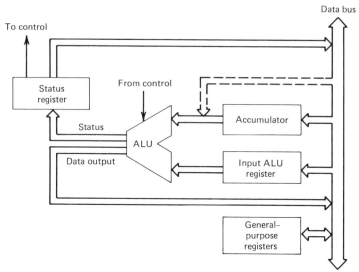

FIGURE 6.8 Typical ALU data paths.

Recalling from Chapter 3 that the ALU is capable of addition, subtraction, comparison, shifting, and logical operations as specified by control inputs, we see that the data paths of Figure 6.8 permit these operations to be performed on a variety of input combinations. The dotted path in Figure 6.8 is not present in some microprocessors and, therefore, one input word to the ALU must always be through the accumulator. Status output bits indicating a negative result, carry generation, comparison results, and others are sent to the status register and to the control logic to implement instructions such as BRANCH on negative result and BRANCH if two compared words are equal. The ALU usually requires storage registers to hold the two input words and a latch (sometimes internal to the ALU) to temporarily hold the results of an ALU operation. The output of the ALU, through the data bus, can be steered by the control circuitry to the accumulator, general-purpose registers, or other destinations. Again, the flexibility and paths allowed are a function of the microprocessor's intended application and design and cost constraints.

6.3 TIMING

The key to understanding the internal operation of any microprocessor is to become familiar with the system timing. The microprocessor is essentially a synchronous sequential machine whose states are determined by instructions, the internal control logic, and, in some cases, external events such as interrupts. Microprocessor timing is accomplished by clock circuitry that provides single or multiphase clock outputs.

6.3.1 Instruction Cycles

Instruction fetching and execution cycles are determined by these clock pulses. An example of an 8-bit, single phase clock microprocessor timing diagram is given in Figure 6.9. A microprocessor internally synchronized by a single phase clock is usually a static device with all on-chip registers and RAM storage composed of static memory cells requiring no refreshing.

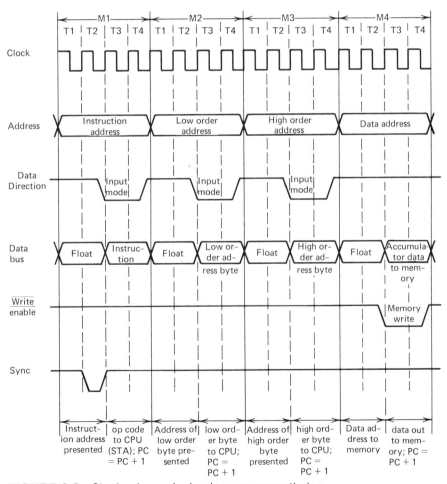

FIGURE 6.9 Single phase clock microprocessor timing.

The hypothetical microprocessor timing in Figure 6.9 illustrates the execution of a STORE ACCUMULATOR IN MEMORY (STA) type instruction. The instruction specifies that the accumulator contents be stored in the 16-bit address specified in the two bytes of memory following the op code. *Machine cycles* are specified as four clock periods or states T1 to T4. In machine cycle 1(M1), in states T1 to T4, the instruction address is presented on the 16-bit address lines of the hypothetical microprocessor. Also at T2 of M1, a SYNC pulse is generated to indicate that a new instruction fetch is being initiated. This SYNC pulse can be used for troubleshooting and in logic to "single-step" the microprocessor though one instruction at a time for debugging purposes. The DATA DIRECTION line indicates the direction of the bidirectional data bus. In this case, a high or logic 1 means that it is in the output mode from the CPU and a low or logic 0 indicates that it is sending instructions or data into the CPU. At the end of T2 in M1, the data bus reverts to the input mode to receive the instruction from memory. Prior to T2, the data bus is in the *high impedance* floating mode. The WRITE ENABLE (WE) line in this example is at a logic 1 when a memory read is being performed and at a logic 0 when a memory write is being executed. During T3 and T4 of M1, the instruction op code is read into the CPU and decoded. Since the instruction requires two more bytes of address indicating where the accumulator contents are to be deposited, these bytes are addressed and returned to the CPU in machine cycles M2 and M3 in a manner similar to the op code fetch. Note that the PC is incremented in T4 of every cycle.

The low order address byte is obtained in M2 and the high order byte in M3.

In machine cycle M4, the two byte address into which the accumulator contents are to be stored is presented on the address bus. Since the write-to-memory portion of this instruction is to be performed during M4, the DATA DIRECTION line remains high throughout M4 and the WRITE ENABLE line goes low at T3 and T4 of M4. This particular processor has no WAIT state, i.e., it assumes that the memory access time is small enough to allow valid accessed information to be available during states T3 and T4 following presentation of the desired address on the address bus during T1 and T2.

Consider another microprocessor that multiplexes (switches between) address and data information on the same bus. In this situation, an address latch external to the microprocessor is necessary to hold the address when the address bus reverts to a data bus. Assume that the address/data bus is 16 bits wide and the microprocessor has a separate 8-bit input/output port for transferring data to and from the outside world. The control signals for the microprocessor are the DATA DIRECTION line (low when data bus is in input mode), a $\overline{\text{WRITE ENABLE}}$ $\overline{\text{(WE)}}$ line (low when writing to memory, a $\overline{\text{READ ENABLE}}$ $\overline{\text{(RE)}}$ line (low when reading from memory, an $\overline{\text{IN}}$ and an $\overline{\text{OUT}}$ line indicating a port input or output operation, and a SYNC line, which indicates the beginning of a new instruction fetch. Timing for this hypothetical processor is by means of a two phase clock with phase two initiating a machine cycle which contains four states. All instructions are executed in either one or two machine cycles. The timing and package diagrams for this microprocessor are given in Figure 6.10. The timing diagram illustrates the fetch and execution of a two cycle instruction sending data out through the output port.

A third and still different microprocessor organization is illustrated in Figure 6.11. This microprocessor has a 16-bit address bus and a 16-bit data bus and is timed by a two phase clock. The control bus for this processor includes Data Direction, $\overline{\text{WRITE ENABLE}}$, READY, WAIT, SYNC, $\overline{\text{MEMAC}}$, HOLD, and HOLD ACKNOWLEDGE (HOLDA) lines. The READY line is pulled to a low state when the memory access time is greater than the time allotted in the microprocessor cycle for the access. The active low READY signal must be produced by logic circuitry associated with the 'slow' memory. The WAIT line is raised to a logic 1 in response to the READY line input and indicates that the processor is in the WAIT state, i.e., the processor idles and does not proceed into the next states until the READY line is raised to a logic 1. The $\overline{\text{MEMAC}}$ (Memory Access) signal becomes a logic 0 when a read from or write to memory is being performed as opposed to a read or write involving an external I/O port. Thus, instructions specifically referencing the I/O ports will not cause $\overline{\text{MEMAC}}$ to go low. The $\overline{\text{MEMAC}}$ can be used in $\overline{\text{CHIP ENABLE}}$ $\overline{\text{(CE)}}$ logic to enable memory circuits as distinguished from I/O circuits. The HOLD input to the microprocessor causes a cessation of its internal operation and places the address and data buses in the tri-state high impedance (floating) mode, thereby effectively isolating the microprocessor from memory and I/O devices. This HOLD state can be used in Direct Memory Access (DMA) operations to allow an external DMA controller to take command of the address and data buses and write to or read from memory directly at a high data rate without involving the microprocessor in slower programmed data transfers. The HOLD ACKNOWLEDGE, HOLDA, output of the microprocessor goes to a logic 1 when the processor enters the HOLD state. Returning the HOLD line to a logic 0 will cause the microprocessor to exit the HOLD state and resume operation in the machine cycle after the last one executed. Both the HOLD and WAIT states are synchronized with the phase clock pulses. The READY line is scanned only when phase one is a logic "1" in state T2 and the HOLD line is sampled when phase two is a logic 1 in state T2 and

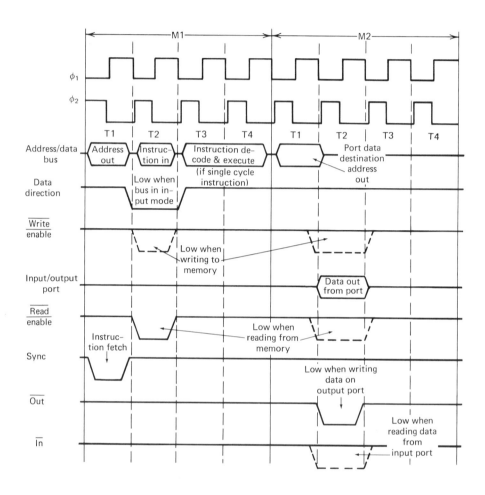

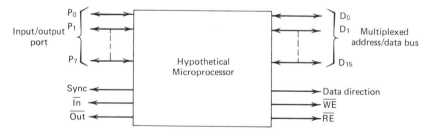

FIGURE 6.10 Hypothetical microprocessor with multiplexed address/data bus.

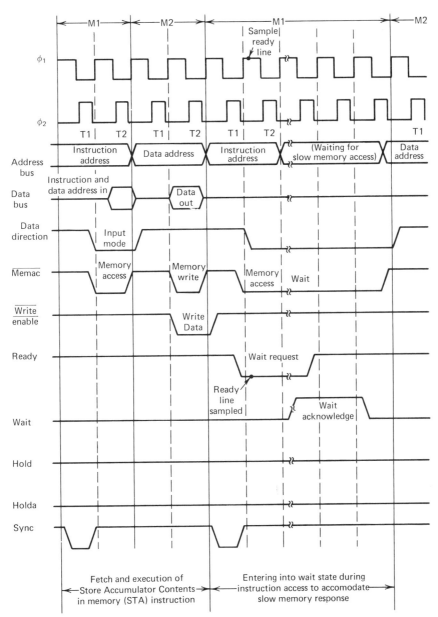

FIGURE 6.11 Timing diagram illustrating instruction fetch, execution, and WAIT state.

completes the current machine cycle before setting HOLDA to a logic 1 and putting the address and data buses in the high impedance state. A STA instruction fetch and execution and a WAIT operation are shown in Figure 6.11 and the HOLD operation is illustrated in Figure 6.12. Note one machine cycle is composed of two states, T1 and T2. The STA instruction is a "zero page" instruction in that 8 of 16 instruction bits represent the lower 8 bits of the address into which the accumulator data are to be stored. The upper 8 bits are assumed to be all 0's, thus, addressing page 0.

6.4 INSTRUCTION SETS

The totality of instructions capable of being executed by a microcomputer is called its *instruction set*. An instruction set can be subdivided into various categories according to the type of operations the instructions perform. The following eight categories will be used to discuss microcomputer instruction sets in this chapter since they cover the major types of instructions.

ARITHMETIC   DATA TRANSFER
BRANCH   LOGICAL
CONTROL   INPUT/OUTPUT
USER OPERATIONS   TIMER/COUNTER

Each of these categories will be discussed in terms of an instruction set for a hypothetical microcomputer. Before proceeding to develop this instruction set, however, we describe the concepts and types of addressing.

6.4.1 Addressing Modes

Addressing modes vary among microcomputers from those providing a large number of addressing options to those providing only one or two. For completeness, the important addressing modes used in microcomputers will be presented here. Be aware that the terminology used varies among manufacturers.

Extended or Absolute or Long Addressing
The addressing mode that permits accessing the entire memory is the extended or absolute or long addressing. For an 8-bit microcomputer (8-bit accumulator, data paths, and memory word) with 16-bit addressing, an instruction with this type of addressing would be:

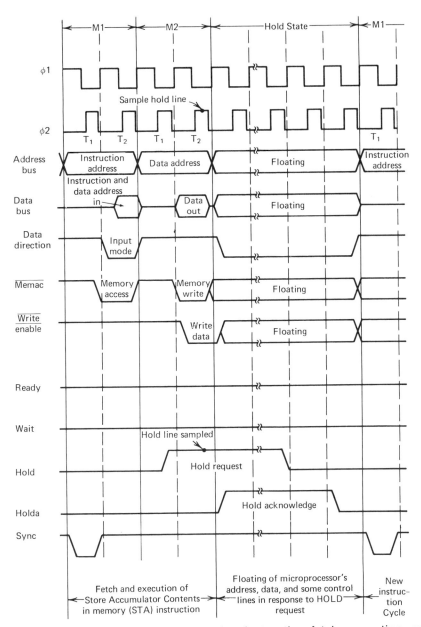

FIGURE 6.12 Timing diagram illustrating instruction fetch, execution, and HOLD State.

7	6	5	4	3	2	1	0	
								Op Code
A7	A6	A5	A4	A3	A2	A1	A0	Low order address
A15	A14	A13	A12	A11	A10	A9	A8	High order address

For a 16-bit microcomputer with 16-bit addressing, the instruction may appear as:

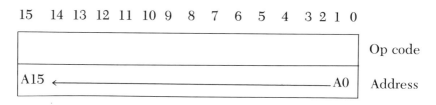

15 14 13 12 11 10 9 8 7 6 5 4 3 2 1 0

Op code

A15 ←——————————————————— A0 Address

Direct or Short Addressing

The instruction specifies a portion of memory that can be accessed. This portion can be on the same page as the instruction itself or, sometimes, on page zero. For example, the following instruction in an 8-bit microprocessor would be interpreted as (1) perform the operation specified using the address $C4_{16}$ on page zero ($00C4_{16}$) or (2) perform the operation specified on the same page as the instruction itself is located ($08C4_{16}$), depending on the op code.

Address	7	6	5	4	3	2	1	0	
$08A1_{16}$									Op code
$08A2_{16}$	1	1	0	0	0	1	0	0	Address ($C4_{16}$)

A 16-bit version would be:

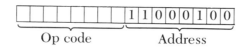

Op code   Address

Immediate Addressing

The data are contained in the instruction. For the 8-bit microcomputer, an immediate instruction is, for example:

Op code

Data

Load data held in second byte to a previously specified location.

For a 16-bit microcomputer, possible immediate instructions are:

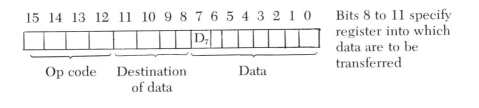

Op code Destination of data Data

Bits 8 to 11 specify register into which data are to be transferred

or

Op code   Destination of data

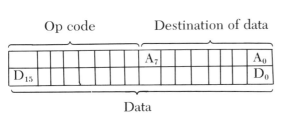

Data

Bits A_0 to A_7 specify memory location or registers into which data are to be transferred or between which an operation is to be performed.

Indexed Addressing

The address contained in the instruction is added to the contents of a register in the microprocessor called the *Index Register*. This computed or *effective* address is then sent out on the address bus in order to access data in memory.

For an 8-bit microcomputer with a 16-bit Index Register:

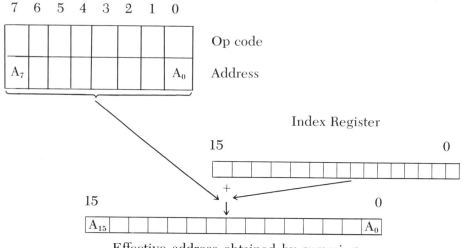

Effective address obtained by summing
A_0 to A_7 and Index Register contents.

For 16-bit microcomputer with 16-bit Index Register:

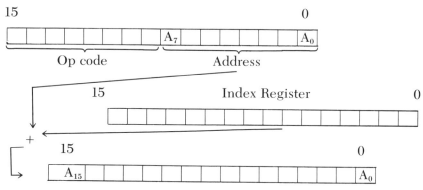

Effective address obtained by
summing A_0 to A_7 and Index Register
contents.

Implied Addressing

Implied addressing is used when operations internal to the microprocessor
are performed or when the memory address is specified by a counter or

register. For example, a CLEAR CARRY instruction sets the CARRY bit in the microprocessor to a 0. Since this bit is internal to the microprocessor, the address is implied. A second example would be an instruction that places the accumulator contents in a memory location specified by a register. The particular register holding the memory address would not be referred to in the instruction but would be implied.

For an 8-bit microcomputer:

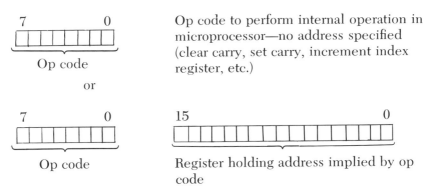

Op code to perform internal operation in microprocessor—no address specified (clear carry, set carry, increment index register, etc.)

or

Op code

Register holding address implied by op code

The 16-bit microcomputer addressing would be identical to the 8-bit unit except for word length of op code.

Indirect Addressing

The memory location specified in the instruction holds the address of the desired data. This concept allows the same instruction to access different memory locations by simply changing the contents of the memory location pointed to by the address in the instruction.

For the 8-bit microcomputer:

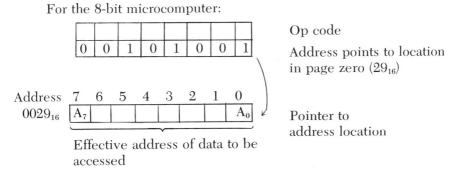

Op code

Address points to location in page zero (29_{16})

Pointer to address location

For the 16-bit microcomputer:

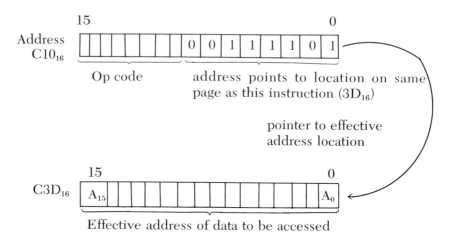

Relative Addressing

An offset word contained in the instruction is algebraically (two's or one's complement) added to the value of the Program Counter. This addition allows addressing of a range around the present instruction being executed. Note that the Program Counter is automatically incremented after fetching the offset value and is pointing to the next memory byte.

For the 8-bit microcomputer:

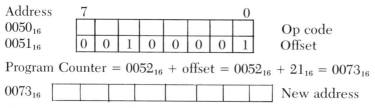

Program Counter = 0052_{16} + offset = 0052_{16} + 21_{16} = 0073_{16}

0073_{16} [_____] New address

If signed two's complement arithmetic is used, the range of the offset is -128_{10} to $+127_{10}$ from the address of the next instruction.

For the 16-bit microcomputer:

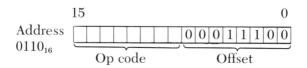

$$PC = 0111_{16} + offset = 0111_{16} + 1C_{16} = 012D_{16}$$

15   0

$012D_{16}$ ⬚⬚⬚⬚⬚⬚⬚⬚⬚⬚⬚⬚⬚⬚⬚⬚ New address

There are variations on, and combinations of, these addressing modes that are too numerous to cover and that are peculiar to particular microprocessors. The addressing modes discussed will, however, provide a basis for understanding these additional addressing techniques when they are encountered.

6.4.2 Input/Output

Transferring data into and out of the microprocessor is an important part of most microprocessor applications. The techniques of interfacing to the outside world are discussed in Chapter 8, but the means of effecting the associated data transfers are closely linked to the architecture and instructions of the microprocessor and, therefore, are discussed in that context.

One method of data transfer is by means of instructions. As illustrated in the timing diagram of Figure 6.10, data can be placed on the Data Bus by an OUTPUT microcomputer instruction. This instruction also produces appropriate control signals such as $\overline{\text{WRITE ENABLE}}$ and $\overline{\text{OUT}}$ that can be used to transfer the data to external latches or other interface chips. Similarly, an INPUT instruction can transfer data onto the data bus from an external device that utilizes control signals such as $\overline{\text{READ ENABLE}}$ and $\overline{\text{IN}}$. These types of data movement are controlled by instructions in a program and are therefore referred to as *programmed I/O*. It is obvious that the rate of data transfer is limited by the instruction execution time. For example, if an INPUT instruction were used to read data into a microprocessor register from a peripheral chip and a MOVE instruction were used to transfer the data from the register into memory, the total time to accomplish this input would be the sum of the two instruction times. If each instruction requires k microseconds to execute, then the maximum frequency of data transfer using programmed I/O would be $1/2k$ MHz. For a NMOS microcomputer with 1-microsecond instruction times for the INPUT and MOVE instructions, the maximum input rate would be 1/2 MHz or 500 KHz. A bipolar microprocessor with instruction times of approximately 0.2 microseconds would have a transfer rate of $1/.4$ MHz or 2.5 MHz.

An alternative to programmed I/O is *Direct Memory Access (DMA)*, in which data are transferred directly to and from memory without utilizing the microprocessor. The address and data lines from the microprocessor to memory and peripheral chips are placed in a high impedance state by a control input (HOLD in Figure 6.12) and data are written to or read from memory directly. These transfers usually take place in a time interval between instructions and the data rate is now limited mainly by the memory cycle time.

There are three principal options in initiating programmed I/O operations. The first is that of writing the I/O sequence into the program and, thus, transferring data when that portion of the program is reached and executed. The second is to include a series of instructions that cause the program to loop on itself while testing for the occurrence of an external event. For example, the microprocessor may have an input line called FLAG that is tested by an instruction (JUMP ON FLAG) and, when active, will cause the program to jump to a new sequence of instructions in a different portion of memory. These instructions will implement the desired response to the occurrence of the external event. A typical response may be the reading of data on the data bus into the microprocessor from a peripheral device. This looping and testing for the FLAG signal occupies the microprocessor completely and prevents it from executing another sequence of instructions during this time. Of course, the program may branch and perform other tasks, but it must return and test for the occurrence of the FLAG signal or the external event may be missed. An alternative to this testing technique is to have the external event interrupt the microprocessor program execution. In this mode, the instruction sequence proceeds until interrupted and then program flow is transferred to another group of instructions that will service the *interrupt request*.

The interrupt request line(s) is an input to the microprocessor chip that, when activated, initiates a response to the interrupt. If there is only one interrupt line to which a number of devices are connected, the interrupting device must be identified. When more than one device is interrupting at a time, a priority scheme must also be used. The interrupting device may place identifying data on the data bus, which is then used by the microprocessor to generate an address vector pointing to the location in memory containing the beginning of the service routine for that particular device. A similar approach is to have separate interrupt lines into the microprocessor. Activation of a particular line causes the program to transfer to a memory location corresponding to the specific interrupt request. Both these types of interrupts are called *vectored interrupts*. If the microprocessor has multiple interrupt capability, a means must exist to prioritize the interrupt requests. This selection is accomplished by priority encoding circuits internal or external to the microprocessor. If the microprocessor chip itself does not contain the interrupt priority logic, interrupt controller chips can be used that provide the priority and control capabilities needed to effectively process multiple interrupts.

A microprocessor that has one interrupt line shared by a number of devices and does not have vectored capability must *poll* each device after an interrupt has occurred to determine which device or devices initiated the interrupt request. An interrupt flip-flop is set by the interrupting device and the microprocessor polling or reading of the flip-flop states will detect the device requesting service. In this *polled mode* of interrupt servicing, the prioritizing is usually accomplished by software that checks the interrupting devices against a programmed priority list.

In the process of responding to an interrupt, the microprocessor must suspend the program it was executing at the time, save the states of the various status flags (Carry, Overflow, etc.) following the last instruction executed in the present program, and save the value of the Program Counter. The contents of the PC are the address of the next instruction to be executed in the present program, following the return from the interrupt service routine. Thus, in addition to restoring the PC, one must return the microprocessor status flags to their preinterrupt values when a return from interrupt is accomplished. The methods chosen to save and restore preinterrupt information greatly influence the architecture of the microprocessor.

The simplest but most time-consuming approach is to save and restore the PC and status information under program control by writing small interrupt save and restore routines. With this method, everytime an interrupt occurs and is serviced, all housekeeping is accomplished by these programs and, thus, the interrupt response time is relatively slow. Assume, for example, that an NMOS microprocessor requires 30 microseconds total to respond to an interrupt, save the PC and status information, and branch to an interrupt service routing while requiring 30 microseconds total to restore the PC and status information and return to the original program. The interrupt servicing overhead time alone (excluding the time taken to execute the interrupt service program itself) would be 60 microseconds.

If this microprocessor were used in an application with a high incidence of interrupts, program execution speed would deteriorate rapidly. This reduction in throughput would be especially critical in real time applications. An improvement of the total software interrupt handling approach is one that detects an interrupt, saves the PC and status registers, and branches to the interrupt service routine address all under hardware control. Return to the interrupted program is accomplished in the same fashion. This method is obviously faster but requires more hardware in the microprocessor chip. An interesting microprocessor architecture used to effectively accomplish hardware interrupt servicing is the *stack architecture*. The most common stack implementation is a Last In First Out (LIFO) stack, which is simply a group of registers into which data words are

PUSHED or *POPPED*. For example, consider a four-deep stack onto which three bytes of data were pushed. Byte 1 was pushed in first, byte 2 second, and byte 3 last. The stack would appear as:

When byte 3 was popped off the stack, it would appear as:

Stacks can be implemented in RAM or in registers inside the microprocessor chip. The location of data pushed onto or popped from a stack implemented in RAM external to the microprocessor chip is determined by an address held in a *Stack Pointer (SP)* register. The contents of the Stack Pointer register specify the stack memory location that will be used by the next push or pop operation. As an example of stack use in servicing an interrupt, assume that an interrupt has occurred and been identified in a microprocessor whose stack is implemented in external RAM. Further assume that the contents of the SP and PC registers are $001B_{16}$ and $01FO_{16,}$ respectively. In responding to the interrupt, the PC and Status registers are pushed onto the stack under hardware control. The Status information is stored as one word referred to as the *Status Word (SW)*. The stack appears as:

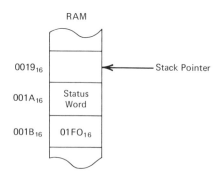

In this microprocessor, the stack "grows downward" and the SP is now pointing at location 0019_{16}. When the return from interrupt instruction is executed, the PC and SW are popped from the stack back to the PC Register and Status Flags in the microprocessor. The SP is now pointing at location $001B_{16}$, ready to accept new data. Note that the Stack Pointer changes by 2 since two words were popped off the stack.

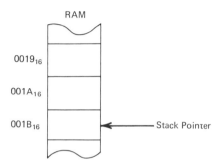

When an interrupt routine itself is interrupted by a higher priority device, the PC and SW associated with the first interrupt routine are pushed onto the stack and program control is transferred to a new routine located at the address vector corresponding to the second interrupting device. The stack in this situation would appear as:

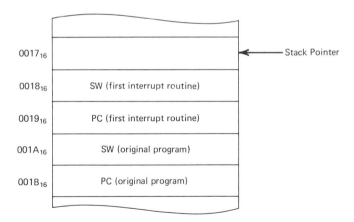

The number of pushes onto a stack that can be performed without losing the data is referred to as the *depth of a stack*. For example, if the stack is contained in the microprocessor chip, its depth must be limited for space reasons. Assuming that a microprocessor on-chip stack has eight registers or is eight deep, then eight pushes or four interrupts (two pushes/interrupt) could be accommodated before data are lost. If four interrupts are being serviced and a fifth, higher priority, request occurs, the PC and SW of the first interrupt will "fall out of the stack" and be lost. An advantage of having the stack on the microprocessor chip is that, in some instances, small microcomputer systems could be implemented without requiring any external RAM and transfers to and from an on-chip stack take less time than external RAM accesses. On the other hand, a stack utilizing external memory provides virtually unlimited depth. Care must be taken, however, to insure that the stack does not "grow" into other portions of data memory and overwrite needed data. To avoid this occurrence, one page of data memory is usually reserved by the programmer for stack operations.

A stack is also useful in storing the return address and, sometimes, status information when a subroutine is called. Recall that a *subroutine* is a program that performs operations or calculations frequently needed by the main or *calling* program. If performance of integer multiplication was frequently needed in an application, a multiply subroutine would be written that could be called from the main program. Thus, the code for the multiply routine would appear only once and would not be duplicated everywhere in the main program that it was needed. A JUMP TO SUBROUTINE or CALL instruction usually initiates the transfer from the main program to the subroutine. Similar to an interrupt, the subroutine call must also save the PC in order to continue with the main program following completion of the subroutine. The SW is not saved in some microcomputers. Stack operations for a subroutine are identical to those for an interrupt. If a second subroutine is called by a subroutine, the PC (and SW) of the first subroutine are saved in the stack along with the PC (and SW) of the main program. This procedure is called *nesting of subroutines.* If the stack has the capability of storing the PC (and SW) associated with four subroutines without losing any of the information, then the microprocessor is said to have the capability of nesting subroutines four deep.

Another approach to transferring program control while saving return parameters is to set up discrete working areas in RAM which are assigned to a particular subroutine or interrupt routine. These working areas could be defined in RAM external to the microprocessor or contained within the microprocessor chip itself. Consider a microprocessor having eight working areas on the chip, each working area consisting of 16 registers. During the main program execution, work area 0 would be used as a scratchpad for storing intermediate results and would supply registers for indexed and

indirect addressing. When an interrupt or subroutine call o
work area, say area 1, would be assigned to the new progr:
and a pointer (PR) to the previous work area would be sav
registers in the new work area. This transfer operation is ....
than the other approaches since any other data which might have to be
saved prior to the transfer are in the previous work area and do not have
to be stored by using time-consuming instructions. Multiple interrupts and
subrouting nesting are handled by simply transferring to new work areas
each time an interrupt or subroutine call occurs. Saving of the PC, SW, and
PR would be accomplished under hardware control during those transfers
and would not require explicit instruction executions. The advantage of
incorporating the work areas in external RAM as opposed to having them
in the microprocessor chip is identical to that of off-chip stack implementation, namely, that an essentially unlimited number of work areas could
be defined. On-board work areas of reasonable size permit many applications that require no external RAM chips and also increase instruction
execution speed since external memory references take more time than
internal register references.

An additional critical I/O consideration is that of *isolated* versus *memory mapped* I/O. In *isolated I/O*, separate INPUT and OUTPUT instructions are used for data transfer from and to external devices. These instructions produce IN and OUT pulses on two pins of the microprocessor chip
and these pulses are used as gating and/or chip select signals for I/O devices (see Figure 6.10). These IN/OUT pulses distinguish between memory addressing and I/O addressing and, therefore, up to the full address
space of the microprocessor can be used for specifying I/O devices as well
as memory addresses. The disadvantage of this method is that only two
instructions, INPUT and OUTPUT, can be used for I/O operations. *Memory mapped I/O* does not distinguish between memory and I/O devices
and the address space is shared between them. Decoders are used with
the address and control lines to select either memory or I/O. Thus, the
space available for program and data memory is reduced in memory
mapped I/O. A common practice is to use the msb of the address (A_{15} in
16-bit addressing) to differentiate between memory and I/O. Memory is
selected when the msb = 0 and I/O is selected when the msb = 1. Thus,
any address less than $32,768_{10}$ in a 16-bit address space will refer to memory
and any address greater than or equal to 2^{15} or $32,768_{10}$ will specify an I/O
device. Memory mapped I/O has the feature, since memory and I/O are
indistinguishable except for address, that any instructions referencing
memory can also reference I/O chips and peripherals. This approach makes
available a significant number of instructions that can be used in I/O operations.

6.4.3 A Microprocessor Design

In order to illustrate the instruction set–architecture interrelationship, we will now proceed to develop a one-chip microprocessor. Naturally, some assumptions must be made initially as to its application and desirable features. The following are proposed:

1. General-purpose use.
2. Extended arithmetic capability.
3. Rapid response to interrupts.
4. Limited number of concurrent interrupts.
5. Both memory-mapped and isolated I/O capability.
6. Ability to add user-defined instructions *without* obsoleting vendor-supported software.
7. On-chip clock, timer/counter, power fail, and restart circuitry.
8. Multiple addressing modes.
9. Ability to be used *without* external RAM in some applications (two-chip applications requiring only microprocessor chip and program memory—ROM, PROM, or EPROM).
10. One microsecond or less minimum instruction cycle.

To state these requirements does not necessarily mean that they can be met. With the technological advances being made in semiconductor fabrication, however, the list is not unrealistic.

To meet the density requirements of such a chip and stay within the speed constraints, NMOS (HMOS) technology is chosen. SOS is also a possible alternative. In order to function without external RAM, internal registers or register banks are needed and, to provide fast interrupt response to a limited number of interrupts, bank switching is used. In this mode, there is no single accumulator register in the microprocessor but banks of registers in which each register can act as an accumulator. To accommodate the on-chip power-fail, restart, timer/counter, and reset functions, internal interrupts are implemented. Isolated I/O can be accomplished by defining an input and an output instruction with two mutually exclusive logic outputs from the microprocessor chip that are active when an input or output instruction is being executed. Extended arithmetic capability is implemented by providing multiply and divide instructions in the instruction set. As a further means of controlling the internal devices and reducing instruction execution times, a 16-bit organization is used.

A microprocessor design that satisfies the requirements is given in Figure 6.13. The design includes eight banks of 16-bit registers with 16 registers per bank. A portion of the program being run will use the registers

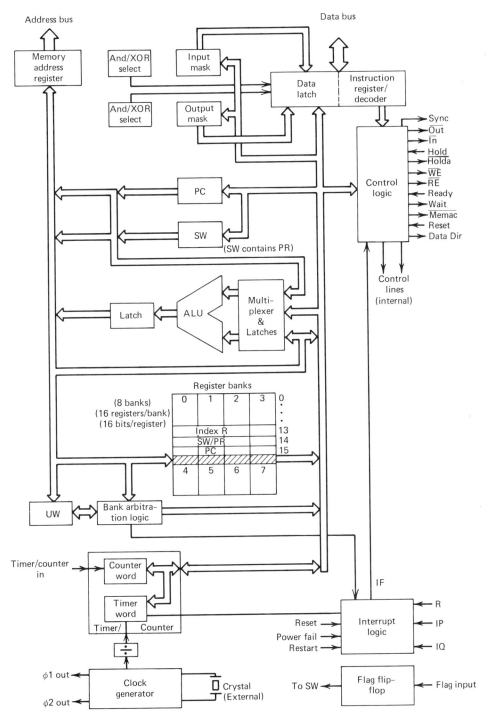

FIGURE 6.13 A microprocessor design.

in one register bank as scratchpads, accumulators, and an index register. When a subroutine is called or an interrupt occurs, another register bank is assigned to the new program and the information associated with the present program remains in the old register bank. This technique eliminates the need to store and retrieve any intermediate results when a transfer is made to another part of the program. The information that must be stored is that of the PC, the Status Word (SW), and the Pointer Register (PR), which is a 3-bit word identifying the bank that was being used before the transfer was initiated. The stores and retrievals can be reduced to two words, the PC and SW, if the PR is included as part of the SW. The SW and PC are stored in registers 14 and 15, respectively, of the new register bank following a program transfer. The format of the SW is:

Condition bits													Pointer Register (PR)		
AB	AR	E	Z	N	IF	P	IP	IQ	B	F	C	V	2^2	2^1	2^0

15   0

where

AB   = 1   when the result of the last operation affecting this flag indicated a < result, assuming the two numbers compared were positive integers;

AR   = 1   same as AB except that numbers compared are treated as both positive and negative numbers in two's complement form;

E   = 1   when last result affecting this flag showed that two numbers compared were equal;

Z   = 1   when result of last operation affecting this flag yielded a zero result;

N   = 1   when result of last operation affecting this flag yielded a negative result;

IF   = 1   if maskable interrupt IF (no vacant register banks) is enabled;

P   = 1   if parity check is odd;

IP   = 1   if maskable interrupt, IP, is enabled;

IO   = 1   if maskable interrupt, IO, is enabled;

F   = 1   if Flag input line to microprocessor = 1;

C   = 1   if Carry bit = 1 following last instruction affecting this bit;

V $= 1$ if Overflow bit $= 1$ following last instruction affecting this bit;

PR $= 0_{10}$ to 7_{10} indicating 1 of 8 register banks selected.

A means of keeping track of which register banks have been used and which ones are available for use must be provided. This bookkeeping is accomplished by the bank Usage Word (UW), in conjunction with the bank arbitration logic. The UW provides up-to-date usage information on the eight register banks and, with the bank arbitration logic, automatically selects vacant banks for use by the interrupt or subroutine programs if the desired bank is not specified by the programmer in the JUMP TO SUBROUTINE (JSR) instruction. In this mode of selection, the bank designation need not be sequential and register banks already in use will be skipped over until an unused bank is found. If no vacant banks are found, an interrupt, IF, is generated to permit the programmer, if he so desires, to transfer the contents of a bank or banks to external memory for temporary storage and, thus, free bank register space for the interrupt or subroutine being executed. Another IF interrupt will also be generated when one executes a RETURN to the interrupted or subroutine calling program to permit restoring the bank register contents to their original condition. The format of the UW is:

```
  7   6   5   4   3   2   1   0 ←── Register bank
 ┌─┬─┬─┬─┬─┬─┬─┬─┬─┬─┬─┬─┬─┬─┬─┬─┐     designation
 │ │ │ │ │ │ │ │ │ │ │ │ │ │ │ │ │
 └─┴─┴─┴─┴─┴─┴─┴─┴─┴─┴─┴─┴─┴─┴─┴─┘
15                              0
```

BIT PATTERN FOR EACH REGISTER BANK

00	Register bank available
01	Register bank in use
10	Register bank available, copy saved in memory
11	Register bank in use, copy saved in memory

This format allows the processor to choose an available register bank when servicing a subroutine or interrupt with unspecified bank designation. When all banks have been used, the IF interrupt will occur (if the IF flag has been set in the SW) allowing the programmer to save banks to memory and free them for continued usage. Also, in order to provide a reference point, the bit pattern of the register bank presently in use is *not* changed in the UW when the UW is loaded with zeros by a LUW (LOAD USAGE WORD) instruction.

Register 13 of the designated register bank is used as the index register in the indexed mode of addressing. This mode is one of eight modes of addressing used. These addressing modes and their instruction formats are:

Word 2 (if required)

MODE	XXX	ADDRESS MODE
1	000	Direct source, direct destination
2	001	Indirect source, direct destination
3	010	Direct source, indirect destination
4	011	Indirect source, indirect destination
5	100	Indexed (through Register 13) source, indexed destination
6	101	Immediate source, direct destination
7	110	Direct source, indirect extended destination
8	111	Indirect extended source, direct destination

A 16-bit PC permits addressing of 2^{16} or 65,536 words of memory. The first 16 locations of memory should be ROM, PROM, or EPROM storage and are designated as interrupt vector locations as follows.

ROM ADDRESS	INTERRUPTS
0000	RESET VECTOR
0001	POWER FAIL VECTOR
0002	RESTART VECTOR
0003	TIMER VECTOR
0004	COUNTER VECTOR
0005	R NON MASK VECTOR
0006	IP MASK VECTOR
0007	IQ MASK VECTOR
0008	IF VECTOR ON JSR
0009	IF VECTOR ON RET
000A	NEA VECTOR FOR NEW INSTRUCTION A

000B	NEB VECTOR FOR NEW INSTRUCTION B
000C	NEC VECTOR FOR NEW INSTRUCTION C
000D	NED VECTOR FOR NEW INSTRUCTION D
000E	NEE VECTOR FOR NEW INSTRUCTION E
000F	SFI VECTOR

The R interrupt is the highest priority interrupt and cannot be disabled. Interrupts IP, IQ, and IF can be *masked* (disabled) and will be ignored until enabled. Interrupt IP has a higher priority than IQ; SFI is a software interrupt and is the lowest priority of all interrupts. Locations A_{16} through E_{16} are vector locations through which program control will be transferred when the OP codes for NEW instructions NEA through NEE are executed. The starting addresses of the subroutines that will implement the user-defined instructions are contained in locations A_{16} through E_{16}.

The timer/counter input pin permits the input to the microprocessor of external events to be counted. The control signals—HOLD, $\overline{\text{HOLDA}}$, $\overline{\text{WE}}$, $\overline{\text{RE}}$, READY, WAIT $\overline{\text{MEMAC}}$, RESET, and DATA DIR are identical to those described in Section 6.3 of this chapter. The Flag Input is a logical level that is tested by a microprocessor instruction.

A possible pin configuration for the microprocessor is shown in Figure 6.14.

6.4.4 Microprocessor Instruction Set

The proper design of a microprocessor should develop from the simultaneous consideration of both hardware and software requirements. An instruction set that evolved from these requirements for the proposed microprocessor is presented. The following symbols are used to concisely represent the operations by the instruction set.

DDDD	Bit pattern representing destination of instruction data manipulation
SSSS	Bit pattern representing source of instruction data manipulation
PR	Pointer Register designating which of eight register banks in microprocessor is being used
PCH	High order eight bits of program counter
PCL	Low order eight bits of program counter
PC	Program Counter
SW	Status Word

UW	Usage Word
m	nth register of 16 registers in register bank pointed to by PR—registers are numbered r0 through r15
r13	Index register in indexed instructions
r14	Register in which Status Word is stored in new register bank when interrupt, Jump To Subroutine, or new instruction is executed
r15	Register in which Program Counter is stored in new register bank when interrupt, Jump To Subroutine, or new instruction is executed
rs	Register in a 16-register bank that is the source of data in an instruction operation
rd	Register in a 16-register bank that is the destination of data in an instruction operation
b_n	The nth bit in designated register
d	Operand bit
D	Operand word
word2	Second 16-bit word of an instruction
( )	Contents of memory or register
((m))	Contents of memory location whose address is contained in m
←	Is replaced by
↔	Is exchanged with
+	Addition
−	Subtraction (two's complement)
*	Multiplication (integer)
÷	Division (integer)
XXX	Three-bit addressing mode pattern representing eight addressing modes or JUMP/RETURN conditions in instruction word.
TW	Sixteen-bit word used by on-chip timer to provide programmed time intervals
CW	Sixteen-bit counter word that is accumulated count of on-chip counter or preset counter word loaded by LCW instruction—The input to the counter is the TIMER/COUNTER IN line on the chip.

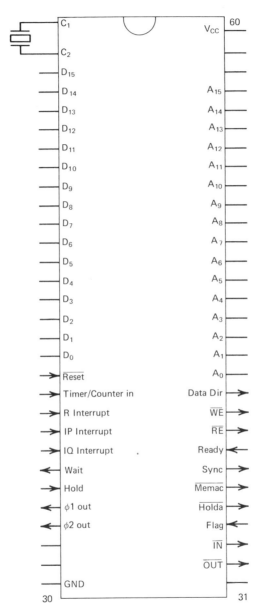

FIGURE 6.14 Microprocessor pin configuration.

Using these symbols, we can describe the instruction set for the microprocessor and the eight addressing modes for each instruction. The instruction set is divided into Arithmetic, Logical, Data Transfer, Branch, Control, Input/Output, Timer/Counter, and User Operations groups. The first instruction, ADD WITH CARRY, in the Arithmetic group and its addressing modes is explained in detail and the subsequent instructions follow the same pattern. The ADD WITH CARRY instruction in mnemonic form is ADD rs,rd where rs and rd are source and destination registers, respectively, for the ADD WITH CARRY operation. The instruction format is:

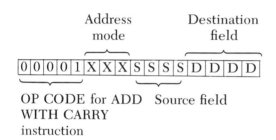

The OP CODE 00001_2 uniquely identifies the ADD WITH CARRY instruction. The three bits specifying the addressing modes are interpreted as follows:

Mode 1

$$(rd) \leftarrow (rd) + (rs) + (C) \qquad XXX = 000$$

The notation (rs) identifies the contents of one of 16 bank registers specified by the 4-bit number in the SSSS field of the instruction. Similarly, (rd) identifies the contents of one of 16 bank registers identified by the 4-bit number in the DDDD field of the instruction. The execution of this instruction will add together the contents of the source register, the contents of the destination register, and the contents of the carry bit and place the result in the destination register.

Mode 2

$$(rd) \leftarrow (rd) + ((rs)) + (C) \qquad XXX = 001$$

The notation ((rs)) identifies the contents of the memory address pointed to by rs (indirect addressing.) The register (rs) can contain any address in the 0 to $65,535_{10}$ range, and, thus, allows any word in memory to be added to the contents of rd along with the carry bit. The result is placed in rd.

Mode 3

$$((rd)) \leftarrow ((rd)) + (rs) + (C) \qquad XXX = 010$$

The contents of rs and carry are added with the contents of the memory location pointed to by rd. The result is then written back out to the memory location pointed to by rd.

Mode 4

$$((rd)) \leftarrow ((rd)) + ((rs)) + (C) \qquad XXX = 011$$

This mode is identical to mode 3 except that both rs and rd are used in the indirect addressing mode.

Mode 5

$$((r13) + (rd)) \leftarrow ((r13) + (rd)) + ((r13) + (rs)) + (C) \qquad XXX = 100$$

This mode is identical to mode 4 when (r13) = 0. When (r13) are not zero, the addresses specified by rs and rd are offset by the value in r13, thus allowing indexed addressing.

Mode 6

$$(rd) \leftarrow (rd) + (Word2) + (C) \qquad XXX = 101$$

In mode 6, the instruction is a two-word instruction, causing the next word in memory to be added, along with carry to the contents of rd. The result is placed in rd. The PC is automatically incremented to fetch Word2 and then incremented again to point to the next instruction.

Mode 7

$$((Word\ 2)) \leftarrow ((Word\ 2)) + (rs) + (C) \qquad XXX = 110$$

The second word of the instruction is used as the indirect address of the destination in this mode. The contents of rs and carry are added to the indirectly addressed data with the result written back to the indirectly addressed location. As in mode 6, the PC is incremented twice during the execution of this instruction.

Mode 8

$$(rd) \leftarrow (rd) + ((Word2)) + (C) \qquad XXX = 111$$

An instruction with this mode of addressing is executed in an identical manner to one with mode 7 except that the contents of rd are added with carry to the location indirectly addressed by (Word2) and the result is stored in rd. A summary of the eight modes along with their assembly language format is as follows.

| | | | ASSEMBLER | |
MODE	CODE	OPERATION	OP CODE	OPERAND
1	000	(rd) ← (rd) + (rs) + (C)	ADD	rd, rs
2	001	(rd) ← (rd) + ((rs)) + (C)	ADD	rd, (rs)
3	010	((rd)) ← ((rd)) + (rs) + (C)	ADD	(rd), rs
4	011	((rd)) ← ((rd)) + ((rs)) + (C)	ADD	(rd), (rs)
5	100	((r13) + (rd)) ← ((r13) + (rd)) + ((r13) + (rs)) + (C)	ADD	Indexed (rd,rs)
6	101	(rd) ← (rd) + (Word2) + (C)	ADD	rd, number in Word2
7	110	((Word2)) ← ((Word 2)) + (rs) + (C)	ADD	(address in Word2), rs
8	111	(rd) ← (rd) + ((Word2)) + (C)	ADD	rd, (address in Word2)

All binary arithmetic is two's complement. The microprocessor has a BCD mode that, when selected by an instruction, will treat register contents as packed BCD numbers (4 BCD numbers/16 bits) in operations. The MULTIPLY and DIVIDE instructions treat numbers as either positive binary numbers or unsigned BCD numbers. The MULTIPLY instruction multiplies two 16-bit binary or two 4-digit BCD numbers together and produces a 32-bit binary or 8-digit BCD result. The DIVIDE instruction divides a positive 32-bit binary or unsigned 8-digit BCD number by a 16-bit or 4-digit BCD number and produces a 16-bit or 4-digit quotient and a 16-bit or 4-digit remainder. The instructions are presented in detail in functional groups, in short form in functional groups, and alphabetically. Explanation of assembly language coding of the instruction set along with specific examples of its use are given in Chapter 7.

6.4.5 Detailed Instruction Set Description for the Microprocessor Design

Arithmetic

ADD WITH CARRY

ADD rd,rs | 0 | 0 | 0 | 0 | 1 | X | X | X | S | S | S | S | D | D | D | D |

ADDRESSING MODES

1	000	$(rd) \leftarrow (rd) + (rs) + (C)$
2	001	$(rd) \leftarrow (rd) + ((rs)) + (C)$
3	010	$((rd)) \leftarrow ((rd)) + (rs) + (C)$
4	011	$((rd)) \leftarrow ((rd)) + ((rs)) + (C)$
5	100	$((r13) + (rd)) \leftarrow ((r13) + (rd)) + ((r13) + (rs)) + (C)$
6	101	$(rd) \leftarrow (rd) + (Word2) + (C)$
7	110	$((Word2)) \leftarrow ((Word2)) + (rs) + (C)$
8	111	$(rd) \leftarrow (rd) + ((Word2)) + (C)$

Status bits affected: Z, N, P, C, V

SUBTRACT WITH BORROW

SUB rd, rs   `0 0 0 1 0 X X X S S S S D D D D`

$(rd) \leftarrow (rd) - (rs) - (C)$

Modes: ALL
Status bits: Z, N, P, C, V

MULTIPLY

MUL rd, rs   `0 0 0 1 1 X X X S S S S D D D D`

High product (rd)
Low product (r[d+1]) $\Big\} \leftarrow (rd) * (rs)$

NOTE: r[d+1] denotes next register number following rd, that is, if rd = r10, r[d+1] = r11.

Modes: ALL
Status bits: Z, P

DIVIDE

DIV rd, rs   `0 0 1 0 0 X X X S S S S D D D D`

Quotient: (rd)
Remainder: (r[d+1]) $\Big\} \leftarrow \dfrac{(rd)*[10{,}000_{10} \text{ or } 65{,}536_{10}] + (r[d+1])}{(rs)}$

Modes: ALL
Status bits: Z, V, P

INCREMENT

INC rd, rs

0	0	1	0	1	X	X	X	S	S	S	S	D	D	D	D

$(rd) \leftarrow (rs) + 1$
Modes: ALL
Status bits: Z, N, P, C, V

DECREMENT

DEC rd, rs

0	0	1	1	0	X	X	X	S	S	S	S	D	D	D	D

$(rd) \leftarrow (rs) - 1$
Modes: ALL
Status bits: Z, N, P, C, V

TWO's COMPLEMENT

TWC rd, rs

0	0	1	1	1	X	X	X	S	S	S	S	D	D	D	D

$(rd) \leftarrow 2^{16} - (rs)$
Modes: ALL
Status bits: Z, N, P, C, V

ONE's COMPLEMENT

ONC rd, rs

0	1	0	0	0	X	X	X	S	S	S	S	D	D	D	D

$(rd) \leftarrow 2^{16} - 1 - (rs)$
Modes: ALL
Status bits: Z, N, P, C, V

Logical

AND

AND rd, rs

0	1	0	0	1	X	X	X	S	S	S	S	D	D	D	D

$(rd) \leftarrow (rs) \text{ AND } (rd)$
Modes: ALL
Status bits: AB, AR, E, Z, N, P

OR

ORR rd, rs   0 1 0 1 0 X X X S S S S D D D D

(rd) ← (rs) OR (rd)
Modes: ALL
Status bits: AB, AR, E, Z, N, P

EXCLUSIVE OR

XOR rd, rs   0 1 0 1 1 X X X S S S S D D D D

(rd) ← (rs) XOR (rd)
Modes: ALL
Status bits: AB, AR, E, Z, N, P

ROTATE LEFT N BITS THROUGH CARRY

RRL rd, rs   0 1 1 0 0 X X X S S S S D D D D

(rd) ← (rd) Shifted left (rs) bits through Carry

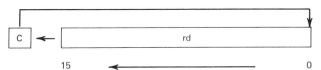

NOTE: Only lower 4 bits of (rs) used to specify N.
Modes: ALL
Status bits: C, P

ROTATE RIGHT N BITS THROUGH CARRY

RRR rd, rs   0 1 1 0 1 X X X S S S S D D D D

(rd) ← (rd) Shifted right (rs) bits through Carry

NOTE: Only lower 4 bits of (rs) used to specify N.
Modes: ALL
Status bits: C, P

ROTATE LEFT N BITS

ROL rd, rs `0 1 1 1 0 X X X S S S S D D D D`

(rd) ← (rd) Shifted left (rs) bits; last bit rotated also retained in C

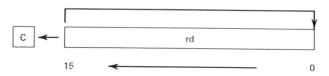

NOTE: Only lower 4 bits of (rs) used to specify N.
Modes: ALL
Status bits: C, P

ROTATE RIGHT N BITS

ROR rd, rs `0 1 1 1 1 X X X S S S S D D D D`

(rd) ← (rd) Shifted right (rs) bits; last bit rotated also retained in C

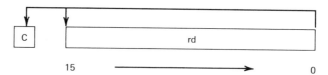

NOTE: Only lower 4 bits of (rs) used to specify N.
Modes: ALL
Status bits: C, P

COMPARE ARITHMETIC

CPA rd, rs `1 0 0 1 0 X X X S S S S D D D D`

(rd) − (rs)
Modes: ALL
Status bits: AR, E

COMPARE LOGICAL

CPL rd, rs `1 0 0 1 1 X X X S S S S D D D D`

(rd) Logically compared to (rs)
Modes: ALL
Status bits: AB, E

Data Transfer

MOVE DATA

MOV rd, rs | 1 | 0 | 0 | 0 | 0 | X | X | X | S | S | S | S | D | D | D | D |

   (rd) ← (rs)
Modes: ALL
Status bits: NONE

EXCHANGE DATA

EXH rd, rs | 1 | 0 | 0 | 0 | 1 | X | X | X | S | S | S | S | D | D | D | D |

   (rd) ↔ (rs)
Modes: 1, 2, 3, 4, 5, 7, 8
Status bits: NONE

LOAD STATUS WORD

LSW rs | 1 | 1 | 1 | 1 | 1 | X | X | X | S | S | S | S | 0 | 0 | 0 | 0 |

   (SW) ← (rs)
Modes: 1, 2, 6, 8
Status bits: ALL

LOAD POINTER REGISTER

LPR rs | 1 | 1 | 1 | 1 | 1 | X | X | X | S | S | S | S | 0 | 0 | 0 | 1 |

   (PR) ← $b_2b_1b_0$ of (rs)
Modes: 1, 2, 6, 8
Status bits: NONE

LOAD USAGE WORD

LUW rs | 1 | 1 | 1 | 1 | 1 | X | X | X | S | S | S | S | 0 | 0 | 1 | 0 |

   (UW) ← (rs)
Modes: 1, 2, 6, 8
Status bits: NONE

GET STATUS WORD

GSW rd | 1 | 1 | 1 | 1 | 1 | X | X | X | D | D | D | D | 0 | 0 | 1 | 1 |

   (rd) ← (SW)
Modes: 1, 3, 7
Status bits: NONE

GET USAGE WORD

GUW rd ⟦1|1|1|1|1|X|X|X|D|D|D|D|0|1|0|0⟧

(rd) ← (UW)
Modes: 1, 3, 7
Status bits: NONE

EXCHANGE STATUS WORD

XSW rd ⟦1|1|1|1|1|X|X|X|D|D|D|D|0|1|0|1⟧

(rd) ↔ (SW)
Modes: 1, 3, 7
Status bits: ALL

EXCHANGE USAGE WORD

XUW rd ⟦1|1|1|1|1|X|X|X|D|D|D|D|0|1|1|0⟧

(rd) ↔ (UW)
Modes: 1, 3, 7
Status bits: ALL

MOVE TO PREVIOUS BANK

MTP rd, rs ⟦1|1|1|0|1|X|X|X|S|S|S|S|D|D|D|D⟧

(Old rd) ← (Current rs)
Modes: ALL
Status bits: NONE

MOVE FROM PREVIOUS BANK

MFP rd, rs ⟦1|1|1|1|0|X|X|X|S|S|S|S|D|D|D|D⟧

(Current rd) ← (Old rs)
Modes: ALL
Status bits: NONE

Branch

JUMP UNCONDITIONAL

JUN rd | 1 | 0 | 1 | 0 | 1 | X | X | X | — | — | — | — | D | D | D | D |

(PC) ← NEWPC (Dependent on Mode)

	MODE	NEWPC
1	000	(PC) ← (PC) + (rd)
2	001	(PC) ← (rd)
3	010	(PC) ← (PC) + ((rd))
4	011	(PC) ← ((rd))
5	100	(PC) ← (PC) + ((r13) + (rd))
6	101	(PC) ← (Word2)
7	110	(PC) ← (PC) + (Word2)
8	111	(PC) ← ((Word 2))

Status bits: NONE

JUMP CONDITIONAL

J—D | 1 | 0 | 1 | 0 | 0 | X | X | X | d | d | d | d | d | d | d | d |

If XXX is TRUE then (PC) ← (PC) + dddddddd (Relative +127, −128 if dddddddd is 2's complement); otherwise (PC) ← (PC) + 1

MODE	XXX	DESCRIPTION	MNEMONIC
1	000	JUMP ON EQUAL	JME D
2	001	JUMP ON LESS THAN	JAL D
3	010	JUMP ON ZERO	JRZ D
4	011	JUMP ON NEGATIVE	JRN D
5	100	JUMP ON PARITY	JOP D
6	101	JUMP ON FLAG	JFL D
7	110	JUMP ON CARRY	JCA D
8	111	JUMP ON OVERFLOW	JOV D

Status bits: NONE

JUMP CONDITIONAL (Inverted)

JN—D | 1 | 0 | 1 | 1 | 0 | X | X | X | d | d | d | d | d | d | d | d |

If XXX is NOT TRUE then (PC) ← (PC) + dddddddd (Relative +127, −128 if dddddddd is 2's complement): Otherwise (PC) ← (PC) + 1

MODE	XXX	DESCRIPTION	MNEMONIC
1	000	JUMP ON NOT EQUAL	JNE D
2	001	JUMP ON NOT LESS THAN	JNL D
3	010	JUMP ON NOT ZERO	JNZ D
4	011	JUMP ON NOT NEGATIVE	JNN D
5	100	JUMP ON NOT PARITY	JNP D
6	101	JUMP ON NOT FLAG	JNF D
7	110	JUMP ON NOT CARRY	JNC D
8	111	JUMP ON NOT OVERFLOW	JNO D

Status bits: NONE

JUMP TO SUBROUTINE

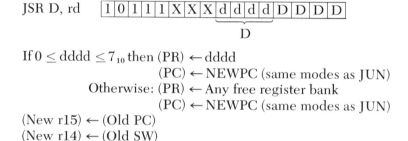

JSR D, rd

$$\boxed{1\,|\,0\,|\,1\,|\,1\,|\,1\,|\,X\,|\,X\,|\,X\,|\,\underbrace{d\,|\,d\,|\,d\,|\,d}\,|\,D\,|\,D\,|\,D\,|\,D}$$
$$D$$

If $0 \leq dddd \leq 7_{10}$ then (PR) ← dddd
$\qquad\qquad\qquad$ (PC) ← NEWPC (same modes as JUN)
$\qquad$ Otherwise: (PR) ← Any free register bank
$\qquad\qquad\qquad$ (PC) ← NEWPC (same modes as JUN)
(New r15) ← (Old PC)
(New r14) ← (Old SW)

NOTE: (OldSW) contains (Old PR). (UW) are also updated. If no free banks are available and the IF interrupt is enabled, an interrupt will occur to permit bank register transfer to external RAM, if desired.

Status bits: NONE

RETURN UNCONDITIONAL

RUN

$$\boxed{0\,|\,0\,|\,0\,|\,0\,|\,0\,|\,-\,|\,-\,|\,-\,|\,-\,|\,-\,|\,-\,|\,-\,|\,0\,|\,0\,|\,1\,|\,1}$$

(SW) ← (r14)
(PC) ← (r15)
Status bits: NONE

If the Current (Old) register bank was saved to memory (according to (UW)), and if the IF interrupt is enabled, an interrupt will occur to permit data transfer from external RAM back to on-chip bank registers.

RETURN CONDITIONAL

R__ | 0 | 0 | 0 | 0 | 0 | X | X | X | — | — | — | — | 0 | 0 | 1 | 0 |

If XXX is TRUE then return (as in RUN)
Otherwise (PC) ← (PC) + 1
XXX is defined as in J__ as are variable mnemonic names
Status bits: NONE

RETURN CONDITIONAL (Inverted)

RN__ | 0 | 0 | 0 | 0 | 0 | X | X | X | — | — | — | — | 0 | 1 | 1 | 0 |

If XXX is NOT TRUE then return (as in RUN)
Otherwise (PC) ← (PC) + 1
XXX is defined as in JN__ as are variable mnemonic names
Status bits: NONE

INCREMENT AND JUMP ON NOT ZERO RESULT

INJ rd, rs | 1 | 1 | 0 | 0 | 0 | X | X | X | S | S | S | S | D | D | D | D |

	MODE	OPERATION	(PC) ON NOT ZERO RESULT
1	000	(rs) ← (rs) + 1	(PC) ← (PC) + (rd)
2	001	(rs) ← (rs) + 1	(PC) ← (rd)
3	010	(rs) ← (rs) + 1	(PC) ← (PC) + (Word2)
4	011	(rs) ← (rs) + 1	(PC) ← (Word2)
5	100	((rs)) ← ((rs)) + 1	(PC) ← (PC) + (rd)
6	101	((rs)) ← ((rs)) + 1	(PC) ← (rd)
7	110	((rs)) ← ((rs)) + 1	(PC) ← (PC) + (Word2)
8	111	((rs)) ← ((rs)) + 1	(PC) ← (Word2)

Status bits: Z, N, P, C, V

DECREMENT AND JUMP ON NOT ZERO RESULT

DEJ rd, rs | 1 | 1 | 0 | 0 | 1 | X | X | X | S | S | S | S | D | D | D | D |

Modes: Identical with INJ except: (rs) ← (rs) − 1 for modes 1–4 and ((rs)) ← ((rs)) − 1 for modes 5–8
Status bits: Z, N, P, C, V

SOFTWARE INTERRUPT

SFI D

$$\underbrace{}_{D}$$

$(PC) \leftarrow (F_{16})$
If $0 \leq dddd \leq 7$ then $(PR) \leftarrow dddd$
Otherwise $(PR) \leftarrow$ any free register bank
$(New\ r15) \leftarrow (Old\ PC)$
$(New\ r14) \leftarrow (Old\ SW)$
Modes: NONE
Status bits: NONE

Control

CONTROL

CTR BIPQF

| 1 | 1 | 1 | 1 | 1 | B | I | P | Q | F | — | — | 1 | 0 | 0 | 0 |

If B = 1 then binary mode is selected;
otherwise decimal mode is selected.

If I = 1 then allow software interrupt;
otherwise disallow software interrupt.
If P, Q, F = 1 then allow interrupts IP, IQ, and/or IF;
otherwise disable interrupts IP, IQ, and/or IF.
EXAMPLE: CTR 01001 would:
     Put processor in decimal mode, allow SFI
interrupt, ignore IP and IQ interrupts, and allow
IF interrupts.

Modes: NONE
Status bits: B, IP, IQ, IF

NO OPERATION

NOP

| 0 | 0 | 0 | 0 | 0 | 0 | 0 | 0 | 0 | 0 | 0 | 0 | 0 | 0 | 0 | 0 |

Mode: NONE
Status bits: NONE

WAIT FOR INTERRUPT

WAT

| 0 | 0 | 0 | 0 | 0 | 0 | 0 | 0 | 0 | 0 | 0 | 0 | 0 | 0 | 0 | 1 |

Mode: NONE
Status bits: NONE

Input/Output

INPUT DATA

INP   rd, rs | 1 | 1 | 0 | 1 | 0 | X | X | X | S | S | S | S | D | D | D | D |

Modes: ALL
Status bits: NONE

NOTE: Identical to MOV, but also places $\overline{IN}$ line of microprocessor in low state.

OUTPUT DATA

OUT   rd, rs | 1 | 1 | 0 | 1 | 1 | X | X | X | S | S | S | S | D | D | D | D |

Modes: ALL
Status bits: NONE

NOTE: Identical to MOV, but also places $\overline{OUT}$ line of microprocessor in low state.

AND DATA BUS DURING I/O

ANB   rs, IO | 0 | 0 | 0 | 0 | 0 | — | I | O | S | S | S | S | 0 | 1 | 0 | 0 |

Modes: ALL
Status bits: NONE

If I = 1 then AND data bus with (rs) during INPUT
If O = 1 then AND data bus with (rs) during OUTPUT
(AND word in rs is stored internal to the microprocessor. Thus, once the AND mask is specified by (rs), (rs) can be changed and mask pattern will still be retained until modified by another ANB instruction.)

XOR DATA BUS DURING I/O

XOB   rs, IO | 0 | 0 | 0 | 0 | 0 | — | I | O | S | S | S | S | 0 | 1 | 0 | 1 |

If I = 1 then XOR data with (rs) on INPUT
If O = 1 then XOR data with (rs) on OUTPUT
(XOR word in rs is stored internal to the microprocessor and, similar to ANB instruction, (rs) can be altered after this instruction and XOR mask pattern will be retained until changed by another XOB instruction.)

Timer/Counter

LOAD TIMER WORD

LTW   rs

1	1	1	1	1	X	X	X	S	S	S	S	1	0	0	1

(TW) ← (rs)
Modes: 1, 2, 6, 8
Status bits: NONE

LOAD COUNTER WORD

LCW   rs

1	1	1	1	1	X	X	X	S	S	S	S	1	0	1	0

(CW) ← (rs)
Modes 1, 2, 6, 8
Status bits: NONE

GET TIMER WORD

GTW   rd

1	1	1	1	1	X	X	X	S	S	S	S	1	0	1	1

(rd) ← (TW)
Modes: 1, 3, 7
Status bits: NONE

GET COUNTER WORD

GCW   rd

1	1	1	1	1	X	X	X	S	S	S	S	1	1	0	0

(rd) ← (CW)
Modes; 1, 3, 7
Status bits: NONE

CONTROL TIMER/COUNTER

CTC   D

1	1	1	1	1	d	d	d	d	d	d	d	1	1	0	1

D

If $ddddddd_2 < 1000000_2$ then timer speed = $1/40 \times$ system clock/
[dddddd + 1] where the dddddd bits in the brackets exclude msb
of D.

Otherwise: Lower 2 bits of ddddddd specify:

00	No operation
01	Start timer counting up (using divided system clock)
10	Start timer counting down (using divided system clock)
11	Stop timer

Next higher 2 bits of dddddddd specify:

00	No operation
01	Start counter up (counting external input pulses)
10	Start counter down (counting external input pulses)
11	Stop counter

Next higher 2 bits of dddddddd specify:

00	No timer/counter interrupts
01	Allow timer interrupt
10	Allow counter interrupt
11	Allow both interrupts

Status bits: NONE

User Operations

| 0 | 0 | 0 | 0 | — | — | — | d | d | d | d | D | D | D | D |

NEA
NEB
NEC
NED
NEE

DDDD = A,B,C,D or E (Hexadecimal) selects instructions NEA through NEE

$(PC) \leftarrow (DDDD)$

If $0 \le dddd \le 7_{10}$ then $(PR) \leftarrow dddd$
Otherwise: $(PR) \leftarrow$ any free register bank
(New r15) $\leftarrow$ (Old PC)
(New r14) $\leftarrow$ (Old SW)
Modes: NONE
Status bits: NONE

6.4.6   Listing of Instructions by Functional Groupings

ARITHMETIC

ADD	rd, rs
SUB	rd, rs
MUL	rd, rs
DIV	rd, rs
INC	rd, rs
DEC	rd, rs
TWC	rd, rs
ONC	rd, rs

LOGICAL

AND	rd, rs
ORR	rd, rs
XOR	rd, rs
RRL	rd, rs
RRR	rd, rs
ROL	rd, rs
ROR	rd, rs
CPA	rd, rs
CPL	rd, rs

DATA TRANSFER

MOV	rd, rs
EXH	rd, rs
LPR	rs
LSW	rs
LUW	rs
GSW	rd
GUW	rd
XSW	rd
XUW	rd
MTP	rd, rs
MFP	rd, rs

BRANCH

JUN	rd
J__ __	D
JN__	D
JSR	D, rd
RUN	
R__ __	
RN__	
INJ	rd, rs
DEJ	rd, rs
SFI	D

CONTROL

CTR	BIPQF
NOP	
WAT	

INPUT/OUTPUT

INP	rd, rs
OUT	rd, rs
ANB	rs, IO
XOB	rs, IO

TIMER/COUNTER

LTW	rs
LCW	rs
GTW	rd
GCW	rd
CTC	D

USER OPERATIONS

NEA, NEB, NEC, NED, NEE

6.4.7 Alphabetical Listing of Instructions and Hexadecimal Tabulation of Instructions

ALPHABETICAL GROUPING OF INSTRUCTIONS

ADD	rd,rs	NEA	
ANB	rs, IO	NEB	
AND	rd, rs	NEC	
CPA	rd,rs	NED	
CPL	rd, rs	NEE	
CTC	D	NOP	
CTR	BIPQF	ONC	rd, rs
DEC	rd, rs	ORR	rd, rs
DEJ	rd, rs	OUT	rd, rs
DIV	rd, rs	R___	
EXH	rd, rs	RN__	
GCW	rd	ROL	rd, rs
GSW	rd	ROR	rd, rs
GTW	rd	RRL	rd, rs
GUW	rd	RRR	rd, rs
INC	rd, rs	RUN	
INJ	rd, rs	SFI	D
INP	rd, rs	SUB	rd, rs
J__ __	D	TWC	rd, rs
JN__	D	WAT	
JSR	D, rd	XOB	rs, IO
JUN	rd	XOR	rd, rs
LCW	rs	XSW	rd
LPR	rs	XUW	rd
LSW	rs		
LTW	rs		
LUW	rs		
MFP	rd, rs		
MOV	rd, rs		
MTP	rd, rs		
MUL	rd, rs		

HEXADECIMAL TABULATION OF INSTRUCTIONS

INSTRUCTION WORD FORMAT

15 11 10 8 7 4 3 0				
OP	MD	S	D	
0	0	0	0	NOP
0	0	0	1	WAT
0	X	0	2	R___
0	0	0	3	RUN
0	X	X	4	ANB
0	X	X	5	XOB
0	X	0	6	RN_
0	X	X	7	
0	X	X	8	
0	X	X	9	
0	0	X	A	NEA
0	0	X	B	NEB
0	0	X	C	NEC
0	0	X	D	NED
0	0	X	E	NEE
0	X	X	F	
1	X	X	X	ADD
2	X	X	X	SUB
3	X	X	X	MUL
4	X	X	X	DIV
5	X	X	X	INC
6	X	X	X	DEC
7	X	X	X	TWC
8	X	X	X	ONC
9	X	X	X	AND
A	X	X	X	ORR
B	X	X	X	XOR
C	X	X	X	RRL
D	X	X	X	RRR
E	X	X	X	ROL
F	X	X	X	ROR

15 11 10 8 7 4 3 0				
OP	MD	S	D	
10	X	X	X	MOV
11	X	X	X	EXH
12	X	X	X	CPA
13	X	X	X	CPL
14	X	X	X	J___
15	X	X	X	JUN
16	X	X	X	JN_
17	X	X	X	JSR
18	X	X	X	INJ
19	X	X	X	DEJ
1A	X	X	X	INP
1B	X	X	X	OUT
1C	X	X	X	
1D	X	X	X	MTP
1E	X	X	X	MFP
1F	X	X	0	LSW
1F	X	X	1	LPR
1F	X	X	2	LUW
1F	X	X	3	GSW
1F	X	X	4	GUW
1F	X	X	5	XSW
1F	X	X	6	XUN
1F	X	X	7	SFI
1F	X	X	8	CTR
1F	X	X	9	LTW
1F	X	X	A	LCW
1F	X	X	B	GTW
1F	X	X	C	GCW
1F	X	X	D	CTC
1F	X	X	E	
1F	X	X	F	

6.5 BIT-SLICE ARCHITECTURE

An architecture used primarily with Schottky bipolar microprocessors is the bit-slice architecture. Since the density of bipolar processing is less than that of MOS and the associated power dissipation is higher, most Schottky bipolar microprocessors are implemented on multiple rather than single chips. A few single chip Shottky bipolar microprocessors are available, however, and are designed mainly for use as controllers (microcontrollers). The I²L bipolar process has made possible true single chip bipolar microprocessors. If the microprocessor is to be divided into a number of chips, it would be desirable to have as few different types of chips as possible. The approach taken is to "cut" an n-bit-wide slice through a conventional microprocessor chip. In most cases $n = 2$ or 4. A typical n-bit slice of a processor or Register Arithmetic Logic Unit (RALU) as it is sometimes called, is shown in Figure 6.15. By concatenating these bit slices, we can assemble a microprocessor of any reasonable word length.

In order to control the instruction fetches and execution, another chip or chips is required. Since the Schottky bipolar processor speed can take advantage of bipolar memories, and space requirements of random sequential control logic can be reduced by using simpler ROM control, bit-slice processors are usually microprogrammable. A microprogrammable microprocessor is one whose control signals necessary to fetch and execute an instruction are generated by the execution of a set of *microinstructions* in user-definable *control memory*, usually ROM. The instructions in the microprocessor instruction set are referred to as *macroinstructions* relative to the microinstructions used to execute the macroinstruction. If, for example, an ADD instruction were to be executed, control signals would have to be sent in a specific sequence to the logic elements in the microprocessor (ALU, PC, Memory Address Register, Accumulator, etc.) in order to implement the instruction fetch and execution. These control signals could be generated by sequential logic circuits or, in a microprogrammed processor, by the execution of a sequence of microinstructions stored in a separate control memory. Thus, address generation, fetching, and, in some cases, decoding of the microinstruction must be accomplished in a manner similar to that for the macroinstruction. Also, conditional branches on status flags, unconditional branches, and subroutine calls and returns can take place in the microprogram. Usually, all of these functions are performed by a single chip, the microprogram control chip, in the bit-slice microprocessor. The block diagram of a microprogram control chip is illustrated in Figure 6.16.

If a single chip microprogram controller is utilized in a bit-slice system, the number of words of microprogram control memory is fixed by the number of bits in the microprogram address bus. Some bit-slice microprocessors permit multiple microprogram controllers to be used to expand the capacity of control memory. In either case, the number of bits, m, in a microprogram instruction word is usually fixed and is independent of the number of control or processor chips. A 16-bit microcomputer comprised of a single microprogram controller, four 4-bit-wide processor sections, and ROM control memory is given in Figure 6.17.

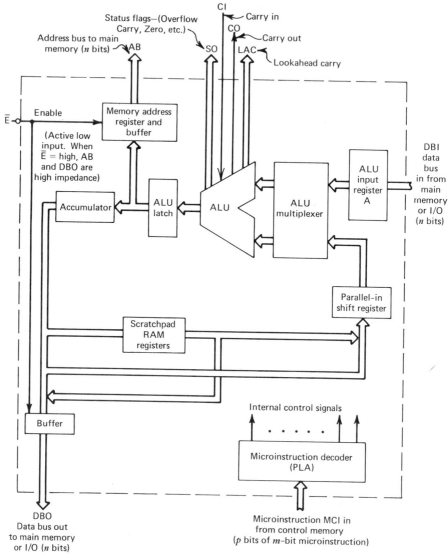

FIGURE 6.15 Typical n-bit-slice processor section.

Note in Figure 6.17 that the data buses to and from macroinstruction memory are built up to 16 bits from the 4 bits of each processor section. Also of importance is that the instruction word fetched from microprogram control memory is split into different groups. In this example, they are the microinstruction bits (MCI) connected in common to provide the microin-

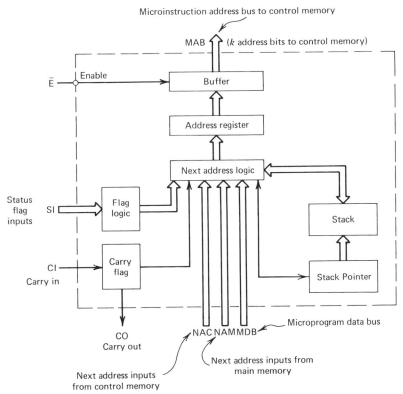

FIGURE 6.16 Microprogram control chip.

struction op code to all processing sections, the microprogram data bus bits (MDB) running to the microprogram control chip, and the next address control inputs (NAC) to the microprogram control chip. The lookahead carry outputs of the processing section are fed into a carry lookahead combinational logic chip to reduce carry propagation delay from the first to the last processing section.

The microprogram instruction length is usually large compared to the macroinstruction length and may range from 16 to 64 bits or larger. A typical 24-bit format might be:

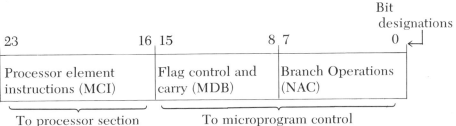

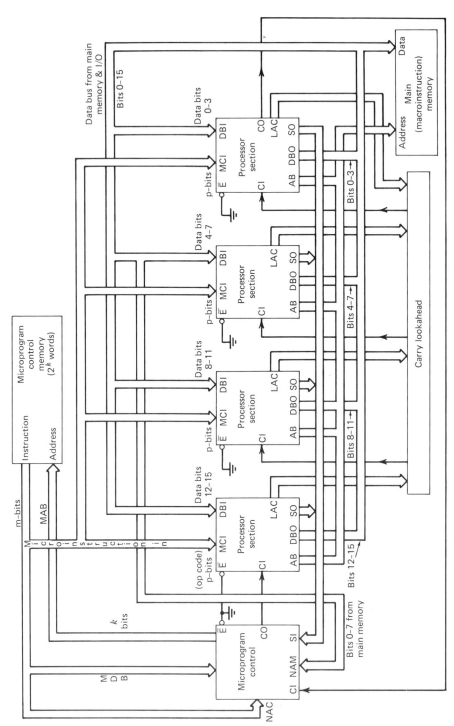

FIGURE 6.17 Bit-slice microprogrammed microcomputer.

The functions of the microprogram control in conjunction with the processor section are to fetch the microinstructions from microprogram memory, to decode and interpret status, carry, main memory next address, and control memory next address information to determine next microinstruction address, and to control microprogram subroutine calls and interrupts. The FLAG CONTROL AND CARRY (MDB) bits of the microinstruction test and control the carry and flag inputs to the microprogram control and the BRANCH OPERATIONS (NAC) bits are branch control and specification bits which affect the microinstruction execution sequence. The bit pattern (MCI) routed to the processor section is used to control operations (*microoperations*) and data paths in this section. If each bit of this MCI pattern is used to control an operation or data path, a large number of bits in the microinstruction may be required. This type of microprogramming, which results in simpler control circuitry but long word lengths, is called *horizontal microprogramming*. If some of the control signals in the processor section are mutually exclusive (only one is active at a time), they can be decoded by a 1 of N decoder that will drastically reduce the number of bits in the microinstruction. The decoder is used in the processor section of Figure 6.15 and is usually a Programmable Logic Array (PLA). This approach, however, results in more complex circuitry in the processor section and is termed *vertical microprogramming*. As the cost of ROM decreases, one may see a trend toward horizontal microprogramming in order to eliminate the decoding circuitry.

Microinstruction cycle times for Schottky bipolar microprocessors are on the order of 100 nsec or less. Further, microinstructions can perform a number of operations in one code, such as reading data from a location in RAM to the accumulator, AND'ing these data with a mask pattern, and writing the AND'ed data back to another location in RAM. The following sequence illustrates the relationship between macroinstruction and microinstruction execution.

MACROINSTRUCTION A (fetched from main memory)
↓
OP CODE of MACROINSTRUCTION A indicates start of microinstruction routine
↓
Microinstructions to implement macroinstruction A are executed from control memory
↓
MACROINSTRUCTION B (fetched from main memory)
↓
and so on

A further extension of microprogramming, called *nanoprogramming,* is also used in some computers, such as the Nanodata QM-1. In nanoprogramming, the microinstruction addresses a lower level *nanostore,* which contains *nanoinstructions.* These nanoinstructions are, effectively, subroutines called by the microinstructions. Schematically, the nanoprogrammed machine instruction sequence may appears as:

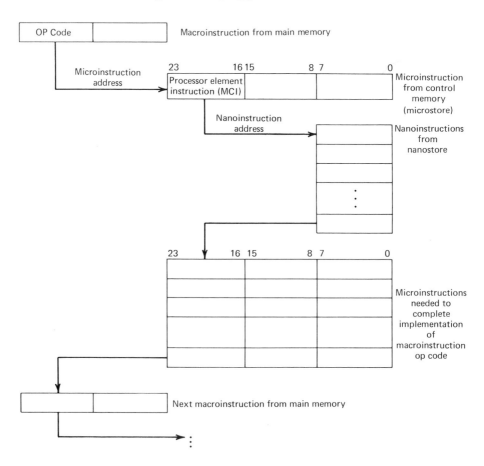

Many macroinstructions may consist of only one or two microinstruction cycles and can, therefore, provide processsng capability 5 to 20 times faster than typical NMOS microprocessor instructions. Also, it is possible for the user to write his own microinstruction sequence or microprogram that will be executed when a newly defined OP code is fetched from main memory. Thus, new instructions can be defined by the user. Consider, for example, the case where, in a process control application, it is necessary to read data from a series of transducers, multiply these data by a constant, and compare the resulting number to a reference number stored in memory. If those operations were to be performed many times, a specialized microprogram could be written to perform those tasks, stored in control memory, and executed every time a newly defined macroinstruction, say, SAMPLE, were encountered in the main program. The only disadvantage to this approach is that the user is, in effect, defining his own unique instruction set that will not be supported by the microprocessor manufacturer.

Another similar application is to define the instruction set of a microprogrammed microprocessor to execute the instruction set of another microprocessor or minicomputer. The microprogrammed microprocessor or *host* machine is said to *emulate* another microprocessor or *target machine*. In general, programs on the host machine take longer to execute than on the original target machine, but there are exceptions to this rule. A good example of computer emulation is the IBM System 360 series in which some models were microprogrammed to emulate the IBM 709 and other models the IBM 1401. Still another twist is to use RAM for the control memory instead of ROM. This modification allows microprograms to be easily modified or replaced. New features can be added to the microprogram and different microprograms can be read into the control memory when required. In some cases, multiple target mechines can be emulated by one host processor by dynamically changing the control memory. Control memory that can be written into is called *Writable Control Store* (WCS).

In summary, Schottky bipolar microprocessors can provide an order-of-magnitude speed increase over most NMOS microprocessors. On the other hand, they normally are bit-slice devices that require more chips than NMOS to build a microprocessor. Since their speed is comparable to bipolar memories, they are usually microprogrammable devices that give the user the option of defining his own instructions in microprograms at the cost of having to support his own software. Implementing the control memory with Writable Control Store permits the emulation of some target machines and provides for ease of field maintenance and changes.

REFERENCES

1. H.S. Stone, *Introduction to Computer Architecture*, SRA, Chicago, Illinois, 1975.

2. Ivan Flores, *Computer Organization*, Prentice-Hall, Englewood Cliffs, N.J., 1969.

3. *Intel Data Catalog 1977*, Intel Corporation, 1977.

SOFTWARE

Developing a microcomputer system requires skills that normally are supplied by more than one person in minicomputer/large-computer-based projects. Even though there had been some overlap in knowledge and experience between specialists, system hardware and software were designed by hardware and software specialists, respectively, with the interface between them, sometimes, being the most difficult part of the project. The microcomputer, on the other hand, requires the user to perform in both the hardware and software arenas to achieve an efficient, cost-effective design that meets the desired goals.

The approach taken to this integration of skills depends upon the experience and education of the individuals involved. The person with the hardware background tends to be wary of the myriad of programming tools and philosophies thrust upon him by minicomputer or large computer programmers. Over the more than 20 years of attempting to remove the drudgery and chances for error from programming, the software component of the computer industry has developed ingenious and tremendously useful programs that have met these goals. It is not unreasonable, then, for software designers with this background to attempt to bring some of these techniques to the relatively infant microcomputer software field. A problem with direct transfer of medium-to-large-system software philosophies to the microcomputer is that the goals of both systems are not the same. In medium and large computer software development, the goal many times is to produce flexible, general-purpose programs that can be used in a large number of applications, some of which may be significantly different. The computer used normally has a core or semiconductor memory ranging from 64K words up to hundreds of K words and byte-saving is not usually a primary concern. The software packages used by the programmer to reduce development and debugging time require large amounts of memory and usually must be run on IBM 360/370-type installations or large minicomputer systems. A few microcomputer manufacturers have developed software that can be executed on *development systems,* which are minicomputer-like systems built around a microcomputer and peripheral devices.

In contrast to the software development viewpoint just described is that of the hardware designer who would like to consider the microprocessor as just another digital chip in his or her repertoire of digital building blocks. Programming in assembly language mnemonics or even *machine language* (the 1 and 0 patterns representing the instructions) of the microprocessor is not a distasteful task to this individual. In fact, working at this low level of programming for small, logic-oriented tasks is merely a variation of the conventional digital hardware design techniques. Counters, gates, registers, data paths, and so on are controlled by 1's and 0's in programmable memory rather than by hard-wired techniques. From this perspective, mastering large software development packages seems to be an unnecessary solution to a problem that does not exist. Another consideration is that a microcomputer may be used in applications where tens of thousands of identical systems will be produced and minimization of the amount of memory will lead to significant cost savings. Since microcomputer memories are, by their nature, discrete blocks of 256, 1K, 4K, 16K, and other, words, a few words of program may mean the difference between requiring chips for the next incremental memory block or saving this cost, which would be multiplied over thousands of systems.

As with most situations, the correct approach to microprocessor program development is dependent on the application, the hardware and software available, and the expertise of the designer. Clearly, a microprocessor application requiring 8K bytes of software would be impractical to develop by directly specifying the 1's and 0's in every byte of program memory. On the other hand, a microprocessor utilized in a logic replacement function with only 50 bytes of program memory is easily implemented at the 1 and 0 level using hexadecimal representation, although this may not be the most desirable method.

7.1 ASSEMBLY LANGUAGE AND ASSEMBLERS

The mnemonics such as ADD, SUB, and MOV of a microprocessor are called its *assembly language.* In assembly language, an instruction mnemonic corresponds one-for-one to the machine language representation of the instruction. Thus, a program with 10 assembly language statements will normally correspond to a machine language program with 10 machine statements. Instead of attempting to write the program in 1 and 0 patterns of machine language, however, we find that the assembly language permits the program to be developed using symbols that correspond to the operation being performed by the instruction. A conversion from the mnemonic to the machine code is still required for program execution on the microprocessor, however, and this is performed by another program called an *assembler.* The assembler takes the program in mnemonic form (the *source* program) and produces a program in machine language form (the *object* program) that can be run on the microcomputer. If there is an adequate amount of memory in the microcomputer system itself to load and execute the assembler object program (approximately 4K to 8K words), the microcomputer can be used to assemble source programs. This type of assembler is referred to as a *resident assembler.* If the assembler is run on another computer such as a minicomputer, the assembler is called a *cross assembler.* Cross assemblers that can run on popular minicomputers and IBM

360/370 series computers are available from most microcomputer manufacturers. Cross assemblers usually have more features than resident assemblers since they are not restricted by memory availability as are most
resident assemblers.

If the location of every instruction and memory reference in the assembly language program must be specified by an absolute address, the
assembler is referred to as an *absolute assembler*. Thus, the resulting machine language program must reside in a particular area of RAM or ROM
and cannot be loaded into another group of locations. Alternately, a *relocatable assembler* generates output object code that is not address dependent. Rather, the location of the particular block of memory is deferred
until the program is loaded by another program called the *loader*. Therefore the program may reside at any available memory block.

7.1.1 Assembler Description

In order to use the assembler software to convert the source program in
assembly language mnemonics to object code of the machine, a set of language rules or *syntax* of the assembler must be followed. In most assemblers, each assembly language instruction can be divided into four parts or
fields that the assembler recognizes. Those fields are the *label, op code,
operand*, and *comment* fields. The label field is a provision for identifying
a particular instruction in the program by a name or label. The op code and
operand fields contain the op code and operand of the assembly language
instruction. The comment field is available for inserting comments relative
to a particular instruction for the programmer's use but is not used by the
assembler. Each manufacturer's assembler has specific rules for the com-
position of each of these fields, but some general guidelines will be discussed.

An example of an assembler statement and the associated fields of the
JRZ (JUMP ON RESULT ZERO) instruction of our microprocessor design
is as follows.

CHECK	JRZ	OFF	CHECK TO SEE IF START SWITCH IS OFF
LABEL	OP CODE MNEMONIC	OPERAND	COMMENT

In some assemblers, delimiting characters such as a colon and semicolon
follow the label and operand fields, repectively.

CHECK: JRZ OFF ;CHECK TO SEE IF START SWITCH IS OFF

In the examples in this chapter, the only delimiting character used is the semicolon, to indicate comments.

The fields must be separated by at least one blank space and must be in the order shown above. The label and comment fields are **optional** and may not appear in every line of assembler code. Also, the label fields are limited to a specific number of characters, n. If a label is written with more than n characters, the excess characters will be ignored. For example, if a label field is defined as being four characters long, the labels BUFF1, BUFF2, and BUFF3 will each be interpreted by the assembler as BUFF. Thus, three statements in the assembly language program will have the same label as seen by the assembler.

If the instruction JRZ BUFF2 (jump to location labeled BUFF2 if the result of previous operation is zero) appears in another part of the program, the assembler will read the statement as JRZ BUFF. Since there are now, effectively, three instructions labeled BUFF, there is not a unique destination for the branch caused by the JRZ instruction. The assembler will, therefore, indicate an error of multiple instructions with the same label.

The op code and operand fields are used to specify the instruction to be executed. In the previous example, JRZ is the op code and BUFF2 is the operand. In the instruction set developed in Chapter 6, the operands may be registers in the register bank, 16-bit memory addresses, 16-bit immediate data, 16-bit input/output addresses, timer/counter information, and control bits. The assembler provides for multiple ways to specify the operand. Some of the commonly used means of specification along with examples utilizing the instruction set from Chapter 6 are:

Decimal Constant—D following the number

```
CALC      ADD      r3,1024D   ;ADD 1024₁₀ TO THE CONTENTS OF
                              ;r3 AND DEPOSIT THE SUM IN r3

LABEL    OP CODE   OPERAND              COMMENT
```

Decimal Constant—D following the number: $;ADD\ 1024_{10}$ TO THE CONTENTS OF r3 AND DEPOSIT THE SUM IN r3

Hexadecimal Constant—H following the number

```
NEW      SUB      r5,10FAH   ;SUBTRACT 10FA₁₆ FROM
                             ;CONTENTS OF r5
                             ;AND DEPOSIT DIFFERENCE IN r5
```

;SUBTRACT $10FA_{16}$ FROM ;CONTENTS OF r5 ;AND DEPOSIT DIFFERENCE IN r5

Binary Constant—B following the number

```
REST    AND    r10,0111000111000111B   ;"AND" BINARY NUMBER WITH
                                        ;THE CONTENTS OF r10 AND
                                        ;DEPOSIT RESULT IN r10
```

Octal Constant—O following the number

```
STRT    LWS    047126O    ;LOAD STATUS WORD WITH
                          ;047126₈
```

In the absence of letter following the number, the number is interpreted by the assembler as a decimal number.

ASCII Constant—characters represented in 7-bit format (American Standard Code for Information Interchange—see Table in Appendix D) are represented by enclosing the character in single quotes.

```
TEXT    MOV    r8, 'N'    ;STORE THE BIT PATTERN FOR
                         ;ASCII CHARACTER N IN r8
```

(The contents of register 8 would appear as 0000000001001110 or $004E_{16}$ where $4E_{16}$ is the ASCII representation of the letter N.

Character String—a string of ASCII characters packed as two characters/16-bit word is represented by enclosing the string in double quotes

```
TEXT MOV r8, "IN"   ;STORE THE TWO ASCII CHARACTERS I AND N IN r8.
                    ;THE CONTENTS OF REGISTER 8 WOULD APPEAR
                    ;AS
                    ;494E₁₆ WHERE 49₁₆ AND 4E₁₆ ARE THE ASCII REPRE-
                    ;SENTATIONS OF THE LETTERS I AND N,
                    ;RESPECTIVELY.
                    ;IF MORE THAN TWO 8-BIT ASCII CHARACTERS
                    ;COMPRISE THE STRING, THE CHARACTERS WILL BE
                    ;STORED IN SEQUENCE IN INCREASING AND
                    ;CONSECUTIVE
                    ;REGISTER OR MEMORY LOCATIONS
```

Symbol—character string of 1 to n characters where n is specific to a particular assembler

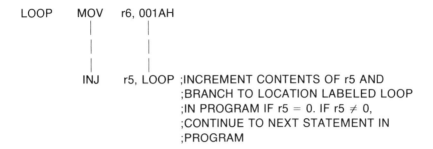

(LOOP is symbol given to address specified by word2 of the INJ instruction).

Expression—an expression can appear in the operand field of the assembly language instruction. The expression will be evaluated by the assembler **prior to** the execution of the object program and converted to a constant for use in the object program. Typical operators and chracters recognized by the assembler and used in expressions are:

+   (add)

−   (subtract)

*   (multiply) usage will distinguish multiply * from * indicating current instruction address (see below)

/   (divide)

**   (exponentiate)

*   or, sometimes, $ (this character is equal to the address of the current instruction)

( )   (parentheses cause expressions contained in them to be evaluated first. For multiple parenthetical expressions, "deepest" parentheses are evaluated first. Parentheses enclosing a register designation or a memory address indicate indirect addressing.)

$$\left.\begin{array}{l} \text{AND} \\ \text{OR} \\ \text{NOT} \\ \text{XOR} \end{array}\right\} \quad \text{(logical operators)}$$

Examples of expressions are:

```
CALC    MOV  r11,(2OD+ 10H)/10B   ;LOAD r11 WITH VALUE OF
                                   ;EXPRESSION
```

(The expression will be evaluated **by the assembler** as $(20_{10} + 10_{16})/10_2$. In all-decimal form, the expression would be $(20 + 16)/2 = 36/2 = 18$. Thus, when the object program is executed, 18_{10} will be loaded into r11).

SUM	ADD	r2, 2**4	;ADD 2^4 or 16_{10} TO THE CONTENTS ;OF r2 AND STORE SUM IN r2
	JRN	*-4	;BRANCH TO LOCATION FOUR ;WORDS ;BEFORE THE FIRST WORD OF ;THIS ;INSTRUCTION
	JRZ	$ + 7	;BRANCH TO LOCATION SEVEN ;WORDS ;PAST THE FIRST WORD OF THIS ;INSTRUCTION
	LPR	07H AND B5H	;LOAD THE POINTER REGISTER ;(PR) ;WITH THE LOGICAL "AND" OF ;07_{16} and $B5_{16}$

(The logical AND, bit by bit, of 07_{16} and $B5_{16}$ is:

$$\begin{array}{ll} 00000111_2 & 07_{16} \\ \underline{10110101_2} & \underline{B5_{16}} \\ 00000101_2 & 05_{16} \end{array}$$

Since the PR is a 3-bit register, the mask provided by 07_{16} insures that no number of more than three bits will be attempted to be loaded into the PR. In this case, the PR would contain 101 after the LPR instruction execution).

Addressing Mode Specification—Since an instruction in our example microcomputer can have up to eight different addressing modes, depending on the value of the three address mode bits in the instruction word, the modes must be distinguished from each other when written in assembly language code. In the first mode, where rd and rs are directly addressed, no special designation is required. In mode 2, the contents of register rs are used in the indirect addressing mode and this is indicated to the assembler by parentheses enclosing rs. The contents of rd are directly addressed and no parentheses are used. Mode 3 utilizes rd in the indirect mode and rs in the direct mode while Mode 4 indirectly addresses memory through both rs and rd. Indexed mode 5 uses r13 as the index register and adds the contents of r13 to the contents of rs and rd to form indirect source and data addresses. If the contents of r13 = 0, mode 5 is functionally equivalent to mode 4. The indexed mode 5 is recognized by the assembler by using a + sign as the first character in the instruction operand. Modes 6, 7, and 8 specify a two word instruction where the second word, word2, is used in direct and indirect addressing. The contents of word2 are directly addressed in mode 6 and used as indirect address pointers in modes 7 and 8. These three modes permit the programmer to specify directly the data or address to be used by the instruction.

In the BRANCH group, the JUMP instructions (JUN, J___ and JN___), two RETURN instructions (R___ and RN___), and the INCREMENT (INJ)/DECREMENT (DEJ) instructions incorporate relative addressing modes. In these modes, the new address in the PC is computed by adding a positive or negative number to the present value of the PC (which is the address of the present instruction +1). Thus, the location to which the program is transferred is calculated *relative* to the value in the PC. The relative mode of addressing is indicated in the assembly language by an asterisk, *, as the first character in the instruction operand. If both relative and indexed addressing are used in the same addressing mode of an instruction [such as mode 5 of the JUN instruction where (PC)←(PC) + ((r13) + (rd)), an * and a + are used in any order as the first characters of the instruction operand.

Examples of the different addressing modes are:

MATH	SUB	(r5), r7	;SUBTRACT THE CONTENTS OF ;REGISTER r7 WITH BORROW FROM ;THE CONTENTS OF THE MEMORY
	(Mode 3)		;ADDRESS POINTED TO BY r5 AND ;DEPOSIT THE DIFFERENCE IN ;ADDRESS POINTED TO BY r5. ;((r5))←((r5))−(r7)−(C)
	SUB	r7, r5	;SUBTRACT THE CONTENTS OF ;REGISTER r5 WITH BORROW FROM
	(Mode 1)		;THE CONTENTS OF REGISTER r7 ;AND DEPOSIT THE DIFFERENCE IN r7 ;(r7)←(r7) — (r5) — (C)
	SUB	+r7, r5	;SUBTRACT WITH BORROW THE CON-;TENTS OF MEMORY LOCATION ;INDIRECTLY

(Mode 5)		;ADDRESSED BY THE SUM OF THE CON- ;TENTS OF REGISTERS r13 and r5 FROM ;THE MEMORY LOCATION INDIRECTLY ;ADDRESSED BY THE SUM OF THE ;CONTENTS OF REGISTERS r13 and r7. ;DEPOSIT THE DIFFERENCE IN MEMORY ;LOCATION INDIRECTLY ADDRESSED BY ;THE SUM OF THE CONTENTS OF r13 and ;r7. ;((r13) + (r7)) ← ((r13) + (r7)) − ;((r13) + (r5)) − (C)
SUB	r5, (AMNT)	;SUBTRACT WITH BORROW THE ;CONTENTS ;OF MEMORY LOCATION INDIRECTLY
(Mode 8)		;ADDRESSED BY WORD2 (REFERRED TO ;AS *AMNT*) FROM THE CONTENTS OF ;REGISTER r5 AND DEPOSIT THE ;DIFFERENCE IN r5. ;(r5) ← (r5) − ((WORD2)) − (C)
SUB	(AMNT), r5	;SUBTRACT WITH BORROW FROM THE ;CONTENTS OF MEMORY LOCATION IN-
(Mode 7)		;DIRECTLY ADDRESSED BY WORD2 (RE- ;FERRED TO AS *AMNT*) THE CONTENTS ;OF REGISTER r5 AND DEPOSIT THE ;DIFFERENCE IN LOCATION INDIRECTLY ;ADDRESSED BY WORD2. ;((AMNT)) ← ((AMNT)) − (r5) − (C)
TEST	JUN +*r3	;JUMP UNCONDITIONAL TO INDEXED ;MEMORY LOCATION (INDICATED BY +) :THAT IS COMPUTED RELATIVE ;(INDICATED
(Mode 5)		;BY *) TO PC. THEREFORE, LOCATION ;TO WHICH JUMP OCCURS IS COMPUTED ;AS (PC) + ((r13) + (r3)).
LOOK	JUN * SAVE	;JUMP UNCONDITIONAL TO ADDRESS ;RELATIVE TO PC (INDICATED BY *). ;ADDRESS IS COMPUTED BY ADD- ;ING CONTENTS OF WORD2 OF INSTRUC- ;TION, CALLED *SAVE,* TO PC. ;(PC) ← (PC) + SAVE
TEST	JOP 50D	;IF PARITY BIT IN SW IS = 1 ;(WHICH INDICATES THAT THE RE- ;SULT OF THE PREVIOUS INSTRUCTION

			;AFFECTING THE PARITY FLAG HAD AN
			;ODD NUMBER OF ONE'S), A BRANCH
			;TO MEMORY LOCATION 50 DECIMAL
			;BEYOND THE PRESENT VALUE OF THE
			;PC WILL OCCUR. NOTE THAT THE
			;PRESENT VALUE OF THE PC IS ALWAYS
			;ONE GREATER THAN THE ADDRESS OF
			;PRESENT INSTRUCTION. IF THE PARITY
			;BIT IN SW = 0 (INDICATING AN EVEN
			;NUMBER OF ONE'S), THEN THE NEXT
			;INSTRUCTION FOLLOWING THE JOP IN-
			;STRUCTION WILL BE EXECUTED.
CHEK	JNF −10		;IF THE FLAG INPUT BIT TO THE
			;MICROPROCESSOR FROM AN EXTERNAL
			;SOURCE IS NOT = 1, (=0), A
			;BRANCH WILL OCCUR TO THE MEMORY
			;LOCATION 10 DECIMAL LOCATIONS LESS
			;(IN NUMERICAL TERMS) THAN THE
			;PRESENT VALUE OF THE PC. IF THE
			;FLAG INPUT LINE IS = 1, THE NEXT
			;INSTRUCTION FOLLOWING THE JNF
			;WILL BE EXECUTED.
GO	JSR	4,CALC	;BRANCH TO SUBROUTINE WHOSE FIRST
			;INSTRUCTION IS AT LOCATION
	(Mode 6		;LABELED *CALC* (ADDRESS OF CALC
	as in JUN)		;CONTAINED IN WORD2 OF THIS
			;INSTRUCTION). REGISTER BANK 4
			;CONTAINING 16 REGISTERS IS
			;DESIGNATED AS NEW "SCRATCH" AREA
			;FOR SUBROUTINE. (PC) ← (WORD2);
			;(PR) ← 4; (new r15) ← (old PC);
			;(new r14) ← (old SW); (UW) updated
GO	JSR	8,CALC	;EXECUTION OF THIS INSTRUCTION IS
	(Mode 6		;IDENTICAL TO THAT OF THE PREVIOUS
	as in JUN)		;EXAMPLE EXCEPT THAT
			;THE OPERAND 8 (NORMALLY ANY NUM-
			;BER FROM 8 TO 15 INCLUSIVE) IN-
			;DICATES TO THE ASSEMBLER THAT THE
			;NEW REGISTER BANK CAN BE ANY FREE
			;REGISTER BANK AS INDICATED BY THE
			;UW. IF THERE ARE NO FREE REGISTER
			;BANKS, THE IF INTERRUPT WILL OCCUR
			;(PROVIDING IT IS ENABLED) WHICH
			;WILL PERMIT THE TRANSFER OF A

	;REGISTER BANK OR BANKS TO
	;EXTERNAL
	;RAM BY SOFTWARE. THIS TRANSFER
	;WILL FREE SOME REGISTER BANKS FOR
	;USE BY THE SUBROUTINE AND/OR
	;SUBSEQUENT EXTERNAL INTERRUPTS
	;OR SUBROUTINE CALLS.
	;(PC) ← (WORD2); (PR) ← FREE REGIS-
	;TER BANK NUMBER, (NEW r15) ←
	;(OLD PC), (NEW r14) ← (OLD SW),
	;(UW) UPDATED.
RUN	;RETURN UNCONDITIONALLY FROM
	;INTERRUPT
	;PROGRAM OR SUBROUTINE TO NEXT IN-
	;STRUCTION TO BE EXECUTED PRIOR TO
	;INTERRUPT OR SUBROUTINE CALL. THE
	;r15
	;OF PRESENT REGISTER BANK CONTAINS
	;OLD PC VALUE AND RESTORES IT TO PC.
	;THE r14 OF PRESENT REGISTER BANK
	;CONTAINS OLD VALUE OF STATUS WORD
	;(WHICH INCLUDES OLD PR VALUE) AND
	;RESTORES IT TO SW AND PR.
	;(PC)←(r15), (SW) ← (r14), PR ALSO
	;RESTORED. IF THE INTERRUPT OR
	;SUBROUTINE CALL THAT CORRESPONDS
	;TO THE
	;RUN INSTRUCTION INITIATED A REGIS-
	;TER BANK TRANSFER TO EXTERNAL
	;RAM, AN IF INTERRUPT WILL BE CAUSED
	;BY
	;THE RUN INSTRUCTION (PROVIDING IT IS
	;ENABLED). THIS IF INTERRUPT WILL
	;PERMIT DATA TRANSFER BACK TO THE
	;CHIP BANK REGISTERS FROM EXTERNAL
	;RAM.
RRN	;THE FUNCTION OF THIS INSTRUCTION
	;IS IDENTICAL TO THAT OF THE PREVIOUS
	;EXAMPLE (RUN) EXCEPT THAT IT WILL
(Mode 4)	;BE EXECUTED ONLY ON THE CONDITION
as in JRN)	;THAT THE RESULT OF THE INSTRUCTION
	;PRECEDING THIS INSTRUCTION IN THE
	;PROGRAM YIELDED A NEGATIVE RESULT.

		;OTHERWISE, THE NEXT INSTRUCTION
		;FOLLOWING THE RRN INSTRUCTION WILL
		;BE EXECUTED. (PC) ← (r15), (SW) ← (r14),
		;and (PR) RESTORED IF RESULT NEGATIVE.
		;OTHERWISE, (PC) ← (PC) + 1.
	SFI 6	;BRANCH TO ROUTINE STARTING AT MEM-
		;ORY ADDRESS CONTAINED IN LOCATION
		;F_{16}.
		;THE ADDRESS CONTAINED IN F_{16} IS
		;USUALLY THE BEGINNING OF A SUBROU-
		;TINE THAT SERVICES THIS SOFTWARE
		;INTERRUPT. EXCEPT FOR THE BRANCH
		;TO THE SPECIFIC MEMORY LOCATION
		;SPECIFIED IN F_{16}, EXECUTION OF THIS
		;INSTRUCTION IS IDENTICAL
		;TO THAT OF THE JSR INTRUCTION
		;IF $0 \leq dddd \leq 7$, (PR) ← ddd, THE 3
		;LEAST SIGNIFICANT BITS OF dddd. IF
		;$8 \leq dddd \leq 15$, (PR) ARE REPLACED BY
		;CODE OF A VACANT REGISTER BANK AS
		;INDICATED IN UW. IF INTERRUPT WILL
		;OCCUR WHEN IT HAS BEEN ENABLED
		;PRIOR TO EXECUTION OF SFI.
	NEA 6	;BRANCH TO ROUTINE WHOSE ADDRESS
		;IS CONTAINED IN MEMORY ADDRESS A_{16}.
		;EXCEPT FOR THE ADDRESS, EXECUTION
		;OF THIS INSTRUCTION IS IDENTICAL
		;TO THAT OF SFI 6 INSTRUCTION
		;EXAMPLE GIVEN PREVIOUSLY. THIS
		;INSTRUCTION,
		;AND INSTRUCTIONS NEB THROUGH NEE
		;WILL BE TREATED AS USER-DEFINED
		;INSTRUCTIONS BY EXECUTING A PRO-
		;GRAM IN A
		;SUBROUTINE THAT IS
		;ACCESSED THROUGH MEMORY
		;LOCATION A_{16} FOR NEA AND LOCATIONS
		;B_{16} THROUGH E_{16} FOR INSTRUCTIONS
		;NEB THROUGH NEE. POINTER REGISTER
		;CONTENTS ARE DEFINED AS IN THE JSR
		;AND SFI INSTRUCTIONS.
SCAN	INP r3, (r9)	;THE CONTENTS OF THE DEVICE OR MEM-
		;ORY LOCATION INDIRECTLY ADDRESSED
		;BY r9 ARE DEPOSITED IN r3,

(Mode 2)		;(r3) ← ((r9)). AN ACTIVE LOW PULSE ;IS PRODUCED ON THE MICRO- ;PROCESSOR ;IN PIN WHEN VALID DATA ARE ASSUMED ;PRESENT ON THE DATA BUS. THE DATA ;DIR PIN IS LOW DURING THIS TIME IN- ;DICATING THAT THE DATA BUS IS IN ;THE INPUT MODE.
SCAN	INP r8, SAVE (Mode 6)	;THE CONTENTS OF THE DEVICE OR MEM- ;ORY LOCATION WHOSE ADDRESS IS IN ;WORD2 (REFERRED TO AS LOCATION ;"SAVE") ARE READ FROM THE DATA BUS ;AND DEPOSITED IN r8, (r8) ← (SAVE). AN ;ACTIVE LOW PULSE IS PRODUCED ON ;THE MICROPROCESSOR IN PIN WHEN ;VALID DATA ARE ASSUMED PRESENT ON ;THE DATA BUS. THE DATA DIR PIN IS ;LOW DURING THIS TIME INDICATING ;THAT THE DATA BUS IS IN THE INPUT ;MODE.
SEND	OUT (r6), (r7) (Mode 4)	;THE CONTENTS OF THE MEMORY LOCA- ;TION INDIRECTLY ADDRESSED BY r7 ARE ;SENT OUT ON THE DATA BUS TO THE DE- ;VICE OR MEMORY LOCATION INDIRECTLY ;ADDRESSED BY r6. AN ACTIVE LOW ;PULSE IS PRODUCED ON THE MICRO- ;PROCESSOR OUT PIN WHEN VALID DATA ;ARE PRESENT ON THE DATA BUS. THE ;DATA DIR PIN IS HIGH DURING THIS TIME ;INDICATING THAT THE DATA BUS IS IN ;THE OUTPUT MODE.
SETM	CTR 00001	;SET MICROPROCESSOR ARITHMETIC ;MODE ;TO BCD, DISABLE SOFTWARE INTERRUPT ;SFI AND MASKABLE INTERRUPTS IP AND ;IQ; ENABLE BANK TRANSFER INTERRUPT ;IF.
ARIT	DIV r7, r4 (Mode 1)	;DIVIDE POSITIVE 32-BIT BINARY OR UN- ;SIGNED 8-DIGIT BCD NUMBER (SPECIFIED ;BY CTR INSTRUCTION AS IN PREVIOUS ;EXAMPLE) BY A 16-BIT OR 4-DIGIT BCD ;NUMBER AND PRODUCE A 16-BIT OR 4- ;DIGIT QUOTIENT AND A 16-BIT OR 4- ;DIGIT REMAINDER. IN PARTICULAR, FOR ;THIS INSTRUCTION, THE NUMBER WHOSE

			;HIGH ORDER PORTION IS IN r7 AND
			;WHOSE LOW ORDER PORTION IS IN r8 IS
			;DIVIDED BY THE NUMBER IN r4. THE
			;QUOTIENT IS STORED IN r7 AND THE RE-
			;MAINDER IS STORED IN r8. IF DECIMAL
			;MODE IS SPECIFIED, THE OPERATION IS
			;AS FOLLOWS:
			;$(r7) \leftarrow [(r7)*10,000_{10}+(r8)]/(r4)$
			;$(r8) \leftarrow$ REMAINDER
			;FOR THE BINARY MODE,
			;QUOTIENT
			;$(r7) \leftarrow [(r7)*65,536_{10}+ (r8)]/(r4)$
			;$(r8) \leftarrow$ REMAINDER
STUP	LSW	(STAT)	;LOAD THE CONTENTS OF THE MEMORY
			;LOCATION SPECIFIED BY STAT (WHICH
	(Mode 8)		;IS WORD2 OF THIS INSTRUCTION) INTO
			;THE SW.
BNK	LUW	TABL	;LOAD THE CONTENTS OF TABL (WHICH IS
			;WORD2 OF THIS INSTRUCTION) INTO
	(Mode 6)		;THE UW. THE 16-BIT PATTERN IN TABL
			;WILL SPECIFY THE AVAILABILITY AND
			;STATUS OF THE EIGHT ON-CHIP
			;REGISTER BANKS.
SWCH	MTP	r8, r5	;MOVE THE CONTENTS OF REGISTER r5 IN
			;THE PRESENTLY SPECIFIED REGISTER
	(Mode 1)		;BANK TO REGISTER r8 IN THE REGISTER
			;BANK SPECIFIED IMMEDIATELY PRIOR
			;TO THE PRESENT BANK. (OLD r8) ←
			;(CURRENT r5)
CHNG	MFP	(LOC1),r2	;MOVE THE CONTENTS OF REGISTER r2 IN
			;THE REGISTER BANK SPECIFIED IMME-
	(Mode 7)		;DIATELY PRIOR TO THE PRESENTLY
			;SELECTED BANK TO THE MEMORY AD-
			;DRESS LOC1 (WORD2 OF THE PRESENT
			;INSTRUCTION). (LOC1) ← (OLD r2)
MSK	ANB	r5, 10B	;PERFORM LOGICAL AND OF THE CON-
			;TENTS OF r5 WITH DATA APPEARING ON
	(MODE 1)		;THE DATA BUS AS A RESULT OF AN INP
			;(INPUT) INSTRUCTION. THE AND MASK
			;PATTERN SPECIFIED BY (r5) WILL BE RE-
			;TAINED IN A SEPARATE MICROPROC-
			;ESSOR REGISTER AND WILL BE AND'ED
			;WITH ALL INPUT DATA FROM INP
			;INSTRUCTIONS UNTIL MODIFIED BY
			;ANOTHER ANB INSTRUCTION.

MSK	ANB	r5, 01B	;EXECUTED IN IDENTICAL MANNER TO
	(Mode 1)		;PREVIOUS EXAMPLE EXCEPT MASKING
			;OCCURS ON OUT (OUTPUT)
			;INSTRUCTION.
EXOR	XOB	r5, 10B	;EXECUTED IN IDENTICAL MANNER TO
	(Mode 1)		;ANB INSTRUCTION EXCEPT DATA BUS IS
			;XOR'ED WITH (r5) INSTEAD OF AND'ED
TMCT	CTC	0010100B	;SET INTERNAL TIMER RATE TO 1/40 ×
			;SYSTEM CLOCK RATE/(20 + 1) OR
			;SYSTEM CLOCK RATE/840. IF, FOR EX-
			;AMPLE, SYSTEM CLOCK RATE IS 2 MHZ,
			;INTERNAL TIMER RATE FOR ON-CHIP
			;TIMER WOULD BE 2×10^6/840 HZ OR
			;2.38×10^3 HZ OR 2,380 COUNTS/SECOND.
			;THIS RATE CORRESPONDS TO A TIMER
			;PULSE EVERY 1/2380 SECONDS OR
			;EVERY 0.4 OF A MILLISECOND.
TICT	CTC	1110110B	;THE LOWEST TWO BITS (10) OF THE
			;OPERAND INITIATE THE TIMER COUNTING
			;DOWN AT A RATE SET BY THE CTC IN-
			;STRUCTION IN PREVIOUS EXAMPLE. IF
			;THE TIMER INTERRUPT IS ENABLED, AN
			;INTERRUPT WILL OCCUR INTERNAL TO
			;THE MICROPROCESSOR WHEN THE
			;TIMER COUNT REACHES 0. THE INTER-
			;RUPT WILL TRANSFER THE PROGRAM
			;EXECUTION TO THE INSTRUCTION
			;LOCATED AT THE ADDRESS SPECIFIED IN
			;3_{16}. THE NEXT HIGHER TWO BITS OF THE
			;OPERAND (01) ALLOW THE INTERNAL
			;COUNTER TO START COUNTING UP. THE
			;COUNT PULSES HAVE TO ORIGINATE
			;FROM AN EXTERNAL SOURCE AND ARE
			;CONNECTED TO THE MICROPROCESSOR
			;THROUGH THE TIMER/COUNTER IN PIN
			;ON THE CHIP. A COUNTER INTERRUPT
			;WILL OCCUR, IF ENABLED, WHEN THE
			;COUNT REACHES A PRESET 16-BIT
			;VALUE SPECIFIED IN THE LCW (LOAD
			;COUNTER WORD) INSTRUCTION. THE
			;INTERRUPT WILL TRANSFER THE PRO-
			;GRAM FLOW TO THE INSTRUCTION
			;WHOSE ADDRESS IS STORED IN 4_{16}.
			;THE REMAINING HIGHER TWO OPERAND
			;BITS (11) ENABLE BOTH THE TIMER AND

			;COUNTER INTERRUPTS. IF THE TIMER
			;IS COUNTING UP AND/OR THE COUNTER
			;IS COUNTING DOWN, INTERRUPTS WILL
			;OCCUR WHEN A TIMER PRESET VALUE
			;OR A COUNT OF ZERO OCCURS,
			;RESPECTIVELY.
LOAD	LTW	r5	;LOAD THE TIMER WORD WITH THE 16-BIT
			;VALUE IN r5. IN THE TIMER COUNT UP
			;MODE, THIS 16-BIT VALUE WILL BE USED
	(Mode 1)		;TO CAUSE A TIMER INTERRUPT WHEN
			;THE TIMER COUNT MATCHES IT. IN
			;THE TIMER COUNTDOWN MODE, THE
			;VALUE IN r5 IS USED AS THE STARTING
			;TIMER VALUE THAT WILL BE DECRE-
			;MENTED AT THE SPECIFIED TIMER RATE.
LOAD	LCW	r5	;EXECUTION OF THIS INSTRUCTION IS
			;IDENTICAL TO THAT OF PREVIOUS IN-
	(Mode 1)		;STRUCTION EXCEPT THAT IT APPLIES TO
			;THE INTERNAL COUNTER INSTEAD OF TO
			;THE TIMER.

7.1.2 Assembler Directives or Pseudo Instructions

In addition to the assembly language instructions, the assembler requires information and directives in order to make it a useful program development tool. This information and these directives are written in the same format as assembly language instructions, but no object code is generated for these instructions during program assembly; hence the name *pseudo instructions*. In these pseudo instructions, a label may either be optional, required, or not permitted. A typical set of pseudo instructions for a microcomputer assembler are:

		ORG	Value or symbol
LABEL	Usually not permitted for ORG instruction	MNEMONIC	OPERAND

This instruction directs the assembler to store the first word of object code in the location specified in the operand of the ORG instruction. The object code of the remaining instructions will be stored in consecutively increasing memory addresses when loaded into the microcomputer memory unless another ORG instruction is encountered later in the assembly language program. The ORG instruction controls a software memory address counter in the assembler by setting this counter to the value of the ORG instruction operand and assigning the object code addresses beginning in this location. For example

ORG 100D

sets the assembler memory address counter to 100 decimal (64 hexadecimal). The object code, therefore, and its corresponding addresses will be assumed by the assembler to be stored in the microcomputer memory locations beginning with location 100 decimal. The pseudo instruction

ORG BEGN

specifies the value of the symbol *BEGN* as the starting address of the object code program. A value must be assigned to the symbol *BEGN* before it is first encountered in the ORG statement.

Expressions can also be used as the operand of the ORG instruction. The following ORG statement directs the assembler to assign the object code of the instructions coming after the ORG instruction to locations beginning at memory address $4C11_{16} + 5_{10}$ or to $4D00_{16}$.

```
Assembler
 address
 counter

4C10 STAY       NOP            ;NO OPERATION INSTRUCTION
4C11            ORG *+5D
  .               .
  .               .
  .               .

                EQU            value
└──────┬──────┘ └────┬────┘   └──┬──┘
LABEL (REQUIRED)   MNEMONIC    OPERAND
```

The EQU pseudo instruction directs the assembler to equate the instruction label to the operand such that, whenever the label is encountered by the assembler, the numerical value of the operand will replace the label. The assembler directives

AMNT	EQU	1016H
VALU	EQU	200D

equate the numerical values of 1016 hex and 200 decimal to the labels *AMNT* and *VALU*, respectively. Then, anywhere in the assembly language program that the labels *AMNT* or *VALU* are encountered, the numerical values assigned to them will be used.

DEFINE name , value
‾‾‾‾‾‾‾‾‾‾‾‾‾
OPERAND

The DEFINE assembler directive as used in this text performs exactly the same function as the EQU instruction but is presented since it is similar to the format of the microprocessor instruction set developed in Chapter 6. Hence, it is used in the illustrative programs later in this chapter. As with EQU, the DEFINE directive causes every occurrence of name to be replaced by value. The DEFINE directive

DEFINE   NUMB, 172H

will cause the value 172 hexadecimal to be used everywhere the label NUMB is encountered.

DATA   value, value, . . .

LABEL (OPTIONAL)   OPERAND

The DATA pseudo instruction places the operand value(s) in consecutive memory locations beginning with the address specified immediately prior to the data statement or at the address specified by the label (one value per location). If the value(s) in the operand are defined as an ASCII string, two values are automatically assigned to each 16-bit memory word as "packed" data in order to conserve memory space.

ORG	0		ORG 0
DATA	100D		DATA 100D, 200D, 300D
DATA	200D	or	
DATA	300D		

The assembler directives above store the value 100 decimal in memory location 0, 200 decimal in memory location 1, and 300 decimal in location 2.

```
         ORG   0                    ORG 0
         DATA  INIT     or          DATA INIT, INIT, INIT
         DATA  INIT                 ORG 2000
         DATA  INIT           INIT: CTR 00000B
         ORG   2000                  .
INIT:    CTR   00000B               .
          .                         .
          .
          .
```

These pseudo instructions store the address labeled *INIT* (2000 decimal) into memory locations 0, 1, and 2.

```
         ORG   20
         DATA  '0', '1', '2', '3', '4', '5'
```

This DATA instruction stores the ASCII value of 0 in memory location 20, the ASCII value of 1 in location 21, the ASCII value of 2 in location 22, and so on

```
         ORG   25
         DATA  "COMMAND:", 0
```

In this form, the DATA directive causes the ASCII representations of the characters of COMMAND: to be stored in the memory locations beginning with address 25 as two ASCII characters per 16-bit memory location. The ASCII characters comprising COMMAND: will take up four 16-bit memory locations (addresses 25 through 28). The second value, 0, in the data command will be stored as a 16-bit quantity in memory address 29.

```
     ‾‾‾‾‾v‾‾‾‾‾  BLOCK       ‾‾size‾‾
        LABEL                 OPERAND
      (OPTIONAL)
```

The BLOCK directive reserves a block of memory for later use by the program. The number of 16-bit memory locations set aside is specified by

the operand. The starting address of the reserved memory block is defined
either by an ORG directive immediately prior to or by the label of the
BLOCK pseudo instruction.

```
        ORG     100
        BLOCK   10H
```

The BLOCK directive in this example reserves 10_{16} or 16_{10} memory locations beginning at memory address 100 decimal.

```
        DEFINE  ARRAY,  100H
          .
          .
          .
ARRAY   BLOCK   20
```

In these instructions, 20 decimal 16-bit memory locations are reserved
beginning at address 100 hexadecimal.

```
        └────┬────┘ END
        NO LABEL
        ALLOWED
```

The END assembler directive indicates to the assembler the end of the
source program list, which must be read. This directive must physically be
the last statement in the source program.

7.1.3   Assembler Macroinstructions

A *macroinstruction* or a *Macro* is a user-defined name that represents a
fixed group of instructions. This name is used as a new instruction and
appears as an op code in the instruction format. Every time the Macro
name is encountered by the assembler, the group of instructions represented by the Macro are actually inserted into the program in place of the
Macro name. Thus, unlike a subroutine call, in which a fixed group of
instructions are stored **only once** in memory and referred to as needed, the
group of instructions defined by a Macro name is inserted into memory
each time the Macro name is encountered in the program. Using a Macro
to represent a series of instructions eliminates the delay associated with
branching to and returning from a subroutine to execute the same instruc-

tions, but usually at the sacrifice of memory space. For example, assume the following sequence of instructions from the microcomputer described in Chapter 6 appears in numerous places throughout a program.

```
MOV    r0, (r1)
ROR    r0, 10
AND    r0, 377
```

A Macro, CHEK, could be defined such that every time CHEK is detected by the assembler, the three instructions shown above are inserted in the program in place of the Macro name CHEK.

A macroinstruction is *defined* in the source program by writing the Macro name in the follow format:

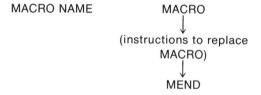

To implement the Macro, CHEK, the definition statement would appear as:

```
CHEK    MACRO
        MOV    r0, (r1)
        ROR    r0, 10
        AND    r0, 377
        MEND
```

Now, if the macroinstruction CHEK were referred to in an assembly language program

```
        .
        .
        .
        JSR    OUTCHR, 10
        CHEK
        .
        .
        .
```

the assembler would perform a *macro expansion* and replace CHEK with
the instructions it represents.

```
        .
        .
        .
    JSR     OUTCHAR, 10
    MOV     r0, (r1)
    ROR     r0, 10
    AND     r0, 377
        .
        .
        .
```

7.1.4 Passing Parameters to Macros and Subroutines

If macroinstructions or subroutines are to be of general use, they sometimes are required to use data that are not known in advance, but are
calculated or obtained by the main program. When this situation occurs,
these data must be *passed* to the macro or subroutine. One method of
accomplishing this *passing of parameters* is to set up *dummy* variables in
the macro or subroutine that correspond positionally to variables in the
Macro or subroutine calling instruction. To accomplish this passing in a
Macro instruction, a Macro definition of the following type is used.

```
              MACRO    parameter 1, parameter 2, etc.
  _____/          _____/
  MACRO NAME                    OPERAND
```

Continuing with the example of macroinstruction CHEK, the following
Macro definition is used to allow passing of two parameters.

```
  CHEK    MACRO    VALU, AMNT
          MOV      r0, (r1)
          ROR      r0, VALU
          AND      r0, AMNT
          MEND
```

In this definition, the numbers to be used in the ROR and AND instructions
are not fixed but take on the values of parameters VALU and AMNT as
supplied by the macroinstruction call. Assembler statements illustrating
this procedure are:

.
.
.
.

```
JSR     OUTCHAR,10
CHECK   15,416
```

When expansion of this Macro is performed by the assembler, the source code would appear as:

```
JSR     OUTCHAR,10
MOV     r0, (r1)
ROR     r0, 15
AND     r0, 416
          .
          .
          .
```

Parameters to be passed to or from subroutines are usually placed in a specific set of registers and accessed by the calling or subroutine program as required. The instruction set defined in Chapter 6 provides an efficient means of parameter passing by use of the MFP and MTP instructions. If a subroutine has been called and requires data from the main program, the MFP rd, rs instruction provides the means to move data from the register bank of the main program to the register bank being used by the subroutine. Thus, data transfer from the calling program to the subroutine is easily accomplished. Similarly, passing of parameters calculated or obtained in the subroutine to the main program is easily performed by the MTP rd, rs instruction. This instruction moves data to the register bank used by the calling program from the register bank of the subroutine.

The techniques described and definitions presented up to this point in Chapter 7 will now be further illustrated by a set of comprehensive examples. A brief description of flowcharts will first be given to aid in the explanation of the algorithms.

7.2 FLOWCHARTS

A useful tool in representing an algorithm is the flowchart. The flowchart is a pictorial diagram of steps involved in an algorithm or problem solution. The flowchart uses different shapes to convey the different functions to be performed. A brief listing of the basic shapes used in a flowchart and their functions is given below.

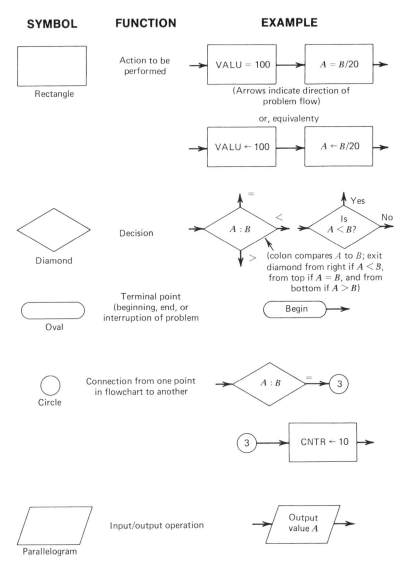

SYMBOL	FUNCTION	EXAMPLE

Rectangle — Action to be performed

VALU = 100 → A = B/20

(Arrows indicate direction of problem flow)

or, equivalenty

VALU ← 100 → A ← B/20

Diamond — Decision

$A : B$; $A < B?$

(colon compares A to B; exit diamond from right if $A < B$, from top if $A = B$, and from bottom if $A > B$)

Oval — Terminal point (beginning, end, or interruption of problem

Begin

Circle — Connection from one point in flowchart to another

$A : B$ ⟶ 3

3 → CNTR ← 10

Parallelogram — Input/output operation

Output value A

An example flowchart for the problem of selecting the largest of four positive integers w, x, y, and z where no two numbers are equal is as follows.

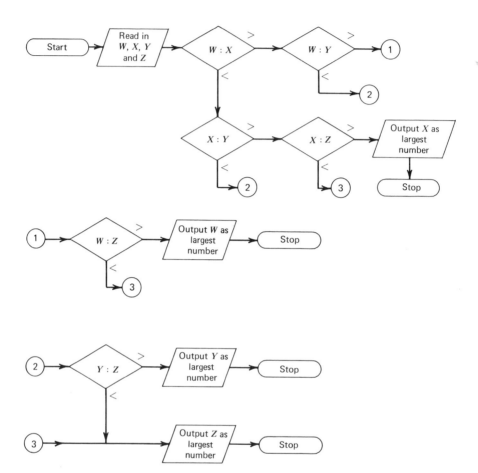

7.3 COMPREHENSIVE EXAMPLES OF USEFUL ALGORITHMS

There are a number of algorithms that are commonly needed by microcomputer users and that, if available, provide a useful reference source. With this need in mind, a set of comprehensive examples based on these algorithms is now given. These algorithms are implemented with the instruction set of Chapter 6 and presented in such a manner as to reinforce the concepts presented earlier in this chapter.

Example 1
Programs for finding N! (In the programs, N = NUM and ANS is desired result.)

(a) Using MULTIPLY instruction:

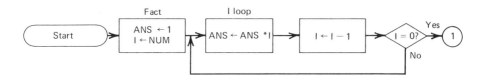

Writing the N! program as a subroutine to be used by a calling program yields:

```
FACT       DEFINE     ANS, r1      ;DEFINE VARIABLES ANS AND I
           DEFINE     I, r0
           MOV        ANS,1        ;INITIALIZE ANS TO 1
           MFP        I,r0         ;INITIALIZE I TO NUM (FROM
                                   ;CALLING ROUTINE)
ILOOP      MUL        ANS,I        ;ANS←ANS * I;
           DEJ        ILOOP,I      ;LOOP UNTIL I EQUALS 0
           MTP        r0,ANS       ;RETURN ANS TO CALLING ROUTINE
                                   ;(PASSING PARAMETER BACK)
           RUN                     ;RETURN
```

This subroutine can be called as:

```
           MOV        r0,20D       ;GET 20 (DECIMAL) FACTORIAL
           JSR        10D,FACT     ;CALL THE FACTORIAL SUBROUTINE
           . . . .                 ;ANSWER IS NOW IN r0
```

(b) Many microprocessors do not have a MULTIPLY instruction. Assuming that we desire to implement the same factorial program without using a MULTIPLY instruction, we give two examples of calculating N! below. The flowchart for one approach is:

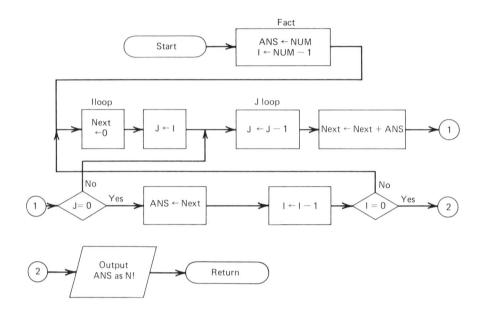

This algorithm has the virtue of being easy to implement and the drawback of being relatively slow. (To multiply by 1000 one has to do 1000 additions!) The following is the code for this algorithm assuming it is to be used as a subroutine in a larger program.

```
FACT      DEFINE    ANS, r0      ;SETUP OUR VARIABLES
          DEFINE    I,r1
          DEFINE    NEXT, r2
          DEFINE    J,r3
          MFP       ANS, r0      ;INITIALIZE ANS TO NUM (FROM
                                 ;CALLING ROUTINE)
          MOV       I,ANS-1      ;INITIALIZE I TO NUM-1
ILOOP     MOV       NEXT,0       ;INITIALIZE NEXT TO 0
          MOV       J,I          ;INITIALIZE J TO I
JLOOP     ADD       NEXT, ANS    ;NEXT ← NEXT + ANS
          DEL       JLOOP,J      ;LOOP UNTIL J = 0
          MOV       ANS, NEXT    ;ANS ← NEXT
          DEJ       ILOOP,I      ;LOOP UNTIL I = 0
          MTP       r0,ANS       ;RETURN ANS IN R0 (PASSING PARA-
                                 ;METER BACK)
          RUN                    ;RETURN
```

(c) A second approach would be to implement a "shift and add" algorithm for the multiply instead of repetitive addition. This method is much faster than the previous one but has the disadvantage of taking up more space and being somewhat more difficult to implement. The flowchart for this approach is:

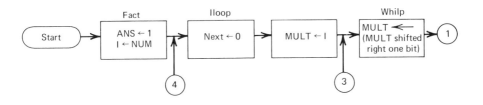

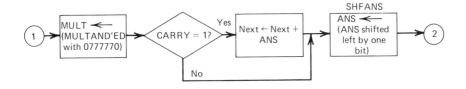

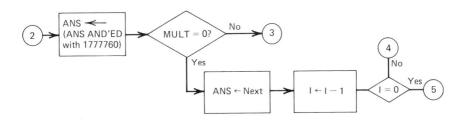

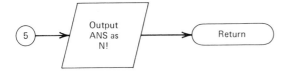

Implementing this algorithm as a subroutine for our microprocessor, we obtain:

```
        DEFINE  ANS, r0
        DEFINE  I, rl
        DEFINE  NEXT, r2
        DEFINE  MULT, r3
FACT    MOV     ANS,1           ;INITIALIZE ANS TO 1
        MFP     I,r0            ;INITIALIZE I TO NUM
ILOOP   MOV     NEXT,0          ;INITIALIZE NEXT TO 0
        MOV     MULT,I          ;INITIALIZE MULT TO I
WHILP   ROR     MULT,1          ;MULT ← (MULT SHIFTED RIGHT 1)
        AND     MULT,077777O    ;MULT ← (MULT AND 077777 OCTAL)
        JNC     SHFANS          ;JUMP IF NO CARRY
        ADD     NEXT, ANS       ;NEXT ← NEXT + ANS
SHFANS  ROL     ANS,1           ;ANS ← (ANS SHIFTED LEFT 1)
        AND     ANS,177760O     ;ANS ← (ANS AND'ED WITH 177776 OCTAL)
        CPA     MULT,0          ;SEE IF WE'RE DONE YET
        JNE     WHILP           ;CONTINUE IF MULT NOT EQUAL 0
        MOV     ANS,NEXT        ;ANS ← NEXT
        DEJ     ILOOP,I         ;LOOP UNTIL I = 0
        MTP     r0, ANS         ;RETURN ANS
        RUN
```

Example 2

Serial Data Transmission Algorithm

Any number of bits may be sent over a single line by sending them one after another spaced evenly apart. If both the sending and receiving end have a clock of the same speed and have some way of recognizing starts and ends of transmission, a very useful means of data communication can be realized. This type of serial transmission is usually termed *asynchronous transmission*.

One typical data format is:

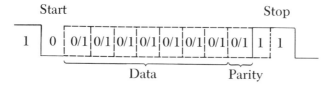

This format allows for the transmission of one 7-bit character with parity. If *odd 1 parity* is desired, a combinational logic circuit (EX-CLUSIVE OR gate) can be used to generate a parity bit (the eighth bit attached to end of the 7-bit character) such that the total number of 1's in the 8-bit word is odd. Other common parity choices are *even 1*, *even 0*, and *odd 0*. In any of these schemes, the receiving circuit can **detect** an error involving the change of one bit **and only one bit** in the transmitted word. In the event of a transmission error of only one bit, a check of parity by the receiver will show, for example, that the eight bit word transmitted with odd 1 parity has an even number of one's. The particular bit in error cannot be identified by this technique, however. To perform error detection and correction additional check bits and techniques are required. The receiving computer waits for a start bit, then pulls in 8 successive bits spaced an even time interval apart. After this character is recreated, the machine can wait for another start bit to occur, and begin the process again. In a common Teletype code, two stop bits are used before the next start bit. A table of the 7-bit ASCII character set is given in Appendix D.

An integral part of any serial data transmission scheme is an accurate timing loop to space the bits evenly apart. This timing can be accomplished in many ways:

(a) Using the timer:

```
        DEFINE   SPEED, NUMBER TO DIVIDE BY

INIT    MOV      r0, TIMINT      ;SET UP TIMER INTERRUPT
        MOV      (3),r0          ;LOAD TIMER VECTOR (LOCATION 3)
        CTC      SPEED           ;SET UP TIMER SPEED
WAITLP  LTW      (WAITVAL)       ;LOAD THE TIME TO WAIT
        CTC      1010010B        ;START TIMER DOWN
        WAT                      ;WAIT FOR THE INTERRUPT
TIMINT  RUN                      ;RETURN
```

(b) Without the timer:

```
WAITLP   MOV     r0,(WAITVAL)    ;GET NUMBER OF LOOPS
WAITLP2  DEJ     WAITLP2,r0
         RUN                     ;THIS ROUTINE HAS SEVERAL
                                 ;DISADVANTAGES.
                                 ;FIRST, WAITVAL HAS TO BE
                                 ;COMPUTED
                                 ;ACCORDING TO THE LENGTH OF
                                 ;TIME
```

```
                                         ;IT TAKES TO PERFORM THE LOOP
                                         ;ITSELF.
                                         ;SECONDLY, THE MAXIMUM VALUE
                                         ;OF WAITVAL
                                         ;IS 65,535 WHICH MAY NOT BE LONG
                                         ;ENOUGH FOR SOME APPLICATIONS.
                                         ;TO OBTAIN A LARGER TIME DELAY,
                                         ;SECOND INNER LOOP CAN BE
                                         ;ADDED:
WAITLP     MOV    r0,(WAITVAL)
WAITLP2    MOV    r1, NUMBER OF INNER LOOPS
WAITLP3    DEJ    WAITLP3,r1
           DEJ    WAITLP2,r0
           RUN
```

One alorithm for *transmitting* serial data and the corresponding assembly language program using the lsb of the data bus as the output is:

- Set up the bus.
- Transmit a start bit.
- Loop 8 times.

    wait for a bit to finish.
    transmit next bit.
    set up for the next bit to transmit.
    go back and loop.

- Transmit two stop bits.

```
SEROUT   MFP    r0,r0          ;GET THE CHARACTER TO DUMP
         ROL    r0,1           ;SET UP FOR SHIFTING OUT THE BITS
         ANB    1,OUT          ;ONLY SEND 1 BIT ON OUTPUT
         MOV    r1,8           ;INITIALIZE FOR 8 LOOPS
         XOR    r2,r2          ;CLEAR r2 (r2 = 0)
         OUT    (SERIAL),r2    ;DUMP OUT A START BIT
SERLP    ROR    r0,1           ;GET NEXT BIT TO DUMP
         JSR    8,WAITLP       ;CALL A WAITING SUBROUTINE
         OUT    (SERIAL),r0    ;OUTPUT THE BIT
         DEJ    SERLP,r1       ;LOOP OUT 8 TIMES
         JSR    8,WAITLP       ;WAIT FOR LAST DATA BIT TO FINISH
```

```
        INC     r2,r2           ;SET UP FOR STOP BIT
        OUT     (SERIAL),r2     ;DUMP THE STOP BIT
        JSR     8,WAITLP
        JSR     8,WAITLP
        RUN                     ;READY FOR NEXT CHARACTER TO
                                ;DUMP
```

An algorithm and assembly language program for *receiving* serial data using the lsb of the data bus as the input is:

- Set up bus.
- Wait for a start bit.
- Loop 8 times, which involves:

  wait for the last bit to finish.
  get a bit.
  shift bit into the result.
  go back and loop.

- Wait for the stop bit.
- Return result.

```
SERIN   MOV     r0,0            ;ZERO OUT THE RETURN VALUE
        ANB     1,INP           ;ONLY LOOK AT 1 INPUT BIT
        MOV     r1,8            ;SET UP FOR 8 LOOPS
GETSTR  INP     r2, (SERIAL)    ;GET A BIT
        CPA     r2,0            ;WAS IT A START BIT
        JNE     GETSTR          ;IF NOT, LOOP
INPLP   JSR     8,WAITLP        ;WAIT FOR LAST BIT TO CLEAR
        INP     r2,(SERIAL)     ;GET THE NEXT BIT
        ORR     r0,r2           ;SET THE BIT IN THE RESULT
        ROR     r0,1            ;GET READY FOR NEXT INPUT
        DEJ     INPLP,r1        ;LOOP 8 TIMES
        MTP     r0,r0           ;RETURN RESULT IN r0
        JSR     8,WAITLP        ;WAIT FOR STOP BIT
        RUN
```

Example 3

Display of an ASCII character
One of the most widely used forms of output is the CRT (Cathode Ray Tube) or TV display. This medium lends itself to computing

through its high speed, versatility, and ease of human interaction. A method of translating the ASCII character code used by the computer to a format that can be displayed by the CRT is needed, and this transformation is usually accomplished by means of a Character Generator ROM. For example, the letter A has an ASCII value of 101 octal or 41 hexadecimal. To display this character, a matrix of dots is formed on the television screen. The most used format of this matrix is the 5-by-7 version, wherein the letter A is formed as:

```
1        X    X    X    X    X
2        X                   X
3        X                   X
4        X    X    X    X    X
5        X                   X
6        X                   X
7        X                   X

         1    2    3    4    5
```

The Character Generator ROM takes the 7-bit ASCII code of the desired character (or, alternately, a 6-bit subset of the code), and the X and Y coordinates of the scan as the input address. The ROM then returns as an output the bit pattern for that particular row. By providing the proper sequence of addresses to ROM, the entire display can be made up of these dots and can appear as a screen filled with text.

7.4 MONITORS

As purchased from a semiconductor supplier, microprocessor chips and memories have no innate "intelligence." Even when its parts are connected in the proper fashion, there is no easy means to communicate with a microcomputer. For this reason, a small number of basic programs are needed to permit even the minimal amount of system design and debugging. A collection of easily accessible subroutines that provide the microcomputer with a minimum "intelligence" level is called a *monitor*. The monitor is usually supplied by the microcomputer manufacturer in a ROM, PROM, or EPROM to purchasers of preassembled microcomputer cards (microcomputer and interface chips mounted on a single card) or development systems (minicomputerlike systems based on a particular microcomputer or microcomputers that support software development and hardware debugging).

Some features of typical monitor programs are reading and interpretation of hexadecimal keyboard entries, loading of object programs, examination and modification of memory locations, asynchronous serial data communication with a Teletype or CRT terminal, and display of information on LED or similar readouts. Execution of the monitor is usually accomplished by entering a letter through a keyboard, Teletype, or a CRT terminal.

In a monitor or as a stand-alone program, the purpose of a loader routine is to provide a means to read a program into memory. A *bootstrap loader* may be entered into the microcomputer by keyboard. More commonly, it is part of a monitor program resident in Read Only Memory. The bootstrap loader can be used to load other types of loaders into memory, such as a *linking loader.* The linking loader works in conjunction with a relocatable assembler to permit loading and executing programs in any area of RAM by completing assembler-originated address calculations.

A small microcomputer monitor program with three commands and written in the assembly language of Chapter 6 is now given as an example. The monitor has the following commands.

I—input data to memory. The user is expected to type an address that will be used as the starting location in memory into which data are to be written. The user then types data words one after another until he has completed his entries. To signify an end of input, the user types any nonlegal number. For example, to enter the numbers 1 through 5 into address 2000, the user would type:
   Command: I2000000100020003000400005/
(The prompting word "Command:" will be presented by the computer on the terminal to indicate to the user that he is in the monitor program and that it is waiting for a command.)

D—display data from memory. The user is expected to type an address that will be used as the starting point from which data are to be read. After each data word is displayed, the user is expected to type a space, which will cause the next word to be shown. Any other response will cause an end of display. For example, to display the data entered in the INPUT example:
   Command: D20000001 0002 0003 0004 0005/ (spaces typed by user)

R—run a procedure in memory. The user is expected to type an address that will be used to initiate a procedure previously stored in memory. The first instruction in the procedure will be at the address entered. For example, to run a procedure at location 2000 octal, type:
   Command: R2000O

NOTE: The monitor considers all numbers to be in HEX unless otherwise specified.

A listing of the assembly language code for the monitor follows. The comments in the comment field of the instructions are used to explain the steps of the program.

MONITOR PROGRAM EXAMPLE

```
        DEFINE   SPACE, 40 O    ;DEFINE THE ASCII VALUE OF A
                                ;SPACE
                                ;START MEMORY WITH 256 WORDS OF
                                ;RAM
        ORG      0              ;START AT TOP OF MEMORY
        DATA     INIT           ;RESET VECTOR
        DATA     INIT           ;POWER FAIL VECTOR
        DATA     INIT           ;RESTART VECTOR
        ORG      2000 O         ;THIS STARTS THE MONITOR ROM
INIT:   CTR      00000B         ;TURN EVERYTHING OFF
        LSW      0              ;CLEAR STATUS WORD
        LUW      0              ;CLEAR USAGE WORD
MAIN:   MOV      r0, PROMPT     ;ASK THE USER WHAT HE WANTS
        JSR      8 ,OUTSTR
        JSR      8 ,INCHAR      ;GET AN INPUT
        CPA      r0,'R'         ;RUN COMMAND?
        JNE      MAIN2
        JSR      8 ,INWORD      ;GET THE ADDRESS TO RUN
        JSR      r0             ;CALL THE USER ROUTINE
        JUN      MAIN
MAIN2:  CPA      r0,'I'         ;INPUT COMMAND?
        JNE      MAIN4          ;
        JSR      8 ,INWORD      ;GET THE ADDRESS TO INPUT
        MOV      r2,r0
MAIN3:  JSR      8, INWORD      ;GET A DATA WORD
        CPA      r1,1           ;WAS THE DATA GOOD?
        JME      MAIN           ;JUMP IF DONE
        MOV      (r2),r0        ;WRITE THE WORD TO MEMORY
        INC      r2,r2          ;SET UP FOR NEXT WRITE
        JUN      MAIN3
MAIN4:  CPA      r0,'D'         ;DISPLAY COMMAND?
        JNE      MAIN           ;COMMAND NOT RECOGNIZED
        JSR      8 ,INWORD      ;GET THE DISPLAY ADDRESS
        MOV      r2,r0
MAIN5:  MOV      r0,(r2)        ;GET A DATA WORD
        JSR      8 ,OUTWRD      ;DUMP OUT THE WORD
        INC      r2,r2          ;SET UP FOR NEXT OUTPUT
```

```
        JSR       8 ,INCHAR        ;GET A CHARACTER
        CPA       r0,SPACE         ;WAS A SPACE TYPED?
        JME       MAIN5
        JUN       MAIN
```

THE REMAINDER OF THE MONITOR IS COMPOSED OF SUBROUTINES FOR
INPUT/OUT. EACH SUBROUTINE WILL BE DESCRIBED AS IT IS
ENCOUNTERED.


```
;INPUT A CHARACTER, THIS SUBROUTINE WAITS UNTIL A KEY
;IS DEPRESSED (SIGNALED BY THE FLAG BIT), AND THEN
;WAITS FOR THE KEY TO BE RELEASED. THE CHARACTER IS RETURNED
;TO r0 OF THE CALLING ROUTINE.

INCHAR:   JNF       INCHAR           ;WAIT FOR THE FLAG BIT
          INP       r0,(KEYBRD)      ;GET THE CHARACTER
          MTP       r0,r0            ;RETURN THE CHARACTER
INCHA2:   JFL       INCHA2           ;WAIT FOR THE FLAG TO CLEAR
```

```
;OUTCHR DIRECTLY FOLLOWS INCHAR CAUSING EVERYTHING BEING TYPED
;TO BE AUTOMATICALLY ECHOED. OUTCHR DUMPS OUT A CHARACTER
;(WHICH SETS A FLAG) AND THEN WAITS FOR THE FLAG TO CLEAR SO THAT
;THE DISPLAY WILL BE READY FOR THE NEXT CALL TO OUTCHR.

OUTCHR:   MFP       r0,r0            ;GET THE OUTPUT CHARACTER
          OUT       (DISPLAY),r0     ;DUMP OUT THE CHARACTER
OUTCH2:   JFL       OUTCH2           ;WAIT FOR THE FLAG TO CLEAR
          RUN
```

```
;OUTSTR IS A SUBROUTINE TO SEND AN ASCII STRING OUT TO THE DISPLAY.
;THE END OF THE STRING IS FOUND BY LOCATING A ZERO. EACH WORD IN
;MEMORY CONTAINS TWO CHARACTERS, THE LOW BYTE IS THE FIRST
;CHARACTER, AND THE HIGH BYTE IS THE SECOND CHARACTER.

OUTSTR:   MFP       r1,r0            ;GET THE STRING ADDRESS
OUTST1:   MOV       r0,(r1)          ;GET A DATA WORD
          AND       r0,377O          ;GET LOW 8 BITS (OCTAL)
          RRZ                        ;RETURN ON END OF STRING
          JSR       8, OUTCHR        ;DUMP OUT THE CHARACTER
          MOV       r0,(r1)
          ROR       r0,100O          ;GET THE TOP 8 BITS
          AND       r0,377O          ;MASK OUT UPPER 8 BITS
          RRZ                        ;RETURN ON END OF STRING
```

```
        JSR     8, OUTCHR       ;DUMP OUT THE CHARACTER
        INC     r1,r1           ;SET UP FOR NEXT DATA WORD
        JUN     OUTST1
```

;OUTDIG DUMPS A SINGLE HEX DIGIT TO THE DISPLAY

```
OUTDIG:  MFP     r0,r0          ;GET THE DIGIT TO DUMP
         AND     r0,17O         ;ONLY DUMP LOW FOUR BITS
         MOV     r1,HEXTAB      ;GET THE CONVERSION TABLE
         ADD     r1,r0          ;r1 = ADDRESS INTO TABLE
         MOV     r0,(r1)        ;GET THE ASCII CHARACTER
         JSR     8 ,OUTCHR      ;DUMP THE CHARACTER
         RUN
```

;OUTWRD SENDS A WORD OF MEMORY TO THE DISPLAY

```
OUTWRD:  MFP     r0,r0          ;GET THE WORD TO DUMP
         ROR     r0,14O         ;GET THE TOP FOUR BITS
         JSR     8 ,OUTDIG
         ROL     r0,4O          ;GET NEXT FOUR BITS
         JSR     8 ,OUTDIG
         ROL     r0,4O          ;GET NEXT FOUR BITS
         JSR     8, OUTDIG
         ROL     r0,4O          ;GET BOTTOM FOUR BITS
         JSR     8, OUTDIG
         RUN
```

;INDIG INPUTS A DIGIT FROM THE KEYBOARD INTO r0, AND CHECKS TO SEE
;THAT IT IS A LEGAL HEX CHARACTER. IF IT IS NOT IT SETS r1 IN THE
;CALLING ROUTINE'S REGISTER BANK, OTHERWISE IT CLEARS IT.

```
INDIG:   JSR     8, INCHAR      ;GET A CHARACTER
         CPA     r0,60 O
         JNL     INDIG2
INDIG1:  MTP     r1,1           ;SET BAD DIGIT
         RUN
INDIG2:  CPA     r0,72 O
         JNL     INDIG4
         AND     r0,17O         ;NUMBER IS BETWEEN 0 and 9
INDIG3:  MTP     r0,r0          ;RETURN THE DIGIT
         MTP     r1,0           ;CLEAR THE SIGNAL
         RUN
INDIG4:  CPA     r0, 101O
         JAL     INDIG1
```

```
        CPA     r0,107O
        JNL     INDIG1
        AND     r0,7O        ;NUMBER IS BETWEEN A AND F
        ADD     r0,11O
        JUN     INDIG3
```

```
;INWORD GETS A FOUR CHARACTER (16 BIT) WORD OF DATA FROM THE
;KEYBOARD. IF ANY ILLEGAL CHARACTER IS TYPED, THE SUBROUTINE
;RETURNS A "SIGNAL" VALUE IN r1, OTHERWISE, r1 IS SET TO 0 AND THE
;DATA ARE RETURNED IN r0.
```

```
INWORD: JSR     8 ,INDIG     ;GET A DIGIT
        MTP     r1,r1        ;PASS BACK r1
        CPA     r1,1         ;WAS THE DATA BAD
        RME
        ROL     r0,140       ;ROTATE CHAR TO HIGH 4 BITS OF
                             ;r0
        MOV     r2,r0

        JSR     8, INDIG
        MTP     r1,r1
        CPA     r1,1
        RME
        ROL     r0,100
        ORR     r2,r0        ;STORE CHAR IN NEXT HIGH 4 BITS
                             ;of r2
        JSR     8 ,INDIG
        MTP     r1,r1
        CPA     r1,1
        RME
        ROL     r0,40
        ORR     r2,r0
        JSR     8,INDIG
        MTP     r1,r1
        ORR     r2,r0
        MTP     r0,r2        ;RETURN THE DATA VALUE
        RUN
```

```
;SOME SYSTEM VARIABLES NEEDED FOR RUNNING:
PROMPT: DATA "Command:", 0
HEXTAB: DATA '0', '1', '2', '3', '4', '5', '6', '7', '8', '9', 'A', 'B', 'C', 'D', 'E', 'F',
        END
```

7.5 INTERPRETERS AND COMPILERS

The assembly language statements in the previous two examples clearly illustrate two points.

(1) A program written in assembly language requires specific knowledge of a particular microcomputer's architecture and instruction set and is, therefore, not machine independent.

(2) Each assembly language instruction corresponds directly to a machine language instruction (one assembly language source instruction produces one machine language object instruction).

Most times it is desirable to utilize a language in which the programmer can specify in almost English-like statements the operations to be performed. Each higher level English-like statement, however, will require many of the more primitive assembly language statements to perform the desired functions and, thus, some sort of transformation process will have to be accomplished. Further, if a translator for the language were available to produce assembly language or machine language code for a large number of microprocessors, then the language would be essentially machine independent. Languages of the type just described are commonly referred to as *high level languages* or *high order languages.* Using a high level language, a user can develop programs much more rapidly and with less errors than with assembly language. A disadvantage of using high level languages is that the machine language program resulting from the high level language is comprised of a larger number of instructions and, therefore, requires more memory. In percentage terms, a high level language may produce machine code requiring 130% to 400% or more memory than that produced by a program written in assembly language. This disadvantage is offset, however, by the plummeting cost of memory and the increase in programmer productivity (sometimes as much as 50 to 200 times). The latter item is extremely important since software development costs are increasing while hardware costs are decreasing.

There are two primary type of programs that take high level statements and convert them to machine code to be executed on a particular microprocessor. These programs are *interpreters* and *compilers.* It is important to note that the characteristics of either type of program are not a function of the high level language being used but of their particular method of operation. *A compiler is a program that translates another program written in a high level language to the assembly language or machine language of a specific computer or microprocessor.* The compiler program itself is specific to a particular microprocessor and, therefore, is written with the assembly language of the particular microprocessor in mind. By writing compilers for a number of different microprocessors, however, we find that the high level language that is translated by the compiler can be machine independent. A distinguishing characteristic of a compiler is that it translates the entire high level source program into microprocessor-specific machine code, which is then loaded into microcomputer memory and executed as a program package.

In contrast to the compiler, *an interpreter is a program which operates on each high level source statement individually and performs the operation indicated by executing a predefined sequence of machine language instructions.* Instead of finally producing a machine language program that is loaded into the microcomputer memory and executed (as with a compiler), *the interpretive process requires both the interpreter program and the high level source program to reside in memory simultaneously.* Then, each high level source instruction is individually interpreted and immediately executed in machine language code. Interpreters are also used in the interactive mode, whereby a user can enter his high level program at a terminal, execute the program, and immediately modify or edit the high level source code if errors occur. With this interactive ability to gain control over the interpreter's execution if an error occurs or if program modification is required, the programmer can verify and debug his software "on line" and achieve more rapid turnaround. Some of the disadvantages of interpreters are that they result in slower program execution times than compilers (because of the interpretation and execution of individual high level statements) and that they do not permit operations that involve the source program's being translated at one time (such as optimization of the code resulting from the interpretive process).

Examples of compiler languages are FORTRAN, ALGOL, PL/I, and COBOL. The most widely used interpretive language is BASIC. The BASIC language resulted from a project begun in 1963 in Dartmouth College and was rapidly adopted by industry as a high level interactive language.

Microprocessors such as the Motorola 68000 and the Zilog Z8000 employ architectures replete with numerous registers, stacks, and other features that support, extensively, high level languages. These features will make high level language programming on these types of microprocessors extremely attractive and more efficient relative to assembly language programming.

In the area of microcomputers, there are relatively few types of compilers and interpreters in use. The most popular of these are the PL/M compiler, produced by Intel Corporation for the 8-bit 8008 and 8080 microprocessors, and the PASCAL and BASIC interpreters.

7.5.1 PL/M

The following paragraphs are excerpts taken directly from the Intel PL/M Programming Manual and provide an overview of the language.

A PL/M program is a sequence of "declarations" and "executable statements".

The declarations allow the programmer to control allocation of storage, define simple textual substitutions (macros), and define procedures. PL/M is a "block structured" language: procedures may contain further declarations which control storage allocation and define other procedures.

The procedure definition facility of PL/M allows modular programming: a program can be divided into sections (e.g., Teletype input, conversion from binary to decimal forms, and printing output messages.) Each of these sections is written as a PL/M procedure. Such procedures are conceptually simple, easy to formulate and debug, and easily incorporated into a large program. They may form a basis for a procedure library if a family of similar programs is being developed.

PL/M handles two kinds of data, its two basic "data types": BYTE and ADDRESS. A BYTE variable or constant is one that can be represented as an 8-bit quantity; an ADDRESS variable or constant is a 16-bit or double-byte quantity. The programmer can DECLARE variable names to represent BYTE or ADDRESS values. One can also declare vectors (or arrays) of type BYTE or ADDRESS.

In general, executable statements specify the computational processes that are to take place. To achieve this, arithmetic, logical (Boolean), and comparison (relational) operators are defined for variables and constants of both types (BYTE and ADDRESS). These operators and operands are combined to form EXPRESSIONS, which resemble those of elementary algebra. For example, the PL/M expressions

$$X * (Y - 3) / R$$

represents this calculation: the value of X multiplied by the quantity Y-3, divided by the value of R. Expressions are a major component of PL/M statements. A simple statement form is the PL/M ASSIGNMENT statement, which computes a result and stores it in a memory location defined by a variable name. The assignment

$$Q = X * (Y - 3) / R$$

first causes the computation to the right of the equals sign, as described above. The result of this computation is then saved in a memory location labeled by the variable name 'Q'.

Other statements in PL/M perform conditional tests and branching, loop control, and procedure invocation with parameter passing. The flow of program execution is specified by means of powerful control structures that take advantage of the block-structured nature of the language. Input and output statements read and write 8-bit values from and to 8008 and 8080 input and output ports. Procedures can be defined which use these basic input and output statements to perform more complicated I/O operations.

A method of automatic text-substitution (more specifically, a "compile-time macro facility") is also provided in PL/M. A programmer can declare a symbolic name to be completely equivalent to an arbitrary sequence of characters. As each occurrence of the name is encountered by the compiler, the declared character sequence is substituted, so the compiler actually processes the substituted character string instead of the symbolic name.

Blanks may be inserted freely around identifiers, reserved words, and special characters. Blanks are not necessary, however, when identifiers or reserved words are separated by special characters or delimiters. Thus the expression

$$X * (Y - 3) / R$$

is equivalent to

$$X*(Y-3)/R$$

Comments

Explanatory remarks should be interleaved with PL/M program text, to improve readability and provide program documentation. This is the purpose of the COMMENT construction. A PL/M comment is a sequence of characters (from the PL/M character set) delimited on the left by the character pair /* and on the right by the character pair */. These delimiters instruct the compiler to ignore any text between them, and not to consider such text as part of the program proper. A comment may appear anywhere a space character may; thus comments may be freely distributed throughout a PL/M program. There is only one restriction on the placement of a comment: it may not begin or end inside a character string. Here is a sample (of a typical) PL/M comment:

/* THIS IS A COMMENT ABOUT COMMENTS */

Basic Constituents of a PL/M Program

PL/M programs are written free-form. That is, the input lines are column-independent and spaces may be freely inserted between the elements of the program.

PL/M Character Set

The character set recognized by PL/M is a subset of both ASCII and EBCDIC character sets. The valid PL/M characters consist of the alpha-numerics

A B C D E F G H I J K L M N O P Q R S T U V W X Y Z

0 1 2 3 4 5 6 7 8 9

along with the special characters

$$ \$ = . / ( ) + - ' * , < > : ; $$

All other characters are unrecognized by PL/M, in the sense that a blank is substituted for each such character.

Special characters and combinations of special characters have particular meanings in a PL/M program, as shown in Appendix E.

Identifiers and Reserved Words

A PL/M identifier is used to name variables, procedures, macros, and statement labels. An identifier may be up to 31 characters in length, the first of which must be alphabetic and the remainder either alphabetic or numeric. Imbedded dollar signs are ignored by the PL/M compiler and are used to improve the readability of an identifier. An identifier containing a dollar sign is exactly equivalent to the same identifier with the dollar sign deleted. Examples of valid identifiers are

X

GAMMA

LONGIDENTIFIERWITHNUMBER3

INPUT$COUNT

INPUTCOUNT

where the PL/M compiler will regard the final two examples as instances of the same identifier.

There are a number of otherwise valid identifiers, whose meanings are fixed in advance. Because they are actually part of the PL/M language, they may not be used as programmer-defined identifiers. A list of such RESERVED WORDS is given in Appendix F.

PL/M Program Organization

STATEMENTS are the building blocks of a PL/M program. A PL/M statement either defines a computational entity or specifies a computation to be performed. For example, the PL/M statement

$$\text{DECLARE } X \text{ BYTE};$$

defines a variable named X that has a single-byte (8-bit) value. The PL/M statement

$$X = 3*(Y + Z);$$

causes the computation of the arithmetic quantity 3 times the sum of Y and Z, and the assignment of that quantity as the new value of the variable X. The PL/M statements are frequently (but not necessarily) written one to a line, and invariably terminate with semicolons.

A PL/M program comprises a sequence of PL/M statements, followed by the special identifier EOF. In the absence of statements specifying otherwise, the statements of a PL/M program are executed sequentially, in the order of their appearance. For example, the following program fragment is a sequence of two statements:

$$X = 3;$$
$$Y = 4 + X;$$

Two successive actions are specified: first, 3 becomes the current value of the variable X; second, a new value for the variable Y is calculated by adding 4 to the current value of X (in this case 3, for a result of 7). It is obvious that, in a different sequence, these two statements could have a very different effect.

The strictly sequential execution of statements is interrupted by, for example, an IF-statement:

$$\text{IF } A > 63 \text{ THEN } X = 3;$$
$$\text{ELSE } X = 9;$$
$$Y = 4 + X;$$

Here the statement "$X = 3$" is executed only if the current value of A is greater than 63; the statement "$X = 9$" is executed only if the current value of A is less than or equal to 63; and the statement "$Y = 4 + X$" is executed always.

Statements may be collected together in groups, delimited by the reserved words DO and END, to form compound statements, or blocks. These blocks are then treated as single statements with respect to the flow of program control. Such a group could, for example, be a part of a conditional statement:

$$\text{IF } A > B \text{ THEN}$$
$$A = B;$$
$$B = C;$$
$$\text{END};$$

This statement performs the two assignments to A and B only if A is greater than B to start with.

Statements may also be grouped to form a "procedure," whose execution may then be called for from elsewhere in the program. The following procedure, for example, calculates the sum of the squares of its two arguments.

```
SUM$SQUARE: PROCEDURE (A, B) ADDRESS;
    DECLARE (A, B) ADDRESS;
    RETURN A*A + B*B;
END SUM$SQUARE;
```

After this procedure has been defined, it is available for use—e.g., for calculating new values for variables. For example, the sequence of statements

```
X = 3;
Y = 5 + SUM$SQUARE (X, 4);
```

results in Y's having the new value 30.

PL/M Data Elements

PL/M data elements can be either variables or constants. Variables are PL/M identifiers whose values may change during execution of the program, whereas constants have fixed values. The expression

$$X * (Y - 3) / R$$

involves the variables X, Y, and R, and the constant 3.

Numeric Constants

A constant is a value known at compile-time, which does not change during execution of the program. A constant is either a number or a character string. Numeric constants may be expressed as binary, octal, decimal, and hexadecimal numbers.

In general, the base (or radix) of a number is represented by one of the letters

$$B \quad O \quad Q \quad D \quad H$$

following the number. The letter B denotes a binary constant; the letters O and Q signal octal constants. The letter D may optionally follow decimal numbers. Hexadecimal numbers consist of sequences of hexadecimal digits (0, 1, 2, 3, 4, 5, 6, 7, 8, 9, A, B, C, D, E, F) terminated by the letter H. The leading character of a hexadecimal number must be a numeric digit, to avoid confusion with a PL/M identifier; a leading zero is always sufficient. Any number not followed by one of the letters B, O, Q, D, or H is assumed to be decimal. Numbers must be representable in 16 bits. The following are valid constants in PL/M:

2   33Q   110B   33FH   55D   55   0BF3H   65535

The dollar sign may be freely inserted between the characters of a constant to improve readability. The two following binary constants are exactly equivalent:

11110110011B
111$1011$0011B

Character String Constants

Character strings are denoted by PL/M characters enclosed within apostrophes. (To include an apostrophe in a string, write it as a double apostrophe: e.g., the string '''Q' comprises 2 characters, an apostrophe followed by a Q.) The PL/M compiler represents character strings in memory as ASCII codes, one 7-bit character code to each 8-bit byte, with a high-order zero bit. Strings of length 1 translate to single-byte values; strings of length 2 translate to double-byte values. For example,

'A'   is equivalent to   41H
'AG'   is equivalent to   4147H

(see the appendix for ASCII character codes). Character strings longer than 2 characters cannot, of course, be used as BYTE or ADDRESS values. But they will turn out to be useful in conjunction with the dot operator, with the INITIAL attribute, and with the DATA declaration.

Variables and Type Declarations

Each variable used in a PL/M program must be declared in a declaration statement before (earlier in the program text than) its use in expressions. This declaration defines the variable and gives necessary information about it.

A PL/M variable takes one of two 'types': type BYTE, or type ADDRESS. Each BYTE data element is an 8-bit, single-byte object; each ADDRESS data element is a 16-bit, double-byte object. The type of each variable must be formally declared in its declaration statement.

A declaration of a variable (or a list of variables) begins with the reserved word DECLARE. Each single identifier, or list of identifiers enclosed in parentheses, is followed by one of the two reserved words BYTE or ADDRESS. Sample PL/M declarations are

DECLARE X BYTE;
DECLARE (Q, R, S) BYTE;
DECLARE (U, V, W) ADDRESS;

Additional facilities are present in PL/M for declaring vectors, macros, labels, and data lists. These facilities are discussed in later sections.

Well-Formed Expressions and Assignments

PL/M expressions can now be more completely defined. A well-formed expression consists of basic data elements combined through the various arithmetic, logical, and relational operators, in accordance with simple algebraic notation. Examples are

$$A + B$$
$$A + B - C$$
$$A*B + C/D$$

Arithmetic Operators

There are 7 arithmetic operators in PL/M. These are

$$+ \quad - \quad PLUS \quad MINUS \quad * \quad / \quad MOD$$

All of the above operators performed unsigned binary arithmetic on either byte or address values.

The operators + and − perform addition and subtraction. If both operands are of type BYTE, the operation is done in 8-bit arithmetic and the result is of type BYTE. If either operand is of type ADDRESS, the other operand, if it is of type BYTE, will be extended by 8 high-order zero bits, and the operation is then performed in 16-bit arithmetic, returning a value of type ADDRESS. A unary '−' operator is also defined in PL/M. Its effect is such that (−A) is equivalent to (0−A). Thus −1, for example, is equivalent to 0−1, resulting in the BYTE value 255 or 0FFH. PLUS and MINUS perform similarly to + and −, but take account of the current setting of the CPU hardware carry flag in performing the operation.

The operators * and / perform unsigned binary multiplication and division, on operands of type BYTE or ADDRESS. The result is always of type ADDRESS. In the event that arithmetic overflow occurs during multiplication, the result is undefined. The division operator always rounds down to an integer result, and the result of division by zero is undefined. (The setting of the 8080 hardware carry flag by these operations is undefined.) MOD performs similarly to /, except that the result of the operation is not the quotient from the division, but the remainder.

Logical Operators

There are 4 logical (boolean) operators in PL/M. They are

$$NOT \quad AND \quad OR \quad XOR$$

These operators perform logical operations on 8 or 16 bits in parallel. NOT is a unary operator, taking one operand only. It produces a result in which each bit is the complement of the corresponding bit of its operand. The remaining operators each take 2 operands, and perform bitwise AND, OR, and EXCLUSIVE OR, respectively. If both operands are of type BYTE, the operation is an 8-bit operation, and delivers a result of type BYTE. If at least one operand is of type ADDRESS, the operation is a 16-bit operation, and delivers a result of type ADDRESS. In this case, the BYTE operand, if any, is first extended to 16 bits by the addition of 8 high-order zero bits. Examples are

```
          NOT  11001100B returns 00110011B
10101010B AND  11001100B returns 10001000B
10101010B OR   11001100B returns 11101110B
10101010B XOR  11001100B returns 01100110B
```

Relational Operators
Relational operators are used to compare PL/M values. They are

<	less than
>	greater than
<=	less than or equal to
>=	greater than or equal to
<>	not equal to
=	equals

Relational operators are always binary operators, taking two operands. The operands may be of type BYTE or ADDRESS. The comparison is always performed assuming that the operands are unsigned binary integers. If the specified relation between the operands holds, a value of 0FFH is returned, otherwise the result is 00H. Thus in all cases the result is of type BYTE, with all 8 bits set to 1 for a true condition, and to 0 for a false condition. For example:

(6 > 5)	returns 11111111B
(6 <= 4)	returns 00000000B
(6 > 5) OR (1 > 2)	returns 0FFH
(6 > (4+5)) OR (1 > 2)	returns 00H

Expression Evaluation
Operators in PL/M have an implied precedence, which is used to determine the manner in which operators and operands are grouped together. A+B*C causes A to be added to the product of B and C. In this case B is said to be "bound" to the operator * rather than the operator +, as a result

of which the multiplication will be performed first. In general, operands are bound to the adjacent operator of highest precedence, or to the left one in the case of a tie. Technically speaking, PL/M does not guarantee the order of evaluation of operands and operations within an expression, but merely defines the association (binding) of operators and operands. Valid PL/M operators are listed below from highest to lowest precedence. Operators listed on the same line are of equal precedence.

$$* \quad / \quad MOD$$
$$+ \quad - \quad PLUS \quad MINUS$$
$$< \quad <= \quad <> \quad = \quad >= \quad >$$
$$NOT$$
$$AND$$
$$OR \quad XOR$$

Parentheses should be used to override the assumed precedence in the usual way. Thus the expression (A + B) * C will cause the sum of A and B to be multiplied by C. For example.

A + B + C + D   is equivalent to ((A + B) + C) + D
A + B * C   is equivalent to A + (B * C)
A + B − C * D   is equivalent to (A + B) − (C * D)

Assignment Statements

Results of computations are stored as values of variables. At any given moment, a variable has only one value—but this value may change with program execution. The PL/M ASSIGNMENT STATEMENT respecifies the value of a variable. Its form is

variable = expression ;

The expression to the right of the equal sign is evaluated, and the resulting value is assigned to the variable named on the left. The old value of the variable is lost.

For example, following execution of the statement

A = 3;

the variable A will have a new current value of 3.

The declared precision (BYTE or ADDRESS) of the assigned variable affects the store operation: if the receiving variable is a BYTE variable, and the expression is a double-byte (ADDRESS) result, the high-order byte is omitted in the store. Similarly, if the expression yields a single-byte result, and the receiving variable is declared type ADDRESS, the high-order byte is filled with zeros.

It is often convenient to assign the same expression to several variables. This is accomplished in PL/M by listing all the variables to the left of the equals sign, separated by commas. The variables A, B, and C could all be set to the value of the expression X + Y with the single assignment statement

$$A, B, C = X + Y;$$

A special form of the assignment is used within PL/M expressions. The form of this 'embedded assignment' is

$$(variable: = expression)$$

and may appear anywhere an expression is allowed. The expression to the right of the := assignment symbol is evaluated and then stored into the variable on the left. The value of the embedded assignment is the same as that of its right half. For example, the expression

$$A + (B := C+D) - (E := F/G)$$

results in exactly the same value as

$$A + (C+D) - (F/G)$$

The only difference is the side effect of storing the intermediate results C+D and F/G into B and E, respectively. These intermediate results can then be used at a later point in the program without calculating them again.

Do Groups

Statements may be grouped together within the bracketing words DO and END, to form a do-group. (DO and END are reserved words.) The simplest do-group is of the form

$$
\begin{aligned}
&\text{DO};\\
&\quad \text{statement-1};\\
&\quad \text{statement-2};\\
&\quad \cdots\\
&\quad \text{statement-n};\\
&\text{END};
\end{aligned}
$$

A group of statements so bracketed may be regarded as a single PL/M statement, and may appear anywhere in a program that a single statement may. The flow of program control is explicitly controlled by other forms of the do-group; these are shown below.

The Do-While Group

The DO-WHILE is a do-group of the form

                DO WHILE expression;
                    statement-1;
                    statement-2;
                    . . .
                    statement-n
                END;

The effect of this statement is: first the expression following the reserved word WHILE is evaluated. If the result is a quantity whose rightmost bit is 1, then the sequence of statements up to the END is executed. When the END is reached, the expression is evaluated again, and again the sequence of statements is executed only if the value of the expression has a rightmost bit of 1. The group is executed over and over until the expression results in a value whose rightmost bit is 0, at which time execution of the statement group is skipped, and program control passes out of the group.

Consider the following example:

                A = 1;
                DO WHILE A <= 3;
                    A = A+1;
                END;

The statement A = A+1 will be executed exactly 3 times. The value of A when program control exits the group will be 4.

It is worth commenting here on the relationship between the logical operators, and the WHILE and IF statements. Recall that the relational operators return a BYTE value of all ones, or all zeros. It may be helpful to consider any BYTE whose least significant (rightmost) bit is 1, as representing a TRUE condition, and any whose least significant bit is 0, as representing a FALSE condition. With this interpretation, we may consider $(1 < 2)$ as returning a value of TRUE. We may also consider that the do-while statement merely executes the statements of its group as long as the while-expression is TRUE. Note that the logical operators AND, OR, and NOT operate bitwise on all the bits of their operands, and in particular perform the standard actions of boolean algebra on the least significant bit, provided a 1 stands for TRUE and a 0 stands for FALSE. For example, with the above definitions,

                NOT(TRUE) is FALSE
                NOT(FALSE) is TRUE

Finally, observe that these conventions cause a complicated expression to take on its most obvious meaning. For example:

DO WHILE (A < 10) AND (A > 4);

. . .

END;

The Iterative Do-Group

An iterative do-group executes a group of statements a fixed number of times. The simplest form of the iterative do-group is

DO var = expr-1 TO expr-2;
    statement-1;
    statement-2;
    . . .
    statement-n;
END;

where 'var' is a variable-name, and 'expr-1' and 'expr-2' are both PL/M expressions. The effect of this statement is first to store the value of expr-1 into the variable var. Second, the value of the variable var is tested, and if it is less than or equal to expr-2, the grouped statements are executed. When the END is reached, the variable is incremented by 1, and the test is repeated. The group is repeatedly executed until the value of the variable is greater than expr-2, when the test fails, execution of the group is skipped, and control immediately passes out of the range of the do-group. An example is

DO I = 1 TO 10;
    A = A+I;
END;

This iterative do-group has exactly the same effect as the following DO-WHILE:

I = 1;
DO WHILE I <= 10;
    A = A+I;
    I = I+1;
END;

The more general form of the iterative do-group allows a stepping value other than 1. This more general form is

```
DO var = expr-1 TO expr-2 BY expr-3;
    statement-1;
    statement-2;
        . . .
    statement-n;
END;
```

In this case, the variable 'var' following the DO is stepped by the value of expr-3, instead of 1, each time the END is reached. An example of this form follows:

```
/*  COMPUTE THE PRODUCT OF THE
    FIRST N ODD INTEGERS */

PROD = 1;
DO I = 1 TO (2*N-1) BY 2;
    PROD = PROD*I;
END;
```

The Do-Case Statement

The final form of the do-group is the DO-CASE statement. Its form is

```
DO CASE expression;
    statement-1;
    statement-2;
        . . .
    statement-n;
END;
```

The effect of this statement is first the evaluation of the expression following the CASE. The result of this is a value K which must lie between 0 and $n-1$. K is used to select one of the n statements of the do-case, which is then executed. The first case (statement-1) corresponds to $K=0$, the second case (statement-2) corresponds to $K=1$, and so forth. After only one statement from the group has been selected and then executed only once, control passes beyond the END of the do-case group. If the run-time value of K is greater than the number of cases, then the effect of the CASE statement is undefined.

An example of the DO-CASE is

```
DO CASE SCORE;
    ;
    CONVERSIONS = CONVERSIONS+1;
    SAFETIES = SAFETIES+1;
```

```
              FIELDGOALS = FIELDGOALS+1;
              ;
              ;
              TOUCHDOWNS = TOUCHDOWNS+1;
         END;
```

When execution of this CASE statement begins, the variable SCORE must be in the range 0 − 7. If SCORE is 0, 4, or 5 then a null statement (consisting of only a semicolon, and having no effect) is executed; otherwise the appropriate variable is incremented.

A more complex example of the DO-CASE is

```
         DO CASE X-5;
              X = X+5;                /* CASE 0 */
              DO;                     /* CASE 1 */
                   X = X+10;
                   Y = X−3;
              END;
              DO I = 3 TO 10;          * Case 2 */
                   A/= A+I;
              END;
              /* END OF CASES */
```

This example illustrates the use of DO-END blocks to group several statements as a single (although compound) PL/M statement.

The If-Statement

The IF-statement provides alternative execution of statements. It takes the form

```
              IF expression THEN statement-1;
              ELSE statement-2;
```

and has the following effect: first the expression following the reserved word IF is evaluated. If the result has a low-order (rightmost) bit of 1, then statement-1 is executed; if the result has a rightmost bit of 0 then statement-2 is executed. Following execution of the chosen alternative, control passes to the next statement following the if-construct. Thus of the two subordinate statements (statement-1 and statement-2) one and only one is executed.

The IF-statement tests the rightmost bit of an expression in the same way as the DO-WHILE statement. The most intuitive interpretation associates TRUE with a rightmost bit of 1, and FALSE with a rightmost bit of 0.

Consider the following program fragment:

IF A>B THEN RESULT=A;
ELSE RESULT=B;

Here RESULT is assigned the value of A or the value of B, whichever is greater. As program control falls through this fragment, there will be exactly one assignment statement executed. RESULT always gets assigned some value; but only one assignment to RESULT will be executed.

Let us return to the most general form of the IF-statement:

IF expression THEN statement-1;
ELSE statement-2;

In the event that statement-2 is not needed, the else-clause may be omitted entirely. Such an IF-statement takes the form

IF expression THEN statement-1;

Here the subordinate statement is executed only if the value of the if-condition has a rightmost bit of 1; otherwise nothing happens, and control falls right through the if-construct.

For example, the following sequence of PL/M statements will assign to INDEX either the number 5, or the value of Y, whichever is larger. The value of X will change during execution of the IF-statement only if Y is greater than 5. The final value of X is always copied to INDEX in any case.

X = 5;
IF Y > X THEN X = Y;
INDEX = X;

The power of the IF construct is enhanced by compound statements. Since a do-group is itself syntactically equivalent to a single statement, each of the two subordinate statements in an IF-construct may be a do-group. For example:

IF A=B THEN
    DO;
    . . .
    END;
ELSE
    DO;
    . . .
    END;

These do-groups can contain further nested if-statements, variable and procedure declarations, and so on.

There is only one restriction on subordinate statements of if-statements: statement-1 (that is, the subordinate statement just following the if-clause) may not itself be an if-statement, unless no ELSE is attached to either of these IF's. In other words, the construction

> IF condition-1 THEN
> > IF condition-2 THEN statement-3;
> ELSE statement-2;

is ambiguous and illegal (to which IF does the ELSE belong?), and must be replaced by one of the two following constructions, depending on the actual intention:

(1) IF condition-1 THEN
>   DO;
>   IF condition-2 THEN statement-3;
>   END;
> ELSE statement-2;

(2) IF condition-1 THEN
>   DO;
>   IF condition-2 THEN statement-3;
>   ELSE statement-2;
>   END;

Arrays

Array Declarations

It is frequently convenient to let one PL/M identifier represent more than one BYTE or ADDRESS value. When this is desired, the identifier must be suitably declared in a DECLARE statement. For example,

> DECLARE X (100) BYTE;

causes the identifier X to be associated with 100 data elements, each of type BYTE. Furthermore,

> DECLARE (A, B, C) (100) ADDRESS;

causes the 3 identifiers A, B, and C each to be associated with 100 data elements of type ADDRESS, so that 300 elements of type ADDRESS have been declared in all. Variables that have been declared in this manner to name more than a single data element are called arrays, vectors, or subscripted variables.

(In the special case that an array is declared to have a length of zero, no space will be allocated for it in memory. As a result, the variable will be a ghost, which refers to memory not specifically reserved for it.)

Subscripted Variables

It is sometimes necessary to refer to each element of an array by name. For example,

$$DECLARE\ X(100)\ BYTE;$$

actually declares 100 data elements of type BYTE, with names $X(0)$, $X(1)$, $X(2)$, and so on up to $X(99)$. If we wish to add the third data element to the fourth, and store the result in the fifth, we can write the PL/M assignment statement

$$X(4) = X(2) + X(3);$$

The index in parentheses, which selects the specific data element of the array, is called an array index, or subscript.

Much of the power of a subscripted variable lies in the fact that its subscript need not be a numeric constant, but can be another variable, or in fact any valid PL/M expression. Thus the following program will sum the elements of the array NUMBERS:

```
DECLARE SUM BYTE;
DECLARE NUMBERS (10) BYTE;
DECLARE I BYTE;

SUM = 0;
DO I = 0 TO 9;
    SUM = SUM + NUMBERS(I);
END;
EOF
```

Subscripted variables are permitted anywhere PL/M permits a simple variable, with the one exception that it is not legal to use one as the control variable of an iterative do-group.

More details on PL/M can be obtained from Intel Corporation, Santa Clara, California.

7.5.2   Basic

As previously stated, BASIC (Beginner's All-purpose Symbolic Instruction Code) is an interpretive language that is commonly used in an interactive mode.

BASIC is written in free format (extra blank spaces are ignored) with each statement consisting of a statement number, instruction, and operand. The following example illustrates the BASIC statements used to calculate the average of six numbers.

```
 5  INPUT G,H,I,J,K,L
10  LET V1 = (G+H+I+J+K+L)/6
15  PRINT V1
20  GO to 5
25  END
```

From this example, it can be seen that the statements of BASIC are easily understood and easy to use. A second example will illustrate some other features of BASIC.

```
20  LET Y = 10
30  READ Z
40  IF Z < = Y THEN 70
50  PRINT "Z IS LARGER THAN"; Y
60  GO TO 30
70  PRINT "Z IS LESS THAN OR EQUAL TO "; Y
80  GO TO 30
90  STOP
```

Statements 50 and 70 are PRINT instructions that print a statement concerning the value of Z relative to Y and also print the value of Y as part of the statement.

BASIC has many more useful features that can be explored by the reader through many excellent references on the subject.*

7.5.3 An Interpretive Adding Machine

A microprocessor programmed to operate as an adding machine is an excellent vehicle with which to illustrate the inner workings of an interpreter program. The adding machine developed is a simple stack-oriented processor and will interpret the following six commands.

* J.G. Kemeney and T.E. Kurtz, *BASIC Programming*, John Wiley and Sons, New York, 1967.

<number>   when a number is typed it is pushed onto the stack (numbers are in BCD)

\+   a plus adds the top two elements of the stack

\-   a minus subtracts the last two elements on the stack

<   copies the top of stack to memory

>   pushes memory onto the stack

C   clear the adding machine

After each operation, the top of stack is displayed, so that a sample run of the program would appear as:

INPUT	DISPLAY	COMMENTS
	0000	machine starts in cleared state
0010	0010	number 10 entered onto stack
0020	0020	number 20 entered onto stack
+	0030	10 + 20 = 30
<	0030	number 30 copied to memory
0073	0073	number 73 entered onto stack
>	0030	bring back 30 from memory
+	0103	73 + 30 = 103

The algorithm for the adding machine is:

- Initialize machine in BCD mode.
- Initialize array pointer (used as stack).
- Store a zero.
- Loop. Display data in array pointer, which involves:

  get an input

  is the flag set? (indicating an operation is being entered)

      no: increment pointer
            array[pointer] ← input
            go to loop

      yes: decrement pointer,
             on the following input, DO the following:

	(Op Code)	
Addition	[0]	(POINTER) ← (POINTER) + (POINTER+1)
		GO TO LOOP
Subtraction	[1]	(POINTER) ← (POINTER) − (POINTER+1)
		GO TO LOOP
Store memory	[2]	INCREMENT POINTER
		MEMORY←(POINTER)
		GO TO LOOP
Get memory	[3]	POINTER←POINTER+2
		(POINTER)←MEMORY
		GO TO LOOP
Clear	[4]	GO TO VERY BEGINNING
Anything else		INCREMENT POINTER
		GO TO LOOP

The code for this procedure in the assembly language of Chapter 6 is:

```
            ORG     0                 ;STARTING ADDRESS FOR
                                      ;THIS PROGRAM IS
                                      ;LOCATION 0
            DEFINE  POINT,r0          ;SET ASIDE VARIABLES, r0 IS
                                      DEFINED AS POINT
            DEFINE  INDAT,r1          ;r1 IS DEFINED AS INDAT
            DEFINE  SCRATCH,r2        ;r2 IS DEFINED AS SCRATCH
            DEFINE  MEMORY,r3         ;r3 IS DEFINED AS MEMORY
ARRAY:      BLOCK   16                ;RESERVE 16 MEMORY
                                      ;LOCATIONS FOR DATA
                                      ;STARTING AT LOCATION 0
MAIN:       CTR     0000B             ;SET UP DECIMAL MODE, NO
                                      ;INTERRUPTS
            MOV     POINT,ARRAY       ;SET UP THE ARRAY POINTER
            XOR     (POINT),(POINT)   ;CLEAR TOP OF STACK
MAINLP:     MOV     SCRATCH,(POINT)   ;GET TOP OF STACK
            OUT     (DISP),SCRATCH    ;DISPLAY THE TOP OF STACK
            INP     INDAT,(KEYBRD)    ;GET AN INPUT
            JFL     YESFLAG           ;JUMP ON FLAG
NOFLAG:     INC     POINT,POINT       ;INCREMENT THE STACK
                                      ;POINTER
            MOV     (POINT),INDAT     ;STORE THE NEW NUMBER
                                      ON THE STACK
            JUN     MAINLP            ;GET ANOTHER INPUT
```

```
YESFLAG:    DEC     POINT,POINT          ;POINT←POINT-1
            CPA     INDAT,0              ;WAS COMMAND A 0?
            JNE     CASE1
            INC     SCRATCH,POINT        ;SCRATCH←POINT+1
            ADD     (POINT),(SCRATCH)
            JUN     MAINLP               ;ADDITION COMPLETED
CASE1:      CPA     INDAT,1              ;WAS COMMAND A 1?
            JNE     CASE2
            INC     SCRATCH,POINT
            SUB     (POINT),(SCRATCH)
            JUN     MAINLP               ;SUBTRACTION COMPLETED
CASE2:      CPA     INDAT,2              ;WAS COMMAND A 2?
            JNE     CASE3
            INC     POINT,POINT
            MOV     MEMORY,(POINT)       ;SAVE TOP OF STACK
            JUN     MAINLP
CASE3:      CPA     INDAT,3              ;WAS COMMAND A 3?
            JNE     MAIN                 ;IF NOT THEN RESTART
            ADD     POINT,2
            MOV     (POINT),MEMORY
            JUN     MAINLP

            END
```

7.5.4 PASCAL

A high level programming language that is finding increasing acceptance among microcomputer manufacturers and users is PASCAL. PASCAL incorporates the methods of program structuring defined by Dahl, Dijkstra, and Hoare (1) and leads the programmer to a disciplined approach to algorithm implementation.

Some subjective and objective reasons for using PASCAL as a general purpose programming language are:

1. PASCAL forces programs to be developed from a general overall point of view and then to successively work down to more specific levels of detail in an orderly manner. This technique is sometimes referred to as *structured programming*. The usual case of a PASCAL program is to have a relatively simplified main program segment that is almost entirely made up of calls to a series of statements known as procedures. The low-level details of a program are executed inside procedures that, themselves, are called from other procedures and the main program. The function of the main program is to direct the overall flow of the program.

2. PASCAL provides facilities that make well written PASCAL programs highly readable, and, as a consequence, maintenance and documentation tend to be simplified. Included is the ability to define new data types, data structuring, and set operations. Programs written in FORTRAN, unless they are scientific application programs oriented to "number crunching," have a tendency to use programming "tricks" that make it difficult for another individual to easily interpret the program flow and the corresponding algorithm.

3. For microcomputer users, PASCAL software portability development work at the University of California at San Diego (UCSD) makes PASCAL especially attractive since moving an application from one microcomputer to another need not entail a new development effort. There is a strong concensus to keep PASCAL standard and not to have different PASCAL implementations as is the case with FORTRAN.

A basic description of the PASCAL language, which was developed by Professor Niklaus Wirth (2,3) at the Eidgenossische Technische Hochschule in Zurich, Switzeland, is presented in the following paragraphs, but the reader should refer to one of the many available texts for a comprehensive coverage of the subject. The following material is intended only as a familiarization with PASCAL.

Structure is obtained in PASCAL by embedding program segments written in PASCAL into a PASCAL *program*. A PASCAL program is comprised of a *heading* and a *block* concluding with a period. The heading begins with the word **PROGRAM**, which is always the first word in a PASCAL program and is reserved by the compiler. The heading is separated from the block by a semicolon. When a word is reserved, it cannot be used in a program other than as prescribed by the language syntax rules. The name of the program follows the word **PROGRAM.** For example, the heading

PROGRAM CONTROL (INPUT, OUTPUT);

identifies the program name as CONTROL and lists the files to be used by the program. In this case, the standard input and output files will be used, which means that data will be read into the program and sent out from the program. This construction and all others can be schematically represented by means of a *syntax diagram* or *syntax chart* which was introduced by Professor Wirth. The syntax chart for a PASCAL program is:

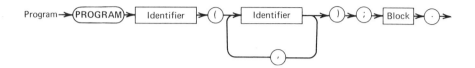

In the syntax diagram, the ovals and circles contain symbols which must appear in the program exactly as they appear in the diagram. As previously stated, the word **PROGRAM** must specifically be the first word in a PASCAL program. A rectangle in the diagram contains names whose formulation rules are themselves defined by another syntax diagram. In the syntax diagram for a PASCAL program it can be seen that the word **PROGRAM** is followed by an identifier that is the program name (CONTROL in the previous example) and then by a pair of parentheses enclosing an identifier or identifiers that are the files used by the program. In the example, these files are input and output files. Note that multiple identifiers can be contained within the parentheses and these identifiers must be separated by a comma as depicted by the "feedback" loop around the second identifier block. The comma symbol in the circle contained in the loop specifies that multiple identifiers must be separated by a comma. The semicolon symbol must follow the closing parentheses of the second identifier and serves to separate the PASCAL program heading from the block of the program.

The block of a PASCAL program contains a list of statements and may also contain declarations of variable and constant types. The statement list must be preceded by the reserved word **BEGIN** and immediately followed by the reserved word **END.** In the syntax diagram, the list of statements bracketed by **BEGIN** and **END** are referred to as a *compound statement* with the syntax diagram as follows:

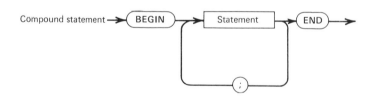

A semicolon serves as a separator between statements and is not a part of a statement. Thus, there is no semicolon between the last statement in the block and the reserved word **END.** The block of a PASCAL program is always terminated by a period. The syntax diagram of a PASCAL program block is:

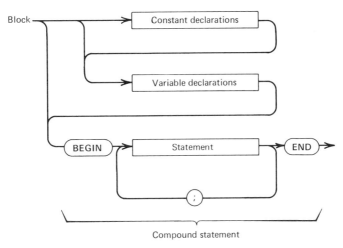

Compound statement

It is important to consider that the syntax diagram of a statement as shown in the block syntax also contains a compound statement. Thus, compound statements can be "nested" in other compound statements.

The six commonly used types of PASCAL statements are given by the statement syntax diagram.

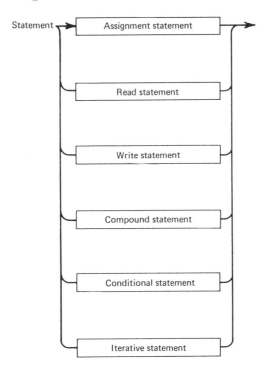

Examples of constant, variable, and type declarations and of the six types of statements will serve to further illustrate the PASCAL syntax. The declaration will be discussed first.

Declaration of a constant or constants in the heading of a PASCAL program must begin with the reserved word **CONST**. The **CONST** declaration must precede the **TYPE** and **VAR** declarations, which are described following **CONST**. Examples of constant declarations are:

```
CONST
    MAX = 200;
    MIN = −50;
    OLD = − YOUNG;
    LETTER = 'A';
```

The reserved symbol = is interpreted as "equals" or "is set equal to." A character enclosed in single quotes ' ' such as A in the above example is interpreted as a character for printing.

Variable declarations must be preceded by the reserved word **VAR**. The four standard types of variables in PASCAL are described by the reserved words INTEGER, REAL, BOOLEAN, and CHAR (character.) Integers are either positive or negative whole numbers such as 222 or −10. Real numbers are numbers such as 15.4, 10.00, and 0.0016. Scientific representation of real numbers is 1.6×10^{-3} or 5.68923×10^{10}. Boolean variables have only two values, TRUE or FALSE. Character variables denoted by CHAR are printable characters. The symbol : separates the variable name or names from the type description. Some example variable declarations are:

```
VAR
    NUM : INTEGER;
    COUNT, INITIAL, FIRST : INTEGER;
    WEIGHT, MAXVAL, MASS : REAL;
    MINTERM, T : BOOLEAN;
    FIRSTCHAR : CHAR;
```

In this description, variables *NUM, COUNT, INITIAL,* and *FIRST* are declared as integers; variables *WEIGHT, MAXVAL,* and *MASS* as real numbers; variables *MINTERM* and *T* as Boolean variables; and variable *FIRSTCHAR* as a character variable.

A third declaration in PASCAL is the **TYPE** declaration. This declaration must appear between the **CONST** and **VAR** declarations and permits the assignment of properties to the range of values that can be assumed by a variable. It can also define the range of values of a variable. The types of variables defined by a **TYPE** statement are the *simple* and *structured* data types. The *simple* data types are made up of the previously described standard scalar PASCAL data types INTEGER, REAL, BOOLEAN, and CHAR and also user-definable scaler and subrange types. In the declaration of a scalar-type variable an ordered set of identifiers are the values that the variable can assume. The subrange-type declaration restricts a variable to an ordered subset of previously defined scalar values. The subrange is made up of two constants that denote the low and high values to which a variable may be assigned. **TYPE** declarations utilize the = sign as do **CONST** declarations. The syntax diagram for the right-hand side of a simple **TYPE** declaration statement is:

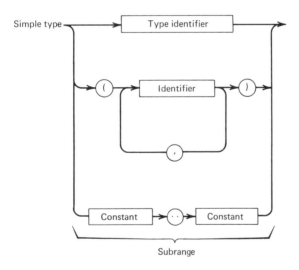

Examples of the three paths in the syntax diagram of a simple **TYPE** declaration are:

```
TYPE
    DAYTYPE = MONDAY;
    TIME = (MORNING, NOON, AFTERNOON, EVENING, MIDNIGHT);
    NUMBER = 1..75;
```

Structured data variables have more than one component where each component is either a simple or a structured data type. The syntax diagrams of the five structured data types used in **TYPE** statements are array, file, record, and set and corresponding examples are:

Array Type

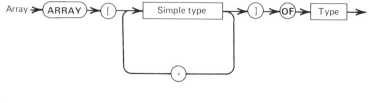

CONST
    MAXNO = 50;
TYPE
    SUBSCRIPT = 1..MAXNO;
    VECTOR = **ARRAY** [SUBSCRIPT] **OF** INTEGER;
VAR

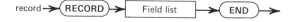

Record Type

record → (RECORD) → | Field list | → (END) →

The record type is a structured data type where RECORD has a number of components associated with an object. It differs from ARRAY in that a record may have different types identified by a name instead of an ARRAY subscript. The components of the record make up the field list. The means of denoting a record are as illustrated.

    TYPE
        PLAYERS =
            RECORD
                NAME : **ARRAY** [1..32] **OF** CHAR;
                POSITION : **ARRAY** [1..16] **OF** CHAR;
                ACTIVE : BOOLEAN;
            END;

Pointer Type
    A pointer type provides a method of accessing elements of a given type. The pointer variables of PASCAL allow for the dynamic creation of

variables. A pointer is bound to a **TYPE**. As an example consider the previously defined RECORD of **TYPE** player. The pointer variable NEXT could be added as a component within the record. i.e.

```
TYPE
    PLAYERS =
        RECORD
            NAME : ARRAY [1..32] OF CHAR;
            POSITION : ARRAY [1..16] OF CHAR;
            ACTIVE : BOOLEAN;
            NEXT : ↑ PLAYER;
        END;
```

The NEXT component of PLAYER could then be used to link the players. It could also be used to "create" new players at run time with the **NEW** primitive. For example:

```
NEW (PLAYER.NEXT);
```

File Type

The file type structured data type occurs where a file is a sequential storage of values of components having a common type and type must not be another file type or a type containing a file type. In the following example, file TEAMFILE is declared in the PASCAL program heading and defined. Also, note that the file is declared as the variable IDENT.

```
            PROGRAM TEAMPOINTS (INPUT, OUTPUT, IDENT)
CONST
    HIGHESTSCORE = 100;
TYPE
    TEAMSCORE = 0..HIGHESTSCORE;
    TEAMNAME = ARRAY [TEAMSCORE] OF CHAR;
    TEAMFILE = FILE OF TEAMNAME;
VAR
    IDENT:TEAMFILE;
```

Set Type

A **SET** in PASCAL is used to represent the mathematical set that is a collection of identifiable objects. The syntax diagram of a PASCAL set is:

The set operators *, +, and −, denote the set intersection, union, and difference, respectively. Also, in PASCAL the symbol > denotes *a set contains,* the symbol < denotes *a set is contained by,* the term IN denotes *inclusion* (ε), the symbol [ ] denotes *the null set,* the symbol ≠ denotes *set inequality,* and the symbol = denotes *set equality.* Examples of two set type declarations (AVAILABLE—ELEMENTS AND ACCOUNT) are: Note that some PASCAL installations permit insertion of the — (underline) character in a string for clarity.

```
CONST
    MAXCOUNT = 150;
TYPE
    ELEMENTS = (HYDROGEN, HELIUM, OXYGEN, CARBON,
        NITROGEN);
    AVAILABLE—ELEMENTS = SET OF ELEMENTS;
    VALUES = 1..MAXCOUNT;
    ACCOUNT = SET OF VALUES;
```

With these brief descriptions of constant, variable, and type declarations, the six common categories of statements can be discussed.

An assignment statement has the syntax diagram:

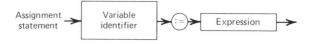

where the reserved symbol := is interpreted as "is assigned the value" or "becomes." A simple assignment statement is

$$Y := 10$$

which is interpreted as "the variable Y is assigned the value of 10." Another assignment statement is:

$$NEWVALUE := NEWVALUE + 2$$

which adds 2 to the present value of variable NEWVALUE and assigns this sum to the variable NEWVALUE, replacing the previous value of NEWVALUE.

If the PASCAL instructions **READ** and **WRITE** are to be used without referring to a specific file name, the standard files INPUT and OUTPUT must be declared in the program heading. An example of a simple PASCAL program illustrating **READ** and **WRITE** used in this manner is:

```
PROGRAM CALCSQR (INPUT,OUTPUT);
    VAR
        Y:INTEGER;
    BEGIN
        READ(Y);
        WRITE(SQR(Y));
    END.
```

In this PASCAL program named $CALCSQR$, which calculates the square of an integer number, the declaration of files INPUT and OUTPUT in the heading indicates the program will read data in and then print data out. The variable Y will be read from an input medium (the actual medium is unknown to the program) by the **READ**(Y) statement and is defined to be an integer value by the assignment statement Y:INTEGER. Calculation of the square of Y is performed by the standard PASCAL function **SQR( )** and the result is sent out to the output medium by the **WRITE( )** statement. The **READ** and **WRITE** statements also accept multiple arguments such as:

```
READ(MIN, AV, MAX) or
WRITE(SUM, DIFF)
```

Since the identifier word **FILE** as used in a PASCAL program is based on magnetic type file operation, a file must be "rewound" prior to reading from it or writing to it. This "rewinding" is accomplished by the PASCAL instruction **RESET**. Before a read or write operation is executed in PASCAL, the instruction **REWRITE** must be invoked in preparation for a read or write. The type of file is declared in a **TYPE** statement such as:

```
TYPE
    ALPHATYPE = ARRAY [1..200] OF CHAR;
    ALPHAFILE = FILE OF ALPHATYPE;
VAR
    DIARY: ALPHAFILE;
```

Note that the file itself can be declared as a variable in the variable declaration statement. Recall that a PASCAL file is a structured data type with the syntax diagram:

where type must not be another file type or a type containing a file type.

An important consideration is that a file variable, even though declared (as *DIARY* above), cannot be assigned a value or referenced directly in an expression. Instead the file variable with the symbol ↑ appended to it serves to reference a file buffer that can be used as an ordinary PASCAL variable. The communication between a file buffer and the file itself is accomplished by the PASCAL procedures **PUT( )** and **GET( )**. The instruction **GET**(*DIARY*) will transfer the next component of file DIARY to the file buffer and **PUT**(*DIARY*) will append the value in the file buffer to the file DIARY. The following statement will fetch data from file *DIARY* through file buffer *DIARY* ↑ and print the data on the output medium.

```
RESET (DIARY);
GET(DIARY);
WRITE(DIARY ↑ );
```

Similarly, to read a variable labeled as Y from the beginning of an input file (previously declared in the program heading) and store the variable in file DIARY, one may use the following instructions.

```
REWRITE (DIARY);
READ(Y)
DIARY ↑ :=Y;
PUT(DIARY);
```

Each time a **GET** operation is performed, a pointer to the data in the file is positioned to be able to retrieve the next value in sequence in the file when the next **GET** operation is executed. In order to provide an end of file indication, a Boolean function, EOF( ), will return a value of TRUE when the end of a file has been reached. The value of EOF( ) can be checked by PASCAL conditional statements that will be described subsequently. The standard PASCAL procedures **READLN( )** and

WRITELN( ) are used to read and write a line of a text file. For example, the instruction

READLN(*MIN, Y, Z*);

will read three values from a line of text from the input buffer and position the input buffer pointer to the start of a new line. **WRITELN** will print a line of text on the output device and transmit a carriage return to the output file. Examples of usage of WRITELN are:

WRITELN ('TIME OF DAY');
WRITELN (*NUMBER*1, *NUMBER*2);

A compound statement has the advantage of being treated as a single entity that is executed when one statement cannot perform the actions required. The reserved words **BEGIN** and **END** bracket the list of statements that are to be executed as a unit. The syntax diagram of a compound statement was previously given in the block syntax diagram and is repeated for convenience.

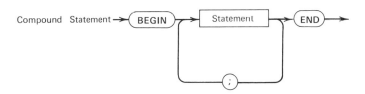

An example of a compound statement in a PASCAL program is:

```
BEGIN
    READ (COST, AMT_IN_BUDGET);
    AMT_IN_BUDGET := AMT_IN_BUDGET - COST;
    WRITELN ('AMOUNT IN BUDGET = ', AMT_IN_BUDGET);
END
```

To develop useful programs in any programming language, *conditional* and *iterative* statements are required. In PASCAL, the syntax diagram of the **IF–THEN–ELSE** conditional statement is:

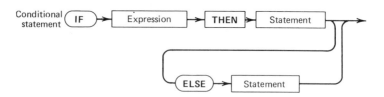

If the expression following the **IF** is true, the statement following the **THEN** statement is executed. Otherwise, the operation in the statement following **ELSE** is performed. If the **ELSE** is omitted and the expression following **IF** is false, nothing occurs as an alternative. The expression in the syntax diagram is a Boolean expression that utilizes the relational PASCAL operators, $<$, $< =$, $=$, $\neq$, $> =$, and $>$, which, as in mathematics, have the meanings of *less than, less than or equal to, equal to, not equal to, greater than or equal to,* and *greater than,* respectively. No semicolons are used within the **IF-THEN-ELSE** statement or after the statement. An example program using this statement follows. The symbol $<>$ is sometimes used in place of inequality ($\neq$).

```
PROGRAM AGECOUNT (INPUT,OUTPUT);
    CONST
  MAXAGE = 60;
    VAR
  AGE, INAGE,OVERAGE : INTEGER;
    BEGIN
```
_____
_____
_____
```
  INAGE := 0;
  OVERAGE:= 0;
  READ (AGE);
  IF AGE < MAXAGE
    THEN INAGE:= INAGE+1
    ELSE OVERAGE:= OVERAGE+1
```
_____
_____
_____
```
  END.
```

The iterative statement provides a means of executing a statement repeatedly. Two statements in PASCAL that provide this capability are the **REPEAT–UNTIL** statement and the **WHILE–DO** statement. The syntax diagrams for these statements are:

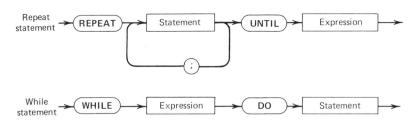

The **REPEAT–UNTIL** statement will execute the statement(s) bracketed by the words **REPEAT** and **UNTIL** until the expression following **UNTIL** is true. The value of the expression will be checked after each cycle of statement execution(s). In the **WHILE–DO** statement, the statement following **DO** is executed if the expression following **WHILE** is true. The expression following **WHILE** is evaluated at the beginning of the cycle, and the termination of the operations following **DO** depends on the condition of the expression at the beginning of each cycle through the loop. Examples of usage of **REPEAT–UNTIL** and **WHILE–DO** statements are as follows.

```
CONST
    MAXNO = 5000000;
VAR
    BINARY:INTEGER;
BEGIN
    BINARY := 2;
    REPEAT
        WRITELN(BINARY)
        BINARY: =2*BINARY;
    UNTIL BINARY > MAXNO
END
```

In the **REPEAT–UNTIL** statement, the words **REPEAT** and **UNTIL** correspond to the words **BEGIN** and **END** in a compound statement, thus permitting semicolons in the statement, between **REPEAT** and **UNTIL**.

or, for **WHILE–DO**

```
CONST
    MAXNO = 5000000;
VAR
    BINARY:INTEGER;
BEGIN
    BINARY:=2;
    WHILE BINARY < MAXNO DO
      BEGIN
        WRITELN(BINARY)
        BINARY:=2*BINARY;
      END
END
```

The **WHILE–DO** statements require the compound statement construct of **BEGIN** and **END** if more than one statement follows **WHILE–DO**.

Comment

Comment is a character string that is ignored by the program and is used to document steps in the program for later reference. Two commonly used notations for delimiting comments are {. . .} and (*. . .*). Any character except the notation which indicates the end of the comment (i.e.} or *)) is permitted in a comment character string. Example:

```
CONST
     MAXNO = 20; {MAXIMUM VALUE OF ORDER NUMBERS}
     UPLIMIT = 100000; {UPPER CREDIT LIMIT}
```

Procedure

Procedure is a PASCAL statement that has been assigned a name or identifier. When the procedure name is invoked or called in the program, the statement will be executed. For example, the following statement will read characters from the array called TEXT until it finds a nonblank character.

```
REPEAT
     READ (TEXT [I]);
     I: = I + 1;
UNTIL TEXT [I] < >' ';
```

This statement could be given the name SKIP-BLANKS and made into a procedure by the following construction.

```
PROCEDURE SKIP-BLANKS (VAR I: INTEGER, TEXT : ARRAY [1..MAX] OF CHAR);
     BEGIN
          REPEAT
               READ (TEXT [I]);
               I: = I + 1;
          UNTIL TEXT [I] < >' ';
     END
```

Now, every time the statement SKIP-BLANKS is written in the PASCAL program, the TEXT will be scanned for the next nonblank character.

Function

PASCAL provides standard functions to the user such as ABS (absolute value), SIN, COS, SQR (square), SQRT (square root), and others. A *custom function* can be defined by the programmer using the following syntax diagram.

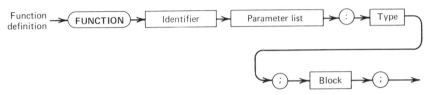

An example of a function defined as MIN is (the second integer reference in the example declaration refers to function MIN):

```
FUNCTION MIN (A,B : INTEGER) : INTEGER;
    BEGIN
        IF A<B THEN
            MIN := A
        ELSE
            MIN : = B
    END;
```

The values assumed by A and B will be determined by the values in the corresponding positions in the function calling statement. For example, the calling statement:

```
SMALLNUMBER := MIN (NUM1, 100)
```

would assign the value of variable NUM1 to A and 100 to B in the function and return the smallest of the two values to the location in memory designated as SMALLNUMBER.

An advantage of PASCAL over some other languages, such as FORTRAN, is the ability of a FUNCTION or PROCEDURE to call itself. This characteristic is known as the *recursive* property. An illustration of the use of *recursion* is shown in the following example of a FUNCTION which calculates N!

```
FUNCTION      FACTORIAL (N: INTEGER) : INTEGER;
BEGIN
    IF N = 1 THEN
        FACTORIAL: = 1
    ELSE
        FACTORIAL: = N * FACTORIAL (N − 1);
END;
```

Since this discussion of PASCAL is intended as an orientation to the language, many concepts and structures could not be developed in the depth necessary to develop skill in using the language. In order to unify the material that has been covered, however, a complete PASCAL program is presented to conclude the PASCAL familiarization.

The problem of sorting a sequence of elements is one which occurs frequently. The sorting problem can be formulated as follows: given a sequence of n elements, find a permutation that will map the sequence into an ascending sequence.

The PASCAL program presented here sorts an array of integers using the heap sort algorithm. The algorithm makes use of an interesting data structure, a heap. A heap is defined to have the following properties. Given that the array A[1], A[2], . . ., A[N] represents a heap, then for every K < N, 2K < N implies that A[K] > A[2 * K] and 2K +1 < N implies that A[K] > A[2 * K + 1].

A heap can best be understood in terms of a binary tree where a father A[K] is greater than or equal to both the left son A[2 * K] and the right son A[2 * K + 1].

This PASCAL example demonstrates the program structuring and detail hiding which can easily be achieved with the language. At the highest level we define two variables and 3 procedures. The variables define the number of elements to be sorted and the array which contains the elements. The procedures read in the data, sort the data, and print the data. Each of the high level procedures contain further refinements. In particular, the sort_list procedure defines an additional variable and three more procedures. The variable defines the number in the heap. The procedures build the initial heap, exchange two values, and reconstruct the heap.

The procedure, make_heap, is a recursive procedure which defines the variable child and another function not_heap. The function not_heap contains further refinements, i.e., the function which returns the larger-child.

The algorithm to sort the array is as follows:

To sort an array A[1], A[2], . . ., A[N] of N elements.

(1) Build a heap with the N elements.
(2) Exchange A[1] (the largest element) with A[N].
(3) If N > 2 then rebuild the heap for N − 1 elements.
(4) Set N = N −1 and repeat steps 2, 3, and 4 until N = 1.

```
PROGRAM   H_SORT (INPUT, OUTPUT);
CONST     MAX = 100;
VAR VALUE: ARRAY[1..MAX] OF INTEGER;
          NUMBER_TO_BE_SORTED: INTEGER;
PROCEDURE READ_LIST;
          VAR I: INTEGER;
BEGIN
          I:= 1;
          READ (VALUE[I]);
          WHILE VALUE[I] <> 9999 DO
          BEGIN
                 I:= I + 1;
                 READ (VALUE [I]);
          END;
          NUMBER_TO_BE_SORTED:= I - 1;
END;
PROCEDURE SORT_LIST;
          VAR NUMBER_IN_HEAP: INTEGER;
          PROCEDURE EXCHANGE (VAR ELEMENT1, ELEMENT 2:
          INTEGER);
                 VAR TEMP: INTEGER;
          BEGIN
                 TEMP:= ELEMENT1;
                 ELEMENT1:= ELEMENT2;
                 ELEMENT2:= TEMP
          END;
          PROCEDURE MAKE_HEAP (PARENT, NUMBER_IN_HEAP: INTEGER);

                 VAR CHILD: INTEGER;
                 FUNCTION NOT_HEAP: BOOLEAN;
                        FUNCTION LARGER_CHILD: INTEGER;
                               VAR BROTHER: INTEGER;
                        BEGIN
                               LARGER_CHILD:= CHILD;
                               IF CHILD < NUMBER_IN_HEAP THEN
                               BEGIN

                                      BROTHER:= CHILD + 1;
                                      IF VALUE [BROTHER] > VALUE
                                      [CHILD] THEN
                                      LARGER_CHILD:= BROTHER;
                               END;
                        END;
```

```
                BEGIN
                        NOT_HEAP:= FALSE;
                        IF CHILD <= NUMBER_IN_HEAP { IS THERE A CHILD?
                        THEN   IF VALUE [PARENT] < VALUE [LARGER_CHILI
                                THEN NOT_HEAP:= TRUE;
                END;
        BEGIN
                CHILD:= PARENT * 2;
                IF NOT_HEAP THEN
                BEGIN
                        EXCHANGE (VALUE[PARENT], VALUE [CHILD]);
                        MAKE_HEAP (CHILD, NUMBER_IN_HEAP);
                END;
        END;
        PROCEDURE BUILD_HEAP;
                VAR PARENT: INTEGER;
        BEGIN
                FOR PARENT:= NUMBER_TO_BE_SORTED DIV 2 DOWNTO 1 [
                        MAKE_HEAP (PARENT, NUMBER_TO_BE_SORTED);
                END;
BEGIN
        BUILD_HEAP;
        FOR NUMBER_IN_HEAP := NUMBER_TO_BE_SORTED DOWNTO 2 D
        BEGIN
                EXCHANGE (VALUE [1], VALUE [NUMBER_IN_HEAP]);
                MAKE_HEAP (1, NUMBER_IN_HEAP - 1);
        END;
END;
PROCEDURE PRINT_LIST;
        VAR I:  INTEGER;
BEGIN
        FOR I := 1 TO NUMBER_TO_BE_SORTED DO
                WRITE (VALUE[I]);
END;
BEGIN
        READ_LIST;
        SORT_LIST;
        PRINT_LIST;
END.
```

7.6 EDITORS AND SIMULATORS

When writing microcomputer programs in assembly language or a high level language, one must have a means available to correct any errors in syntax or logic flow. A program which provides these and additional facilities is called an *Editor*. The Editor normally has two modes of operation—the *text* mode and the *command* mode. In the text mode, the user enters his program text, which is then stored in a *text buffer* (read/write memory locations set aside for text storage). In the command mode, the user specifies control commands to the Editor. Some typical Editor commands are:

- READ—read from the input file into the text buffer.
- WRITE—write text from text buffer to output file.
- FIND—search an input file for the occurrence of a text string as specified in the FIND command.
- INSERT—this command will insert additional text immediately following a specified line of text already in the buffer.
- DELETE—delete a specified number of characters.
- MODIFY—replace specific text in buffer with other text material.
- PUNCH—punch the contents of text buffer onto paper tape.

Editors are available that run on microcomputer development systems as well as on minicomputers and large computers. Generally, the larger the computer and amount of memory available, the more features that can be provided by the Editor.

Once the program has been edited and successfully assembled, the ultimate test of its correctness is to run the program on the microcomputer. The program can be entered into the microcomputer either by loading the program in RAM (using a loader program or a monitor incorporating a loader) or by "burning" the program in EPROM or PROM and then plugging it into the microcomputer card. Execution is accomplished by setting the Program Counter to the address of the first instruction in the program and starting the system. This starting feature is usually included in microcomputer monitors.

When the program runs, it may be completed in milliseconds and, if an error occurs, it would be impossible to trace unless some troubleshooting capabilities were available in the system. Some typical troubleshooting approaches are to have the microcomputer execute one instruction at a time (single step) so that the effect of each instruction could be monitored on input/output ports or on the address and data lines of the microprocessor. Additional methods have a second microcomputer monitoring the important buses and registers of the microcomputer under test and storing or displaying their contents for analysis. Still a third approach to the problem of debugging a microcomputer program is a simulator. A *simulator* is a program that is usually run on a minicomputer or a larger computer system and provides software simulation of the microprocessor or microprocessor(s) it is designed to support. Simulators are usually written in a high level language such as FORTRAN IV.

A simulator accepts machine code produced by an assembler or a high level language such as PL/M and executes the program as if it were being run on the microcomputer itself. During the execution, registers can be monitored and *breakpoints* set (points in the program where it is desired to stop execution and examine contents of the accumulator, registers, etc.). Other features are provided to permit tracing of CPU operations and interaction with the input/output portions of the microcomputer program.

Some typical commands available in simulators are:

- LOAD—loads microprocessor machine code and symbol tables into simulated microcomputer memory.
- SET—sets contents of memory locations, registers, or input/output ports to a designated value.
- GO—runs microprocessor code.
- INT—simulates microprocessor interrupt.
- BKPT—sets breakpoint in program that causes program to stop whenever a particular memory location is accessed.
- EXAM—displays contents of registers, memory locations, and input/output ports.
- CLOCK—displays number of simulated microprocessor cycles.
- STOP—stops the simulated microprocessor after a specified number of cycles.
- TRACE—permits tracing of particular portions of microcomputer program when they are executed. This tracing includes display of microprocessor register contents whenever a previously specified instruction is executed. Some simulators store and display the microprocessor's register contents and decoded instructions for a number of cycles preceding the instruction specified in the TRACE command.
- INP—provides data to simulated input port.
- PUNCH—produces machine code output in specified code.
- END—ends simulation.

7.7 DEVELOPMENT SYSTEMS

Assemblers, editors, and high level microcomputer languages such as PL/M are supported on microcomputer *development systems* in addition to being available for use on minicomputers and larger computers. A *development system* is a microprocessor-based computing system that is enhanced by hardware and software to permit hardware and software development and debugging.

A development system with a full complement of peripherals is shown in Figure 7.1. The development system in the figure (second from left) is supported by a dual floppy disk storage system (extreme left), a CRT interactive terminal (used by operator), and a line printer (extreme right).

The floppy disk system utilizes two recordlike diskettes that each provide in IBM sectioned format approximately 250,000 bytes of storage single density or 500,000 bytes dual density. These numbers will increase as magnetic storage technology is improved.

An IBM compatible diskette is divided into 77 circular tracks with a rotational speed of 360 rpm. The average latency time to read new data on the same track is approximately 83 millisec. The time to access a random track is a function of the time to move from track to track (approximately 10 msec) and the time for the magnetic read head to lower and settle (approximately 10 msec). The worst case time is ½ second for typical floppy disk drives. Once a track has been accessed, data can be read out at a typical speed of 250,000 bits/second.

The development system contains a microprocessor card, memory,

FIGURE 7.1 Microcomputer development system. (Courtesy of Intel Corp.)

I/O facilities, and support software such as an assembler, editor, debugging programs, and, in some cases, a high level language such as PL/M. An operating system program stored on disk is used to control and interact with the development system and its software.

The interactive CRT display typically has a data transfer rate of up to 9600 baud and provides a display of 80 characters across by 25 lines on the screen.

A typical printer used with a development system prints 80 or 132 characters per line at a rate of 55 lines/minute.

The cost of each of the four devices described (floppy disk drive, development system, CRT terminal, and printer) typically ranges from $3K to $4K.

7.8 EVALUATION TECHNIQUES

Critical areas that should be evaluated prior to undertaking a microcomputer-based project are the language to be used and the cost, performance, and support of the microcomputer relative to its intended application. The last two sections of this chpater will attempt to quantify these two areas so that an intelligent choice regarding their use can be made. Before proceeding, however, a word of caution is in order. Since any method of attempting to quantify characteristics (some of which may be subjective) is inexact, the results obtained should be weighted by the experience of the user relative to his particular application and product line.

7.8.1 High or Low Level Language Considerations

As a rule of thumb, assembly language programming for microcomputers pays off when it is important to save bytes of program memory. This criterion usually extrapolates to mean the application where a large number (thousands) of systems are to be produced. The speed and ease of programming with a high level microcomputer language such as PL/M or PASCAL outweigh its relative inefficient memory usage compared to assembly language programming where one or a few microcomputer-based systems are to be produced.

The decision on which programming method to use for systems whose numbers fall between these two limits is a function of the programmer's skill, memory cost/bit, and system production volume.

An empirical derivation of the crossover points from assembly language to high level language programming can be obtained by the following method. Let c = the cost/program memory bit/microcomputer system; let n = the number of program memory bits/microcomputer system; let m

= the total number of microcomputer systems to be built; and let k = cost per memory bit to write the program to be used by each microcomputer system in high level language (all microcomputer systems are assumed to use the same program). In addition, let us assume that, on the average, twice as much machine code will be generated by a high level language compiler than by a programmer writing in assembly language and that five times as much programming time is required to write the same program in assembly language than in a high level language. Now, the total cost, T_H, of programming m systems in a high level language can be written as

$$T_H = 2ncm + nk$$

and the total cost, T_L, of programming m systems in assembly language as

$$T_L = ncm + 5nk$$

The crossover point is found by setting $T_H = T_L$ or $2ncm + nk = ncm + 5nk$. Eliminating n and reducing:

$$2cm + k = cm + 5k$$
$$cm = 4k$$

An average value of k is approximately 5¢ bit. Therefore,

$$cm \cong 20$$

In other words, at the crossover point between assembly language and high level language programming, the product of cost/memory bit/system and the number of systems to be produced is approximately a constant value of 20 for the average values assumed above. A family of curves of language choice versus number of units to be produced with cost/memory bit as a parameter is given in Figure 7.2.

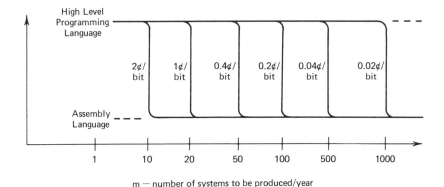

FIGURE 7.2 High level versus assembly language choice.

Again, note that the data on the chart are guidelines only and should not be used as absolute criteria in language selection but as factors to be considered along with the type of application, maintenance philosophies and previous organizaional experiences. To utilize the chart, the annual production volume and the system memory cost per bit must be determined or estimated. With those two parameters, the choice of high or low level language will be indicted by the chart. For example, if an annual production volume of 600 units were predicted and memory cost were 0.1¢/bit, the choice indicated would be assembly language. (A point on the graph to be right of a memory cost-per-bit parameter line specifies assembly language and a point to the left of this line specifies a high level language.)

7.8.2 Microprocessor Cost, Performance, and Support Evaluation

In evaluating a microprocessor, many areas have to be considered. The importance or weight given to these areas is heavily dependent on and varies with the application. The most important of these evaluation areas are:

1. Instruction set, including arithmetic capability.
2. Interrupt capability.
3. Word size.
4. Speed (evaluated by maximum clock frequency).
5. Minimum chip system.
6. Software support.
7. Hardware support.
8. Power requirements.
9. Input/output capability.
10. Memory size.
11. Peripheral chips available.
12. Cost.

If a number (minimum of 0 and maximum of 5) is assigned to each of these areas and this number is weighted by the relative importance of the area to a particular application, a weighted sum can be obtained as a figure of merit for a particular application. If k_i is a number between 0 and 5 assigned to the ith area of the 12 evaluation areas and w_i is the relative importance weight assigned to each of these evaluation areas, the figure of merit, F, of a particular microprocessor is:

$$F = w_1 k_1 + w_2 k_2 + \cdots + w_{12} k_{12}$$

$$= \sum_{i=1}^{12} w_i k_i$$

The w_i's can be chosen to have a range of values from 0 to 10. The k_i's are defined as follows.

1. Instruction set/arithmetic capability $\qquad\qquad k_1$

basic accumulator instructions	1
accumulator-to-memory instructions, BCD capability	2
register-to-memory instructions, BCD capability	3
memory-to-memory instructions, BCD capability	4
memory-to-memory instructions, BCD capability, multiply/divide	5

2. Interrupt capability $\qquad\qquad k_2$

no interrupt capability	0
single-level interrupt (add 1 for vectored capability)	1
multi-level interrupt (add 1 for vectored capability)	2
multi-level vectored interrupt implemented internally	3

3. *Word size* $\qquad\qquad k_3$

2-bit	1
4-bit	2
8-bit	3
16-bit	4
Bit-slice, expandable	5

4. Speed (max clock frequencies) $\qquad\qquad k_4$

Clock < 1 MHz	1
$1 \leq$ Clock < 2 MHz	2

$2 \leq$ Clock ≤ 4 MHz	3
Clock > 4 MHz	4

5. Minimum Chip System $\qquad k_5$

Minimum of 5 or more additional chips	0
Minimum of 4 or more additional chips	1
Minimum of 3 or more additional chips	2
Minimum of 2 or more additional chips	3
Minimum of 1 or more additional chips	4
Minimum of 0 or more additional chips	5

6. Software support $\qquad k_6$

Very little	0
Assemblers, Editors, some applications	1
High Level languages, applications	2
Operating systems, support in many areas	3
Operating systems, massive program libraries	4

7. Hardware support $\qquad k_7$

CPU Single source	1
CPU Multiple sources	2
CPU, Memory, Multiple sources	3
CPU, Memory, applications peripherals, Multiple sources	4

8. Power requirements $\qquad k_8$

3 or more supplies	1
2 supplies	2
1 supply	3
1 supply, variation tolerant	4

9. Input/output capability $\qquad k_9$

0	No I/O instructions or I/O capability	0

1	I/O instructions or memory mapped I/O	1
2	Interface support or separate I/O data bus	2
3	Features of (2)+software	3

10. Memory size k_{10}

<64K bits memory	0
64K bits (8 bits × 8k)	1
128K bits (8 bits × 16K)	2
128K <#bits < 512K (16 bits × 32K), (8 bits × 64K)	3
>512K bits	4

11. Peripheral chips available (compatibility with other manufacturer's families—add 1) k_{11}

No peripheral chips	0
Minimum peripheral chips	1
Family of peripherals	2
Family of peripherals and compatibility with other support chips	3

12. Cost k_{12}

a. Microprocessor cost > $100	0
b. Microprocessor cost ≤ $100	1
c. Microprocessor cost ≤ $50	2
d. Microprocessor cost ≤ $25	3
e. Microprocessor cost ≤ $10	4

Using these twelve areas, we develop two contrasting examples. Suppose it is desired to evaluate a microprocessor for applicaion as a traffic light controller and as a high-speed arithmetic processor. The proposed values of the w_i's for these two applications are:

EVALUATION AREA	TRAFFIC LIGHT w_i	ARITHMETIC w_i
1. Instruction set/arithmetic	4	10
2. Interrupt	6	1
3. Word size	2	8
4. Speed	4	10
5. Minimum chip system	10	3
6. Software support	5	9
7. Hardware support	8	4
8. Power	8	2
9. Input/output	9	1
10. Memory size	2	7
11. Peripheral chips	6	4
12. Cost	10	5

With these values of w_i established, let us now proceed to develop the values of k_i for some existing microprocessors. These values are presented in Table 7.1 and are derived from the specifications of the individual microprocessors.

Using the specified w_i's and the k_i values in Table 7.1, we find that the best values of F for the two applications are:

F (traffic light)	Microprocessor	F (arithmetic)	Microprocessor
233	8085A	208	LSI-11
227	6800	205	6809
227	Z-80	200	8085

This method incorporates the important aspects to be considered in microprocessor selection in a weighted fashion. It results in a reasonable guide to microprocessor evaluation relevant to a particular application **provided** that accurate k_i data are entered into the table **and** realistic weightings, w_i, are used. Note that in the selection process, factors other than purely architectural considerations influence the choice of microprocessors. Specifically, software support, hardware support, and availability of peripheral chips are important elements that must be weighed when evaluating a microprocessor.

TABLE 7.1 Values of k_i for Some Existing Microprocessors

	INSTRUCTION SET ARITHMETIC	INTERRUPT	WORD SIZE	SPEED	MINIMUM CHIP SYSTEM	SOFTWARE SUPPORT	HARDWARE SUPPORT	POWER	INPUT/OUTPUT	MEMORY SIZE	PERIPHERAL CHIP FAMILY	COST	TRAFFIC LIGHT	ARITHMETIC
INTEL 8748	3	2	3	2	5	1	4	3	3	1	2	1	197	145
INTEL 8085A	3	3	3	3	3	3	4	3	3	3	4	3	233	200
MOS TECHNOLOGY 6502	3	2	3	3	3	2	4	3	3	3	4	3	222	190
MOTOROLA 6800	3	2	3	3	3	3	4	3	3	3	4	3	227	199
RCA COSMAC	2	2	3	1	2	1	2	4	2	3	1	2	151	124
TI 9900	5	3	4	3	2	3	2	2	2	3	2	1	166	196
AMD 2900	1-5 (4)	0-3 (2)	5	4	0	3	3	3	0-2 (2)	0-4 (3)	2	2	159	190
FAIRCHILD F8	2	2	3	3	4	1	4	2	2	3	2	3	195	163
DEC LSI-11	5	3	4	3	0	4	4	2	3	3	2	1	176	208
ZILOG Z-80	3	2	3	3	3	3	4	3	3	3	4	3	227	199
MOTOROLA 6809	4	3	3	3	3	3	4	3	3	3	4	2	226	205

Problems

(Where assembly language programs are required, use assembly language of Chapter 6.)

1. Given a group of 8 positive numbers (in memory), write a subroutine that returns the largest number in the group in r0.

2. Given a group of 8 positive numbers (in memory), write two subroutines to find their average. One subroutine should use the divide instruction, and the other should use only shifts and adds.

3. Write a subroutine that will divide a positive 16-bit number by a power of 2 and return the quotient in r0. (Do not use the DIV instruction.)

4. Write a subroutine that will divide a 16-bit positive number by another 16-bit positive number, and return the quotient in 40. (Do not use the DIV instruction.)

5. Write a subroutine to generate the number of combinations of N items taken R at a time. Use the FACT subroutine from the text.

$$\text{Combinations:} \binom{N}{R} = \frac{N!}{R!(N-R)!}$$

6. Write a program that takes a board position in TIC-TAC-TOE and generates a legal move.
   Board is kept in nine memory locations with:

$$0 = \text{empty square}$$
$$1 = \text{computer's move}$$
$$2 = \text{opponent's move}$$

7. Same as problem (6) except that the board is kept in two memory locations as:

SQUARES   9   8   7   6   5   4   3   2   1

									(MEM)
									(MEM+1)

For each square

(MEM) (MEM+1)

0	0 = empty
0	1 = computer's move
1	0 = opponent's move

8. Develop a strategy and a complete program to play the game of NIM. Use calls to the sample monitor in the text for Input and Output.

NIM: (1) There is a pile of nine sticks.

(2) Each player may remove one or two sticks.

(3) Players alternate moves.

(4) Opponent goes first.

Goal: The person who takes the last stick loses.

9. Write a subroutine that reads a stream of data from memory and interprets it as follows.

<CARRIAGE RETURN>	all done
``	start of character string (terminated with a zero)
,	the next word contains a single character
#N	the next *n* characters make up a STRING
%	the next word contains a number

All characters are packed 2 per word (low byte first). The interpreter's output should be handled by calls to the sample monitor.

Example: (ASCII characters are in octal code; data are stored in 16-bit memory locations with two 8-bit words per memory location.)

ADDRESS	MEMORY		OUTPUT
n	101	``	
n + 1	103	102	
n + 2	40	104	
.	,	0	
.	—	105	
.	3	#	
.	61	60	
.	%	62	
.	101	101	
		<CR>	ABCD E01240501

10. Write a program that simulates a J-K flip-flop, defined as follows.

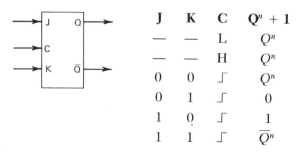

J	K	C	$Q^n + 1$
—	—	L	Q^n
—	—	H	Q^n
0	0	⌐	Q^n
0	1	⌐	0
1	0	⌐	1
1	1	⌐	$\overline{Q^n}$

(Q^n is logic state of Q output of flip-flop prior to application of clock to input C. Then Q^{n+1} is logic state of Q output of flip-flop after application of clock to input C. Flip-flop responds only to leading edge (low-to-high) transition of clock (C) input.)

11. Write a program to implement the following random number generation algorithm.

THE TAUSWORTHE RANDOM NUMBER GENERATOR

Let A and B be registers.

A = B = Last random number (called: SEED).

B = B Shifted right 4 places.

A = A EXCLUSIVE OR B.

B = B Shifted left 11D places.

A = A EXCLUSIVE OR B.

A = A AND 777770.

Store A as new SEED.

Return A.

REFERENCES

1. O.J. Dahl, E. W. Dijkstra, and C. A. R. Hoare, *Structured Programming*, Academic Press, 1972.

2. N. Wirth, "The Programming Language PASCAL," *Acta Informatica*, Vol. 1, pp. 35-63, 1971.

3. K. Jensen and N. Wirth, *PASCAL User Manual and Report* (Second Edition), Springer Verlag, 1976.

4. *Intel 8080 Assembly Language Programming Manual,* Intel Corporation, 1976.

5. C. Weitzman, *Minicomputer Systems,* Prentice-Hall, Inc. Englewood Cliffs, N.J., 1974.

6. *Intel PL/M Programming Manual,* Intel Corporation, 1976.

INTERFACING

The material in the previous chapters of this text was aimed at providing an understanding of microcomputer hardware and software and, to some extent, of communicating with external devices. The latter subject is of such importance that this chapter is devoted completely to the standards and techniques for accomplishing this data transfer and control.

The boundary that is shared between the microprocessor and another device such as a printer or CRT terminal is called the *interface. Interfacing* is defined as accomplishing the data transfer across this shared boundary.

8.1 OBJECTIVES

As a revolution in the electronics industry was brought about by the microcomputer, a second revolution is occurring in the area of microcomputer peripheral chips. These devices are, in many cases, more complex than the microprocessor itself and are programmable either through the microprocessor or independently. The goal of these peripheral LSI circuits is to reduce the number of chips necessary to transfer data in and out of a microprocessor and to provide capabilities that will allow the user to easily implement complex interfaces without large investments of time and labor. A good example of such a peripheral chip is a communications interface that can enable a microprocessor to receive or send data using a number of complex protocols such as SDLC (Synchronous Data Link Control) or BISYNC (Bisynchronous Control). If such a chip were not available, the designer would have to develop a detailed understanding of the protocol used and produce software and/or hardware to control the data link and perform error checking and recovery functions. In many cases, the software approach would not be fast enough to handle the incoming information and a communications interface would have to be built or purchased at an expense far exceeding that of the microcomputer being used.

The objectives of this chapter, then, are to examine:

1. the methodology of interfacing.
2. the types and means of microprocessor data transfers.
3. peripheral interface chips.

8.2 METHODOLOGY

The general block diagram of a microprocessor coupled to an external device is given in Figure 8.1.

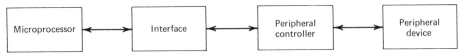

FIGURE 8.1 General requirements for microprocessor communication to a peripheral device.

The microprocessor interface provides data and control information to the peripheral device through a *peripheral controller*. The controller acts as a converter of data and control information from the microprocessor interface to the specific signals required by the peripheral device. For example, if the peripheral device were an impact printer, the controller would have to take the output of the microprocessor interface and produce such signals as character select, print hammer drive, line feed, and print position. Current drive capability not available at the microprocessor interface output may also have to be provided by the controller.

In many cases, the functions of the interface and controller are combined into one chip. This trend is the result of the development of microprocessor-oriented peripherals that are designed specifically for the use with microprocessors in terms of their performance, architecture, size, and cost. These types of chips can receive and/or transmit data by means of a data bus with bidirectional and tri-state capability, have control inputs and outputs compatible with microprocessor control outputs and inputs, and have chip select and/or chip enable inputs to permit the connection of multiple devices to the microprocessor data bus. Some popular devices of this type are data acquisition chips that convert analog signals (voltages) to digital form (bits) and vice versa. These devices are referred to as *A/D (Analog-to-Digital)* and *D/A (Digital-to-Analog)* converters, respectively. Another such chip is the *floppy disk controller*, which interfaces directly to the microprocessor. The controller enables the microprocessor to control floppy disk track position, head loading, disk selection, and data transfers. Peripheral chips of this level of sophistication are often more complex than the microprocessor itself. In fact, many of these chips are based on mask-programmed microprocessors complemented with special function logic subsystems.

8.2.1 Distributed I/O Control and Data Transfer

With the emergence of intelligent peripheral chips, a large portion of the I/O processing load is being removed from the CPU to permit the microprocessor to handle a large number of I/O tasks without significantly reducing system throughput. In the limit, as the peripheral devices approach, reach, and surpass the complexity and performance of microcomputers, multi-microcomputer systems will implicitly or explicitly result. In fact, the option of using a microprocessor or microcomputer as a peripheral of another microcomputer should not be overlooked. For compatibility with microprocessors, most peripheral chips are made to appear as memory or as an I/O port that has a specific address. Data are transferred by means of the microprocessor's bidirectional data bus (Figure 8.2)

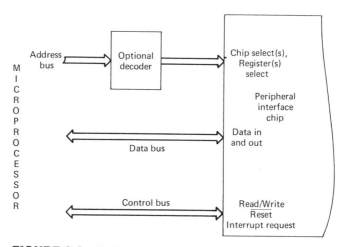

FIGURE 8.2 Peripheral interface chip connections.

Since each manufacturer has defined his own connections between the microprocessor and peripheral devices, there is no accepted standard for peripheral chips. The Motorola 6821 Peripheral Interface Adapter (PIA) and the Intel 8255A Programmable Peripheral Interface (PPI), however, are in such widespread use that they may establish *de facto* standards for peripheral interface chips. The block diagrams of these chips are given in Figure 8.3.

The Motorola PIA is a byte-oriented peripheral chip that communicates with the microprocessor via the miroprocessor's 8-bit data bus and its control bus. The PIA is organized as two sets (A and B) of data direction registers (DDRA and DDRB), control registers (CRA and CRB), and data buffers (DBA and DBB) with associated control lines CA1, CA2, CB1, and CB2. The two data direction registers define the direction of data transfer (input or output) for their corresponding data buffers relative to the outside world. The control registers, CRA and CRB, are used to set up the data direction registers and to define the responses for the corresponding data buffer registers and control lines CA1, CA2, and CB1, CB2. Since there are only two register select lines (RS0 and RS1) available to the microprocessor to select these six separate locations, a bit (b_2) in each of the two control registers is used in conjunction with RS0 and RS1 to specify the registers or data buffers.

The six addressing options of the 6821 are selected as follows:

EXTERNAL REGISTER SELECT LINES		BIT B_2 OF CONTROL REGISTER		LOCATION ADDRESSED
RS0	RS1	CRA	CRB	
0	1	X	X	Control Register A (CRA)
0	0	0	X	Data Direction Register A(DDRA)*
0	0	1	X	Data Buffer A (DBA)
1	1	X	X	Control Register B (CRB)
1	0	X	0	Data Direction Register B(DDRB)*
1	0	X	1	Data Buffer B (DBB)

NOTE: X denotes "don't care."
*a 0 written in a bit position on a data direction register will define the corresponding bit position in the data buffer as an input line and a 1 in the bit position will define the corresponding bit position in the data buffer as an output.

The three chip select lines (CS0, CS1, and $\overline{CS2}$) are identical to chip select lines in memory chips and permit I/O expansion using multiple 6821's. The chip select and register select inputs are obtained directly or derived from the microprocessor address lines with direction of data transfer between the microprocessor and PIA determined by the R/W (Read/Write) line. An E (Enable) input to the PIA is used for timing of peripheral control signals and conditioning of interrupt control. The E line is usually tied to the Ø2 clock pulse when used with the 6800 microprocessor. The A and B ports (PA0-PA7 and PB0-PB7) of the 6821 provide 8-bit connections for the data buffers to external devices. The four control lines, CA1, CA2, CB1, and CB2, can be programmed as interrupts to the 6821 or as control lines between the external device and the PIA to set up and acknowledge the exchange of data. In the latter mode, the CA1, CA2, CB1, and CB2 control lines are used for *handshaking* between the ports and an external device. These control lines can be programmed to operate in a variety of modes as determined by the two 8-bit (bits b_0 through b_7) control registers, CRA and CRB, in the PIA. Control Register A(CRA) and Control Register B (CRB) appear as two separate 8-bit memory locations to the microprocessor and can be written into by a memory write instruction. A typical handshake input mode is to program, by means of the CRA register,

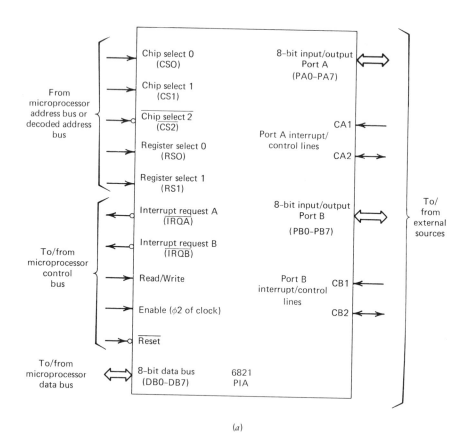

(a)

FIGURE 8.3 Block diagrams of 6821 and 8255A interface chips. (a) Motorola 6821 Peripheral Interface Adapter (PIA). (b) Intel 8255A Programmable Peripheral Interface (PPI).

line CA2 as an output line that is set to a LOW ($\cong 0.4$ volts) following a microprocessor **read** of external data. This handshake mode is established by setting bits b_3 and b_4 of CRA to a 0 and bit b_5 to a 1. This LOW state on CA2 informs the external device that its data have been read. The external device can acknowledge CA2 = LOW (data read) by applying either a positive or negative transition on CA1 (positive transition if bit b_1 of CRA = 1 and negative transition if bit b_1 of CRA = 0), which will, in turn, set an interrupt request flag, IRQA1, in the CRA register. Output line CA2 will also be returned to a HIGH level at this time. If the interrupt is enabled, (bit b_0 of CRA = 1) this flag will initiate an interrupt to the mi-

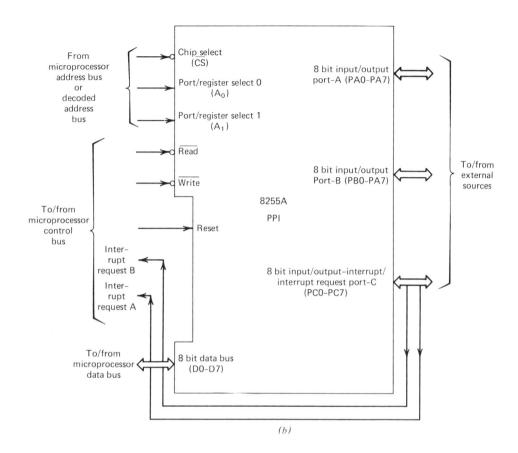

(b)

croprocessor through the PIA interrupt output line $\overline{\text{IRQA}}$ and allow the processor to initiate another data transfer cycle.

In the PIA handshake mode (bits b_3 and b_4 of CRB set to 0 and bit b_5 set to 1), line CB2 associated with Port B is set to a LOW following a microprocessor WRITE to an external device. Line CB1 can then be used as an input to the PIA to indicate that the data have been accepted by the external device and it is now ready for the next data transfer cycle. As with line CA1, line CB1 can be programmed to respond to either a positive or negative-going transition by setting bit b_1 of CRB to a 1 or 0, respectively. Line CB1 will then set its corresponding interrupt request flag, IRQB1, in

CRB to a 1 and also will return CB2 to a HIGH output level. If bit b_0 of CRB is = 1, then interrupt $\overline{\text{IRQB}}$ will be enabled and transmitted to the microprocessor by going LOW when flag IRQB1 is set. These read and write handshake operations are summarized in the diagrams of Figure 8.4.

CRA: $b_5 = 1$ (establishes CA2 as output)

$b_3 = b_4 = 0$ (establishes handshake mode)

$b_1 = 0$ (CA1 responds to negative-going transition)

$b_1 = 1$ (CA1 responds to positive-going transition)

$b_0 = 0$ (IRQA interrupt request line to microprocessor disabled)

$b_0 = 1$ (IRQA interrupt request line to microprocessor enabled)

The 8255A PPI has three I/O ports (Ports A, B, and C) that can be programmed in three main modes of operation. This programming is accomplished by writing a control word to an 8-bit control buffer in the 8255A.

In mode O, each port can perform simple I/O. All 8 lines into each of Ports A and B must be inputs or outputs, but not both. In other words, inputs and outputs cannot be mixed on Port A or on Port B in mode O. In this mode, however, Port C can be subdivided into two subgroups of 4 bits each and each subgroup can either be defined as inputs or outputs with no mixing allowed in a subgroup. This mode is illustrated as follows:

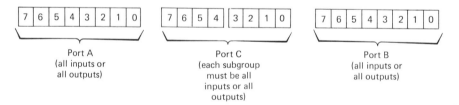

Mode 1 establishes Ports A and B as in mode O, but bits 4, 5, 6, and 7 of Port C are assigned as handshake control signals for Port A and bits 0, 1, 2, and 3 of Port C provide the handshake control for Port B. Mode 1, the handshake mode, appears as

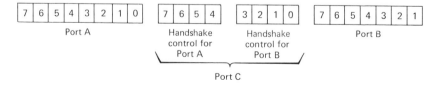

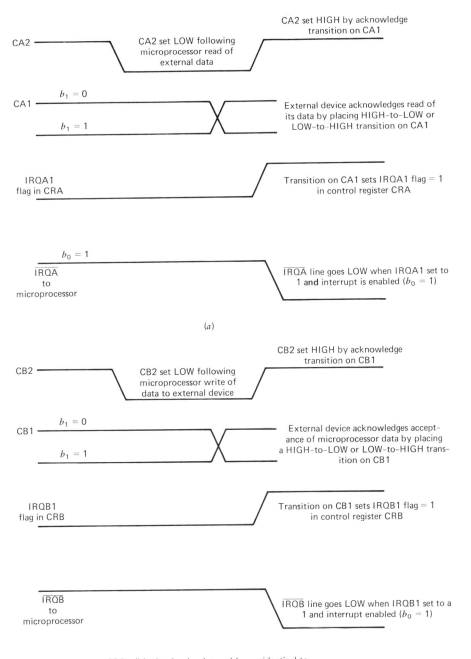

FIGURE 8.4 6821 PIA read and write handshake operations. (*a*) Read (input) data handshake operation. (*b*) Write (output) data handshake operation.

The third mode of operation of the 8255A PPI sets up a single Port A, to be a bidirectional data port and defines 5 bits of Port C as a control port.

The I/O port definitions are made through the control word which, when transmitted from the microprocessor to the 8255A, is interpreted in the following manner.

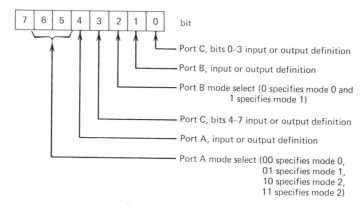

In the control word, a 1 specifies a port as an input and a 0 specifies a port as an output.

The three I/O ports and the control word buffer are addressed through inputs A0 and A1 as shown in the following table (assuming $\overline{CS}$ = 0 which selects the 8255A.)

EXTERNAL SELECT LINES		LOCATION ADDRESSED
A0	A1	
0	0	Port A
1	0	Port B
0	1	Port C
1	1	Control Buffer (Write Only)

As previously discussed, handshaking is implemented in the 8255A in mode 1. In this mode, two 12-bit groups, Group A and Group B, are defined. Each group contains an 8-bit data port and a 4-bit control and status port. The 8-bit data port of Group A, Port A, and the 8-bit data port of Group B, Port B, can be individually defined as either input or output in mode 1. For the purposes of illustration, assume Port A is programmed as an input port and Port B as an output port.

In the read or input data handshaking operation, bit 4 of Port C (PC_4) is used as an active LOW strobe input, $\overline{STB}_A$. The external device will place its 8 bits of data on the 8 input lines of Port A and then set $\overline{STB}_A$ to a LOW. This procedure will load the 8 bits of external data to Port A. Receipt of these data are acknowledged by a resulting HIGH output on bit 5 of Port C (PC_5), which is designated as the IBF_A (Input Buffer Full) line. IBF_A is set to a HIGH by $\overline{STB}_A$ going LOW and is reset by the positive-going edge of the active LOW READ line, $\overline{RD}$, from the microprocessor. Bit 3 of Port C (PC_3) can be used as an active HIGH interrupt line, $INTR_A$, to the microprocessor, indicating that data have been read into PORT A from an external device. The INTRA is set HIGH if $\overline{STB}_A$ is HIGH, IBF_A is HIGH, and the PORT A interrupt enable flip-flop (INTE A) is HIGH. The $INTR_A$ is reset to a LOW by the negative-going transition of $\overline{RD}$.

In the write or output data handshaking operation, bit 1 of Port C (PC_1) will go LOW when the microprocessor has written 8 bits of data into PORT B. This line is called the $\overline{OBF}_B$ line (Output Buffer Full) and is set LOW by the positive-going edge of the active LOW WRITE line, $\overline{WR}$, from the microprocessor. When the external device has accepted the data from PORT B, it places a LOW on bit 2 of Port C (PC_2). This data-accepted response is called the $\overline{ACK}_B$ (Acknowledge) input from the external device. An interrupt request ($INTR_B$) to the microprocessor can also be generated on bit 0 of Port C (PC_0) to indicate that the external device has accepted the data from PORT B. This active HIGH interrupt request is generated on PC_0 when $\overline{ACK}_B$ is HIGH, $\overline{OBF}_B$ is HIGH, and the PORT B interrupt enable flip-flop (INTE B) is HIGH. The $INTR_B$ is reset to a LOW by the negative-going edge of $\overline{WR}$. The 8255A pin functions and handshaking operations for this example are given in Figure 8.5.

Even though there are no microprocessor interface standards, there are two instrumentation interface and bus standards in existence that permit rapid and more economical system design and development. These standards are the IEEE Standard 488-1975 for programmable instruments (Hewlett-Packard Interface Bus)* and IEEE Standards 583, 595, and 596 (relating to CAMAC). The IEEE Standard 488-1975 has been recently revised to IEEE Standard IEEE 488-1978 with minor functional changes from the 1975 version. The final revisions were not available at the time of preparation of this section.

* IEEE Standard Digital Interfaces for Programmable Instrumentation, Standard 488-1975, IEEE Standards, 345 E. 47 St. N.Y. N.Y., 10017.

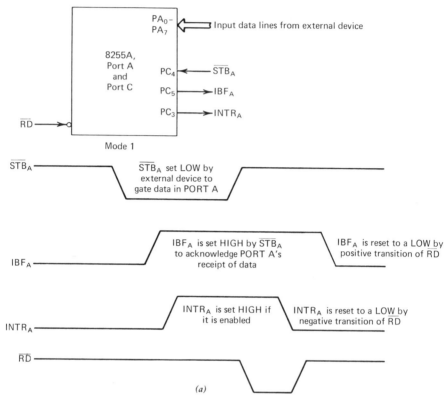

FIGURE 8.5 8255A PPI read and write handshake operations. (*a*) Read (input) data handshake operation. (*b*) Write (output) data handshake operation.

8.2.2 IEEE 488-1975 Interface Standard

IEEE Standard 488 was originally developed by Hewlett-Packard as a standard for instrument interfacing. The basis for this standard is the *Hewlett-Packard Interface Bus (HP-IB), which consists of 16 signal lines functionally grouped as an 8-line data bus, a 3-line handshake or transfer bus, and a 5-line general interface management bus as shown in Figure 8.6.* This last bus is used as the means of connection among a number of instruments, each of which may be idle, a talker, a listener, or a controller to arbitrate among and designate talkers and listeners. A *talker* sends data over the bus to a listener or listeners and a *listener* receives data. It is important to note that the bus is passive and the circuitry associated with talking, listening, and controlling is contained within the instruments connected to the bus. Not all roles need be incorporated in an instrument.

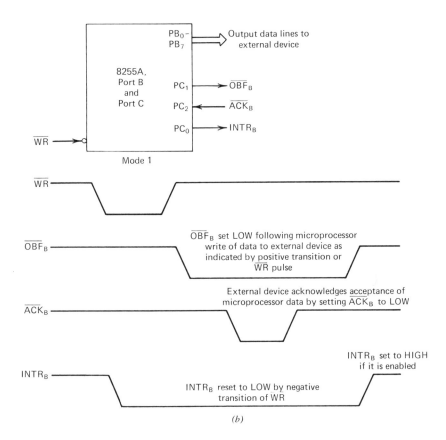

(b)

The three-line transfer bus is used for handshaking, that is, the means by which a talker and listener coordinate and verify the transmission of data between them. The transfer bus consists of a Data Valid line (DAV), a Not Ready for Data line (NRFD), and a Data Not Accepted line (NDAC). The logic levels used on these and the other bus lines are TTL levels (LOW ≤ 0.8V and HIGH ≥ 2.4V). The HP–IB utilizes a LOW = TRUE (Logic 1) convention. Initially, a listener would set the NRFD and NDAC lines LOW (indicating NOT READY FOR DATA) while the talker would set the DAV line HIGH indicating that data are being changed on the data lines and are not yet ready for transmission. The listener would then set NRFD HIGH indicating that it is aware that data are being changed and that it is ready to receive data as soon as DAV is LOW. If there are multiple listeners, NRFD will be HIGH only if all listeners set their respective

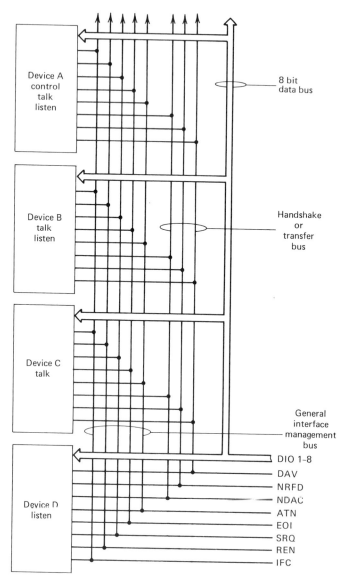

FIGURE 8.6   HP-IB bus. (Courtesy of Mr. Al Devilbiss, Hewlett-Packard, Colorado Springs.)

NRFD outputs to a HIGH. Also, if both NRFD and NDAC are set HIGH simultaneously, an error condition is indicated. When the talker senses that NRFD is HIGH, it will indicate that valid data are available on the data lines by pulling DAV low. The listener that first accepts the data byte on the data lines sets NRFD LOW and releases NDAC to allow it to go to a HIGH. NDAC will not be set to a HIGH until all listeners accept the data byte and release NDAC allowing it to go HIGH. When NDAC is HIGH, this level indicates to the talker that all listeners have accepted the data. Then, the talker sets DAV HIGH again in order to allow for changing of data on the data lines. The first listener to sense DAV = HIGH sets NDAC LOW to acknowledge that data are being changed and to prepare for the next cycle of data transmission. A diagram of these operations for single and multiple listeners is given in Figure 8.7.

The HP–IB can also be described by means of a state diagram of the three wire handshake lines—DAV, NRFD, and NDAC. A normal handshake cycle consists of six distinct states where LOW = TRUE or Logic 1 and HIGH = 0 and is shown in Figure 8.8.

A state diagram as shown in Figure 8.9 of HP–IB handshake sequences can be developed from the handshake cycle to depict normal (solid line) operation and abnormal (dotted line) operation. A HIGH is denoted as a 0 and a LOW as a 1 in the state diagram.

The general interface management bus is used primarily by the instrument acting as the controller. The controller transmits interface messages to other instruments on the bus to direct them in talking and/or listening. Messages can be sent by means of the eight data lines (*multiline* messages) or by means of one of the five interface management bus lines (*uniline*). The interface management lines are labeled as follows.

IFC	Interface Clear
ATN	Attention
SRQ	Service Request
REN	Remote Enable
EOI	End or Identify

The *Interface Clear line* (IFC) is used by the controller to initialize all the instruments to an idle state in which they are neither talkers nor listeners but simply monitors of the bus. All instruments must go into the idle state *relative to the bus* (they can still be functioning) within 100 microseconds following setting of IFC to a LOW. The *Attention (ATN) line* defines the eight data lines as being in either the data mode (when ATN = HIGH) or the command mode (when ATN = LOW). In the command mode, the data lines are used to transfer control information while the data mode is used to transfer data between talkers and listeners. At any

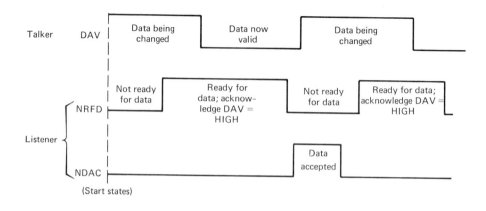

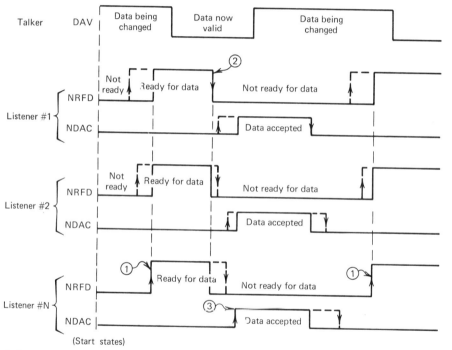

FIGURE 8.7 Handshaking operations for single and multiple listeners. (a) Transfer bus handshake cycle—single listener. (b) Transfer bus handshake cycle—multiple listeners.

* NOTE:
1 NRFD set HIGH only when last listener (listener #N in this example) releases NRFD line indicating ready for data.
2 NRFD set LOW by first listener to accept data (listener #1 in this example).
3 NDAC set HIGH only when last listener releases NDAC line.

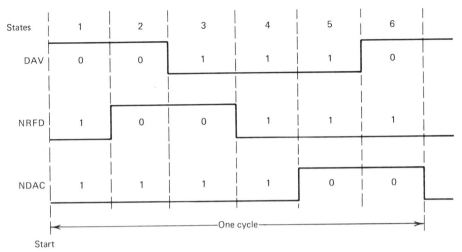

FIGURE 8.8 Normal handshake cycle of HP-IB.

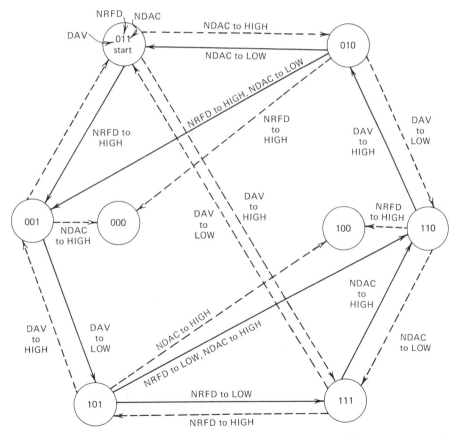

FIGURE 8.9 State diagram representation of HP–IB handshake sequences. For clarity, only transitions to new states are depicted in the diagram. (Courtesy of Al Devilbiss of Hewlett-Packard Corporation, Colorado Springs, Colorado.)

time, the controller can set ATN to a LOW from a HIGH to "gain the attention" of the instruments on the bus. The instruments must then respond by setting NDAC and NRFD LOW within 200 nsec of ATN going LOW, although NRFD is permitted to go HIGH immediately thereafter. A talker that may have been using the bus must release it. This operation would be employed if the controller had been interrupted by the SRQ (Service Request) line and had to initiate a serial poll to determine which instrument had requested service. The *Service Request line* is an interrupt line to the controller that permits an instrument to request access to the bus. This line is activated by an instrument pulling it to a LOW value. The controller then determines which instrument or instruments initiated the interrupt request. The *Remote Enable line* (REN) is pulled LOW by the controller if it is desired to disable the front panel control of an instrument and revert to remote control operation. The LOW state of REN permits an instrument that receives its listen address and is capable of HP–IB remote operation to enter the REMOTE State. When this remote control is terminated by setting REN to a HIGH, the instrument must return to the front panel mode within 100 microseconds. The *End or Identify line* (EOI) along with the ATN line is used to implement a parallel poll of the instruments on the bus that have corresponding facilities for this type of operation. If ATN and EOI are pulled to a LOW simultaneously by the controller, an instrument can transmit one bit of information on a previously assigned line of the eight-line data bus. Thus, when the SRQ line is pulled LOW by an instrument to interrupt the controller, the controller can initiate a parallel poll of up to eight instruments by pulling ATN and EOI LOW simultaneously and sampling the individual lines of the data bus to determine which instrument(s) initiated the interrupts. The instrument(s) must respond by pulling their respective data line(s) LOW within 200 nanoseconds of ATN and EOI going LOW. The availability of one data line for each instrument when ATN and EOI are simultaneously set to a LOW can also be used to transmit status information between the controller and an instrument. The EOI = LOW can also be used to indicate an end of transmission when the data lines are in the data mode of operation.

The 16 bus lines of this IEEE Standard 488 are, then:

———————DIO 1 ⎫ ———————DIO 2 ⎬ ————⋮———DIO 8 ⎭	Eight-line data bus—in data mode when ATN = HIGH and in command mode when ATN = LOW.
———————DAV ⎫ ———————NRFD ⎬ ———————NDAC ⎭	Three-line transfer bus—DAV = LOW when valid data are available from talker; NRFD = HIGH when listener is ready for data; NDAC = HIGH when listener has accepted data.

_____IFC	Five-line interface management bus—
_____ATN	IFC = LOW puts instruments in idle
_____SRQ	state with respect to bus (instruments can
_____REN	still be operating); ATN = HIGH puts
_____EOI	data bus in data mode and ATN = LOW

puts data bus in command mode; SRQ = LOW interrupts controllers; REN = LOW disables instrument's front panel local controls and enables remote control operation; EOI = LOW can be used by talker to indicate end of transmission in data mode of operation or EOI and ATN = LOW simultaneoulsy permits an instrument to use one specified line of eight-line data bus to transmit one bit as information or as a response to controller when an interrupt parallel poll is being conducted.

When the controller desires to select a particular instrument as a talker, the data lines are put into the command mode (ATN = LOW), and a talk address is sent out on the data lines in the following talk command format.

DIO 8	DIO 7	DIO 6	DIO 5	DIO 4	DIO 3	DIO 2	DIO 1
X	1	0	A_5	A_4	A_3	A_2	A_1

where DIO 1 through DIO 8 are data line designations, A_1 through A_5 are the _talk address_ in binary form, and X can either be a 1 or 0. Any talk address code can be used **except** 11111, which is defined as an _untalk command_. The standard specifies that only one talker can be defined at any time. Thus, any talker whose address does not match the talk address sent out when ATN = LOW is disabled from talking. Since a talker can have any address except 11111, sending out 11111 as a talk address disables all instruments from sending data and, therefore, accomplishes an _untalk_ operation. A talk command does not affect the previously defined status of listeners. A _listen address_ can be transmitted on the data lines when ATN = LOW and will select an instrument as a listener. Multiple listeners can be selected in sequence and a listen command will not affect previously selected listeners or disable listeners. The format of a listen command is:

$$X \ 0 \ 1 \ A_5 \ A_4 \ A_3 \ A_2 \ A_1$$

when the stipulation that address 11111 is reserved for the _unlisten_ command. An unlisten command, similar to an untalk command, will disable **all** previously selected listeners.

A third type of command is the *univeral* command, which affects all instruments (whether or not they have been addressed) connected to the bus providing they are equipped to carry out the command. The three lines, IFC, ATN, and REN, of the interface management bus are uniline universal commands while the data lines in the command mode (ATN = LOW) can be used for multiline commands. The format of a multiline universal command is:

$$X \ 0 \ 0 \ 1 \ A_4 \ A_3 \ A_2 \ A_1$$

where A_1 through A_4 specify a particular universal command.

A fourth type of command is the *addressed* command, which is multilined and similar to an universal command except that only instruments that have been addressed as talkers and/or listeners are affected. The format of the addressed command is

$$X \ 0 \ 0 \ 0 \ A_4 \ A_3 \ A_2 \ A_1$$

The last type of command is the *secondary* command, which is multilined and is used following an addressed, universal, or address (talk or listen) command to provide additional bits for expanding their respective codes.

The 16 line bus can accept up to 15 instruments and a maximum total cable length among all instruments of 20 meters. The maximum length of any cable between instruments is 2 m subject to the 20-m maximum total length for 15 instruments. Under these constraints, the data transfer rate is a minimum of 250K bytes per second. Some optimized designs can achieve a data transfer rate of 1 Megabyte per second on a burst basis.

Since the bus logic levels are TTL compatible, they can be easily interfaced using TTL compatible devices. Standard TTL circuits can be used as bus receivers. If higher noise immunity is required, Schmitt trigger gates should be employed. Open collector TTL circuits capable of sinking 48 ma at 0.4 volts should be used for driving the bus. A standard interface to the bus is given Figure 8.10. The connector to the instrument is a 24 pin Cinch or Amphenol-type 56 microribbon connector with pin designations as shown by the circled numbers in the figure. The interface circuits shown in the figure are the basic ones necessary for coupling the instruments to the bus.

Another solution to implement the interface is to use a General Purpose Interface Bus (GPIB) transceiver integrated circuit such as the Motorola MC3446. The MC3446 Quad Interface Bus transceiver provides four open collector drives and four receivers for interfacing the HP–IB. A dia-

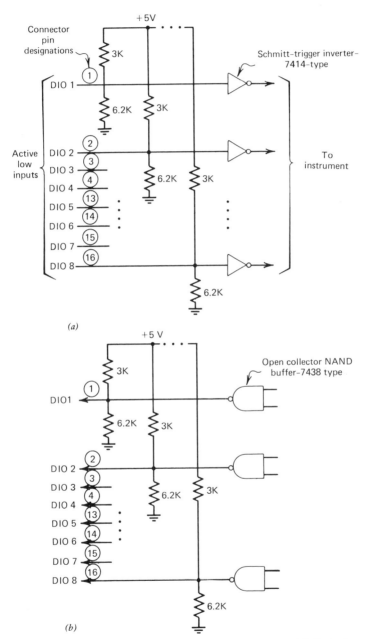

FIGURE 8.10 Interface circuits for IEEE 488-1975 bus. (a) Data bus receiver interface. (b) Data bus driver interface. (c) Bidirectional data bus interface. (d) Multi-lines interface. (e) Listen address detection and unlisten detection.

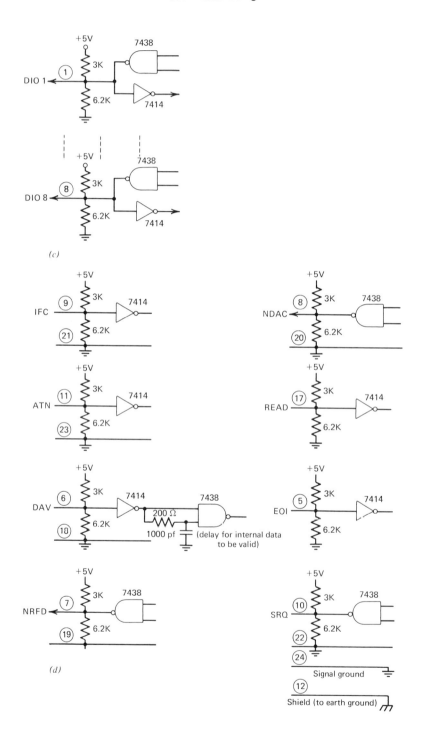

(c)

(d)

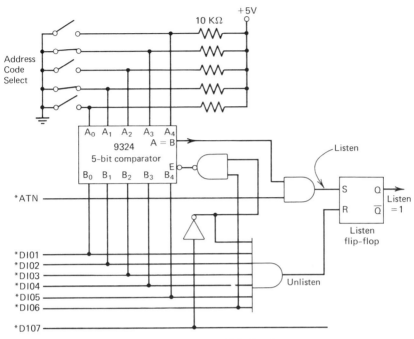

* ATN and DIO lines as shown are outputs of Schmitt–trigger gates.

(e)

gram of the MC3446 is given in Figure 8.11 and typical portions of an interface using the MC3446 are shown in Figure 8.12. An additional useful circuit for interfacing to the bus is the Motorola MC3448A bus transceiver to be used in conjunction with the Motorola MC68488 General Purpose Interface Adapter (GPIA). These devices are shown in Figure 8.13.

8.2.3 CAMAC Interface Standard

A second widely used standard for instrumentation is the CAMAC Standard (IEEE Standards 583-1975, 595-1975, and 596-1975). CAMAC was developed by the ESONE (European Standards on Nuclear Electronics) Committee in 1969.*† The CAMAC Standard has been adopted by the

* EURATOM Report EUR 4100e, 1972, CAMAC—A Modular Instrumentation System for Data Handling, Description and Specification.

† U.S. AEC Report TID-25878, CAMAC—A Modular Instrumentation System for Data Handling, Description and Specification.

PIN CONNECTIONS

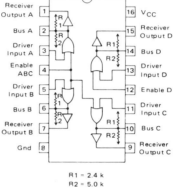

R1 = 2.4 k
R2 = 5.0 k

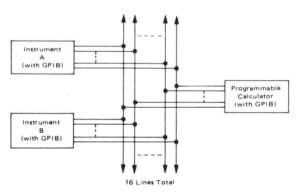

16 Lines Total

FIGURE 8.11 Motorola MC3446 Quad Interface Bus Transceiver. (Courtesy of Motorola Inc., Integrated Circuit Division)

NIM (National Instrumentation Methods) Committee in the United States and has been widely used in the area of nuclear instrumentation.

The basic elements of the CAMAC Standards are a *single width module* (≅ 0.7 in. wide × 8¾ in. high by 12 in. deep) that contains a printed circuit board with integrated circuits; a *double width module* that usually contains printed circuit boards or a single wire wrap board with integrated

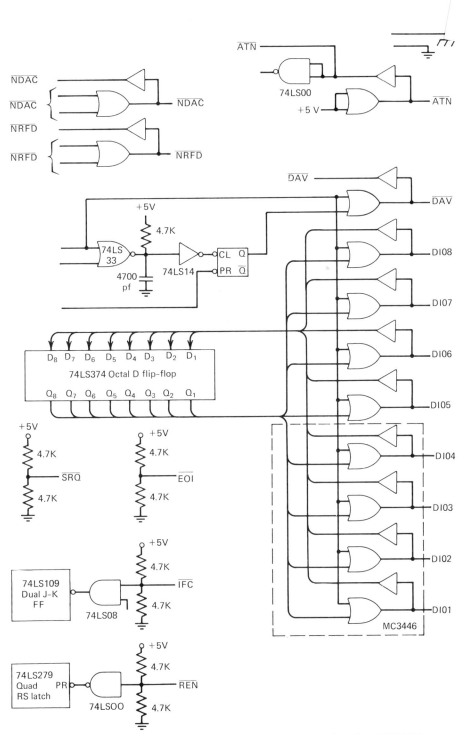

FIGURE 8.12 A typical portion of an HP–IB interface using the MC3446.

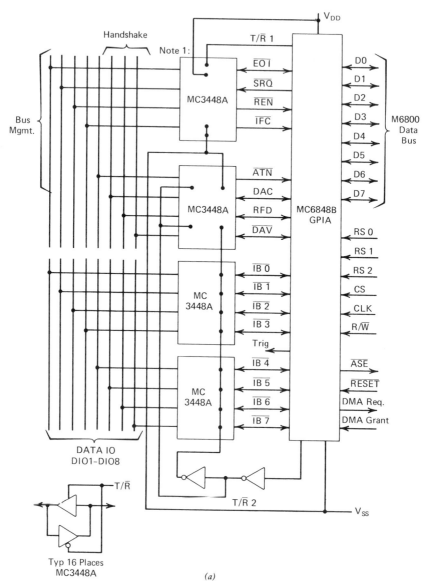

FIGURE 8.13 (a) MC3448A use with MC68488GPIA (Courtesy of Motorola, Inc., Integrated Circuit Division)

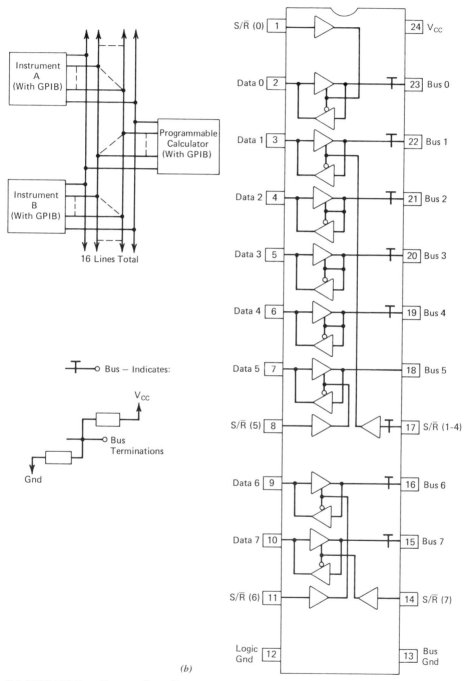

(b)

(*b*) MC3447 Bus Transceiver (Courtesy of Motorola, Inc., Integrated Circuit Division)

circuit sockets); a *crate* or *bin* containing 25 single width module slots and 25 *connectors* into which the modules can be plugged; a *crate controller* module that controls the CAMAC system; and a *Dataway* or interconnection means from the controller to the modules and for supplying power to the modules. Each of the 25 connectors in the crate has 86 pins that mate to edge connectors on the modules. A portion of the Dataway is bused among module slots or *stations* numbers 1 through 24 from left to right as viewed from the front or open end of the crate with stations 24 and 25 occupied by the crate controller. The bused portion of the dataway is comprised of:

1. five function code lines (F1, F2, F4, F8, F16).
2. four subaddress lines (A1, A2, A4, A8).
3. four unaddressed command lines (Z, C, I, and B) applying to all modules in a crate. Line Z initializes registers and functions in a module to a defined state such as is required at system Power On; line C is used to clear specific registers in modules without affecting other states of the module; line I inhibits certain activities within a module; and line B is used by the controller to indicate that a Dataway operation is in progress.
4. two timing signals, S1 and S2.
5. 24 write lines for transfer of data from the crate controller to a module or modules.
6. 24 read lines for transfer of data from a module to the crate controller.
7. one bit X line that is used as a command-accepted acknowledgement from a module to the controller.
8. one bit Q line that is available to the system designer to use as desired.

There are two other Dataway lines, L (Look-At-Me) and N (Station Number) that are not bused but are run directly from the crate controller to the individual modules. Each module is selected by a separate N line that, when active, designates that module as the recipient of the command that is present on the function and subaddress lines. The L lines run directly from individual modules to the crate controller and are used by each module to request service from the controller.

A summary of the Station Positions and the Dataway is given in Figure 8.14. The Dataway signals are all TTL levels with connections from modules to the Dataway lines accomplished with 7401-type open collector gates.

The modules in the CAMAC crate are normally listen only devices and cannot send commands to the controller or other modules. The exception to this is the module's assertion of the L (Listen-To-Me) line, which is used to request service from the controller. The crate controller is the central intelligence of the crate and issues commands to individual modules to coordinate system operation. Commands are sent to respective modules by means of five function code lines. As an example, the function command pattern 1 0 0 0 0 (binary 16) is referred to as F(16) and is a write-to-module command. The subaddress lines A_1 through A_4 are used to designate one of 16 subentities in the module such as a particular register. A pattern of 1 1 0 0 on the subaddress lines would designate register 12 in the address module and is denoted by A(12). Thus, F(16), A(12) would mean write to register 12 in the designated module. A module is selected by means of the N line running from the controller to the module. Module 2 would be denoted as N (2). To write data to register 12 in module 2, an *NAF command* of N(2) A(12) F(16) would be issued on the Dataway and the data would be transferred over the data read lines to the module. In order to distinguish between data registers in a module and control registers, function codes referring to registers in a module are divided into Group 1 and Group 2 codes. Group 1 codes should refer to data registers and Group 2 codes should refer to control registers. In the previous example, F(16) is a Group 1 write command. F(17) is a Group 2 write command. Some other CAMAC function codes are:

F(0)   Group 1 read register command
F(1)   Group 2 read register command
F(9)   Clear Group 1 register
F(10)   Clear Look-At-Me
F(11)   Clear Group 2 register
F(25)   Execute (the module may initiate an action like putting out a logic level change or a pulse)

The L line acts as an interrupt line to the controller and, since it runs directly from the module to the crate controller, the source of the interrupt is identified at once by the controller.

A microcomputer can serve as the basis of a CAMAC module or the crate controller or as an external central control unit that communicates with the crate through the crate controller. The crate controller, then, can serve as an interface between an external computer and the crate modules. An alternative approach is to establish an interface that is independent of the crate controller and, in fact, can permit an external computer to communicate with a number of crates. This interface is termed a *Branch*

Driver, and it enables an external computer to communicate with up to seven crates by means of a 24-line *Branch Highway* that is routed to the individual crate controllers. The Branch Highway includes seven crate address lines that permit individual selection of any one of the seven crates connected to the Highway. An addressing command to a crate in a multi-crate system is now a CNAF command where the C identifies one out of a possible seven crates on the Branch Highway. If single wire and ground (single-ended) transmission is used for the Branch Highway, the maximum length of the Highway should be approximately 25 meters. Differential transmission can extend this limit to a few kilometers.

8.3 MICROPROCESSOR I/O STRUCTURES

The PIA and PPI interface chips discussed in Section 8.2.1 are LSI programmable, bidirectional I/O devices. To provide an understanding of the interfaces implemented in these chips, in single chip microcomputers, and in microcomputers utilizing SSI and MSI devices, the basic classes of mi-

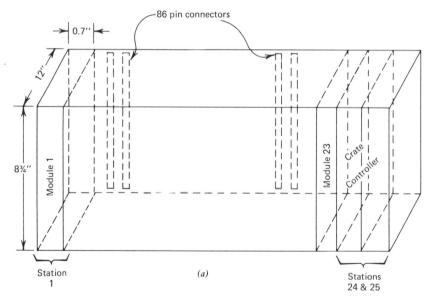

FIGURE 8.14 Summary of CAMAC crate station positions and Dataway. (*a*) CAMAC crate and station positions (front view of crate). (*b*) CAMAC Dataway (rear view of crate). (Standard voltages of ± 6 volts, and ± 24 volts are also bused on the Dataway. Pins for special voltages of ± 12, + 200, and 117 volts AC have also been designated.)

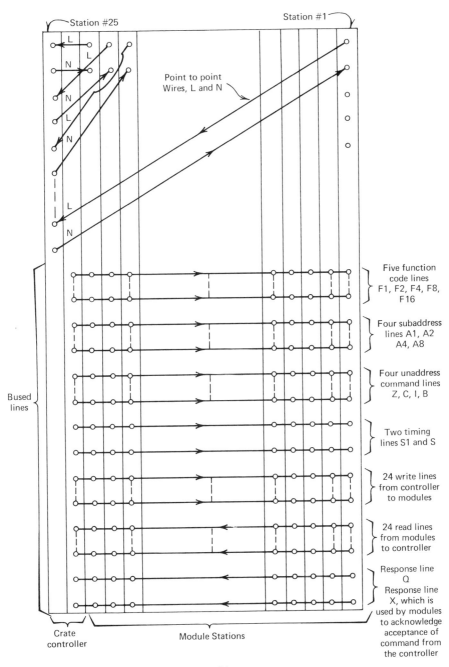

Station #25

Station #1

L

L

N

N

N

L

N

Point to point
Wires, L and N

L

N

L

N

Five function
code lines
F1, F2, F4, F8,
F 16

Four subaddress
lines A1, A2
A4, A8

Four unaddress
command lines
Z, C, I, B

Bused
lines

Two timing
lines S1 and S

24 write lines
from controller
to modules

24 read lines
from modules
to controller

Response line
Q

Response line
X, which is
used by modules
to acknowledge
acceptance of
command from
the controller

Crate
controller

Module Stations

(b)

croprocessor I/O structures are presented. As necessary, associated I/O terms are also defined.

8.3.1 I/O Addressing

The concepts of memory and I/O addressing and decoding were presented and illustrated in Section 5.4.2. The I/O operations in general and relative to the instruction set of Chapter 6 were discussed in Section 6.4.2. Reviewing and expanding on those concepts, we find that there are two basic types of I/O architectures—*isolated I/O* and *memory-mapped I/O*. *Isolated I/O* utilizes specific instructions in the instruction set for input and output. In the instruction set of Chapter 6, these instruction mnemonics are INP for input and OUT for output. A commonly used pair of mnemonics in microprocessors with isolated I/O capability is IN and OUT. The operand of these instructions is an address that is transmitted on the address bus when one of the instructions is executed and that defines a specific I/O port. A typical format for the IN and OUT instructions of an 8-bit microprocessor with isolated I/O is:

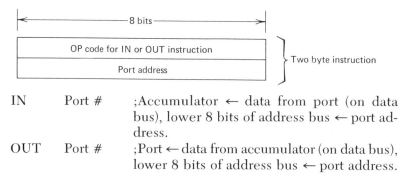

| IN | Port # | ;Accumulator ← data from port (on data bus), lower 8 bits of address bus ← port address. |
| OUT | Port # | ;Port ← data from accumulator (on data bus), lower 8 bits of address bus ← port address. |

When the IN or OUT instructions are executed, an input or output pin, respectively, on the microprocessor is also activated. These pins are normally active LOW and are labeled $\overline{\text{IN}}$ and $\overline{\text{OUT}}$ on the microprocessor chip developed in Chapter 6. Alternative designations commonly used for these pins are $\overline{\text{IOR}}$ (INPUT/OUTPUT READ) and $\overline{\text{IOW}}$ (INPUT/OUTPUT WRITE). Since these two lines are activated only when an input or output instruction is executed, they can be used to distinguish a port address on the address bus from a memory address on the address bus. Thus, the full address space is available for memory and is not affected by I/O port addressing. A typical utilization of the $\overline{\text{IN}}$ and $\overline{\text{OUT}}$ ($\overline{\text{IOR}}$ and $\overline{\text{IOW}}$) lines to separate memory addresses from I/O addresses is given in Figure 8.15. The 8255A PPI described in Section 8.2.1 is used as three I/O ports.

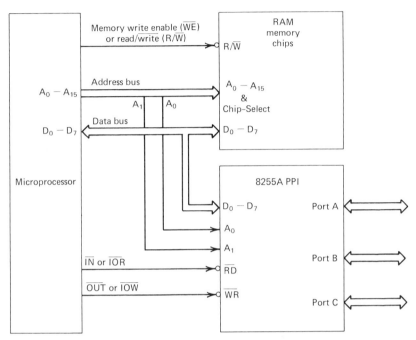

FIGURE 8.15 Use of $\overline{\text{IN}}$ and $\overline{\text{OUT}}$ lines to isolate I/O addressing from memory addressing.

A microprocessor with isolated I/O architecture usually has only two I/O instructions, thereby restricting the number of I/O data transfer alternatives. However, these instructions are usually executed in less time than most other microprocessor instructions in the instruction set.

Memory-mapped I/O does not distinguish between memory and I/O address space and treats all addresses in the space as memory. In order to select I/O devices, a portion of the address space must be set aside for I/O. A commonly used method is to use the most significant address bit, bit A_{15} in 16 bit addresses, to separate I/O from memory. When $A_{15} = 1$, the addresses $\geqslant 32,768_{10}$ and $\leqslant 65,535_{10}$ are selected as I/O addresses and when $A_{15} = 0$, addresses $< 32,768_{10}$ are designated as memory locations. The chip select (CS) lines on the memory and I/O decoders or devices are, respectively, enabled and disabled when $A_{15} = 0$. This technique is illustrated in Figure 8.16.

In either memory-mapped or isolated I/O, if a large number of ports will never be required, each bit of the port address appearing on the address lines can be used to select a port. Thus, an 8-bit port address can be used to select one out of a maximum of 8 ports and eliminate the necessity

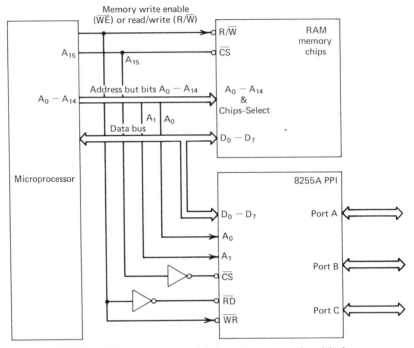

FIGURE 8.16. Memory-mapped I/O addressing using bit A_{15}.

of using a decoding circuit. This technique is referred to as *linear select* addressing. It is important to note that, in any method of port selection, one port can be used for both input and output. Therefore, if 8 port addresses are available, 8 input ports and 8 output ports can be selected.

The basic I/O circuits for a microprocessor utilize tri-state buffers to couple the input to the data bus and a latch to hold data from the data bus for the output. These two circuits are illustrated in Figure 8.17 and are typical of some of the modes of operation of devices such as the 6821 PIA and 8255A PPI.

An interesting variation of the basic I/O circuits is the pseudobidirectional I/O port in which the lines to the external device can be either input or output lines. One implementation of this type of port is shown in Figure 8.18.

This type of port, like the one depicted in Figure 8.17, has latched outputs and nonlatched inputs. Each I/O line can be used for either input or output. The I/O line is pulled up to a logic 1 through approximately a 50K-ohm resistance to +5 volts. This arrangement can provide adequate source current to a TTL device and can be pulled low by a standard TTL

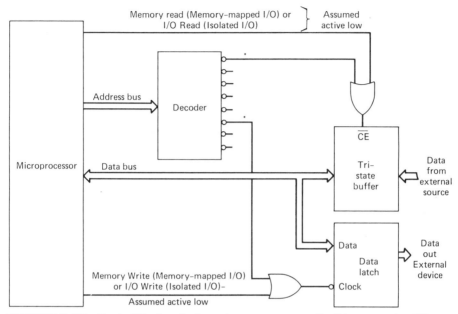

FIGURE 8.17 Basic I/O circuits for microprocessors. *In this example, different addresses and, therefore, different decoder outputs are used for data input and output. The same decoder output could be used for both input and output and, thus, an input port and an output port would be selected by the same address.

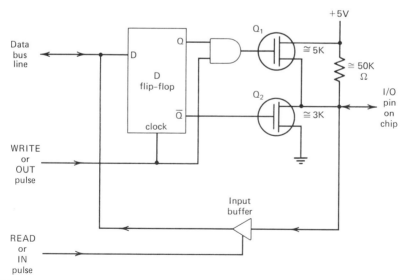

FIGURE 8.18 One bit of pseudobidirectional I/O port. (Copyright Intel Corporation, 1977, all rights reserved)

gate without excessive current sinking by the gate. To program the line as an input, a logic 1 is written to the D flip-flop corresponding to that line as shown in Figure 8.18. This logic 1 is sent to the D input of the flip-flop via one of the microprocessor data bus lines and will appear at the Q output when clocked by the WRITE- (or OUT-)type pulse on the clock input of the flip-flop. If the I/O line was setting at a logic 0 output (Q_2 ON and Q_1 OFF), the logic 1 on the Q output of the D flip-flop will turn ON the MOS transistor Q_1 (Q_2 will be turned OFF by $\overline{Q} = 0$), which will provide a rapid 0 to 1 transition on the I/O line. The Q_1 is switched in to the circuit momentarily (500 nsec) since, because of the AND gate, Q_1 will only remain ON for the duration of the WRITE pulse. Thus, a low impedance ($\cong$ 5K) bypass to the 50K-ohm resistance is inserted to improve the 0 to 1 transition time on the I/O line and then removed.

A logic 0 written into the D flip-flop will result in $Q = 0$ and $\overline{Q} = 1$. Then $\overline{Q} = 1$ turns ON the MOS transistor Q_2 while $Q = 0$ turns OFF transistor Q_1. Thus, the I/O line is at a logic 0 (pulled down to ground through the approximately 3K-ohm ON resistance of Q_2) and provides TTL current sinking capability to external devices. When programmed as an input line ($Q = 1$, $\overline{Q} = 0$), the I/O line is pulled up to +5 volts through a 50K-ohm resistance in the static mode. This line will respond to a TTL logic 1 input by remaining at a HIGH value ($\geqslant$ + 2.4 volts) and to a TTL logic 0 input by sourcing current to the external device and falling to a TTL LOW value ($\leqslant$ 0.4 volts). One of these two levels is clocked into the data bus through an input buffer by means of a READ- (or IN-)type pulse. In addition to serving the purpose of programming the port direction, the D flip-flop is used to specify a 1 or 0 output from the port.

A third type of I/O port configuration is a *pulsed* or *strobed* I/O, which is used when the data are to be transferred at a particular instant of time determined by the occurrence of a *strobe* pulse. For example, if data available at a port input are valid only at a specific time, a strobe pulse can be used to read the data into the port at this time. A strobed input circuit is given in Figure 8.19 and a strobed output circuit is given in Figure 8.20.

The strobed input and output circuits of Figures 8.19 and 8.20 are similar to the ones utilized in LSI interface circuits. The input circuit clocks data into an input latch with an INPUT STROBE pulse that simultaneously sets an interrupt flip-flop (if enabled) and sets an input buffer full flip-flop. When the input data are read into the microprocessor by the Memory or I/O Read line and decoder output lines both being LOW, the two flip-flops are reset. The interrupt request is then removed and the buffer full flip-flop provides an INPUT BUFFER EMPTY signal to the external device.

The output circuit writes data into a data latch from the microproces-

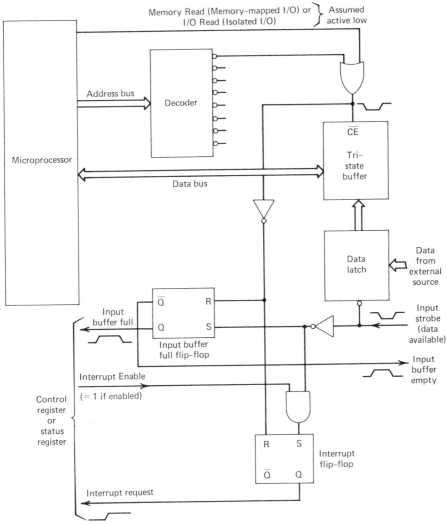

FIGURE 8.19 Strobed input circuit.

sor when Memory or I/O Write and the decoder output are both LOW. Simultaneously, the output buffer full flip-flop is set and provides an OUT-PUT BUFFER FULL signal to the external device. Any previously existing interrupt request from the interrupt flip-flop is also removed at this time. When the external device reads the data from the latch, it provides an OUTPUT DATA RECEIVED pulse. This pulse removes the OUTPUT BUFFER FULL signal by resetting the output buffer full flip-flop and sets

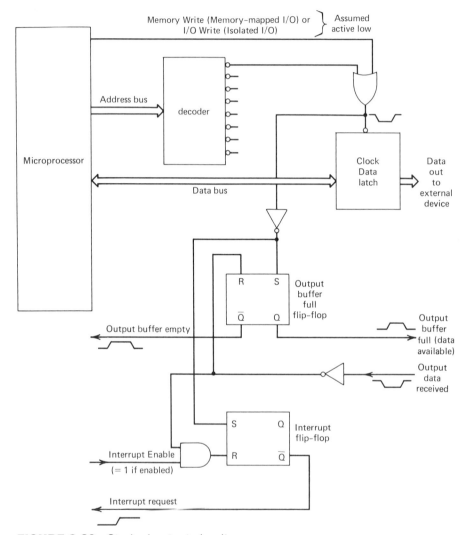

FIGURE 8.20 Strobed output circuit.

the interrupt request flip-flop output $\overline{Q}$ to a 1, producing an interrupt request for more output data.

8.4 COMMUNICATIONS CONSIDERATIONS

Since microcomputers are inexpensive and relatively small in size, one mode of their application is to distribute them and use multiple devices to perform subtasks of a main task. Similarly, a number of microcomputers in a process control environment may be tied in to a central minicomputer for process monitoring and adjustment. In these types of applications, it is necessary to communicate among microcomputers or from a number of microcomputers to a central microcomputer or minicomputer. An important consideration in the usage of multiple microcomputers is the means and type of communication to be established among them.

8.4.1 Basic Communication Terms

If data can be transmitted in *one direction only* on a communication line, the line is defined as a *simplex* line. A second transmission mode is *half-duplex*. In this type of link, data can be transmitted in two directions, but not simultaneously. Half-duplex transmission is implemented by *two wire circuits. Full duplex* transmission or lines that are capable of transmission in both directons are normally implemented using *four wire* circuits. Since digital data are transmitted serially as a stream of bits on these lines, synchronization is required between the source and destination of the data. Information streams containing additional synchronizaton bits (usually start/stop bits) that identify the beginning and end of a character are called asynchronous. A Teletype® operates in this manner with one start bit preceding 8 bits of data, that are followed by 2 stop bits. (See example in Chapter 7.) In some cases, 1 or 1.42 stop bits are used. The stop bits provide time for the equipment to resynchronize, and electromechanical equipment such as Teletypes, therefore, usually require 2 stop bits. Some later electromechanical terminals have been developed, however, which use only 1 stop bit. An alternative method that is capable of higher transmission rates is *synchronous* transmission. In this method, no start/stop bits are sent and, thus, more data are transmitted per unit time. Synchronous transmission requires the transmission of a clock signal with the data or a known character or set of known characters that can be used by the receiver as a means of synchronization with the transmitter. In other words, the transmitter and receiver must use a synchronized common clock signal.

The voice channel of a conventional dial-up telephone line can transmit frequencies from 300 Hz to 3 KHz and is said to have a bandwidth of approximately 3 KHz. As a rule of thumb, this *voice grade channel*, as it is called, can transmit data **asynchronously** at rates of up to 2000 bits per second (bps). A channel with a larger frequency range than a voice grade channel is termed a *wideband* channel. In order to make efficient use of some wideband channels, a number of voice grade channels are fit into the channel bandwidth of the wideband channel and, in fact, wideband channels are often characterized by the number of voice grade channels they can accommodate.

If data are to be transmitted at a rate above 2000 bps on a dial-up voice grade line, **synchronous** data transmission should be used. The synchronous upper bit-rate limit of a voice grade dial-up line is normally taken as 4800 bps, but rates of 9600 bps are possible. Higher data transmission rates can be achieved by leasing special lines from the common carrier that permit rates of up to 19,200 bps. In digital terms, a wideband line is one that is capable of transmitting synchronous data at rates above 9600 bps (such as 19,200 bps).

Other characterizations of data transmission rates have emerged. These characterizations are: 0 to 600 bits per second (*low speed*), 1200 to 4800 bits per second (*medium speed*), and 9600 bits per second and above (*high speed*). These ranges are commonly used, and represent typical numbers.

In addition to bits per second, data transmission rates are specified in terms of *baud* or *baud rates*. A *baud* is a unit of signaling speed that is equal to the number of discrete events occurring per second. If binary signals are used, which implies only two possible discrete events or levels, one baud is equal to 1 bit per second. If, for example, quaternary logic were utilized and four possible logic levels were possible, one baud would be equivalent to 2 bits per second that represent one of four possible states. The baud rate of a Teletype that transmits at 10 characters per second and represents a character by 11 bits (a start bit, 8 data bits, and 2 stop bits) is:

$$11 \text{ bits/character} \times 10 \text{ characters/second}$$
$$= 110 \text{ baud or } 110 \text{ bits/second}$$

Because 3 of the 11 bits are used for synchronization, the actual data rate is 8 bits/character × 10 characters/second = 80 bits/second. Another definition of *baud rate* is the reciprocal of the time in seconds occupied by the shortest element of the code being transmitted. If the shortest element of a code occupied 10 millisec, the baud rate would be 100 baud. The word baud is derived from the five-level Baudot Code.

When a telephone line is used to transmit data, means are necessary to couple the computing system to the line. The most common devices used to accomplish this coupling are modems, acoustic couplers, and data sets.

A *modem* or *modulator/demodulator* is used to convert digital signals to analog signals (modulation) capable of being transmitted over the telephone line and to recover these signals (demodulation) when received from a telephone line. Low speed modems accomplish the modulation by converting the digital 1 and 0 inputs to MARK and SPACE frequencies, respectively, which are transmitted as tones over the telephone lines. This technique is referred to as *FSK modulation* or *Frequency Shift Keying*. The demodulation process is accomplished by filtering and amplifying the incoming FSK information to discriminate between the MARK and SPACE frequencies and produce the corresponding 1 and 0 level outputs.

An example of a microprocessor-compatible modem is the Motorola MC6860 Low Speed Modem. This FSK modem is implemented on an LSI chip but requires external filters and analog circuits for operation. The 6860 implements the modulation by digitally synthesizing a transmitting carrier from a 1-MHz crystal source. The 6860 modem originating the data transmission call transmits a 1270-Hz tone for a MARK and a 1070-Hz tone for a SPACE. The return or ANSWER tones from the called 6860 are different from the transmitted tones and are 2225 Hz for MARK, 2025 Hz for SPACE. These are standard frequencies used in FSK modulation. At higher transmission rates (normally above 9600 bps), 4, 8, or 16 *Phase Shift Keying (PSK)* is employed. Modems utilize either synchronous or asynchronous transmission schemes with synchronous transmission usually used at 2000 bps rates and above.

Common carries such as Bell Telephone supply a number of different types of modems that are referred to as *data sets.* Three classes of these data sets are the 100, 200, and 300 series. There are a number of models in each series and the figures in Table 8.1 represent the ranges covered by the models of a particular series.

An *acoustic coupler* permits serial interfacing from a computing device or terminal to a dial-up line through the handset of a conventional telephone. The line connection is made by manually dialing the number of the remote location and then placing the handset of the telephone into a "cradle" on the coupler. The coupler converts MARK and SPACE electrical signals from the terminal or computer to tones that are transmitted serially and asynchronously over the telephone line to the remote location through the handset mouthpiece. Conversely, tones are received from the

TABLE 8.1   Summary of Characteristics of Popular Bell Data Sets

BELL SERIES	TIMING	DUPLEX	MAX SPEED (BPS)	TYPE OF LINE
100	Asynchronous	Full	300	D.D.D.[a]
200	Asynchronous or synchronous	Full or half	9600	D.D.D.[a] or leased
300	Synchronous	Full or half	460.8K	Leased

[a]D.D.D. denotes Direct Distance Dialing.

remote location through the handset earpiece and converted to MARK and SPACE electrical signals for the terminal or computer.

Standard interfaces to couplers, modems, terminals, and similar equipment are the *20-milliamp current loop,* the Electronic Industries Association (EIA) RS-232-C standard (*1*), the International Telegraph and Telephone Consultative Committee (CCITT) recommendation V.24 (*2*), and the Military Standard MIL-STD-188C (low level) (*3*). The 20-ma current loop uses the presence of current to denote a MARK or 1 and the absence of current to represent a SPACE or 0. Because data are represented by current, this type of connection has immunity to noise and can be used over relatively long distances with direct wire connections. A 20-ma current loop interface to a microprocessor from a Teletype is shown in Figure 8.21, utilizing a 4N33 optical coupler.

The EIA RS-232-C and CCITT V.24 standards are essentially equivalent. Some important parameters of this standards are given in Table 8.2. Special interface circuits are manufactured to meet the requirements of the RS-232-C/CCITT V.24 standard. These circuits include the Motorola MC1488 and MC1489 line driver and receiver, the Fairchild 9616 and 9617 line driver and receiver, and the Signetice 8T15 and 8T16 line driver and receiver. The interface for this standard is a simplex, single-ended con-

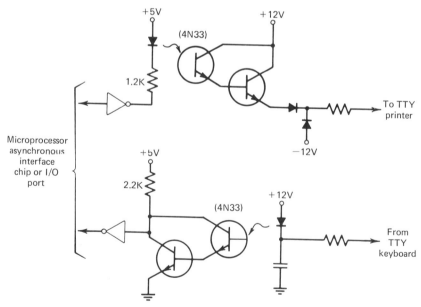

FIGURE 8.21 20-ma current loop interface using optical couplers.

TABLE 8.2 Some Important Parameters of EIA RS-232-C and CCITT V.24 Standards.

PARAMETER	SYMBOL	MIN	MAX	UNITS	COMMENTS
Driver output voltage with load resistance					
Logic 0	V_{OH}	5	15	Volts	
Logic 1	V_{OL}	−15	−5	Volts	$7K\,\Omega \geqslant R_L \geqslant 3K\Omega$
Driver output voltage open circuit					
Logic 0	V_{OH}		25	Volts	
Logic 1	V_{OL}	−25			
Receiver input threshold					
MARK output from driver		−3		Volts	
SPACE output from driver			+3	Volts	
Driver source resistance					
Power on	R_O		Not specified		
Power off	R_O		300	Ohms	$2V \geqslant V_{out} \geqslant -2V$
Driver output short circuit current		−500	500	mA	
Driver output switching characteristics					
Slew rate			30	Volts/μsec	
Rise & fall time			± 14%	of pulse interval	
Bit rate		0	20K	Hz	
Receiver input resistance	R_{IN}	3K	7K	Ohms	$25V \geqslant V_{in} \geqslant 3V$
Receiver input voltage		−25	25	Volts	

nection with no terminations. Reflections are reduced by limiting the slew rate as shown in Table 8.2.

The interface connector used with the RS-232-C standard is a standard 25-pin male connector such as the Amp 205207-1, Amphenol 17-10250-1, or the Cinch DC-255. The pins and corresponding signals on the connector are as follows:

SIGNAL	PIN	SIGNAL	PIN
Chassis ground	1	Supervisory send data (SSD)	11
Transmitted data (TD)	2	Transmitter signal element	
Received data (RD)	3	timing (TSET)	15
Request to send (RS)	4	Data terminal ready (DTR)	20
Clear to send (CTS)	5		
Data set ready (DSR)	6		
Signal ground	7		

A typical EIA RS-232-C interface circuit using the Fairchild 9616 and 9617 chips is shown in Figure 8.22. Maximum cable length of the RS-232-C interface is normally taken as 50 feet.

TABLE 8.3 Summary of RS-422 and RS-423 Interface Standard Specifications

	PARAMETER	CONDITIONS	MIN	MAX	UNITS
V_0	Driver Unloaded Output Voltage			6	V
V_0				-6	V
V_T	Driver Loaded Output Voltage	$R_T = 100\ \Omega$	2		V
V_T				-2	V
R_S	Driver Output Resistance	Per Output		50	Ω
I_{os}	Driver Output Short-Circuit Current	$V_0 = 0$ V		150	mA
	Driver Output Rise Time			10	% Unit Interval
I_{ox}	Driver Power OFF Current	-0.25 V $\leqslant V_0 \leqslant$ 6 V		± 100	μA
V_{TH}	Receiver Sensitivity	$V_{CM} = \pm 7V$		200	mV
V_{CM}	Receiver Common-Mode Voltage		-12	12	V
	Receiver Input Offset		± 3		V

RS-422

TABLE 8.3 Continued

	PARAMETER	CONDITIONS	MIN	MAX	UNITS
V_o	Driver Unloaded Output Voltage		4	6	V
V_o			−4	−6	V
V_T	Driver Loaded Output Voltage	$R_L = 450\ \Omega$	3.6		V
V_T			−3.6		V
R_S	Driver Output Resistance			50	Ω
I_{OS}	Driver Output Short-Circuit Current	$V_o = 0\ V$		±150	mA
	Driver Output Rise and Fall Time	Baud Rate $\leqslant$ 1K Baud		300	μs
		Baud Rate $\geqslant$ 1k Baud		30	% Unit Interval
I_{OX}	Driver Power OFF Current	$V_o = ±6\ V$		±100	μA
V_{TH}	Receiver Sensitivity	$V_{CM} \leqslant ±7V$		±200	mV
V_{CM}	Receiver Common-Mode Range			±10	V
R_{IN}	Receiver Input Resistance		4000		Ω
	Receiver Common-Mode Input Offset			±3	V

RS-423

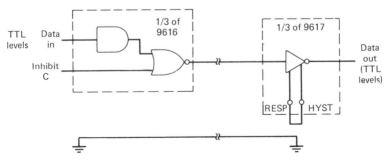

FIGURE 8.22 Typical EIA RS-232-C interface circuit using 9616 and 9617 line driver and receiver.

TABLE 8.4   Some Important Parameters of MIL-STD-188C (Low Level) Standards

PARAMETER	SYM-BOL	MIN	MAX	UNITS	COMMENT
Driver output voltage, open circuit					
Logic 0	V_{OH}	5	7	Volts	
Logic 1	V_{OL}	−7	−5	Volts	
Receiver input threshold					
MARK output from driver			0.1	mA	
SPACE output from driver			−0.1	mA	
Driver source resistance					
Power On	R_O		100	Ohms	$i_{out} \leqslant 10$ ma
Power Off	R_O		Not specified		
Driver output short circuit current			100	mA	To ground
Driver output switching characteristics rise & fall time			±5% of pulse interval		
Bit rate			4K	Hz	Normal rate given
Receiver input resistance	R_{IN}		6K	Ohms	

An upgrade from RS-232-C has been made by EIA to the newer electrical interface standards RS-422* and RS-423.† Standard 423 applies to single-ended transmission at modulation rates up to 1 kiloband (1 ms pulse width) while 422 relates to balanced data transmission at modulation rates up to 10 megaband (0.1 μs pulse width). The characteristics of standards RS-422 and RS-423 are summarized in Table 8.3. These two standards specify the electrical characteristics of a new standard, RS-449 which also

*EIA Standard RS-422: *Electrical Characteristics of Balanced Voltage Digital Interface Circuits,* Electronic Industries Association, April 1975.
†EIA Standard RS-423: Electrical Characteristics of Unbalanced Voltage Digital Interface Circuits, Electronic Industries Association, April 1975.

includes the mechanical and functional characteristics of the interface be-tween the data terminal equipment (DTE) and data circuit terminating equipment (DCE).

The MIL-Standard-188C (low level) interface standard has some spec-ifications that are within the EIA RS-232-C standard such that line drivers and receivers can be manufactured that can be used to implement either interface. Usually an external capacitor must be added to the EIA driver and either an external resistance network or, if provided, different input pins must be used on the EIA receiver to achieve MIL compatibility. Some important parameters of the MIL-STD-188C (low level) standards are given in Table 8.4.

A typical MIL-STD-188C interface circuit is illustrated in Figure 8.23.

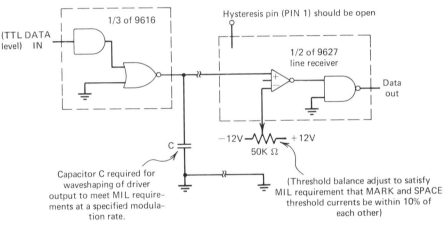

FIGURE 8.23 Typical MIL-STD-188C interface circuit using 9616 and 9627 line driver and receiver.

8.4.2 SDLC Network Communications Protocol

If a message is to be sent over a data communications link, a *protocol* or *discipline for management of information transfer over a data commu-nications channel* must be established. This protocol serves the purposes of assigning message source and destination identification, error detection and recovery, transmitter and receiver control, and communication path control. One such popular protocol is IBM's *Synchronous Data Link Con-trol* (SDLC).* SDLC is becoming pervasive in many types of communi-cations applications and is being supported for microprocessors by SDLC controller peripheral interface chips such as the Intel 8273. As its name implies, SDLC is a synchronous data transmission protocol and, unlike the

* IBM, SDLC General Information Manual, GA27-3093-1, File No. GENL-09 May, 1975.

earlier IBM Binary Synchronous Communication (BSC or BISYNC) procedure, is bit oriented rather than character oriented.

In SDLC, one station acts as a primary node and the others as secondaries. Data transmission can be initiated by a secondary node as well as the primary, but transmissions are always to or from a primary node. SDLC can be used in half- or full duplex mode.

The unit of SDLC transmission is called a *frame*. A standard SDLC frame consists of six fields as shown in Figure 8.24. These fields in the order of their transmission are the 8-bit FLAG (F), 8-bit ADDRESS (A), 8-bit CONTROL (C), variable bit length (in multiples of 8 bits) INFORMATION (I), 16-bit FRAME CHECK SEQUENCE (FCS), and the 8-bit FLAG (F).

The SDLC frames fall into three categories—*Nonsequenced (management)* frames, *Supervisory* frames, and *Information* frames. A *Nonsequenced* frame conveys commands and responses. It is used for control of secondary nodes and indication of transmission errors. This type of frame is sent by the primary or by the secondary as a response to a primary poll.

A *Supervisory* frame is used for supervisory functions such as acknowledgements, busy indications, and calls for retransmission. The data or information to be transmitted are contained in the *Information* frame.

Each field in a frame serves a unique purpose and the characteristics of each field are what make SDLC a flexible and effective protocol. The initial *FLAG* in the frame or *Open FLAG*, as it is sometimes called, signals the beginning of a new frame. It provides a reference for the following fields and signals that **all bits following the FLAG field**, with the exception of the *Close FLAG* and inserted zeros, **should be included in error checking procedures**. The FLAG pattern is a constant pattern of 01111110 and must not occur anywhere else in the frame except in the last or *Close FLAG* at the end of the frame. If this pattern is present in any other fields of the frame to be transmitted, SDLC protocol requires that a zero be inserted after every group of five consecutive 1's before the data are entered into the I field. Consequently, these inserted zeroes must be deleted by the receiver SDLC interface. SDLC assumes synchronism is provided by a modem or *DTE* (Data Terminal Equipment). The DTE is considered as

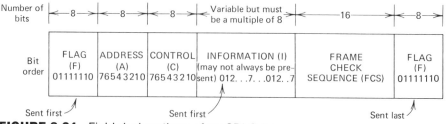

FIGURE 8.24 Field designations of an SDLC frame.

the origin or destination of transmitted data. If timing for received data is not performed by a modem, *NRZI* (Non-Return to Zero Inverting) code is used. In this code, the signal level remains unchanged for the transmission of a 1 while a transition to the opposite level represents a 0. Since the transitions of the signal level can be used for resynchronization between transmitter and receiver, the insertion of a 0 after five consecutive 1's guarantees transitions to opposite levels during long strings of 1's and, thus, eliminates relatively long periods without any level changes. Since the FLAG pattern is known by the receiver, this pattern is used for synchronization of the clocks between the transmitter and receiver. The *Address* field designates the destination or destinations of the frame sent by a primary station. A secondary station will synchronize only if its address is present in the address field. No address field is required when sending from a secondary station to the primary.

The *Control* Field has three different formats, corresponding to either an Information, Supervisory, or Nonsequenced (Management) frame. If the leftmost bit (bit 7), of the Control field is 0, the Control field of an Information frame is identified. If bit 7 of the Control Field is a 1, the Control field of a Supervisory frame is specified by bit 6 = 0 and the Control field of a Nonsequenced frame is specified by bit 6 = 1. The Control field of an Information frame provides for one of the important features of SDLC, namely, **that multiple frames can be transmitted without necessarily waiting for an acknowledgment from the receiver following each frame transmission.** In fact, up to seven frames can be transmitted without acknowledgments. Following the seventh frame, if no acknowledgment has been received, the transmitter will wait for an acknowledgment from the receiver in terms of the number of frames correctly received or request an acknowledgment. Actually, the acknowledgment sent back to the transmitter is the number, N_r, that corresponds to the next frame expected by the receiver. The number of frames transmitted is denoted by the symbol, N_S. For example, if frames 0, 1, and 2 have been transmitted and none immediately thereafter, N_S would equal 2, indicating frames 0, 1, and 2 have been transmitted, and N_r would be 3 if the **three frames were received without error.**

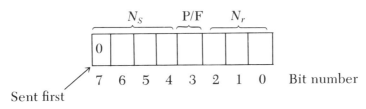

FIGURE 8.25 Control Field of Information Frame

Since the control field of each frame contains the values of N_S and N_r known by a station, SDLC has the feature of a station's being able to verify and acknowledge another station's transmission while continuing to transmit. Of the three types of frames, Information frames are the only ones that are counted for N_S and N_r counts. This type of frame is also referred to as a *Sequenced frame*. A flowchart illustrating a procedure for Information frame transmission, verification, and retransmission is given in Figure 8.26.

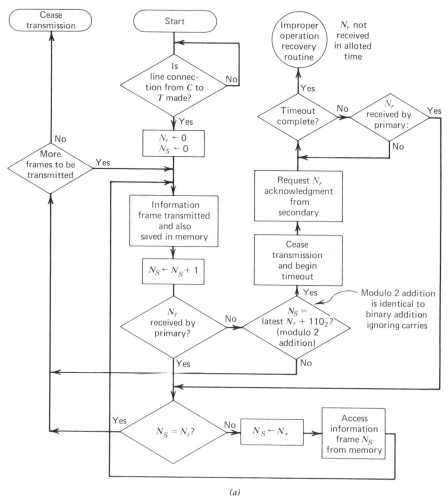

(a)

FIGURE 8.26 Flow charts of SDLC information frame transmission and reception. (a) Information frame transmission procedure flowchart for primary station. C). (b) Information frame reception procedure flowchart for terminal, T.

Related examples are given in Figure 8.27. In these two figures, a central microcomputer, C, is the primary station and is transmitting data to a secondary terminal, T.

The Poll/Final (P/F) bit of the Control field, as shown in Figure 8.25, serves two purposes. If the frame is being sent from a primary station to a secondary station, P/F = 1 requests (polls) the secondary to confirm the

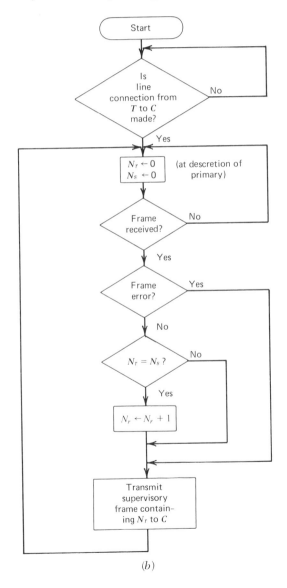

(b)

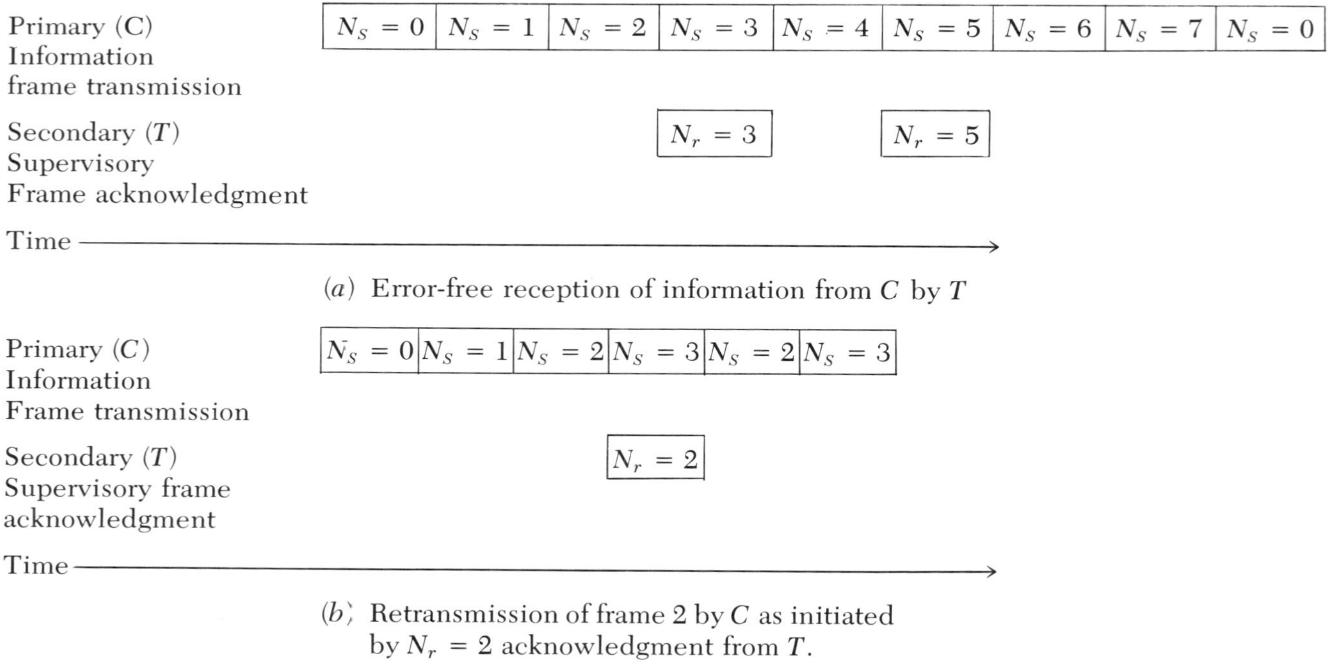

$N_S = 0$	$N_S = 1$	$N_S = 2$	$N_S = 3$	$N_S = 4$	$N_S = 5$	$N_S = 6$	$N_S = 7$	$N_S = 0$

Primary (C)
Information
frame transmission

$N_r = 3$ $N_r = 5$

Secondary (T)
Supervisory
Frame acknowledgment

Time ——————→

(a) Error-free reception of information from C by T

$N_S = 0$	$N_S = 1$	$N_S = 2$	$N_S = 3$	$N_S = 2$	$N_S = 3$

Primary (C)
Information
Frame transmission

$N_r = 2$

Secondary (T)
Supervisory frame
acknowledgment

Time ——————→

(b) Retransmission of frame 2 by C as initiated
by $N_r = 2$ acknowledgment from T.

FIGURE 8.27 Examples of SDLC frame transmissions from C to T.

present N_s count. The P/F is also set to 1 in the final frame of transmission by a secondary station transmitting to a primary to indicate an End of Transmission (EOT).

A Supervisory frame control field has, as previously noted, bit 7 = 1 and bit 6 = 0. The remainder of the field consists of a P/F bit, two bits for Command/Response functions, and three N_r bits (Figure 8.28).

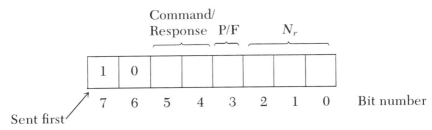

FIGURE 8.28 Control field of supervisory frame.

The Command/Response functions of the Supervisory frame and their Control field patterns are:

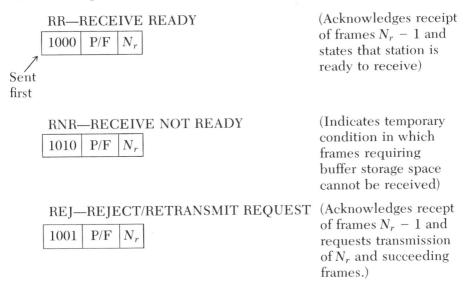

RR—RECEIVE READY

(Acknowledges receipt of frames $N_r - 1$ and states that station is ready to receive)

RNR—RECEIVE NOT READY

(Indicates temporary condition in which frames requiring buffer storage space cannot be received)

REJ—REJECT/RETRANSMIT REQUEST

(Acknowledges recept of frames $N_r - 1$ and requests transmission of N_r and succeeding frames.)

The Nonsequenced frame Control field contains five Command/Response bits, in addition to identification bits 7 and 6, and a P/F bit. This type of frame is sent only by a primary or as a response to a primary poll. **Nonsequenced and Supervisory frames are not counted as N_r and N_s transmissions** (Figure 8.29).

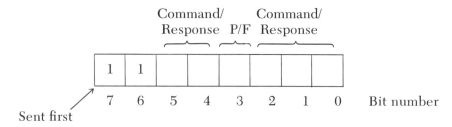

FIGURE 8.29 Control field of a Nonsequenced frame.

The Command/Response functions of a Nonsequenced frame along with their Control field pattern are:

Sent   NSI
first | 1100 | P/F | 000 |

NONSEQUENCED INFORMATION (Response to or command for nonsequenced information; NSI frames are not acknowledged)

SNRM
| 1100 | P | 001 |

SET NORMAL RESPONSE MODE (Primary station command designating secondary station; limits secondary to solicited transmissions only; Normal Response Mode condition changed by DISC or SIM command; N_S and N_r counts of primary and secondary are reset to 0; expected response is NSA)

SIM
| 1110 | P | 000 |

SET INITIALIZATION MODE (Command from primary station resetting N_S and N_r counts of primary and secondary to 0; begins prespecified procedures at secondary; expected response is NSA)

DISC
| 1100 | P | 010 |

DISCONNECT (Command from primary station putting secondary station off line and terminating other modes; secondary station can be reconnected by SNRM or SIM command; expected response to DISC is NSA)

NSA
| 1100 | F | 110 |

NONSEQUENCED ACKNOWLEDGMENT (Confirming acknowledgment to SNRM, SIM, or DISC commands; additional transmissions are at discretion of primary)

RQI
| 1110 | F | 000 |

REQUEST FOR INITIALIZATION (Secondary station request for SIM command; any response other than SIM command by primary will initiate another RQI by secondary)

CMDR
| 1110 | F | 001 |

COMMAND REJECT (Response by secondary station to nonvalid command; nonvalid commands include unassigned commands and, optionally, an I field that contains too many bits for receiving buffer storage)

ROL
| 1111 | F | 000 |

REQUEST ON LINE (Secondary station response indicating that it is presently off line)

XID
| 1111 | P/F | 101 |

EXCHANGE STATION IDENTIFICATION (Command to or response for the address of the receiving secondary station; an optional I field may be included in the frame to identify transmitting or responding station)

NSP
| 1100 | 1/0 | 100 |

NONSEQUENCED POLL (Transmission request by primary to secondary, this request is a command if P/F is a 1, but response is optional if P/F = 0; I field is not permitted)

TEST
| 1100 | P/F | 111 |

TEST (Command to or response for testing purposes; an optional I field can be included in the command that will then elicit a TEST Nonsequenced frame from the receiver that will contain the same I field)

The Information (I) field itself contains the data to be transmitted in multiples of 8 bits. For each individual 8-bit grouping, the high order bit is transmitted **last** in time.

The Frame Check Sequence (FCS) field or *Block Check (BC)*, contains a 16-bit pattern that is computed by the transmitter and that is a function of previous bits in the frame. To generate the FCS, the bits transmitted after the Open FLAG and before the Close FLAG (excluding inserted zeros) are considered to be coefficients of a polynomial in X. For n coefficients, the order of the polynomial is $n - 1$. The FCS field follows the Information field (if there is one) in Information and Nonsequenced frames or the Control field in all other situations.

Consider the eight-bit "message" 10010011. This message could be considered as the polynomial

$$M(X) = (1)X^7 + (0)X^6 + (0)X^5 + (1)X^4 + (0)X^3 + (0)X^2 + (1)X^1 + (1)X^0$$

or

$$M(X) = X^7 + X^4 + X + 1, \text{ where } n = 8.$$

Now, for a general polynomial $M(X)$, a series of 16 check bits corresponding to the FCS is to be added to the message before transmission and used by the receiver to verify that a valid transmission has occurred. In order to obtain and prepare for the 16 check bits that are to be added to $M(X)$, $M(X)$ must effectively be shifted 16 bit positions to the left or, equivalently, multiplied by X^{16} while ignoring any carries during multiplication (modulo 2 multiplication). In SDLC, the vacant 16 bit positions to the right of $M(X)$ are set to 1's and the resulting bit string including $M(X)$ is divided (modulo 2, ignoring carries or borrows) by a polynomial, $G(X)$. Then $G(X)$ is known as the *generating polynomial*.

The generating polynomial must have an order equal to the number of check bits that, for SDLC, is 16. The generating polynomial is constant for a particular coding scheme and for SDLC is $X^{16} + X^{12} + X^5 + 1$. The quotient, $Q(X)$, of the division is ignored and the one's complement of the remainder, $R(X)$, becomes the FCS field. It is important to note that, in carrying out the modulo 2 division, we perform modulo 2 subtraction. Furthermore, modulo 2 addition and subtraction are identical since carries and borrows are ignored. Both operations are the EXCLUSIVE OR function of corresponding bits of the two words involved. The appending of the FCS field to the other fields involved in error checking will product a polynomial to be transmitted, $T(X)$. Then $T(X)$ is divided (modulo 2) at the receiver by $G(X)$, where $T(X)$ includes the transmitted FCS field. The remainder obtained at the receiver is a constant and is characteristic of the divisor. For the $G(X)$ of SDLC, this remainder must always be 1111000010111000 for a correct transmission indication. If this constant is not obtained after division at the receiver, the frame is assumed to be in error and is not accepted. Then N_r is not incremented.

This procedure is summarized as:

$M(X)$ message polynomial in X of order n
$G(X)$ generating polynomial in X of order 16
$N(X)X^{16}$ message polynomial shifted 16 bit positions to the left with vacant positions filled by 0's.
$M(X)X^{16} + 65,535_{10}$ $M(X)X^{16}$ with vacant positions filled by 1's
$(M(X)X^{16} + 65,535_{10})/G(X) = Q(X) + R(X)/G(X)$

$R(X)$ 16-bit series that is remainder of
$(M(X)X^{16} + 65,535_{10})/G(X)$

$R(X)'$ one's complement of $R(X)$ **and is FCS field**

$T(X)$ transmitted word

$T(X) =$ $M(X)X^{16} + R(X)'$ At the receiver, $T(X)$ is divided by $G(X)$. For an error-free transmission to be assumed by the receiver, $T(X)/G(X)$ must yield 1111000010111000.

A code obtained in the manner just described is referred to as a *CRC* or a *Cyclic Redundancy Check*.

The modulo 2 division process is accomplished serially using shift registers and EXCLUSIVE OR gates. The shifting process performs the alignment of the highest order nonzero divisor bit with the highest order bit of the dividend. The first modulo 2 subtraction is implemented by an EXCLUSIVE OR function between each pair of bits of corresponding weight. This procedure is then accomplished repeatedly in the loading and shifting process of the shift register with the $M(X)X^{16} + R(X)'$ sum exiting serially from the shift register.

A block diagram of a shift register CRC generator for the SDLC generating polynomial $X^{16} + X^{12} + X^5 + 1$ is given in Figure 8.30. The flip-flops comprising the shift register are D type with shift/preset control. The CRC generator can be used at both the transmitting and receiving stations.

At the transmitting station, the shift register is initialized to all 1's by momentarily placing the SHIFT/PRESET line in the PRESET logic level. Then, with the SHIFT/PRESET line at the SHIFT logic level and the CALCULATE FCS line at a HIGH level, output AND gate 1 will be enabled and the Message consisting in order of the Address, Control, and Information (when desired and permitted) fields will appear at the Data out line in bit sequential form. These bits bypass the shift register and will be clocked out sequentially until completely transmitted. As this transmission is occurring, the Message bits are also being shifted into the shift register EXCLUSIVE OR string which was PRESET with 1's. This shifting process will perform the serial division of the message by $G(X) = X^{16} + X^{12} + X^5 + 1$. This division is accomplished by virtue of the recirculation of the output of flip-flop 15 (corresponding to X^{16}) through an EXCLUSIVE OR gate to the input (corresponding to X^0 or 1) and the placement of other EXCLUSIVE OR gates at the inputs of flip-flops X^5 and X^{12}. In the transmitting station, the FCS bits will appear following the last message bit at the Data out line as the CALCULATE FCS line is brought LOW following the last message bit output, thus switching out AND gate 1 and switching in AND gate 2. The 16-bit FCS character is formed by inverting the remainder, $R(X)$, which emerges from the output of flip-flop X^{15} after the last message bit is transmitted.

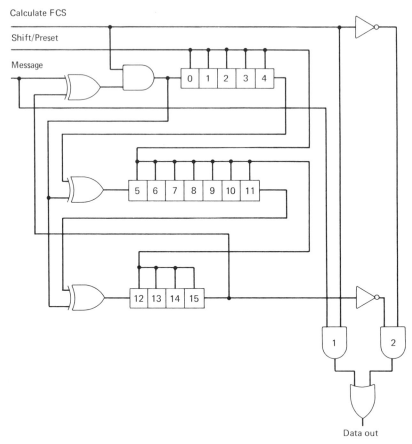

FIGURE 8.30 CRC generator shift register for

$$G(X) = X^{16} + X^{12} + X^5 + 1.$$

At the receiving station, the circuit of Figure 8.30 is utilized in the same manner as at the transmitting station except that the FCS character is included in the division with the Message data. As with the transmitting station, inserted zeros are not included in the CRC generation. The remainder, $R(X)'$, of this operation must be the 16-bit sequence 1111000010111000 for the receiving station to assume that no error has occurred. In this sequence of bits, the leftmost bit corresponds to X^0 and the rightmost bit to X^{15}.

In order to keep a data link open and maintain an active line state, a series of contiguous FLAG characters can be sent by the transmitting station. A station sending in this manner is called an *Idle Station*. This action can be used to prevent the occurrence of timeouts at the other station on the link. For example, the primary station may transmit a frame with a Control field requesting a response from the secondary. If response is not received within a specified time interval or an unintelligible response is received, recovery procedures may be initiated. Some typical timeout intervals are 900 millisec, or 3 sec to 20 sec.

If it is desired to break a data link at any time, the transmitting station and only the transmitting station can transmit an ABORT signal by sending eight consecutive 1's. No FCS field or Close FLAG are produced after an ABORT.

8.5 USARTS AND UARTS

Since asynchronous or synchronous data communications are almost always required in a microcomputer system, a general-purpose synchronous/asynchronous interface chip is commonly used for this function. This type of chip is called a *Universal Synchronous/Asynchronous Receiver/Transmitter or USART.* If the chip implements asynchronous communication only, it is termed a *Universal Asynchronous Receiver/Transmitter (UART)* or an *Asynchronous Communications Interface Adapter (ACIA).* The conventional USART can be used with some difficulty for SDLC transmission, but a chip such as the Intel 8273 SDLC protocol controller should be employed for this type of communication. Because the USART has both asynchronous and synchronous capabilities, a discussion of its operation will describe the UART. A block diagram of a USART, the Intel 8251A, which was designed specifically for use with a microcomputer, is given in Figure 8.31.

The 8251A utilizes a +5 volt power supply and is packaged in a 28 pin, Dual-In-Line package.

8.5.1 Asynchronous Transmission Mode

In the asynchronous or UART mode of operation, the 8251A can accept from five to eight data bits from the microprocessor data bus and transmit them serially as part of a character on the Transmitter Data (T×D) output. The transmitted character is composed of a start bit, the five to eight data bits, a *parity* bit that is optional, and either one, one and one-half, or two stop bits. A logic 1 is represented by a HIGH level. The character begins with a HIGH-to-LOW transition signalling the onset of the start bit. The start bit is a LOW level for one bit time followed by the five to eight data bits (least significant bit first.) The data bits are followed in turn by an optional even or odd parity bit and the end of the character is indicated by a HIGH level stop bit(s). If *even parity* is selected, the parity bit will be used to insure that there are an even number of 1's (including the parity

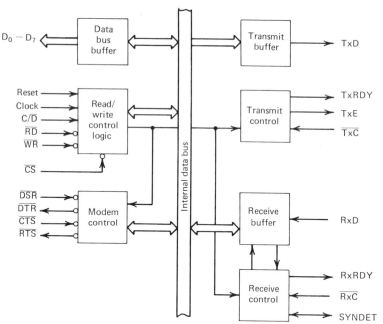

FIGURE 8.31 Block diagram of Intel 8251A. (Reprinted by permission of Intel Corporation, Copyright 1978)

bit) transmitted between the start and stop bits. A selection of *odd parity* will use the parity bit to cause an odd number of 1's (including parity) to be transmitted. If another character is to be transmitted immediately following the previous character, a HIGH-to-LOW transition start bit is initiated following the last stop bit(s). If a character is not transmitted immediately following another character, any number of idle bits (HIGH level) can be transmitted until a new character transmission is indicated by a start bit.

Transmission of characters with a start bit, seven data bits, a parity bit, and two stop bits is depicted in Figure 8.32.

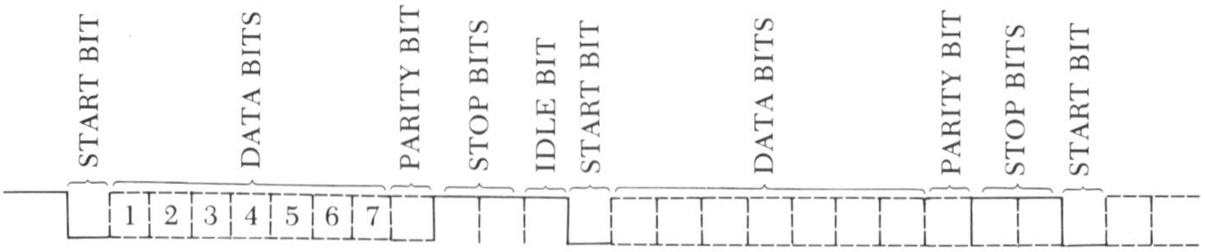

FIGURE 8.32 One format of asynchronous data transmission.

The USART mode and data format are programmable by the microcomputer through mode and command instructions. If the Control/Data (C/$\overline{\text{D}}$) input is a 1, the byte on the data bus is interpreted as command or status information. The data bus contents are read as data if C/$\overline{\text{D}}$ is a 0. The mode selection and control words, respectively, must immediately follow a RESET of the 8251A either by an external input to the RESET pin or by a RESET command from the microprocessor. The format of the command and status words is discussed in Section 8.5.4, Synchronous Reception Mode.

The format of the mode select word that must be sent to the 8251A on the data bus for asynchronous operation is shown in Figure 8.33.

Stop Bit Specification D7 D6	Even/odd parity select D5	Parity enable D4	Data word length D3 D2	Baud rate factor D1 D0
0 1 (1 bit)	1 (Even parity)	1 (Enable)	0 0 (5 bits)	0 0 (Synchronous)
1 0 (1½ bits)			0 1 (6 bits)	1 1 (1x)
1 1 (2 bits)	0 (Odd parity)	0 (Disable)	1 0 (7 bits)	1 0 (16x)
0 0 (invalid)			1 1 (8 bits)	1 1 (64x)

where the Baud rate factor is the multiple of the transmission and reception rate at which the transmission clock $\overline{\text{T} \times \text{C}}$ and reception clock $\overline{\text{R} \times \text{C}}$ are set.

FIGURE 8.33 Asynchronous mode selection word formats.

If, for example, the USART were to operate in the asynchronous mode with even parity and were to transmit data in the form of Figure 8.32, the mode selection word would appear as (Figure 8.34):

D_7	D_6	D_5	D_4	D_3	D_2	D_1	D_0
1	1	1	1	1	0	1	0

2 stop bits	Even parity	Parity enable	7 bits of data specified	$\overline{T \times C}$ and $\overline{R \times C}$ are 16 × baud rate

FIGURE 8.34   Asynchronous mode selection example.

In this mode specification, the baud rate factor is defined as 16, which means that the external transmitter and receiver clock inputs have a frequency 16 times the baud rate. Thus, the character(s) to be transmitted are shifted out serially at a rate 1/16 of the transmitter clock input, $\overline{T \times C}$. The $\overline{T \times C}$ and $\overline{R \times C}$ clock signals can be nicely supplied by a Baud Rate Generator chip.

Following the asynchronous mode instruction, a command instruction can be sent from the microprocessor to the 8251A. Both the mode and command instructions are sent to the 8251A as a memory or I/O Write from the microprocessor utilizing the $\overline{CE}$ (Chip Enable) and $\overline{WR}$ (Write) lines of the 8251A. Similarly data are read from the 8251A by means of the $\overline{CE}$ and $\overline{RD}$ (Read) lines of the USART as a memory or I/O Read. The command instruction specifies operations such as transmit or receive enable, error reset, and modem controls. (See Section 8.5.4, Synchronous Reception Mode, for details.) The modem control lines affected by the command instruction are Data Terminal Ready (DTR) and Request-to-Send (RTS) lines. The DTR and RTS outputs of the 8251A can be used directly for the DTR and RTS signals needed for typical modems. The other two modem control lines, Data Set Ready ($\overline{DSR}$) and Clear to Send ($\overline{CTS}$) are inputs to the 8251A. $\overline{DSR}$ is used by the microprocessor to monitor the DSR line of the modem and the $\overline{CTS}$ input is used as a qualifier to enable serial data transmission. The transmitter employs *double buffering*, which is accomplished by having a separate buffer register and shifting register in the transmitter. With these two registers, the next word to be transmitted can be entered into the buffer register while the word presently being transmitted is shifted out of the shifting register. The Transmitter Ready (T × RDY) output from the 8251A indicates to the microprocessor that the buffer register can now accept another character. This character is written to the 8251A by the processor executing a memory or I/O Write (RD = 1, WR = 0, $\overline{CS}$ = 0) with $\overline{C/D}$ = 0. The Transmitter Empty (T × E) line is LOW when characters are available to the 8251A for transmission but is set HIGH when there are no characters to be transmitted.

8.5.2   Asynchronous Reception Mode

When the 8251A is receiving data in the asynchronous mode, it must check for proper character format, check for parity errors (if the parity bit is used), and provide the data bits in parallel to the data bus lines of the receiving microprocessor. The receiver portion of the USART will synchronize on the HIGH to LOW transition of the received character start bit, sample the center of the start bit to insure that it is a LOW level and, thus, a valid start, and sample the approximate centers of the remaining bits of the character. If parity is used and a parity error occurs, a *Parity Error (PE)* flag is set in the status word of the 8251A. Similarly, if the stop bit level is sampled by the receiver and is determined to be a LOW instead of a HIGH, a *Framing Error (FE)* flag is set in the status word. Double buffering is also utilized in the receiver when a valid character is transferred from the receiver input shift register to a separate buffer register for reading by the microprocessor. The Receiver Ready (R × RDY) output of the 8251A goes HIGH whenever a character is available in the receiver buffer register and can be used as an interrupt or poll output to the microprocessor. If a new character is received and transferred to the receiver buffer register before the previous character is read by the microprocessor, the previous character is written over and an *Overrun Error (OE)* flag is set in the 8251A status word. The Framing Error, Parity Error, and Overrun Error flags in the 8251A status word can be read at any time by the microprocessor by setting C/D = 1 and executing a Read from the 8251A device address.

8.5.3   Synchronous Transmission Mode

In the synchronous mode, the Baud rate factor is always 1× and, thus, the baud rate is equal to the frequency of $\overline{T \times C}$. In a typical synchronous transmission, the first character sent is usually the SYNC character which is a known pattern to be used by the receiver to synchronize its clock to that of the transmitter. Prior to the first character transmission, T × D is HIGH. The SYNC character is transmitted when the Clear-to-Send (CTS) input to the 8251A goes LOW. All following data are continuously sent out at the $\overline{T \times C}$ frequency. Since, in synchronous transmission, data must continually be sent until the End of Transmission (EOT), the 8251A will fill in "blanks" in the data stream with SYNC characters if the microprocessor does not keep the USART "filled" with data words to be transmitted. In synchronous operation, the Transmitter Empty (T × E) line goes HIGH when the 8251A is supplying SYNC characters for transmission in the absence of data from the microprocessor. The T × E goes HIGH at the last bit time of each SYNC character as it is transmitted and goes LOW again when the SYNC character has been completely shifted out. The format for synchronous data transmission is one or two SYNC characters followed by data characters of five to eight bits each (Figure 8.35).

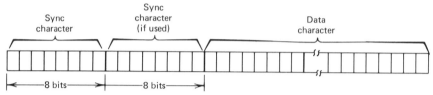

FIGURE 8.35 Format of synchronous data transmission.

Mode selection for the synchronous mode is accomplished similarly to that for the asynchronous mode with the synchronous mode selection shown in Figure 8.36.

Number of sync charac- ters	Sync detect	Even/odd parity select	Parity enable	Character length		Synchronous mode select	
D_7	D_6	D_5	D_4	D_3	D_2	D_1	D_0
1 (Single Sync)	1 (External Sync)	1 (Even)	1 (Enable)	0	0 (5 bits)		
				0	1 (6 bits)	0	0
0 (Double Sync)	0 (Internal Sync)	2 (Odd)	2 (Disable)	1	0 (7 bits)		
				1	1 (8 bits)		

FIGURE 8.36 Synchronous mode selection word format.

8.5.4 Synchronous Reception Mode

For the receiver to correctly interpret the incoming synchronous data, its internal clock must be synchronized with the transmitting clock. When the two clocks are synchronized, the receiver will sample, on the LOW to HIGH transition of R × C, the serial input data stream on pin Receiver Data (R × D) at the proper times and intervals to effect a valid interpretation of the logic levels on the line. If an explicit clock signal is not transmitted along with the data (as is the case when one is using a USART), the receiver clock can obtain synchronism with the transmitter clock (the transmitted frequency is known) by "hunting" in clock phase until a known transmitted synchronizing (SYNC) character is identified. The 8251A transmitter, as previously described, can be programmed to transmit one SYNC character or two (BI-SYNC transmission). In the synchronous mode selection word, bit D_7 will specify a single SYNC character transmission and reception ($D_7 = 1$) or a double SYNC character ($D_7 = 0$). Bit D_6 of the selection word selects SYNC character detection by either an external means ($D_6 = 1$) or by the 8251 itself ($D_6 = 0$). If external synchronizing means are selected, the SYNC Detect (SYNDET) pin on the 8251A is programmed as an input. In this situaion, the 8251A will assume clock synchronism has been achieved when a LOW to HIGH transition appears on the SYNDET pin and remains HIGH for a minimum time equal to the period of $\overline{R} \times C$. Data characters will be interpreted on the HIGH-to-LOW $\overline{R} \times C$ transition immediately following the LOW-to-HIGH transition on SYNDET. When internal synchronizaton is specified, ($D_6 = 0$), the SYNDET pin is programmed as an output that will be set to a HIGH when synchronism has been achieved. SYNDET is reset to a LOW whenever the 8251A is RESET by applying a HIGH to the RESET input pin or when a Status Read operation is executed.

The SYNC character or characters (if BI-SYNC is used), must be programmed into the 8251A **immediately after the mode selection word is written from the microprocessor into the 8251A.** As with writing the asynchronous selection word from the microprocessor to the USART, a RESET (external or internal) of the 8251A must precede the writing of the synchronous mode selection word to the 8251A and the C/$\overline{D}$ pin must be set to a 1. Following the SYNC characters, command instructions (C/$\overline{D}$ still set to 1) can be written to the 8251A as in the asynchronous mode. For either the asynchronous or synchronous mode, a mode selection word can be written into the 8251A at any time by setting a bit in the command instruction word that will cause an internal RESET of the USART. The command instruction word for either mode or operation is as follows.

Enter Hunt Mode	Internal Reset	Request to Send	Error Reset	Send back character	Receive Enable	Data terminal ready	Transmit Enable
D_7	D_6	D_5	D_4	D_3	D_2	D_1	D_0
1 (Hunt)	1 (Reset)		1 (Reset Parity, Overrun	1 (T $\times$ D $\rightarrow$ 0) 0 (Normal	1 (Receive Enable)	1 ($\overline{\text{DTR}}\rightarrow$0)	1 (Transmit Enable)
		1 (RTS$\leftarrow$0)	& Framing Error Flags)	Operation)	0 (Disable)		0 (Disable)

FIGURE 8.37 Command instruction word format.

Overrun and Parity errors are checked and flagged in the synchronous mode as in the asynchronous mode. Framing Error check is not utilized in synchronous transmission. The presence of an error or other status conditions is determined by a Status Read command from the microprocessor to the 8251A. This command is a microprocessor Read command with C/$\overline{\text{D}}$ = 1 and its execution will result in the status word's being read into the microprocessor on the data bus. The format of the status word is the same for both the asynchronous and synchronous modes of transmission (Figure 8.38).

8.5.5   USART Connection to Microprocessor

A typical connection of the 8251A USART to a microprocessor is shown in Figure 8.39.

8.6   DIRECT MEMORY ACCESS (DMA)

If it is desired to move data from a peripheral device to memory or vice versa, there are two alternatives. One is to execute MOVE-type instructions transferring one word at a time or, equivalently, LOAD ACCUMULATOR

Data set ready	SYNC detect	Framming Error (async only)	Overrun Error	Parity Error	Trans- mitter Empty	Receiver Ready	Trans- mitter Ready
D_7	D_6	D_5	D_4	D_3	D_2	D_1	D_0
*	*	FE = 1 when valid stop bit is not detected.	OE = 1 when character receiver buffer is written over.	PE = 1 when parity error occurs	*	*	○

*These status bits are identical in definition to corresponding pins on 8251A chip

○This status bit has same meaning as T × RDY pin on 8251A except that the T × RDY pin output is AND'ed with CTS and T × EN but the status bit is not.

NOTE: The occurrence of any error does not inhibit continued operation of the 8251A.

FIGURE 8.38   Status word format.

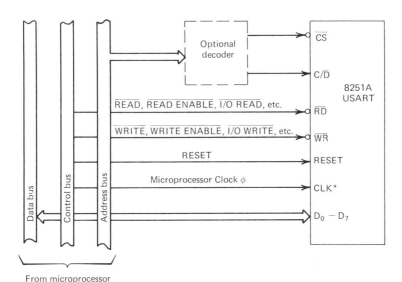

FIGURE 8.39 USART connection to microprocessor. *The CLOCK (CLK) input of the 8251A is used for internal timing and is not used for transmission and reception reference timing. The frequency of CLK must, however, be greater than 4.5 times $\overline{T \times C}$ or $\overline{R \times C}$ for asynchronous operation and greater than 30 times $\overline{T \times C}$ or $\overline{R \times C}$ for the synchronous mode. For the 8080A, CLK is ϕ_2 (TTL) output of 8224 clock generator.

FROM MEMORY and INPUT/OUTPUT ACCUMULATOR CONTENTS instructions. This alternative ties up the CPU and the data rate is limited by the execution times of the instructions required to effect the transfer. Direct Memory Access, or DMA as it is sometimes called, effectively bypasses the microprocessor and transfers data directly between a peripheral and memory.

To accomplish the data movement, the peripheral device must essentially "take over" the address, data, and control lines to memory from the microprocessor and produce the proper address and control signals to implement the data transfer.

8.6.1 Bandwidth Sharing

When the memory access time is significantly less than the processor clock period and the microprocessor timing permits, the memory can be waiting, unutilized, for the next processor memory access. On some microprocessors, the instruction cycle states are such than an external device could use this memory "dead time" to transfer data by DMA. This type of operation can be referred to as *bandwidth sharing* (Figure 8.40).

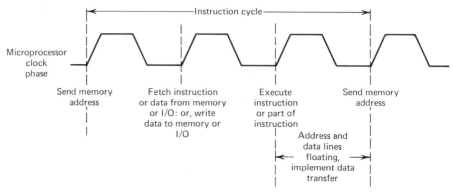

FIGURE 8.40 Bandwidth sharing.

If it is possible to transfer data between memory and a peripheral during a time when the microprocessor is not using memory, there would be, ideally, no degradation in system throughput. Because of delays and settling time requirements, throughput may actually be 5% to 10% less than ideal.

8.6.2 Cycle Stealing

If there is no time to transfer data between memory and peripheral in the instruction cycle, the DMA operation must supplant some instruction cycles. This interference will reduce the microprocessor throughput to a greater degree than bandwidth sharing. The DMA transfer during a time when an instruction would normally be executed is called *cycle stealing*.

8.6.3 DMA Control

The DMA transfer by a peripheral device must include control of the memory address lines and data lines. This control includes providing the correct and proper number of memory addresses involved in the data transfer, control of the data bus, and, where applicable, control of the mode of data transfer, which may vary among peripherals.

A typical monolithic DMA controller designed for use with a microprocessor is given in Figure 8.41. Typical data rates for DMA transfer range from 200K to 1.5M bytes per second depending on the microprocessor instruction cycle timing, memory access time, and buffering techniques utilized.

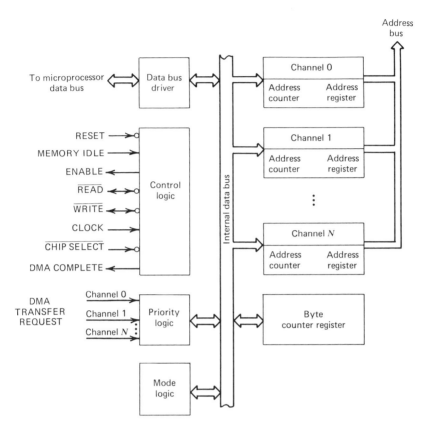

FIGURE 8.41 Typical DMA controller chip.

Even though the particulars of a DMA chip vary among manufacturers, the following functions as illustrated in Figure 8.41 are typical of those performed in DMA transfers.

1. CHANNEL ADDRESS REGISTER(S)—register(s) holding address in memory of data to be transferred on a particular channel.
2. CHANNEL ADDRESS COUNTER—counter associated with each channel address register that is incremented or decremented to produce the next channel address.
3. BYTE COUNT REGISTER—register into which is loaded number of bytes to be transferred by DMA. This register is normally decremented after each byte transfer until it is zero. Individual byte count registers could also be associated with each channel.
4. MODE LOGIC—logic that selects particular channel to be used in

DMA transfer, channel properties, special timing, and transfer termination condition.

5. PRIORITY LOGIC—determines priority of servicing DMA TRANSFER REQUESTS on Channels 1 through N.

6. ENABLE—logic level to microprocessor initiating tri-state floating condition on microprocessor address and data bus lines so that DMA Controller Chip address and data bus lines can control memory accesses and data transfers.

7. MEMORY IDLE—acknowledgement that memory address, data, and required control lines are free for use by DMA Controller Chip.

8. READ and WRITE LINES—lines to and from DMA Controller Chip enabling the programming of DMA operations by the microprocessor by reading/writing from/to the DMA Controller Chip. In addition, these lines are used by the DMA chip as READ and WRITE lines to memory for control of data transfers.

9. RESET—initializes DMA Controller Chip and sets internal registers and counters to known states.

10. CHIP SELECT—input which enables READ and WRITE inputs into DMA chip when it is being programmed or read by the microprocessor. The CHIP SELECT level is derived from the microprocessor address bus in a manner identical to that of memory chip select. When the DMA chip is providing addresses on the address lines, CHIP SELECT for the DMA chip must be disabled lest the chip select itself.

11. ADDRESS BUS—address lines to memory or peripheral device involved in data transfer. These lines normally have tri-state capability.

12. DATA BUS—bus for transmitting data and programming information to and from the DMA chip. The DMA chip is programmed by the microprocessor's sending start address information to the chip over the data bus. In addition, the number of bytes to be transferred are also sent to the DMA chip from the microprocessor.

13. DMA COMPLETE—output from DMA chip to microprocessor indicating DMA transfer is complete and normal microprocessor program execution can resume.

14. CLOCK—microprocessor clock phase for synchronization of DMA chip.

A typical DMA sequence would be as follows.

(a) Microprocessor programs DMA chip through data bus. This programming includes enabling of particular channels, specifying the start address in memory to/from which data are to be transferred, and specifying the number of bytes to be transferred.

(b) When peripheral activates a DMA TRANSFER REQUEST for a particular channel, the DMA chip activates the ENABLE line to the microprocessor to place the microprocessor address and data lines in tri-state condition.

(c) When memory address, data, and control lines are free for use by DMA chip, MEMORY IDLE input to DMA chip is activated.

(d) The DMA chip now controls the data transfer by sending out the appropriate addresses to memory along with the $\overline{READ}$, $\overline{WRITE}$ control signals. The DMA Controller sequentially transfers the bytes to/from memory while decrementing the byte count register until it is zero, indicating that all bytes have been transferred. When the DMA transfer is complete, a DMA COMPLETE signal is provided to the microprocessor so that normal program execution can resume.

8.7 MAGNETIC BUBBLE MEMORY INTERFACE

The high density and nonvolatility of the magnetic bubble memory will lead to its increased use as a reliable magnetic disk replacement. Since the magnetic bubble memory device can be mounted in Dual In-Line Packages (DIP's), the memory system can be implemented in a smaller space than can conventional disks.

8.7.1 Bubble Memory System

A specific example of an early bubble memory chip is the Texas Instruments TBM 0101 device, which contains 92 Kilobytes of memory in a 14 pin DIP package. Its useful capacity is 92,304 bits organized as 144 minor loops of 641 bits each. (See Chapter 5 for description of magnetic bubble memories). The maximum data I/O rate of the TBM 0101 is 50 kilobits/sec with an average access time to the first bit of 4 msec. The average cycle time of a 144 bit block (minor loop) of data is 12.8 msec.

The TBM 0101 requires current pulses to generate, replicate, and transfer magnetic domains. It also needs triangular current drives that are 90° out of phase for two internal coils. Coil drivers and a diode array satisfy the latter requirement while a function driver chip provides the generate, replicate, and transfer drives. Timing for the current drive circuits is generated by a function timing generator. In addition to the current drive/timing functions, an interface controller to the microprocessor must be provided. The TI TMS9916JL controller chip can be used for this task.

On the output side of the magnetic bubble memory chip, the logic signal is typically 3 millivolts. This signal has to be shaped by an RC network and then fed into a sense amplifier. The output of the sense amplifier is then stored in a flip-flop.

A summary of these circuits showing the interface to a microprocessor is given in Figure 8.42.

Some newer developments in the bubble memory area include the Intel Magnetics 7110 solid state memory with a normal data capacity of 1,048,576 bits. This memory is supported by a family of interface circuits. These circuits are the 7220 bubble memory controller, the 7242 formatter/sense amplifier, the 7230 current pulse generator, and the 7250 coil pred-

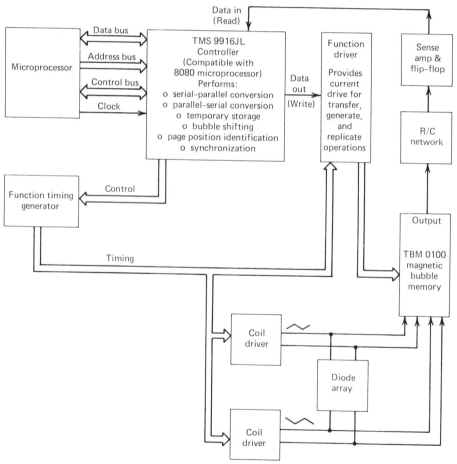

FIGURE 8.42 Magnetic bubble memory interface circuit.

river. This system is designed for use with microprocessors and provides the user with the devices to implement relatively large-scale bubble memory systems with minimal interfacing requirements.

8.8 COMPREHENSIVE INTERFACE EXAMPLE

This chapter concludes by presenting an example of two methods of microcomputer input/output: programmed I/O and DMA I/O in a video processing environment. In so doing, we illustrate the relative merits and disadvantages of each method in a practical application.

The combination of a television camera and a microprocessor can result in a powerful tool for solving many industrial problems. Since the total amount of real-time data presented by a video source can be very large, preprocessing is required to reduce the data content of an image without removing the desired information. A video interface system that returns some length measurement of an object in the image field could be used to obtain dimensional information of various products in a manufacturing environment. Dimensional information may be obtained from a video image by measuring the length of time a particular horizontal video scan line remains above a given reference value. This time is proportional to the length of an object in the video field. By collecting the lengths from each horizontal scan line in a video image, we can then construct an overall length profile of an object. This data content is drastically reduced from the original video image but contains dimensional data that may be used in production and quality control in an industrial manufacturing environment. The resolution of such a system is strictly a function of the clock frequency used to count the time of one horizontal sweep from one end of the video field to the other. For example, the time for a full horizontal scan can be chosen so that the full length corresponds to 256 counts. This scale will generate one byte of data per horizontal scan line. To further simplify matters, it can be assumed that only one of the two interlaced images making up a standard 525-line video frame will be used in the processing. Thus, an image made up of 256 horizontal scan lines of one byte each can be used to represent a frame and, again, is a simplification of the standard 525-line video image.

With this information in mind, it is possible to discuss in detail the two methods of inputting the video information into a microcomputer system for further processing and control application.

Data Rates

A new interlaced video image is generated every 1/30 of a second from a standard vidicon camera operating under NTSC standards. This image is broken up into one interlace image made up of 525/2 horizontal lines every 1/60 sec. Thus a horizontal line is scanned every 63.5 microseconds. Since one horizontal scan generates one byte of data, the basic data rate of such a system is 63.5 microsec per byte. Whatever method of I/O is chosen, it must be capable of accepting data from the interface at such a rate. Fortunately, this is not a strict limitation in itself since most microprocessors have basic clock rates higher than this value. Using programmed I/O implies that the total number of instructions necessary to move one byte of data from an I/O port to the microcomputer memory must be executable in less than 63.5 microseconds. The horizontal and vertical syncs that are present in a video signal are used to synchronize the processor to the image available from the video signal. The vertical sync signals the start of an image frame and the horizontal sync signals the availability of one byte of data after each horizontal scan.

8.8.1 Interface Development for Programmed I/O

For programmed I/O, it is necessary for the program to test the vertical and horizontal signals before acquiring the bytes of data from each horizontal scan line. The vertical sync assures that consistent, whole frames of data are acquired. The horizontal sync is used to signal the availability of one byte of data from the interface. The microprocessor of Chapter 6 has a convenient test flag input to which the horizontal sync signal can be connected. This flag provides a simple test for data ready.

The interface has a 16-bit device register that can be read from the microprocessor. One byte of data is located at bits 8 through 15. The separated vertical sync is at bit 0 of the device register for easy testability through signed processor test instructions. Bits 1 through 7 of the device interface register are not used.

With these requirements in mind, it is now possible to design the video interface for programmed I/O operation as shown in Figure 8.43.

The video signal is first separated into two paths. In the first path, the vertical and horizontal syncs are separated and made compatible with the microcomputer signal levels. The horizontal sync is then applied to the microprocessor flag input line. The vertical sync is gated to bit position 0 of the interface device register.

The other path is sent to a video level discriminator circuit, which in turn controls the counters that count the length of time the video signals remain above a given signal level. The horizontal sync from the sync separator controls the timer reset and gating functions. Analog comparators are used to turn counters on and off. The output of the counters is gated to bits 8 to 15 of the device interface register.

Using this interface design, we may use the following program segment to acquire one image frame consisting of 256 bytes of data and store these data into 256 contiguous microcomputer words.

```
;TV is the address of the video interface device register
;Initialization
        MOV     R2, BUFF     ;Place address of buffer to hold
                             ;image into Register 2
        MOV     R0,256       ;Place number of input words to be
                             ;read from the interface in Register 0
;Now Wait for Vertical Sync transition to signal start of new frame
VERT1   INP     R1,(TV)      ;Read interface device register into
                             ;Register 1
        CPA     R1,0         ;Test the vertical sync bit
        JAL     VERT1        ;Stay here until vertical sync changes
VERT2   INP     R1,(TV)      ;Read the register again
        CPA     R1,0
        JNL     VERT2        ;This ensures consistently high-low transition
;Now wait on high low transition from flag (horizontal sync)
HOR1    JFL     HOR1
HOR2    JNF     HOR2
        INP     R1,(TV)      ;Now read the interface
        AND     R1,FF00      ;Save only 8 bits
        MOV     (R2),R1      ;Put in memory
        INC     R2           ;Increment to next memory location
        DEJ     HOR1,R0      ;Decrement count, back to HOR1
                             ;if not done yet.
```

8.8.2 Interface Development for DMA I/O

In DMA I/O, the CPU of the microprocessor is not involved in the actual movement of data during the I/O process. As a matter of fact, the CPU is not aware that the I/O has taken place until notified by the DMA controller.

The I/O through DMA requires at least two setup operations before the I/O can begin. First, the DMA hardware must be initialized with the memory address of the microcomputer at which the I/O operation is to take place and with the number of data words to be transferred. Second, the interface must be initialized to start the I/O operation. After this setup, the I/O operation is conducted without CPU intervention until the desired number of transfers has occurred. The external device interface notifies the DMA controller whenever the device has a word to transfer into the microcomputer main memory. The DMA controller seizes control of the microcomputer address and data buses and permits the device interface to

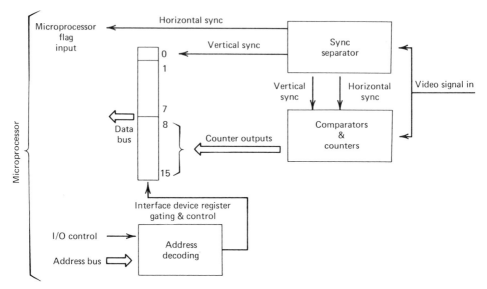

FIGURE 8.43 Programmed I/O video interface.

move a single byte or block of bytes into the microcomputer memory (Figure 8.44).

The horizontal sync signal is used to notify the DMA controller of the availability of one byte of data. The interface must not activate the DMA operation until the I/O operation has been initiated by the CPU. To assure this condition, the horizontal sync, therefore, is gated to the DMA controller only after the video interface has been activated and the vertical sync has been sensed by the video interface.

The design of the DMA version of the video processing interface can now be given. To start the I/O transfer, the DMA controller must first be initialized with a memory address and the data count. These data are written into the DMA internal registers using I/O instructions of the microcomputer. Next, the video interface is armed to start the input operation after the occurrence of the next vertical sync signal. At this time, each occurrence of the horizontal sync notifies the DMA controller that the video interface has a data byte ready to be transferred into the microcomputer memory. The DMA controller seizes control of the address and data buses (the microprocessor address and data buses are now in high impedance mode) to move the contents of the video interface device register into the memory address specified by the internal DMA address register. The DMA controller increments its address register and decrements the count register. When the count register value becomes zero, indicating the end

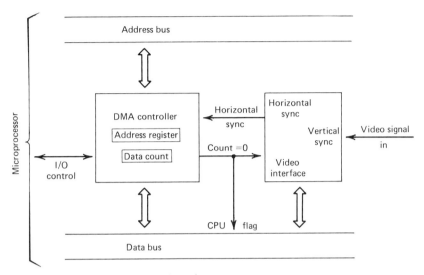

FIGURE 8.44 DMA video interface.

of I/O operation, the DMA controller asserts the microprocessor's flag line to notify the CPU of the completion of the DMA operation and at the same time disables the video interface from activating the DMA controller on further horizontal syncs.

The following program segment can be used to input one video frame of data using the DMA controller video interface.

```
;TVDMA1—address of DMA memory address register
;TVDMA2—address of DMA count register
;INIT—control word to start to interface
;Initialize the DMA controller
            OUT     (TVDMA1), BUFF      ;memory buffer
            OUT     (TVDMA2), 256       ;data count
            OUT     (TV), INIT          ;set init word to TV
WAIT        JFL     WAIT                ;wait here for flag
                                        ;to know it is done
```

Although ordinarily one would not use the flag input to sense when the I/O operation has been completed, in this case it can be seen that the DMA version results in greatly compacted code compared to the programmed I/O approach. Normally, the DMA controller would notify the CPU of the completion of the I/O through the interrupt system or through a DMA input to the microprocessor.

8.8.3   Comparison between Programmed I/O and DMA

Using programmed I/O, the CPU is intimately involved in the I/O process since it must execute instructions to transfer each piece of data from the device register to the microcomputer memory. There is an inherent speed limitation based on the number of instructions the microprocessor must execute for each word of data moved from the device to the memory. Since this must include the overhead bookkeeping instructions such as those to increment addresses and to keep track of numbers of data words moved, the total data bandwidth is limited. Furthermore, since the microprocessor must execute instructions to effect the I/O, the CPU is not free to perform other operations while I/O takes place. In contrast, the DMA approach, once properly initiated, is limited in speed mainly only by the time it takes for the DMA controller to gain control of the bus and the memory cycle time. In practice, this can approach the bandwidth of the data bus. Also, since the microprocessor is not used during the I/O operation, the CPU is free to accomplish other internal tasks in the interim. The penalty in using DMA is in the additional complexity of the hardware required. This includes the additional hardware of the DMA controller itself as well as of the interface required.

The choice of DMA versus programmed I/O is based primarily on two factors.

1. Speed of the I/O transfer required.
2. Effect of CPU intervention during the I/O process resulting in the exclusion of other tasks.

REFERENCES

1. *EIA RS-232-C; Interface Between Data Terminal Equipment and Data Communication Equipment Employing Serial Binary Data Interchange,* Electronics Industries Association, August, 1969.
2. *CCITT, White Book,* Volume 8, International Telecommunication Union, recommendation V. 24 (revised and reissued as V.28), 1969.
3. *MIL-STD-188C,* Department of Defense, Low Level Interface, November, 1969.
4. Ken Pine, "Troubleshooting with Logic Analyzers," Digital Design, October, 1977.
5. *AMD Advanced Interface Specifications,* AMD, Inc., 1966.
6. *The TTL Data Book for Design Enginners,* Texas Instruments Inc., 1976.
7. *Intel 8048 User's Manual,* Intel Corp., 1976.

BINARY-TO-DECIMAL CONVERSION TABLE

Powers of Two

2^n	n	2^{-n}
1	0	1.0
2	1	0.5
4	2	0.25
8	3	0.125
16	4	0.062 5
32	5	0.031 25
64	6	0.015 625
128	7	0.007 812 5
256	8	0.003 906 25
512	9	0.001 953 125
1 024	10	0.000 976 562 5
2 048	11	0.000 488 281 25
4 096	12	0.000 244 140 625
8 192	13	0.000 122 070 312 5
16 384	14	0.000 061 035 156 25
32 768	15	0.000 030 517 578 125
65 536	16	0.000 015 258 789 062 5
131 072	17	0.000 007 629 394 531 25
262 144	18	0.000 003 814 697 265 625
524 288	19	0.000 001 907 348 632 812 5
1 048 576	20	0.000 000 953 674 316 406 25
2 097 152	21	0.000 000 476 837 158 203 125
4 194 304	22	0.000 000 238 418 579 101 562 5
8 388 608	23	0.000 000 119 209 289 550 781 25
16 777 216	24	0.000 000 059 604 644 775 390 625
33 554 432	25	0.000 000 029 802 322 387 695 312 5
67 108 864	26	0.000 000 014 901 161 193 847 656 25
134 217 728	27	0.000 000 007 450 580 596 923 828 125
268 435 456	28	0.000 000 003 725 290 298 461 914 062 5
536 870 912	29	0.000 000 001 862 645 149 230 957 031 25
1 073 741 824	30	0.000 000 000 931 322 574 615 478 515 625
2 147 483 648	31	0.000 000 000 465 661 287 307 739 257 812 5

APPENDIX B

POWERS OF SIXTEEN TABLE

Table of Powers of Sixteen

16^n	n	16^{-n}
1	0	$0.10000\ 00000\ 00000\ 00000 \times 10$
16	1	$0.62500\ 00000\ 00000\ 00000 \times 10^{-1}$
256	2	$0.39062\ 50000\ 00000\ 00000 \times 10^{-2}$
4 096	3	$0.24414\ 06250\ 00000\ 00000 \times 10^{-3}$
65 536	4	$0.15258\ 78906\ 25000\ 00000 \times 10^{-4}$
1 048 576	5	$0.95367\ 43164\ 06250\ 00000 \times 10^{-6}$
16 777 216	6	$0.59604\ 64477\ 53906\ 25000 \times 10^{-7}$
268 435 456	7	$0.37252\ 90298\ 46191\ 40625 \times 10^{-8}$
4 294 967 296	8	$0.23283\ 06436\ 53869\ 62891 \times 10^{-9}$
68 719 476 736	9	$0.14551\ 91522\ 83668\ 51807 \times 10^{-10}$
1 099 511 627 776	10	$0.90949\ 47017\ 72928\ 23792 \times 10^{-12}$
17 592 186 044 416	11	$0.56843\ 41886\ 08080\ 14870 \times 10^{-13}$
281 474 976 710 656	12	$0.35527\ 13678\ 80050\ 09294 \times 10^{-14}$
4 503 599 627 370 496	13	$0.22204\ 46049\ 25031\ 30808 \times 10^{-15}$
72 057 594 037 927 936	14	$0.13877\ 78780\ 78144\ 56755 \times 10^{-16}$
1 152 921 504 606 846 976	15	$0.86736\ 17379\ 88403\ 54721 \times 10^{-18}$

(Courtesy Fairchild Camera and Instrument Corp., 464 Ellis St., Mountain View, Ca. 94042)

HEXADECIMAL-DECIMAL INTEGER CONVERSION

The table below provides for direct conversions between hexadecimal integers in the range 0-FFF and decimal integers in the range 0-4095. For conversion of larger integers, the table values may be added to the following figures:

HEXADECIMAL	DECIMAL	HEXADECIMAL	DECIMAL
01 000	4 096	20 000	131 072
02 000	8 192	30 000	196 608
03 000	12 288	40 000	262 144
04 000	16 384	50 000	327 680
05 000	20 480	60 000	393 216
06 000	24 576	70 000	458 752
07 000	28 672	80 000	524 288
08 000	32 768	90 000	589 824
09 000	36 864	A0 000	655 360
0A 000	40 960	B0 000	720 896
0B 000	45 056	C0 000	786 432
0C 000	49 152	D0 000	851 968
OD 000	53 248	E0 000	917 504
0E000	57 344	F0 000	983 040
0F 000	61 440	100 000	1 048 576
10 000	65 632	200 000	2 097 152
11 000	69 632	300 000	3 145 728
12 000	73 728	400 000	4 194 304
13 000	77 824	500 000	5 242 880
14 000	81 920	600 000	6 291 456
15 000	86 016	700 000	7 340 032
16 000	90 112	800 000	8 388 608
17 000	94 208	900 000	9 437 184
18 000	98 304	A00 000	10 485 760
19 000	102 400	B00 000	11 534 336
1A 000	106 496	C00 000	12 582 912
1B 000	110 592	D00 000	13 631 488
1C 000	114 688	E00 000	14 680 064
1D 000	118 784	F00 000	15 728 640
1E 000	122 880	1 000 000	16 777 216
1F 000	126 976	2 000 000	33 554 432

(Courtesy Fairchild Camera and Instrument Corp., 464 Ellis St., Mountain View, Ca. 94042)

Hexadecimal-decimal integer conversion, Continued

	0	1	2	3	4	5	6	7	8	9	A	B	C	D	E	F
000	0000	0001	0002	0003	0004	0005	0006	0007	0008	0009	0010	0011	0012	0013	0014	0015
010	0016	0017	0018	0019	0020	0021	0022	0023	0024	0025	0026	0027	0028	0029	0030	0031
020	0032	0033	0034	0035	0036	0037	0038	0039	0040	0041	0042	0043	0044	0045	0046	0047
030	0048	0049	0050	0051	0052	0053	0054	0055	0056	0057	0058	0059	0060	0061	0062	0063
040	0064	0065	0066	0067	0068	0069	0070	0071	0072	0073	0074	0075	0076	0077	0078	0079
050	0080	0081	0082	0083	0084	0085	0086	0087	0088	0089	0090	0091	0092	0093	0094	0095
060	0096	0097	0098	0099	0100	0101	0102	0103	0104	0105	0106	0107	0108	0109	0110	0111
070	0112	0013	0114	0115	0116	0117	0118	0119	0120	0121	0122	0123	0124	0125	0126	0127
080	0128	0129	0130	0131	0132	0133	0134	0135	0136	0137	0138	0139	0140	0141	0142	0143
090	0144	0145	0146	0147	0148	0149	0150	0151	0152	0153	0154	0155	0156	0157	0158	0159
0A0	0160	0161	0162	0163	0164	0165	0166	0167	0168	0169	0170	0171	0172	0173	0174	0175
0B0	0176	0177	0178	0179	0180	0181	0182	0183	0184	0185	0186	0187	0188	0189	0190	0191
0C0	0192	0193	0194	0195	0196	0197	0198	0199	0200	0201	0202	0203	0204	0205	0206	0207
0D0	0208	0209	0210	0211	0212	0213	0214	0215	0216	0217	0218	0219	0220	0221	0222	0223
0E0	0224	0225	0226	0227	0228	0229	0230	0231	0232	0233	0234	0235	0236	0237	0238	0239
0F0	0240	0241	0242	0243	0244	0245	0246	0247	0248	0249	0250	0251	0252	0253	0254	0255
100	0256	0257	0258	0259	0260	0261	0262	0263	0264	0265	0266	0267	0268	0269	0270	0271
110	0272	0273	0274	0275	0276	0277	0278	0279	0280	0281	0282	0283	0284	0285	0286	0287
120	0288	0289	0290	0291	0292	0293	0294	0295	0296	0297	0298	0299	0300	0301	0302	0303
130	0304	0305	0306	0307	0308	0309	0310	0311	0312	0313	0314	0315	0316	0317	0318	0319
140	0320	0321	0322	0323	0324	0325	0326	0327	0328	0329	0330	0331	0331	0333	0334	0335
150	0336	0337	0338	0339	0340	0341	0342	0343	0344	0345	0346	0347	0348	0349	0350	0351
160	0352	0353	0354	0355	0356	0357	0358	0359	0360	0361	0362	0363	0364	0365	0366	0367
170	0368	0369	0370	0371	0372	0373	0374	0375	0376	0377	0378	0379	0380	0381	0382	0383
180	0384	0385	0386	0387	0388	0389	0390	0391	0392	0393	0394	0395	0396	0397	0398	0399
190	0400	0401	0402	0403	0404	0405	0406	0407	0408	0409	0410	0411	0412	0413	0414	0415
1A0	0416	0417	0418	0419	0420	0421	0422	0423	0424	0425	0426	0427	0428	0429	0430	0431
1B0	0432	0433	0434	0435	0436	0437	0438	0439	0440	0441	0442	0443	0444	0445	0446	0447
1C0	0448	0449	0450	0451	0452	0453	0454	0455	0456	0457	0458	0459	0460	0461	0462	0463
1D0	0464	0465	0466	0467	0468	0469	0470	0471	0472	0473	0474	0475	0476	0477	0478	0479
1E0	0480	0481	0482	0483	0484	0485	0486	0487	0488	0489	0490	0491	0492	0493	0494	0495
1F0	0496	0497	0498	0499	0500	0501	0502	0503	0504	0505	0506	0507	0508	0509	0510	0511
200	0512	0513	0514	0515	0516	0517	0518	0519	0520	0521	0522	0523	0524	0525	0526	0527
210	0528	0529	0530	0531	0532	0533	0534	0535	0536	0537	0538	0539	0540	0541	0542	0543
220	0544	0545	0546	0547	0548	0549	0550	0551	0552	0553	0554	0555	0556	0557	0558	0559
230	0560	0561	0562	0563	0564	0565	0566	0567	0568	0569	0570	0571	0572	0573	0574	0575
240	0576	0577	0578	0579	0580	0581	0582	0583	0584	0585	0586	0587	0588	0589	0590	0591
250	0592	0593	0594	0595	0596	0597	0598	0599	0600	0601	0602	0603	0604	0605	0606	0607
260	0608	0609	0610	0611	0612	0613	0614	0615	0616	0617	0618	0619	0620	0621	0622	0623
270	0624	0625	0626	0627	0628	0629	0630	0631	0632	0633	0634	0635	0636	0637	0638	0639
280	0640	0641	0642	0643	0644	0645	0646	0647	0648	0649	0650	0651	0652	0653	0654	0655
290	0656	0657	0658	0659	0660	0661	0662	0663	0664	0665	0666	0667	0668	0669	0670	0671
2A0	0672	0673	0674	0675	0676	0677	0678	0679	0680	0681	0682	0683	0684	0685	0686	0687
2B0	0688	0689	0690	0691	0692	0693	0694	0695	0696	0697	0698	0699	0700	0701	0702	0703
2C0	0704	0705	0706	0707	0708	0709	0710	0711	0712	0713	0714	0715	0716	0717	0718	0719
2D0	0720	0721	0722	0723	0724	0725	0726	0727	0728	0729	0730	0731	0732	0733	0734	0735
2E0	0736	0737	0738	0739	0740	0741	0742	0743	0744	0745	0746	0747	0748	0749	0750	0751
2F0	0752	0753	0754	0755	0756	0757	0758	0759	0760	0761	0762	0763	0764	0765	0766	0767

Hexadecimal-decimal integer conversion, Continued

	0	1	2	3	4	5	6	7	8	9	A	B	C	D	E	F
300	0768	0769	0770	0771	0772	0773	0774	0775	0776	0777	0778	0779	0780	0781	0782	0783
310	0784	0785	0786	0787	0788	0789	0790	0791	0792	0793	0794	0795	0796	0797	0798	0799
320	0800	0301	0802	0803	0804	0805	0806	0807	0808	0809	0810	0811	0812	0813	0814	0815
330	0816	0817	0818	0819	0820	0821	0822	0823	0824	0825	0826	0827	0828	0829	0830	0831
340	0832	0833	0834	0835	0836	0837	0838	0839	0840	0841	0842	0843	0844	0845	0846	0847
350	0848	0849	0850	0851	0852	0853	0854	0855	0856	0857	0858	0859	0860	0861	0862	0863
360	0864	0865	0866	0867	0868	0869	0870	0871	0872	0873	0874	0875	0876	0877	0878	0879
370	0880	0881	0882	0883	0884	0885	0886	0887	0888	0889	0890	0891	0892	0893	0894	0895
380	0896	0897	0898	0899	0900	0901	0902	0903	0904	0905	0906	0907	0908	0909	0910	0911
390	0212	0913	0914	0915	0916	0917	0918	0919	0920	0921	0922	0923	0924	0925	0926	0927
3A0	0928	0929	0930	0931	0932	0933	0934	0935	0936	0937	0938	0939	0940	0941	0942	0943
3B0	0944	0945	0946	0947	0948	0949	0950	0951	0952	0953	0954	0955	0956	0957	0958	0959
3C0	0960	0961	0962	0963	0964	0965	0966	0967	0968	0969	0970	0971	0972	0973	0974	0975
3D0	0976	0977	0978	0979	0980	0981	0982	0983	0984	0985	0986	0987	0988	0989	0990	0991
3E0	0992	0993	0994	0995	0996	0997	0998	0999	1000	1001	1002	1003	1004	1005	1006	1007
3F0	1008	1009	1010	1011	1012	1013	1014	1015	1016	1017	1018	1019	1020	1021	1022	1023
400	1024	1025	1026	1027	1028	1029	1030	1031	1032	1033	1034	1035	1036	1037	1038	1039
410	1040	1041	1042	1043	1044	1045	1046	1047	1048	1049	1050	1051	1052	1053	1054	1055
420	1056	1057	1058	1059	1060	1061	1062	1063	1064	1065	1066	1067	1068	1069	1070	1071
430	1072	1073	1074	1075	1076	1077	1078	1079	1080	1081	1082	1083	1084	1085	1086	1087
440	1088	1089	1090	1091	1092	1093	1094	1095	1096	1097	1098	1099	1100	1101	1102	1103
450	1104	1105	1106	1107	1108	1109	1110	1111	1112	1113	1114	1115	1116	1117	1118	1119
460	1120	1121	1122	1123	1124	1125	1126	1127	1128	1129	1130	1131	1132	1133	1134	1135
470	1136	1137	1138	1139	1140	1141	1142	1143	1144	1145	1146	1147	1148	1149	1150	1151
480	1152	1153	1154	1155	1156	1157	1158	1159	1160	1161	1162	1163	1164	1165	1166	1167
490	1168	1169	1170	1171	1172	1173	1174	1175	1176	1177	1178	1179	1180	1181	1182	1183
4A0	1184	1185	1186	1187	1188	1189	1190	1191	1192	1193	1194	1195	1196	1197	1198	1199
4B0	1200	1201	1202	1203	1204	1205	1206	1207	1208	1209	1210	1211	1212	1213	1214	1215
4C0	1216	1217	1218	1219	1220	1221	1222	1223	1224	1225	1226	1227	1228	1229	1230	1231
4D0	1232	1233	1234	1235	1236	1237	1238	1239	1240	1241	1242	1243	1244	1245	1246	1247
4E0	1248	1249	1250	1251	1252	1253	1254	1255	1256	1257	1258	1259	1260	1261	1262	1263
4F0	1264	1265	1266	1267	1268	1269	1270	1271	1272	1273	1274	1275	1276	1277	1278	1279
500	1280	1281	1282	1283	1284	1285	1286	1287	1288	1289	1290	1291	1292	1293	1294	1295
510	1296	1297	1298	1299	1300	1301	1302	1303	1304	1305	1306	1307	1308	1309	1310	1311
520	1312	1313	1314	1315	1316	1317	1318	1319	1320	1321	1322	1323	1324	1325	1326	1327
530	1328	1329	1330	1331	1332	1333	1334	1335	1336	1337	1338	1339	1340	1341	1342	1343
540	1344	1345	1346	1347	1348	1349	1350	1351	1352	1353	1354	1355	1356	1357	1358	1359
550	1360	1361	1362	1363	1364	1365	1366	1367	1368	1369	1370	1371	1372	1373	1374	1375
560	1376	1377	1378	1379	1380	1381	1382	1383	1384	1385	1386	1387	1388	1389	1390	1391
570	1392	1393	1394	1395	1396	1397	1398	1399	1400	1401	1402	1403	1404	1405	1406	1407
580	1408	1409	1410	1411	1412	1413	1414	1415	1416	1417	1418	1419	1420	1421	1422	1423
590	1424	1425	1426	1427	1428	1429	1430	1431	1432	1433	1434	1435	1436	1437	1438	1439
5A0	1440	1441	1442	1443	1444	1445	1446	1447	1448	1449	1450	1451	1452	1453	1454	1455
5B0	1456	1457	1458	1459	1460	1461	1462	1463	1464	1465	1466	1467	1468	1469	1470	1471
5C0	1472	1473	1474	1475	1476	1477	1478	1479	1480	1481	1482	1483	1484	1485	1486	1487
5D0	1488	1489	1490	1491	1492	1493	1494	1495	1496	1497	1498	1499	1500	1501	1502	1503
5E0	1504	1505	1506	1507	1508	1509	1510	1511	1512	1513	1514	1515	1516	1517	1518	1519
5F0	1520	1521	1522	1523	1524	1525	1526	1527	1528	1529	1530	1531	1532	1533	1534	1535

Hexadecimal-Decimal Integer Conversion (Continued)

	0	1	2	3	4	5	6	7	8	9	A	B	C	D	E	F
600	1536	1537	1538	1539	1540	1541	1542	1543	1544	1545	1546	1547	1548	1549	1550	1551
610	1552	1553	1554	1555	1556	1557	1558	1559	1560	1561	1562	1563	1564	1565	1566	1567
620	1568	1569	1570	1571	1572	1573	1574	1575	1576	1577	1578	1579	1580	1581	1582	1583
630	1584	1585	1586	1587	1588	1589	1590	1591	1592	1593	1594	1595	1596	1597	1598	1599
640	1600	1601	1602	1603	1604	1605	1606	1607	1608	1609	1610	1611	1612	1613	1614	1615
650	1616	1617	1618	1619	1620	1621	1622	1623	1624	1625	1626	1627	1628	1629	1630	1631
660	1632	1633	1634	1635	1636	1637	1638	1639	1640	1641	1642	1643	1644	1645	1646	1647
670	1648	1649	1650	1651	1652	1653	1654	1655	1656	1657	1658	1659	1660	1661	1662	1663
680	1664	1665	1666	1667	1668	1669	1670	1671	1672	1673	1674	1675	1676	1677	1678	1679
690	1680	1681	1682	1683	1684	1685	1686	1687	1688	1689	1690	1691	1692	1693	1694	1695
6A0	1696	1697	1698	1699	1700	1701	1702	1703	1704	1705	1706	1707	1708	1709	1710	1711
6B0	1712	1713	1714	1715	1716	1717	1718	1719	1720	1721	1722	1723	1724	1725	1726	1727
6C0	1728	1729	1730	1731	1732	1733	1734	1735	1736	1737	1738	1739	1740	1741	1742	1743
6D0	1744	1745	1746	1747	1748	1749	1750	1751	1752	1753	1754	1755	1756	1757	1758	1759
6E0	1760	1761	1762	1763	1764	1765	1766	1767	1768	1769	1770	1771	1772	1773	1774	1775
6F0	1776	1777	1778	1779	1780	1781	1782	1783	1784	1785	1786	1787	1788	1789	1790	1791
700	1792	1793	1794	1795	1796	1797	1798	1799	1800	1801	1802	1803	1804	1805	1806	1807
710	1808	1809	1810	1811	1812	1813	1814	1815	1816	1817	1818	1819	1820	1821	1822	1823
720	1824	1825	1826	1827	1828	1829	1830	1831	1832	1833	1834	1835	1836	1837	1838	1839
730	1840	1841	1842	1843	1844	1845	1846	1847	1848	1849	1850	1851	1852	1853	1854	1855
740	1856	1857	1858	1859	1860	1861	1862	1863	1864	1865	1866	1867	1868	1869	1870	1871
750	1872	1873	1874	1875	1876	1877	1878	1879	1880	1881	1882	1883	1884	1885	1886	1887
760	1888	1889	1890	1891	1892	1893	1894	1895	1896	1897	1898	1899	1900	1901	1902	1903
770	1904	1905	1906	1907	1908	1909	1910	1911	1912	1913	1914	1915	1916	1917	1918	1919
780	1920	1921	1922	1923	1924	1925	1926	1927	1928	1929	1930	1931	1932	1933	1934	1935
790	1936	1937	1938	1939	1940	1941	1942	1943	1944	1945	1946	1947	1948	1949	1950	1951
7A0	1952	1953	1954	1955	1956	1957	1958	1959	1960	1961	1962	1963	1964	1965	1966	1967
7B0	1968	1969	1970	1971	1972	1973	1974	1975	1976	1977	1978	1979	1980	1981	1982	1983
7C0	1984	1985	1986	1987	1988	1989	1990	1991	1992	1993	1994	1995	1996	1997	1998	1999
7D0	2000	2001	2002	2003	2004	2005	2006	2007	2008	2009	2010	2011	2012	2013	2014	2015
7E0	2016	2017	2018	2019	2020	2021	2022	2023	2024	2025	2026	2027	2028	2029	2030	2031
7F0	2032	2033	2034	2035	2036	2037	2038	2039	2040	2041	2042	2043	2044	2045	2046	2047
800	2048	2049	2050	2051	2052	2053	2054	2055	2056	2057	2058	2059	2060	2061	2062	2063
810	2064	2065	2066	2067	2068	2069	2070	2071	2072	2073	2074	2075	2076	2077	2078	2079
820	2080	2081	2082	2083	2084	2085	2086	2087	2088	2089	2090	2091	2092	2093	2094	2095
830	2096	2097	2098	2099	2100	2101	2102	2103	2104	2105	2106	2107	2108	2109	2110	2111
840	2112	2113	2114	2115	2116	2117	2118	2119	2120	2121	2122	2123	2124	2125	2126	2127
850	2128	2129	2130	2131	2132	2133	2134	2135	2136	2137	2138	2139	2140	2141	2142	2143
860	2144	2145	2146	2147	2148	2149	2150	2151	2152	2153	2154	2155	2156	2157	2158	2159
870	2160	2161	2162	2163	2164	2165	2166	2167	2168	2169	2170	2171	2172	2173	2174	2175
880	2176	2177	2178	2179	2180	2181	2182	2183	2184	2185	2186	2187	2188	2189	2190	2191
890	2192	2193	2194	2195	2196	2197	2198	2199	2200	2201	2202	2203	2204	2205	2206	2207
8A0	2208	2209	2210	2211	2212	2213	2214	2215	2216	2217	2218	2219	2220	2221	2222	2223
8B0	2224	2225	2226	2227	2228	2229	2230	2231	2232	2233	2234	2235	2236	2237	2238	2239
8C0	2240	2241	2242	2243	2244	2245	2246	2247	2248	2249	2250	2251	2252	2253	2254	2255
8D0	2256	2257	2258	2259	2260	2261	2262	2263	2264	2265	2266	2267	2268	2269	2270	2271
8E0	2272	2273	2274	2275	2276	2277	2278	2279	2280	2281	2282	2283	2284	2285	2286	2287
8F0	2288	2289	2290	2291	2292	2293	2294	2295	2296	2297	2298	2299	2300	2301	2302	2303

Hexadecimal-Decimal Integer Conversion (Continued)

	0	1	2	3	4	5	6	7	8	9	A	B	C	D	E	F
900	2304	2305	2306	2307	2308	2309	2310	2311	2312	2313	2314	2315	2316	2317	2318	2319
910	2320	2321	2322	2323	2324	2325	2326	2327	2328	2329	2330	2331	2332	2333	2334	2335
920	2336	2337	2338	2339	2340	2341	2342	2343	2344	2345	2346	2347	2348	2349	2350	2351
930	2352	2353	2354	2355	2356	2357	2358	2359	2360	2361	2362	2363	2364	2365	2366	2367
940	2368	2369	2370	2371	2372	2373	2374	2375	2376	2377	2378	2379	2380	2381	2382	2383
950	2384	2385	2386	2387	2388	2389	2390	2391	2392	2393	2394	2395	2396	2397	2398	2399
960	2400	2401	2402	2403	2404	2405	2406	2407	2408	2409	2410	2411	2412	2413	2414	2415
970	2416	2417	2418	2419	2420	2421	2422	2423	2424	2425	2426	2427	2428	2429	2430	2431
980	2432	2433	2434	2435	2436	2437	2438	2439	2440	2441	2442	2443	2444	2445	2446	2447
990	2448	2449	2450	2451	2452	2453	2454	2455	2456	2457	2458	2459	2460	2461	2462	2463
9A0	2464	2465	2466	2467	2468	2469	2470	2471	2472	2473	2474	2475	2476	2477	2478	2479
9B0	2480	2481	2482	2483	2484	2485	2486	2487	2488	2489	2490	2491	2492	2493	2494	2495
9C0	2496	2497	2498	2499	2500	2501	2502	2503	2504	2505	2506	2507	2508	2509	2510	2511
9D0	2512	2513	2514	2515	2516	2517	2518	2519	2520	2521	2522	2523	2524	2525	2526	2527
9E0	2528	2529	2530	2531	2532	2533	2534	2535	2536	2537	2538	2539	2540	2541	2542	2543
9F0	2544	2545	2546	2547	2548	2549	2550	2551	2552	2553	2554	2555	2556	2557	2558	2559
A00	2560	2561	2562	2563	2564	2565	2566	2567	2568	2569	2570	2571	2572	2573	2574	2575
A10	2576	2577	2578	2579	2580	2581	2582	2583	2584	2585	2586	2587	2588	2589	2590	2591
A20	2592	2593	2594	2595	2596	2597	2598	2599	2600	2601	2602	2603	2604	2605	2606	2607
A30	2608	2609	2610	2611	2612	2613	2614	2615	2616	2617	2618	2619	2620	2621	2622	2623
A40	2624	2625	2626	2627	2628	2629	2630	2631	2632	2633	2634	2635	2636	2637	2638	2639
A50	2640	2641	2642	2643	2644	2645	2646	2647	2648	2649	2650	2651	2652	2653	2654	2655
A60	2656	2657	2658	2659	2660	2661	2662	2663	2664	2665	2666	2667	2668	2669	2670	2671
A70	2672	2673	2674	2675	2676	2677	2678	2679	2680	2681	2682	2683	2684	2685	2686	2687
A80	2688	2689	2690	2691	2692	2693	2694	2695	2696	2697	2698	2699	2700	2701	2702	2703
A90	2704	2705	2706	2707	2708	2709	2710	2711	2712	2713	2714	2715	2716	2717	2718	2719
AA0	2720	2721	2722	2723	2724	2725	2726	2727	2728	2729	2730	2731	2732	2733	2734	2735
AB0	2736	2737	2738	2739	2740	2741	2742	2743	2744	2745	2746	2747	2748	2749	2750	2751
AC0	2752	2753	2754	2755	2756	2757	2758	2759	2760	4761	2762	2763	2764	2765	2766	2767
AD0	2768	2769	2770	2771	2772	2773	2774	2775	2776	2777	2778	2779	2780	2781	2782	2783
AE0	2784	2785	2786	2787	2788	2789	2790	2791	2792	2793	2794	2795	2796	2797	2798	2799
AF0	2800	2801	2802	2803	2804	2805	2806	2807	2808	2809	2810	2811	2812	2813	2814	2815
B00	2816	2817	2818	2819	2820	2821	2822	2823	2824	2825	2826	2827	2828	2829	2830	2831
B10	2832	2833	2834	2835	2836	2837	2838	2839	2840	2841	2842	2843	2844	2845	2846	2847
B20	2848	2849	2850	2851	2852	2853	2854	2855	2856	2857	2858	2859	2860	2861	2862	2863
B30	2864	2865	2866	2867	2868	2869	2870	2871	2872	2873	2874	2875	2876	2877	2878	2879
840	2880	2881	2882	2883	2884	2885	2866	2887	2888	2889	2890	2891	2892	2893	2894	2895
850	2896	2897	2898	2899	2900	2901	2902	2903	2904	2905	2906	2907	2908	2909	2910	2911
B60	2912	2913	2914	2915	2916	2917	2918	2919	2920	2921	2922	2923	2924	2925	2926	2927
B70	2928	2929	2930	2931	2932	2933	2934	2935	2936	2937	2938	2939	2940	2941	2942	2943
B80	2944	2945	2946	2947	2948	2949	2950	2951	2952	2953	2954	2955	2956	2957	2958	2959
B90	2960	2961	2962	2963	2964	2965	2966	2967	2968	2969	2970	2971	2972	2973	2974	2975
BA0	2976	2977	2978	2979	2980	2981	2982	2983	2984	2985	2986	2987	2988	2989	2990	2991
BB0	2992	2993	2994	2995	2996	2997	2998	2999	3000	3001	3002	3003	3004	3005	3006	3007
BC0	3008	3009	3010	3011	3012	3013	3014	3015	3016	3017	3018	3019	3020	3021	3022	3023
BD0	3024	3025	3026	3027	3028	3029	3030	3031	3032	3033	3034	3035	3036	3037	3038	3039
BE0	3040	3041	3042	3043	3044	3045	3046	3047	3048	3049	3050	3051	3052	3053	3054	3055
BF0	3056	3057	3058	3059	3060	3061	3062	3063	3064	3065	3066	3067	3068	3069	3070	3071

Hexadecimal-Decimal Integer Conversion (Continued)

	0	1	2	3	4	5	6	7	8	9	A	B	C	D	E	F
C00	3072	3073	3074	3075	3076	3077	3078	3079	3080	3081	3082	3083	3084	3085	3086	3087
C10	3088	3089	3090	3091	3092	3093	3094	3395	3096	3097	3098	3099	3100	3101	3102	3103
C20	3104	3105	3106	3107	3108	3109	3110	3111	3112	3113	3114	3115	3116	3117	3118	3119
C30	3120	3121	3122	3123	3124	3125	3126	3127	3128	3129	3130	3131	3132	3133	3134	3135
C40	3136	3137	3138	3139	3140	3141	3142	3143	3144	3145	3146	3147	3148	3149	3150	3151
C50	3152	3153	3154	3155	3156	3157	3158	3159	3160	3161	3162	3163	3164	3165	3166	3167
C60	3168	3169	3170	3171	3172	3173	3174	3175	3176	3177	3178	3179	3180	3181	3182	3183
C70	3184	3185	3186	3187	3188	3189	3190	3191	3192	3193	3194	3195	3196	3197	3198	3199
C80	3200	3201	3202	3203	3204	3205	3206	3207	3208	3209	3210	3211	3212	3213	3214	3215
C90	3216	3217	3218	3219	3220	3221	3222	3223	3224	3225	3226	3227	3228	3229	3230	3231
CA0	3232	3233	3234	3235	3236	3237	3238	3239	3240	3241	3242	3243	3244	3245	3246	3247
CB0	3248	3249	3250	3251	3252	3253	3254	3255	3256	3257	3258	3259	3260	3261	3262	3263
CC0	3264	3265	3266	3267	3268	3269	3270	3271	3272	3273	3274	3275	3276	3277	3278	3279
CD0	3280	3281	3282	3283	3284	3285	3286	3287	3288	3289	3290	3291	3292	3293	3294	3295
CE0	3296	3297	3298	3299	3300	3301	3302	3303	3304	3305	3306	3307	3308	3309	3310	3311
CF0	3312	3313	3314	3315	3316	3317	3318	3319	3320	3321	3322	3323	3324	3325	3326	3327
D00	3328	3329	3330	3331	3332	3333	3334	3335	3336	3337	3338	3339	3340	3341	3342	3343
D10	3344	3345	3346	3347	3348	3349	3350	3351	3352	3353	3354	3355	3356	3357	3358	3359
D20	3360	3361	3362	3363	3364	3365	3366	3367	3368	3369	3370	3371	3372	3373	3374	3375
D30	3376	3377	3378	3379	3380	3381	3382	3383	3384	3385	3386	3387	3388	3389	3390	3391
D40	3392	3393	3394	3395	3396	3397	3398	3399	3400	3401	3402	3403	3404	3405	3406	3407
D50	3408	3409	3410	3411	3412	3413	3414	3415	3416	3417	3418	3419	3420	3421	3422	3423
D60	3424	3425	3426	3427	3428	3429	3430	3431	3432	3433	3434	3435	3436	3437	3438	3439
D70	3440	3441	3442	3443	3444	3445	3446	3447	3448	3449	3450	3451	3452	3453	3454	3455
D80	3456	3457	3458	3459	3460	3461	3462	3463	3464	3465	3466	3467	3468	3469	3470	3471
D90	3472	3473	3474	3475	3476	3477	3478	3479	3480	3481	3482	3483	3484	3485	3486	3487
DA0	3488	3489	3490	3491	3492	3493	3494	3495	3496	3497	3498	3499	3500	3501	3502	3503
DB0	3504	3505	3506	3507	3508	3509	3510	3511	3512	3513	3514	3515	3516	3517	3518	3519
DC0	3520	3521	3522	3523	3524	3525	3526	3527	3528	3529	3530	3031	3532	3533	3534	3535
DD0	3536	3537	3538	3539	3540	3541	3542	3543	3544	3545	3546	3547	3548	3549	3550	3551
DE0	3552	3553	3554	3555	3556	3557	3558	3559	3560	3561	3562	3563	3564	3565	3566	3567
DF0	3568	3569	3570	3571	3572	3573	3574	3575	3576	3577	3578	3579	3580	3581	3582	3583
E00	3584	3585	3586	3587	3588	3589	3590	3591	3592	3593	3594	3595	3596	3597	3598	3599
E10	3600	3601	3602	3603	3604	3605	3606	3607	3608	3609	3610	3611	3612	3613	3614	3615
E20	3616	3617	3618	3619	3620	3621	3622	3623	3624	3625	3626	3627	3628	3629	3630	3631
E30	3632	3633	3634	3635	3636	3637	3638	3639	3640	3641	3642	3643	3644	3645	3646	3647
E40	3648	3649	3650	3651	3652	3653	3654	3655	3656	3657	3658	3659	3660	3661	3662	3663
E50	3664	3665	3666	3667	3668	3669	3670	3671	3672	3673	3674	3675	3676	3677	3678	3679
E60	3680	3681	3682	3683	3684	3685	3686	3687	3688	3689	3690	3691	3692	3693	3694	3695
E70	3696	3697	2698	3699	3700	3701	3702	3703	3704	3705	3706	3707	2708	3709	3710	3711
E80	3712	3713	3714	3715	3716	3717	3718	3719	3720	3721	3722	3723	3724	3725	3726	3727
E90	3728	3729	3730	3731	3732	3733	3734	3735	3736	3737	3738	3739	3740	3741	3742	3743
EA0	3744	3745	3746	3747	3748	3749	3750	3751	3752	3753	3754	3755	3756	3757	3758	3759
EB0	3760	3761	3762	3763	3764	3765	3766	3767	3768	3769	3770	3771	3772	3773	3774	3775
EC0	3776	3777	3778	3779	3780	3781	3782	3783	3784	3785	3786	3787	3788	3789	3790	3791
ED0	3792	3793	3794	3795	3796	3797	3798	3799	3800	3801	3802	3803	3804	3805	3806	3807
EE0	3808	3809	3810	3811	3812	3813	3814	3815	3816	3817	3818	3819	3820	3821	3822	3823
EF0	3824	3825	3826	3827	3828	3829	3830	3831	3832	3833	3834	3835	3836	3837	3838	3839

Hexadecimal-Decimal Integer Conversion (Continued)

	0	1	2	3	4	5	6	7	8	9	A	B	C	D	E	F
F00	3840	3841	3842	3843	3844	3845	3846	3847	3848	3849	3850	3851	3852	3853	3854	3855
F10	3856	3857	3858	3859	3860	3861	3862	3863	3864	3865	3866	3867	3868	3869	3870	3871
F20	3872	3873	3874	3875	3876	3877	3878	3879	3880	3881	3882	3883	3884	3885	3886	3887
F30	3888	3889	3890	3891	3892	3893	3894	3895	3896	3897	3898	3899	3900	3901	3902	3903
F40	3904	3905	3906	3907	3908	3909	3910	3911	3912	3913	3914	3915	3916	3917	3918	3919
F50	3920	3921	3922	3923	3924	3925	3926	3927	3928	3929	3930	3931	3932	3933	3934	3935
F60	3936	3937	3938	3939	3940	3941	3942	3943	3944	3945	3946	3947	3948	3949	3950	3951
F70	3952	3953	3954	3955	3956	3957	3958	3959	3960	3961	3962	3963	3964	3965	3966	3967
F80	3968	3969	3970	3971	3972	3973	3974	3975	3976	3977	3978	3979	3980	3981	3982	3983
F90	3984	3985	3986	3987	3988	3989	3990	3991	3992	3993	3994	3995	3996	3997	3998	3999
FA0	4000	4001	4002	4003	4004	4005	4006	4007	4008	4009	4010	4011	4012	4013	4014	4015
FB0	4016	4017	4018	4019	4020	4021	4022	4023	4024	4025	4026	4027	4028	4029	4030	4031
FC0	4032	4033	4034	4035	4036	4037	4038	4039	4040	4041	4042	4043	4044	4045	4046	4047
FD0	4048	4049	4050	4051	4052	4053	4054	4055	4056	4057	4058	4059	4060	4061	4062	4063
FE0	4064	4065	4066	4067	4068	4069	4070	4071	4072	4073	4074	4075	4076	4077	4078	4079
FF0	4080	4081	4082	4083	4084	4085	4086	4087	4088	4089	4090	4091	4092	4093	4094	4095

ASCII CODES

GRAPHIC OR CONTROL	ASCII (HEXA-DECIMAL)	GRAPHIC OR CONTROL	ASCII (HEXA-DECIMAL)	GRAPHIC OR CONTROL	ASCII (HEXA-DECIMAL)
NULL	00	ACK	7C	1	31
SOM	01	Alt. Mode	7D	2	32
EOA	02	Rubout	7F	3	33
EOM	03	!	21	4	34
EOT	04	"	22	5	35
WRU	05	#	23	6	36
RU	06	$	24	7	37
BELL	07	%	25	8	38
FE	08	&	26	9	39
H. Tab	09	'	27	A	41
Line Feed	OA	(	28	B	42
V. Tab	OB	)	29	C	43
Form	OC	*	2A	D	44
Return	OD	+	2B	E	45
SO	OE	'	2C	F	46
SI	OF	-	2D	G	47
DCO	10	.	2E	H	48
X-On	11	/	2F	I	49
Tape Aux. On	12	:	3A	J	4A
X-Off	13	;	3B	K	4B
Tape Aux. Off	14	<	3C	L	4C
Error	15	=	3D	M	4D
Sync	16	>	3F	N	4E
LEM	17	?	3F	O	4F
S0	18	[	5B	P	50
S1	19	/	5C	Q	51
S2	1A	]	5D	R	52
S3	1B	↑	5E	S	53
S4	1C	←	5F	T	54
S5	1D	@	40	U	55
S6	1E	blank	20	V	56
S7	1F	0	30	W	57
				X	58
				Y	59
				Z	5A

(Courtesy Fairchild Camera and Instrumentation Corp., 434 Ellis St., Mountain View, Ca. 94042)

PL/M SPECIAL CHARACTERS

SYMBOL	NAME	USE
$	Dollar sign	Compiler toggles, number and identifier spacer
=	Equal sign	Relational test operator, assignment operator
:=	Assign	Imbedded assignment operator
.	dot	Address operator
/	slash	Division operator
/*		Left comment delimiter
*/		Right comment delimiter
(	Left paren	Left delimiter of lists, subscripts, and expressions
)	Right paren	Right delimiter of lists, subscripts, and expressions
+	Plus	Addition operator
−	Minus	Subtraction operator
'	Apostrophe	String delimiter
*	Asterisk	Multiplication operator
<	Less than	Relational test operator
>	Greater than	Relational test operator
<=	Less or equal	Relational test operator
>=	Greater or equal	Relational test operator
<>	Not equal	Relational test operator
:	Colon	Label delimiter
;	Semicolon	Statement delimiter
,	Comma	List element delimiter

PL/M RESERVED WORDS

RESERVED WORD	USE
IF THEN ELSE	Conditional tests and alternative execution
DO PROCEDURE INTERRUPT END	Statement grouping and procedure definition
DECLARE BYTE ADDRESS LABEL INITIAL DATA LITERALLY BASED	Data declarations
GO TO BY GOTO CASE WHILE	Unconditional branching and loop control
CALL RETURN HALT ENABLE DISABLE	Procedure call Procedure return Machine stop Interrupt enable Interrupt disable
OR AND XOR NOT	Boolean operators
MOD PLUS MINUS EOF	Remainder after division Add with carry Subtract with borrow End of input file (compiler control)

INDEX